MODERN RESPONSA

JPS ANTHOLOGIES
OF JEWISH THOUGHT

University of Nebraska Press
LINCOLN

Modern Responsa

An Anthology of Jewish Ethical *and* Ritual Decisions

PAMELA BARMASH

The Jewish Publication Society
PHILADELPHIA

© 2024 by Pamela Barmash

Acknowledgments for the use of copyrighted material appear on pages 331–37, which constitute an extension of the copyright page.

All rights reserved. Published by the University of Nebraska Press as a Jewish Publication Society book.

Library of Congress Cataloging-in-Publication Data
Names: Barmash, Pamela, 1966– editor compiler, writer of supplementary textual content.
Title: Modern responsa: an anthology of Jewish ethical and ritual decisions / Pamela Barmash.
Description: Lincoln: University of Nebraska Press; Philadelphia: Jewish Publication Society, 2024. | Series: JPS anthologies of Jewish thought | Includes bibliographical references and index.
Identifiers: LCCN 2024021607
ISBN 9780827615588 (paperback)
ISBN 9780827619241 (epub)
ISBN 9780827619258 (pdf)
Subjects: LCSH: Responsa—1948– | Jewish law. | Judaism—Customs and practices. | BISAC: RELIGION / Judaism / Rituals & Practice | SOCIAL SCIENCE / Jewish Studies
Classification: LCC BM522.A1 M633 2024 | DDC 296.1/85—dc23/eng/20240604
LC record available at https://lccn.loc.gov/2024021607

Designed and set in Merope by L. Welch.

In memory of my dear sister,
Marilyn B. Weinberger
"Say to Wisdom, 'You are my sister'" (Prov. 7:4)

CONTENTS

Acknowledgments ... xiii

Introduction: Understanding Responsa ... xv

How to Use This Book ... xxvii

Notes on Translation ... xxxi

1. Personal and Business Ethics ... 1

TEXT 1.1. Cardin and Reisner, "On the Mitzvah of Sustainability" ... 2

TEXT 1.2. Leff, "Whistleblowing: The Requirement to Report Employer Wrongdoing" ... 9

TEXT 1.3. Weiss, "About Commercial Encroachment" ... 18

TEXT 1.4. Somekh and Al-Ḥakam, "On Commerce in the Markets of Malabar" ... 21

TEXT 1.5. Barmash, "Veal Calves" ... 29

2. Ritual ... 37

TEXT 2.1. Sofer, "On Using the Vernacular in Prayer" ... 38

TEXT 2.2. Halevi, "What Are the Chances That Our Prayers Are Answered by God?" 46

TEXT 2.3. CCAR Responsa Committee, "A Sex Offender in the Synagogue" 51

3. Personal Status 57

TEXT 3.1. Oshry, "The Case of a *Mamzer* Rabbi" 58

TEXT 3.2. Spitz, "*Mamzerut*" 65

TEXT 3.3. Mesas, "A *Pesak Din* in a Matter of *Mamzerut*" 73

TEXT 3.4. CCAR Responsa Committee, "Patrilineal and Matrilineal Descent" 81

TEXT 3.5. Yosef, "On the Status of Ethiopian Jews" 87

TEXT 3.6. Barmash, "The Status of the *Ḥeresh* [Deaf Mute] and of Sign Language" 93

4. Women 101

TEXT 4.1. Lauterbach, "Shall Women Be Ordained Rabbis?" 102

TEXT 4.2. Herzog, "*Takkanot* on Marriage and *Yibbum*" 110

TEXT 4.3. Roness, "When Staining Renders a Woman *Niddah*" 115

TEXT 4.4. Rembaum, "Regarding the Inclusion of the Names of the Matriarchs in the First Blessing of the *Amidah*" 120

TEXT 4.5. Barmash, "Women and Mitzvot" 128

5. LGBTQIA+ ... 139

TEXT 5.1. Roth, "Homosexuality" ... 140

TEXT 5.2. Dorff, Nevins, and Reisner, "Homosexuality, Human Dignity and Halakhah" ... 148

TEXT 5.3. CCAR Responsa Committee, "Same-Sex Marriage as *Kiddushin*" ... 157

TEXT 5.4. Sharzer, "Transgender Jews and Halakhah" ... 162

6. Medical Ethics ... 175

TEXT 6.1. Sternbuch, "A Woman Suffering from Alzheimer's Disease Whose Husband Wishes to Divorce Her" ... 176

TEXT 6.2. Mevorakh, "Eating on Yom Kippur When a Person Is Suffering from an Eating Disorder (Anorexia)" ... 179

TEXT 6.3. Waldenberg, "On Abortion in General" ... 186

TEXT 6.4. Waldenberg, "On the Abortion of a Fetus with Tay-Sachs Disease" ... 196

TEXT 6.5. Grossman, "'Partial Birth Abortion' and the Question of When Human Life Begins" ... 198

7. The COVID-19 Pandemic ... 205

TEXT 7.1. Co-chairs, Committee on Jewish Law and Standards, "Halakhic Guidance from CJLS about Coronavirus" ... 206

TEXT 7.2. CCAR Responsa Committee, "Virtual Minyan in Time of COVID-19 Emergency" 209

TEXT 7.3. Iggud Ḥakhmei ha-Ma'arav be-Eretz Yisrael, "On a Seder via Zoom" 212

TEXT 7.4. Schachter, "Washing on Tisha b'Av" and "Regarding the Rule of 'God Protects the Simple'" 216

TEXT 7.5. Barmash, "Ethics of Gathering When Not All of Us May Attend in Person" ... 221

8. Relationships with the Other 229

TEXT 8.1. Shapira, "Engaging in a Public Fast in Sympathy with German Jews" 230

TEXT 8.2. Weinberg, "On the Burial of a Person Converted by Liberal Rabbis" 234

TEXT 8.3. Halevi, "Transcendental Meditation" 237

TEXT 8.4. Hirsch and Rapport, "Yoga as a Jewish Worship Practice: *Chukat Hagoyim* or Spiritual Innovation?" 245

TEXT 8.5. Hammer, "The Status of Non-Jews in Jewish Law and Lore Today" 252

9. The Modern State of Israel 263

TEXT 9.1. Goren, "The Siege on Beirut in Light of Halakhah" 264

TEXT 9.2. Halevi, "The Law of 'the One Who Comes Forth to Kill You, Kill Him First' in Our State Affairs" 274

TEXT 9.3. Friedman, "A Responsum on the Issue of 'the Greater Land of Israel' and Halakhah" ... 283

TEXT 9.4. Yosef, "Ceding Territory from the Land of Israel When There Is *Pikku'aḥ Nefesh*" ... 290

TEXT 9.5. Yisraeli, "Ceding Territory because of *Pikku'aḥ Nefesh*" ... 298

10. Life in the United States ... 307

TEXT 10.1. Committee on Responsa of the Committee on Army and Navy Religious Activities, "Responsa in War Time" ... 307

TEXT 10.2. Feinstein, "American Thanksgiving" ... 316

TEXT 10.3. Kalmanofsky, "Participating in the American Death Penalty" ... 320

Source Acknowledgments ... 331

Glossary ... 339

Notes ... 347

Index ... 369

ACKNOWLEDGMENTS

Rabbi David Ellenson brought me into this modern responsa anthology project in another iteration and shared with me the introduction he had prepared, parts of which I have gratefully used. Many others offered sage and useful advice when I shared my musings as the manuscript was coming together. Rabbi David J. Wise evinced great enthusiasm for this project from the start and discussed many aspects of it with me. Rabbi Joan Friedman, chair of the CCAR Responsa Committee, provided me with a list of significant CCAR responsa and answered my questions about them. Rabbi Harold Kravitz recommended Rabbi Theodore Friedman's responsum on "The Greater Land of Israel" for this anthology. Hannah Davidson shared sources on the reaction to the Zoom ruling of the Iggud Ḥakhmei ha-Ma'arav be-Eretz Yisrael. Beverly Gribetz and Prof. Edward L. Greenstein acquainted me with the *bagrut* (the Israeli high school matriculation exam) on responsa. Prof. Martin Jacobs, Housni Bennis, and Younasse Tarbouni analyzed how the family name of Rabbi Shalom Mesas is pronounced in Morocco. Prof. Hillel J. Kieval discussed Rabbi Moshe Feinstein's *teshuvot* on Thanksgiving and various matters of modern Jewish history with me. Rabbi Amy Levin provided a quiet space to write the glossary. W. David Nelson shared with me his experience in publishing with The Jewish Publication Society. Rabbi Deborah Silver assisted with UK geography. Shifra Mescheloff sent me her dissertation on Rabbi Shlomo Goren. Rabbi Irving Elson provided information about the volume *Responsa in War Time*. Rabbi Marc Angel conferred with me on the writings of Rabbi Ḥayyim David Halevi. Rabbis Dalia Marx and Galia Sadan responded to my queries about Reform Judaism in Israel. Rabbi Jan Uhrbach strongly supported this project. My research assistant Jonathan Mack ably procured primary and secondary source materials.

Many of the living rabbinic decisors responded positively to my request for their biographies: Rabbis Nina Beth Cardin, Elliot Dorff, Susan Grossman, Liz P.G. Hirsch, Jeremy Kalmanofsky, Barry Leff, Tomer Mevorakh, Daniel Nevins, Yael Rooks Rapport, Avram Reisner, Joel Rembaum, Joel Roth, Leonard Sharzer, and Elie Spitz. The families of Rabbis Theodore Friedman and Reuven Hammer also responded positively to my request for biographies.

This book would not have been possible without the Interlibrary Loan staff at Washington University in St. Louis; their speed and extraordinary ability to find obscure items in Hebrew is amazing.

During the time I was writing this book, the Memorial Foundation for Jewish Culture awarded me a fellowship, and Washington University in St. Louis granted me a research leave.

I would like to thank Rabbi Barry Schwartz, director emeritus of The Jewish Publication Society (JPS), for his strong advocacy of this book and his wise counsel during its planning stages; Joy Weinberg, JPS managing editor, for assiduously editing the manuscript for publication; and Elias Sacks, then JPS director, for his stalwart support of the anthology. I also thank the University of Nebraska Press staff for publishing this volume, especially Leif Milliken, Debra Corman, and Abigail Kwambamba for skillfully shepherding the book in its final stages.

During the writing of this book, my dear sister, Marilyn B. Weinberger, passed away. She always supported my rabbinic career, and her joie-de-vivre remains ever vivid in my memory. I dedicate this book to her in sadness and love.

INTRODUCTION *Understanding Responsa*

Studying and applying halakhah (Jewish law, broadly defined) have been hallmarks of virtually every Jewish community. Judaism has always been a religion and culture rooted in text and law. In our day both Conservative/Masorti Judaism and the various expressions of Orthodoxy abide by a long-standing commitment to the binding nature of halakhah. More liberal movements such as Reform and Reconstructionist Judaism do not view halakhah as authoritative, but still eternalize Judaism's focus on text, both by studying ancient texts and composing new ones, including legal ones.

Early on, Judaism met the interpretive challenge implicit in its commitment to Jewish law through the various sources of biblical law, followed by interpretation of the Bible and the development of Rabbinic texts: Mishnah, Talmud, midrash, and more. Once these texts were codified, the primary literary locus for the development of Jewish law shifted in the early Middle Ages to a genre of texts known as *she'eilot uteshuvot* (Hebrew for "questions and answers," usually referred to in Hebrew as *teshuvot* and in English as responsa). Leading rabbinic decisors issued a ruling and explanation of Jewish law to rabbinic colleagues. Sometimes these responsa (singular, responsum) were published for public dissemination, serving as guidance for analogous cases that might arise in the future.

The advent of the modern world significantly transformed patterns of Jewish religion and identity. The political autonomy of the premodern Jewish community ceased to exist in the West and began to dissolve in the East. Rabbis no longer functioned as civil magistrates, with the sole authority to adjudicate financial and property disputes in their communities. The cultural context further complicated this situation: Jews imbibed non-Jewish culture in a way that influenced them deeply. Even Jews who thought they were living a traditional life unchanged from before modernity lived in multiple cultural worlds, navigating between different values and modes of living. Many Jews abandoned a commitment to the traditional belief in an eternal, unchanging Jewish law revealed by God to Moses and varied their commitment to observance. All of this posed a challenge to the classical foundations and beliefs that supported the influence of responsa.

Given this reality, one might have anticipated that the writing of responsa as expressions of Jewish law would have diminished or even disappeared altogether. Yet, amazingly, this genre of Jewish legal literature remains vital in our era. The production of countless responsa continues unabated in nearly every circle of the Jewish community.

Indeed, as moral commitments, technology, and sociological realities rapidly changed, Jewish communities across the globe had to address unprecedented halakhic questions and to reexamine issues that once seemed resolved. Rabbinic decisors (Hebrew *posek*, plural *posekim*) from diverse streams of Judaism recognized they had critical roles to play in instituting new Jewish laws for their times. Their opinions have remained influential among many Jews who affirm a commitment to Judaism and seek guidance from masters of rabbinic law to understand what Judaism requires of them.

Structure and Content of Responsa

Though responsa are legal documents, the basic form of responsa is as letters. Employing epistolary style for a legal document is medieval in origin; it was common convention in the Middle Ages to utilize letters as legal devices (e.g., papal bulls and royal decrees in Christian Europe and the fatwa in the Islamic world).

Some responsa are in the form of a letter with greetings and salutation. Modernity has prompted another form: an essay format, with an introduction, exposition of sources and analysis of those sources, footnotes or endnotes, and a conclusion. Some responsa resemble brief, even hastily penned, correspondence; others mirror academic papers in style, length, and complexity.

Responsa generally follow a standardized format. They begin with the issue at hand: generally put forth as a question, and less often in a summary, declarative form. Then comes the analysis of sources and exposition, a discussion of variable length invoking legal precedents and sources relevant to the disposition of the particular matter. Finally, once the classical literary structure (citation and discussion of relevant sources and resolution of difficulties in the sources) has been observed, the rabbinic decisor issues a definitive ruling (Hebrew *pesak din*), and the responsum is completed.

The content of responsa may vary greatly. Rabbinic decisors sort through the Bible and Talmud as well as codes of Jewish law,[1] commentaries, and other responsa to find precedents; they weigh the pertinence and significance of earlier sources and devise arguments that interweave the traditional sources of Jewish law with modes of analysis that speak to their community. Each responsum is an individual reflection of the interpretations, principles, insights, and precedents provided by the texts of the Jewish past to the urgent and often unprecedented issues of a new time period. Responsa are in conversation with a complex and deeply layered textual heritage of classical Jewish literary tradition (Bible, Talmud, and occasionally midrash) and later rabbinic texts (codes, responsa, and occasionally commentaries, philosophy, pietistic literature, and mystical texts), as well as with contemporary social, psychological, intellectual, and ethical factors and thinking. They invoke the Jewish textual tradition and, in so doing, reinvent it for a new context: responsa embody both historical interconnection and creativity in a rich, new way.

The Character of Responsa: Judicial, Persuasive, Educational

The content of responsa is judicial, with the closest analogue in other legal systems being the opinion of a judge who decides a case. This comparison must be made with caution. While some authorities accept the identification and speak of the responsa literature as the "case law" of the Jewish legal tradition, others emphasize the differences. The author of responsa is not a judge who wields the institutional power to dispose of the instant case, but rather a scholarly rabbi who pens a learned discourse upon an issue for which advice has been requested.

Understanding responsa only as judicial decision-making misses crucial aspects. Responsa are not just rulings. Perhaps the exception proves the rule: Rabbi Ḥayyim Kanievsky, a contemporary *haredi* non-Hasidic Ultraorthodox rabbinic decisor, is famous for replying with one- or two-word rulings on a postcard.[2] Still, in general, rabbinic decisors offer opinions bolstered by citations of sources and analysis, some brief, others at great length, in order to persuade readers to find the responsum meaningful and follow the rulings. And even when responsa are written as private responses to questions from individuals, communal leaders, or other rabbis, when rabbinic decisors publish them, they are seeking to convince other rabbis and communities to follow their opinion and rulings. Rabbinic decisors aspire to persuade and educate.[3] They promote a particular view of halakhah over other plausible interpretations. They seek to teach others the fresh patterns of meaning and Jewish observance that they have illuminated in their responsa.

In order to make their ideas cogent and convincing to others, rabbinic decisors make a variety of choices about the types of sources and the tone of communication. They invoke differing modes of argumentation. Conservative and Reform responsa cite academic scholarship. Reform and Conservative responsa, and sometimes Modern Orthodox ones, cite scientific publications. The decisors of all the movements generally adduce medical science.

When rabbinic decisors disagree, sometimes this is expressed in harsh and strongly negative language, and other times in neutral, even respectful, tones. The attitude of one movement's attitude toward another is also reflected in the decisors' choices whether to cite sources from other movements. Some rabbinic decisors see Judaism as pluralistic, whereas others see their movement as the sole arbiters of religious law and divine truth. Conservative and Reform responsa refer to responsa across the movements, but Orthodox decisors, ranging from Modern Orthodox to Ultraorthodox, will never cite responsa from other movements, except perhaps in scorn.

The ideology rabbinic decisors share with others in their movement naturally shapes their argumentation and rulings. Ultraorthodox decisors generally seek to increase the stringency and specificity of religious laws, to promote social separation of Ultraorthodox Jews and Jewish communities, and to reject, even demonize, the culture of the surrounding society, even demonizing it.[4] Conservative decisors often articulate their aim to navigate between traditional halakhah and modern ethical ideas, while Orthodox decisors may do so without explicitly articulating it.[5]

Responsa in the Twentieth and Twenty-First Centuries

A number of significant changes in the publication and dissemination of responsa have occurred during the modern period covered by this volume.

While earlier responsa were written solely by individual rabbinic decisors, the last century has witnessed the development of responsa committees, authorized mostly by national and international rabbinic organizations, to decide matters of halakhic policy.

The Central Conference of American Rabbis, the rabbinic organization of Reform rabbis, established its Responsa Committee in 1906.[6] Agudat Yisrael, the worldwide Ultraorthodox organization, created Mo'etzet Gedolei Hatorah (Council of Great Torah Experts) in 1912. The Rabbinical Assembly, the international organization of Conservative/Masorti rabbis, founded the Committee on Jewish Law in 1917 and its successor, the Committee on Jewish Law and Standards, in 1927. The Rabbinical Council of America, the association of Modern Orthodox rabbis, launched its Va'ad Halacha (Committee on Halakhah) in the late 1930s. At the outbreak of World War II, the Jewish Welfare Board–sponsored Committee on Army and Navy Religious Activities, aiming to address questions from Jews serving in the U.S. military, created a unique, transdenominational Committee on Responsa—one consisting of rabbis from the Reform, Conservative, and Orthodox movements. In the 1980s, Po'alei Agudat Yisrael created its own Mo'etzet Gedolei Hatorah in a break with Agudat Yisrael, and the Shas political party in Israel also established Mo'etzet Ḥakhmei Hatorah (Council of Torah Sages). The Conservative/Masorti movement in Israel established a Va'ad Halakhah to answer Israeli halakhic questions in 1986.

These committees enhance the authority of the rabbinic decisors who issue responsa with the endorsement of a committee and are themselves enhanced by the reputation and writings of the rabbis on the committees. Some committees formally approve responsa by vote, and some do not. Some restrict the availability of their responsa to their members, some publish their responsa openly, and some have switched from a policy of restrictive to open readership.

Perhaps inspired by non-Jewish scholarly journals, general rabbinic journals have appeared, as well as periodicals devoted to practical halakhah, a number with specializations, such as medical issues or technology. A number of *posekim* publish versions (sometimes preliminary ones) of their responsa in these journals.

New technology of the twentieth and twenty-first century has also influenced how responsa are written and disseminated. Radio shows popularized the responsa of a number of Sefardic/Mizraḥi rabbis, such as Rabbi Ḥayyim David Halevi and Rabbi Ovadiah Yosef, and inspired them to publish books of responsa more easily understood by lay readers. The online Bar Ilan Responsa Project (in Hebrew, https://www.responsa.co.il/home.he.aspx; in English, https://www.responsa.co.il/home.en-US.aspx), a Bar Ilan University initiative, has made available responsa and other halakhic works from the past that were difficult to obtain, with its search capability transcending the earlier system of hard-copy volumes listing and indexing.[7] This has facilitated the integration of prior responsa text into more recent responsa, as rabbinic decisors see more easily and quickly how other decisors have ruled. Other online resources (see this book's study guide at https://jps.org/study-guides) have also broadened the availability of responsa material.

Technology has additionally streamlined the dissemination of contemporary responsa. Questions that were sent to rabbinic decisors via post and telephone are now sent by email, with speedy replies. Completed responsa are posted on the official websites of movements and organizations and on private websites far more rapidly than those published in printed volume or sent by post and are further shared via social media and email with web links. Interestingly and fairly recently, the use of technology to publicize responsa was especially effective early in the COVID-19 pandemic, when they were written posthaste as Purim and Passover approached and quickly posted and shared.

About This Volume

Focusing on the last one hundred years or so of responsa (with a handful from the nineteenth century), this anthology showcases the vitality of Jewish law in modernity. *Modern Responsa* sheds light on how the halakhic process has evolved in the modern period, highlights the dynamism and creativity of Jewish legal writings on matters significant to modern Jews, and provides insight into the dynamic nature of Judaism and the multidimensionality of Jewish religious experience and identity in modernity. It also speaks to the spiritual power of responsa. When rabbinic decisors interweave Jewish tradition with a modern sensibility in response to contemporary quandaries, they offer Jews conceptual frameworks that help them understand themselves as well as how they relate to God and other human beings.

To introduce lay readers to this mode of Jewish literature and facilitate the teaching of these responsa by rabbis and educators, this volume is organized by subject; it is not an anthology organized chronologically or with brief chapters highlighting a single rabbinic decisor in a kind of literary parade. Rather, each of its ten chapters is devoted to a topic: personal and business ethics (chapter 1), ritual (chapter 2), personal status (chapter 3), women (chapter 4), LGBTQIA+ (chapter 5), medical ethics (chapter 6), the COVID-19 pandemic (chapter 7), relationships with the other (chapter 8), the modern State of Israel (chapter 9), and life in the United States (chapter 10).

Diverse responsa on the given topic, selected from across the Jewish movements and from both Ashkenazic and Sefardic/Mizraḥi *posekim*, showcase how the rabbinic decisors who wrote them handled the quandaries of modernity for their communities. Notably, the majority of these responsa have never before been translated into English. As a result, my translations in this volume open up the vast realm of modern responsa literature to new readers.

Generally, only one responsum addresses a given issue, but for some issues, I have included two or more responsa to show how rabbinic decisors disagree—or, perhaps more surprisingly, rule similarly, despite having differing backgrounds and ideological commitments.

Each chapter starts with a brief introduction to the topic and the types of challenges the issue presents—in other words, why responsa are needed. An overview of the chapter's responsa on that topic follows. A brief biography of the rabbinic decisors, foregrounding their individual responsum, sheds additional light on these decisors' intellectual, ethical, and religious commitments and on how their life story may have influenced their writings and rulings. To overcome possible difficulties in understanding these responsa—often they were written by experts for experts and assume background knowledge (including uncommon abbreviations)—I offer summaries and analyses of each responsum, as well as definitions of terms and identities of figures, section by section, as needed. A glossary at the back of this volume defines terms and concepts as they are employed in this volume's responsa.

Challenges and Choices

The number of responsa is colossal. I could have easily produced a volume (or a set of volumes) with completely different responsa. The ten topics I focus on represent the broad array of areas that modern *posekim* address, from individual behavior to communal practice and from specifically Jewish matters to universal concerns. I have also selected areas of special concern and transformation in modernity: personal status, women, LGBTQIA+, the modern State of Israel, and life in the United States.

In selecting the individual responsa, I had the following goals:

1. To reflect on how *posekim* answer current dilemmas. Responsa on sustainability, transgender Jews, "partial birth abortion," and the COVID-19 pandemic, among others, address the issues of today. They attest to the vitality of responsa in navigating vexing quandaries of contemporary society.

2. To illustrate how *posekim* address the classic issues of Jewish life. The status of *mamzer*, a Jew of problematic family lineage, has been a source of distress and disquiet for millennia. In dealing with the case of a young rabbi who finds himself to

be a *mamzer*, Rabbi Ephraim Oshry expresses sadness and sympathy for the young rabbi's plight but complies with the tradition's severe restrictions on a *mamzer*. Rabbis Shalom Mesas and Elie Spitz, by contrast, seek rulings to prevent a person from being deemed a *mamzer* (see chapter 3).

3. To show how classic discussions of halakhah address issues that remain vexing today. For example, how far along the chain of commerce does responsibility for fraud lie? Rabbis Abdallah Somekh and Rabbi Joseph Ḥayyim Al-Ḥakam deal with nineteenth-century merchants (see chapter 1), but the underlying moral issue persists in our time: if a store buys an item from a manufacturer that mistreats its employees, is the purchaser along the chain of commerce responsible at least partially for the offense?

4. To introduce readers to a diversity of rabbinic decisors, from across the movements and from both Ashkenazic and Sefardic/Mizraḥi backgrounds. I have sought to include the major *posekim* of modern times as well as less well-known ones, but I have not included texts from the Reconstructionist movement.[8] These *posekim* do include women, who did not write responsa before the late twentieth century and are still few in number.

5. To point out when *posekim* from different movements rule similarly, even though their differing ideological commitments might lead to the assumption that they would issue divergent rulings. Based on their movement affiliations, one might expect Rabbi Ḥayyim David Halevi and the team of Rabbis Liz P.G. Hirsch and Yael Rooks Rapport to issue contradictory conclusions on the acceptability of Jews practicing transcendental meditation and yoga, but the decisors' concerns about foreign religious practices concomitant with their openness to new ideas impel them to permit restricted use of both modalities (see chapter 8).

6. To manifest how ethics and policy are incorporated into legal argumentation. Confronted with an offender who won't obey a rabbinic ruling, Rabbi Isaac Jacob Weiss extends the prohibition of competition to another person in order to be fair to the injured party (chapter 1). Rabbi Moses Sofer rules that Hebrew must be the language of prayer (chapter 2) despite the long-standing rule that prayer may be in any language, because of the central place Hebrew holds in Jewish life.

7. To address matters of theology, not just law narrowly defined. Rabbi Ḥayyim David Halevi reflects on whether God answers prayer (chapter 2), and Rabbi Reuven Hammer analyzes theological attitudes toward non-Jews (chapter 8).

Given space constraints, most of the responsa have been abbreviated, with the intent of clarifying the rabbinic decisors' arguments and stance toward the halakhic process. Opening readers to the variety of responsa in the volume also required excluding some of the decisors' original arguments. I hope that in so doing I have not created a misleading version. Readers can ascertain whether arguments have been omitted from a given responsum by checking whether the last endnote pertaining to that responsum mentions omitted arguments; if it does not, then the full argument appears. Both source notes and these endnotes indicate where the texts can be found in their original language and their entirety.

If the original responsum was titled, I retained that title; if it was untitled, I created a title and point to this in the first endnote pertaining to that responsum. If a given responsum was not already divided into sections with subheadings, I did so to facilitate teaching how the line of argumentation leads to the legal ruling (Hebrew *pesak din*). Also, for increased clarity, in one case, I substituted my own subheadings, and for better organization, in a couple of cases I supplemented the preexisting subheadings with one or two of my own. Whenever my own section headings appear, I indicate this in the notes. About half of the original responsa do not begin with a question (optional in responsa); this is not notated, as it will be self-evident. In three instances, I took the liberty of reorganizing a responsum in order to clarify the logic of its argument; that has been noted here[9] and within the individual responsa as well.

This book makes repeated reference to Sefardic/Mizraḥi Jews, a designation for Jews whose family origins are in North Africa and the Middle East, which is a complicated matter. The term "Sefardic" refers to Jews whose families came from Spain and Portugal by the end of the fifteenth century. The Jews of the Middle East and North Africa generally referred to themselves as members of specific communities, such as Baghdadi Jews, who lived in Iraq and India, or Kurdish Jews, who lived in northern Iraq. The term "Mizraḥi" (easterner) has become the term for non-Ashkenazic Jews who have created a more unified identity since the modern State of Israel came into being, but the term is somewhat problematic because the Jews of North Africa lived to the west of the Land of Israel.[10] Ashkenazic Jews are easier to classify: Jews whose family origins are from Europe, generally from the Rhineland in the Middle Ages, except for those from the Iberian peninsula, Italy, and parts of Europe under the rule of the Ottoman empire. As needed, I refer to other groups of Jews who do not identify either as Ashkenazic or Sefardic/Mizraḥi as they arise in the responsa, such as Ethiopian Jews.

Although it is usual to designate streams within Judaism as Reform, Orthodox, Conservative, and Ultraorthodox as if they are monolithic, it must be emphasized that each one is diverse within itself.

I have tried to cite English sources whenever possible, even though most of the cutting-edge scholarship on modern responsa and halakhah is in Hebrew. Sometimes, however, it was not possible to find an English publication equivalent to the Hebrew source.

Ultimately I hope that readers and teachers of this volume will feel inspired to continue their journey through responsa.

HOW TO USE THIS BOOK

This book is appropriate for classes at the level of continuing education, college, and university; day schools at the middle school and high school level; and individuals reading on their own.

For Teachers
An exciting way to teach the volume is to jump right into a chapter of responsa and start with an introduction to a responsum: what is the question the rabbinic decisor is addressing, and what are the halakhic and ethical principles at stake.

These ten questions may be used to deepen your students' understanding of each responsum:

1. What is the real question being asked of the rabbinic decisor?
2. How might the rabbinic decisor's background inform the approach to the subject?
3. How does the rabbinic decisor start to answer? How might that influence the *pesak din* (final ruling)?
4. Which rabbinic sources are cited, and how are these used to persuade the reader?
5. Which other sources are cited? Why does the rabbinic decisor think these are important?
6. Does the *posek* (rabbinic decisor) address contesting points of view, and if so, how are these refuted?

7. Sketch out the flow of the *posek*'s points — why does the *posek* think this is convincing?
8. Which assumptions has the rabbinic decisor made? What does this say about the rabbinic decisor and the community being addressed?
9. How well does the *pesak din* answer the question posed at the beginning?
10. If there are multiple responsa on an issue, how do these differ? Do they use the same sources, and if so, do they interpret them the same way? How do their arguments vary? How and why do they come to the same or different conclusions?

Some students may be eager to engage in a short discussion as to what their intuition and prior knowledge tell them would be significant in a rabbinic decisor's thinking. Others may be keen to start studying and discussing the responsum. Two modes of teaching, seminar-style discussion as a group and small-group study in *ḥavruta*, are compatible and may be combined in a single class session.

Educators may wish to first study the complete original source, whether in Hebrew or English. I have indicated in a note at the end of each responsum where it is published.

To deepen understanding of the responsa in this book, I am providing a complimentary study guide at https://jps.org/study-guides. You'll find additional questions and comments to help understand the significance of each responsum and to use in furthering group discussions, links to websites that contain responsa (which I shall update from time to time as new websites are launched and others disappear), and an annotated bibliography of suggested reading for both laypeople and educators.

For Those Reading on Their Own

In reading this book on your own, I recommend downloading the complimentary study guide (https://jps.org/study-guides/), which provides additional, focused questions for studying the responsa, and using the glossary at the back of this book.

You may find it fun and engaging to read this volume with a study partner or in a small group. Reading the responsa together will allow you to dive deeper in understanding why and how a rabbinic decisor makes a decision and creates a persuasive line of reasoning. The suggested questions above will help you start discussing, and the questions in the study guide, focused on individual responsa, may help you gain more in-depth understanding.

Feel free to read the book in order or start with the topic or responsum that interests you.

NOTES ON TRANSLITERATION AND TRANSLATION

Both *ḥeit* and *ṭeit* are transliterated with a diacritical dot, and an apostrophe has been inserted where two vowels could be misread as one. Vocal sheva is indicated by e. The spelling of names follows the *Encyclopaedia Judaica* and the *Encyclopedia of Jews in the Islamic World*; however, the spelling in other publications cited has not been changed.

MODERN RESPONSA

Personal and Business Ethics   1

We are all confronted by ethical dilemmas, and in this chapter we delve into the ethical predicaments that arise in our daily lives as human beings. These quandaries can result from a clash between deeply ingrained ethical values or from the complexities of real-world situations, which may make it challenging or even impossible to adhere to our ethical principles. When faced with conflicting ethical values, how do we determine which ones to prioritize? Moreover, what do we do when all options seem to present ethical issues? In situations where following our ethical ideals could result in the loss of a job or being blacklisted or worse, how much are we willing to sacrifice? How do we apply Jewish ethics to contemporary circumstances that were unimaginable in earlier Jewish history? *Posekim* (rabbinic decisors) provide guidance on how to navigate competing ethical values and resolve them with integrity in tune with the realities of everyday life.

We begin with the burning issue of climate change and sustainability. Rabbis Nina Beth Cardin and Avram Israel Reisner offer an inventive reading of the Creation stories in the Bible and discuss the practical steps they urge Jews and Jewish communities to take. Next, Rabbi Barry Leff tackles the ethical dilemma of blowing the whistle on corporate wrongdoing, even if it may lead to negative consequences for the whistleblower, such as losing a job or being sued or blacklisted by an employer. Rabbi Isaac Jacob Weiss offers advice to a *beit din* (Jewish court of law) as to how it can remedy unfair business practices when the offender refuses to follow the *beit din*'s ruling. In a late nineteenth-century responsum, Rabbis Abdallah Somekh and Joseph Ḥayyim Al-Ḥakam peruse how far along a chain of commerce the responsibility for ethical violations should run. Rabbi Pamela Barmash investigates whether the way veal calves are raised violates principles of Jewish law and therefore whether it is or is not acceptable for Jews to consume, sell, or purchase veal.

Text 1.1. Cardin and Reisner, "On the Mitzvah of Sustainability"

COMMITTEE ON JEWISH LAW AND STANDARDS OF THE RABBINICAL ASSEMBLY, ḤOSHEN MISHPAṬ 175:26

Rabbi Nina Beth Cardin earned a BA at Connecticut College and an MA in Talmud and Rabbinics from the Jewish Theological Seminary (JTS). She worked to open the doors of its rabbinical school to women and was admitted as a member of the first class of women. She founded the Jewish Women's Resource Center and the Pregnancy Loss Peer Counseling Program and was also one of the founders of the New York Jewish Healing Center. Rabbi Cardin worked as the director of Jewish life at the Greater Baltimore JCC, and she founded both the Baltimore Orchard Project and the Maryland Campaign for Environmental Human Rights. She believes our texts are the spine that supports and animates the Jewish body politic.

Rabbi Avram Israel Reisner earned bachelor's degrees from Columbia University and JTS and spent a year in Israel studying at Yeshivat Mercaz Harav. Ordained at JTS, he also earned a PhD in Talmud there as well as a master's degree in bioethics at the University of Pennsylvania. He was a congregational rabbi in New Milford, New Jersey, and Baltimore. He has served since 1987 on the Conservative movement's Committee on Jewish Law and Standards and was also appointed to the Joint Beit Din of the Conservative/Masorti movement and the Maryland State Stem Cell Research Commission. Rabbi Reisner maintains that the way to interpret law is to study the precedent, without prejudice, in order to determine the ideational basis upon which prior law was decided and then to apply those ideas freely to the current situation without undue regard to the concrete application in the past. He has been drawn toward the application of halakhah to cutting-edge issues. He is married to Rabbi Nina Beth Cardin, his coauthor on this *teshuvah* (responsum).

QUESTION

In a responsum approved by the Committee on Jewish Law and Standards in 2019, Rabbis Cardin and Reisner contend that we must deal with a quandary whose global scope we human beings have never faced—accelerating climate change caused by human activity—and address this question:

> In a world facing the urgent challenges of climate change and environmental degradation, how should a Jew live? What does Jewish law teach and require in the matter of sustainability?

SECTION A: THE UNDERSTANDING THAT GROUNDS THIS *TESHUVAH*[1]

Rabbis Cardin and Reisner start their responsum by offering an innovative interpretation of two of the most famous stories of the Bible: the first and second Creation stories. The first Creation story assumes that the earth exists at humanity's pleasure to be used and even abused, while in the second story, humanity is embedded in nature and is responsible for ensuring that nature flourishes. The rabbis argue that we human beings have followed the viewpoint of the first Creation story, but now in light of climate change, we must adopt the thinking of the second Creation story:

Humanity's first mission upon being created is... described in... two distinct creation stories. In Gen. 1:28, God creates humans and says: "Be fruitful and multiply. Fill the world and subdue it. Gain control over the fish of the sea, the birds of the sky and every animal that roams on the earth."...

In the second version of creation the primary mission is described in Gen. 2:15: "God took the human and placed him in the Garden of Eden to work and protect it."

Thus in both stories, in different ways, the first mission of humankind is to establish the world as a hospitable place for humankind. The question is: how? In Genesis One, the Earth is a bounty of ever-renewing life to which we may help ourselves; in Genesis Two... we are tasked to take care of it... so that it may take care of us....

Genesis One tells the story, step by step, of how the world was made.... Life... was born with the capacity of self-renewal in an environment that was created to support and sustain it. Each generation was born with the seeds that promise to bring forth the next generation. If left undisturbed, if allowed to live out the plan of the Creator, life would continue, one generation cascading into another, forever.... For humans, the depiction was a bit different.... "God blessed them and God said to them, 'Be fertile and increase, fill the earth and master it; and rule the fish of the sea, the birds of the sky, and all the living things that creep on earth.'"... Our footprint was small and our vulnerability great.... The big take-away from Genesis One over the generations seems to have been that... humankind had great latitude to work the earth as we saw fit. So we did, for thousands of years. We tamed the rivers and felled the trees; distilled potions from the plants to reduce our fevers and ease our pains; we built cities, roads and museums. We planted and harvested and gathered in, changing the land, flora and watercourses as we went. We were fruitful and multiplied.... Genesis One is an anthropocentric vision of creation, where humans are beneficiaries seeking to flourish in an eternally self-regenerating world....

But that was then. We are, in many ways, past that now.... Our footprint is larger than it ever was. Over the last 150 years we have already profoundly altered elements of the world's operating systems in ways that are irreparable in any meaningful human timeframe. Genesis One was the story for the first era of human development. But having fulfilled that promise, that mandate, we need another story to guide our next steps. And we have that story in the very next verses of the Torah: Genesis Two....

Genesis Two places humans deeply embedded within, and as an essential contributing part of, earth's complex operating system. Our job in Genesis Two is not to consume and subdue the world's goodness so that we may thrive, but to bring the earth into its own full fecundity and manage its richness and resources wisely. We were created for the Earth's sake.... We are not sovereigns as we seem to be in Genesis One but caretakers; concerned for the needs of the place in which we live and upon which we depend.... Humanity no longer lives in the era of Genesis One. We abide in the era of Genesis Two. We must come to terms with the geophysical powers we wield and must develop an ethic that can honor, restrain and guide those powers so we and future generations can live in a thriving world.

SECTION B: DEFINING THE PROBLEMS

Rabbis Cardin and Reisner delineate the ways we are harming the environment:

The following areas [of human behavior]... threaten the functioning of the world:

1) Resource Depletion. Resources are depleted when they are extracted or consumed at a faster pace than the earth is able to replenish them. Some resources, like fossil fuels and rare earth elements, require timeframes for renewal that are so vast they are essentially considered non-renewable. Still other resources, like water and soil, or wild fish and forests, are renewable but are being consumed or otherwise depleted faster than they can be restored. Every year since 1969 . . . we now use up more than 1.7 times earth's renewal capacity each year.
2) Climate Disruption. . . . We have known since the mid-20th century that greenhouse gases, especially but not exclusively CO_2 and methane, are causing the atmosphere to retain heat and thus warm the planet beyond the temperature ranges that . . . sustain civilization. . . . Our urgent task is to reduce greenhouse gas emissions before they cause an ever-accelerating feedback loop that defies our ability to arrest climate disruption.
3) Species Extinction. . . . The earth is on track to prematurely lose one million species due to human impact on the environment. . . . The effects of such massive die-offs are dire, jeopardizing . . . our economies, livelihoods, food security, health, and quality of life worldwide. . . .

These three crises . . . are largely the consequences of three activities by humanity that demand our response . . . 1) Resource extraction. . . . Currently, most of our methods of resource extraction contribute to the eventual destruction and depletion of the very resources we seek, as well as to the degradation of the environment that sustains them. . . . 2) Resource consumption. . . . Up to 40% of food produced in the United States, and 1.6 billion tons of food world-wide goes to waste somewhere between field and fork. . . . 3) Waste management. . . .

> The quest for sustainability is immediate and urgent. The best of science is telling us that we are running out of time.... Expressed in Jewish terms, are we truly behaving as... the human that God placed in the Garden to work and tend well to the earth?

SECTION C: "DO NOT DESTROY"

Rabbis Cardin and Reisner introduce the halakhic principle of *bal tashḥit*, a halakhic principle derived from Deuteronomy 20:19 that forbids the destruction of fruit trees when besieging a city during war. In the Middle Ages and early Modern period, rabbis broadened its scope to prohibit gratuitous destruction of natural and manufactured objects but permitted the broad use of resources for human benefit in the short term. While it has not been taken to apply to the use of resources over the long term, Rabbis Cardin and Reisner argue that it must be extended to prohibit harming nature over a sustained period:

> We believe that *bal tashḥit*, as it has traditionally been understood, has been too narrowly construed. Yet applied anew to the issue of sustainability... it can offer us the over-arching guidance we need.... The traditional parameters of *bal tashḥit* have been interpreted exclusively within the model of Genesis One.... Our challenge... is to consider *bal tashḥit* as reflected through the prism of Genesis Two, that is, in a natural environment whose health and generativity are affected by and dependent upon human behavior. In that model, *bal tashḥit* is measured in terms of harm over the long-term, for no generation has a greater claim to earth's resources than any other generation.
>
> Our mission not to destroy... is both a positive command and negative command. Our difficulty is determining in the specificity of the moment what is demanded. But at every

moment, the demands of those mitzvot are urgent and immediate. We must be as dedicated to attending to them as to reciting the Shema and building a *sukkah* . . . or avoiding unkosher food or ḥametz on Pesaḥ.

PESAK DIN (RULING)

Rabbis Cardin and Reisner urge us to take specific actions:

All of us, as individuals and institutions, must:

1) Respond with urgency. It is past the time when we can accommodate the sensitivities and restraints of political expediency. . . . The longer we wait, the more costly it will be—in lives, health, environmental degradation and the economy. . . .
2) Inform ourselves about sustainability issues.
3) Talk with family, friends, colleagues and co-workers, those in your congregations, schools and other arenas of your social orbit about the necessity and ways of living sustainably. Institutional leaders must speak with their counterparts in sister institutions. . . . People will act with urgency if and when they feel the collective sense of urgency. We care most about what we talk most about.
4) Make all our decisions align with the goals of sustainability. Individuals and families should create their own sustainability "credo" articulating their values and ideal practices. On a broader level, institutions should create and develop ways to abide by sustainability policies. Our institutions should conduct energy, resource and food consumption audits, including what we use, how much we use and how we discard what is left over. . . .
5) Advocate for sustainable practices in business and government. . . . We must work to align all of society's practices and policies with nature's demands. . . .

Institutions must:

6) Appoint someone to hold a designated sustainability portfolio. Synagogues, schools, camps, federations, agencies and other Jewish institutions should designate sustainability offices and officers (just as we have fiscal advisors, IT advisors...) and designate a portion of their budget to that end....
7) Develop and incorporate texts, teachings and values of Jewish environmentalism in the curricula of our formal and informal education.... These should be taught from pre-school to rabbinical school....

We recognize that this teshuvah does not offer specific halakhic directives for sustainable living. It does not decree the propriety of local eating or a 100% plant-based diet, create a mandate for composting, or determine transportation options. That is because the landscape of sustainable options is constantly changing and does not lend itself to solutions that work for everyone everywhere, both today and tomorrow.[2]

Text 1.2. Leff, "Whistleblowing: The Requirement to Report Employer Wrongdoing"

COMMITTEE ON JEWISH LAW AND STANDARDS OF THE RABBINICAL ASSEMBLY, ḤOSHEN MISHPAṬ 410:8.2007

Rabbi Barry Leff served with the U.S. Army Security Agency as an electronic warfare specialist. After completing a BS degree at the State University of New York, he went on to a twenty-year-long career in Silicon Valley and earned MBA and DBA degrees from Golden Gate University. Ordained as a rabbi at American Jewish University, he served congregations in Vancouver and Toledo prior to making *aliyah* in 2007. In Israel, he returned to the business world, serving as general manager for the Israeli subsidiary of a U.S.-based outsourcing company. He served as chairman of the

Board of Rabbis for Human Rights in Israel from 2011 to 2013 and on the board of directors of the rabbinical seminary at the Schechter Institute for Jewish Studies since 2011. He has a special interest in business ethics and is fascinated by halakhah, seeing it as the intersection between what Jews believe and what Jews do.

QUESTION

In a responsum approved by the Committee on Jewish Law and Standards in 2007, Rabbi Leff addresses the question:

> To what extent does an employee have an obligation to report wrongdoing on the part of his or her employer?

SECTION A: THE SCOPE OF CORPORATE MALFEASANCE[3]

Stressing the importance of addressing the issue of whistleblowing, Rabbi Leff enumerates instances of corporate malfeasance that resulted in personal ruin and death. He points to competing halakhic principles and rules: we must help a person in need and not be an innocent bystander, yet we are warned against gossip. Furthermore, in general, whistleblowers act at the risk of their jobs, future employment, and a possible lawsuit (by violating non-disclosure agreements).

To reach a ruling, it is noteworthy that Rabbi Leff investigates halakhic rules applying to how an individual behaves toward another individual, and not toward an organization. He does not apply halakhic rules about cheating in business; presumably, he deems that the halakhic principles requiring one to speak up when seeing a wrong and acting when a life is in danger (*pikku'aḥ nefesh*) are more powerful:

> The beginning of the 21st century has seen an unprecedented wave of corporate financial scandals which resulted in thousands of people becoming unemployed and billions of dollars being

lost.... Employers who fail to follow the law are not only found in the corporate world—the public sector has also been hit with its fair share of scandals in the last decade, including numerous cases of attempted cover-ups of embarrassing facts to the government which went so far as to include obstruction of justice, bribery, and misuse of public funds. Companies have lied about or hidden data about their products that have cost lives.... In many cases, problems only came to light through the efforts of insiders who reported on the wrongdoing—"whistleblowers."...

There are also cases where we wish there had been a whistleblower. Ford Motor Company knew they had a defect in the Pinto gas tank design that would result in an estimated 180 deaths over the planned production run of the car. But Ford management decided that the cost to repair the defect, about $11 per car, was higher than the cost of the 180 deaths, so they did not fix it. Twenty-seven people died before a lawsuit brought the facts to light and Ford was forced to recall the vehicles and make the repairs. Those lives quite possibly could have been saved if a whistleblower would have reported on Ford's cold calculations on the value of a human life....

Whether to report employer wrongdoing is a very complicated question. On the one hand, from the principle of "do not stand idly by the blood of your neighbor" (Lev. 19:16) we know the Jewish tradition does not countenance being an innocent bystander to wrongdoing. At the same time ... Jews are warned against gossip and are taught not to go around sharing tales of the misdeeds of others....

Whistleblowers ... face possible retaliation from their employer: they could be fired, denied promotion, reassigned to a less desirable assignment, etc.... Potential whistleblowers face tremendous obstacles beyond direct employer retaliation. They know, for example, that bringing massive, Enron-style fraud to light could potentially lead to their current employer's implosion. Moreover, whistleblowers may fear blacklisting from future employers who suspect disloyalty, as well as social ostracism from their coworkers. Additionally, the psychological burdens associated with whistleblowing, including the effects of public criticism and a lengthy stay in litigation's limelight, cannot be ignored. Finally, employees may be contractually or otherwise bound in a way that deters them from blowing the whistle.

SECTION B: WHISTLEBLOWING AND *LASHON HARA*

Rabbi Leff discusses whether whistleblowing violates the prohibition of *lashon hara*, "improper speech":

> Engaging in *lashon hara*—broadly speaking, all forms of "improper speech," including gossip, slander, etc.—is considered a very serious violation under halakhah. Rabbi Israel Meir Hakohen Kagen [known as the Ḥafetz Ḥayyim, 1838–1933, Poland], lists 17 negative commandments and 14 positive commandments that can be violated through improper speech.... [He] goes on to state that if someone sees someone doing something wicked to another, like stealing from him, and it is known to him that the goods have not been returned, etc., it is permissible to tell people to help those who have been transgressed against. He goes on to list seven conditions that should be met before conveying the information to others:
>
> 1) It should be something he saw himself, not based on hearsay;
> 2) He should reflect carefully that he is certain the behavior he saw met the requirements of being considered theft or damage;
> 3) He should first gently rebuke the wrongdoer;
> 4) He shouldn't make the transgression greater than what it really was;

5) He should be clear about his motives—that this is being done to benefit the one who was sinned against, and that the one who is reporting the matter is not going to benefit from the damage he is about to inflict to another, or that he is doing it because he hates the transgressor;
6) If he is able to accomplish the effect through some other means without having to engage in *lashon hara*, he should do so, and not speak of the matter;
7) His speaking about this should not result in greater damage to the transgressor than if the matter had come before a beit din. . . .

The important point here is that the rules about *lashon hara* do not provide an excuse or a barrier NOT to report employer wrongdoing.

SECTION C: THE RESPONSIBILITY TO REBUKE

Rabbi Leff investigates the rule that a person must rebuke another when one sees a wrong being committed, considering whether it is dependent on whether it will be heeded and on the whistleblower's rank in an organization:

> The Torah charges us with an obligation to rebuke our neighbor when we see him doing something wrong to us. Leviticus 19:17 commands us: "You shall not hate your brother in your heart, you shall surely rebuke your neighbor, and not bear sin on his account." . . .
>
> When we see something wrong being done, we have a responsibility to speak up. . . . One factor in determining whether or not there is an expectation that the rebuke would be listened to is the culture of the corporation. Some companies make a real effort to solicit input from employees and to be responsive to that input. Other companies follow a much more rigidly hierarchical model, or have a CEO who is known not to take criticism well.

However, a mere general sense that a rebuke will not be listened to is not sufficient to relieve a person of the responsibility to rebuke a wrong-doer. In general, a high level executive is not only responsible for his particular department, but he is part of a team leading the corporation, and the expectation is that his advice will at least be listened to, even if it won't always be followed. Therefore, unless there were truly unusual circumstances, an executive would be expected to rebuke his employer (tactfully, of course), whereas a lower level employee could argue that the CEO would not listen to criticism coming from someone lower down in the organization....

We learn from the Talmud that we are each responsible to correct others who are within our sphere of influence [Babylonian Talmud *Shabbat* 54b].... We conclude that an executive (but not necessarily a lower-level employee) is obligated to rebuke his employer in a case of wrongdoing; for a lower-level employee, it is admirable, but not necessarily obligatory to rebuke his employer in the case of wrongdoing. However, if a lower level employee refrains from rebuking his employer because he does not believe he will be listened to, there may still be an obligation to report the wrongdoing to others.... If one's superior was not responsive to a rebuke, the next question is whether an employee is required to notify others, such as those higher up in a corporation, the corporation's board of directors, or someone outside the corporation, like legal authorities.

SECTION D: THE RESPONSIBILITY TO REPORT CASES OF *PIKKU'AḤ NEFESH* (LIFE IS ENDANGERED)

Rabbi Leff argues that if an employer's wrongdoing may result in death, the principle of *pikku'aḥ nefesh*, the requirement to save a life in immediate danger, is involved and, therefore, whistleblowing is required:

The nature of the employer's wrongdoing clearly is an important factor in deciding whether or not to report it. A design flaw that could lead to the loss of hundreds of lives—or a drug with dangerous side effects that could lead to thousands of deaths—is obviously in an entirely different category than a low level fraud that costs a company a few thousand dollars.

Clearly, the most serious situation is one in which lives are threatened.... It is well known that as a matter of halakhah, "nothing stands in the way of *pikku'aḥ nefesh* (to save a life)— save for the three cardinal sins of public idol worship, sexual transgressions, and murder." Not only does saving lives take precedence over any other commandment—including, for example, the commandments relating to *lashon hara*—but under the principle of do not stand idly by the blood of your neighbor, one is OBLIGATED to violate other commandments to save a life.

There are those who read *pikku'aḥ nefesh* very narrowly, and claim that *pikku'aḥ nefesh* only applies in situations where there is a specific life that one can point to that will be saved.... Others read the concern for *pikku'ah nefesh* in a broader, more inclusive fashion.... We rule that cases where it is known that a product is dangerous and people will be harmed are included under the rubric of *pikku'aḥ nefesh*. As such, not only are commandments such as *lashon hara* set aside, but there is a positive requirement to report the information, in keeping with the biblical injunction "not to stand idly by the blood of one's neighbor" (Lev. 19:16).

SECTION E: THE RESPONSIBILITY TO REPORT CASES OF FINANCIAL LOSS

It is less clear which halakhic principle regulates the response to financial misdeeds. Therefore, Rabbi Leff argues that the halakhic requirement to blow the whistle on financial misdeeds is less definitive and, therefore, disclosing wrongdoing may not be required:

Financial misdeeds in the corporate world have come under increasing scrutiny. There are many kinds of financial misbehavior in the corporate world. Sometimes companies engage in illegal practices, such as bribery or theft. The most common form of corporate theft is undoubtedly misappropriation of another company's intellectual property. In many other cases, companies engage in "creative accounting." . . .

If a person knows that his company is stealing from individuals or from another company, he knows that someone is being harmed. This could be seen as a case of "finding a lost object," which the Torah instructs us to return with not just one but two commandments (Deut. 22:1 and 22:8).

Many cases of corporate misdeed involve intellectual property, which is intangible, hence there is no "object" to return. . . . The commandment to return a lost object includes a requirement to save another person's money. . . . Maimonides [1135–1204, Spain, Egypt] adds in his *Sefer Hamitzvot* (Negative Commandments, no. 297) that the commandment "do not stand idly by" applies to a person who sees his friend's money in danger and he must prevent the loss by testifying in court. Even though there may be an obligation to save others from a loss if one can do so at no cost, one is not obligated to lose wages to save someone else a loss. This is understood by at least some poskim as meaning one does not have to forgo potential profits to return a lost item. The relevance of this to whistleblowing is that if the employee feared that reporting the loss would jeopardize his job (a potential loss of not only profits, but his very livelihood), he would NOT be obligated to inform. . . .

One potential barrier to reporting the activity is that most employees, especially executives, have to sign non-disclosure agreements, which they would breach if they reported the wrongdoing to a third party, which very likely could get the employee fired, and possibly make him the subject of a lawsuit.... Since one is not obligated to injure one's self financially to save someone else's money, an important factor in the decision about whether to whistleblow is proportion. Someone would not be required to endanger his livelihood to protect someone against a small loss.... On the other hand, in a case where the sums involved are large—and in some cases, the money involved can be staggering, in the billions of dollars—while one might not be strictly obligated under halakhah to report the wrongdoing, one who does so is praiseworthy. We are charged to "do what is right and good in the eyes of the LORD" (Deut. 6:18).

PESAK DIN

Rabbi Leff concludes:

1) In any case of wrongdoing, there is an obligation to rebuke the person doing wrong if it can be assumed there is a reasonable chance the rebuke will be listened to, and the rebuke can be administered without substantial personal cost to the reporter.
2) In cases of *pikku'aḥ nefesh*, where there is a certainty or substantial likelihood of loss of life if information is withheld, one is obligated to report the information to appropriate authorities, even at substantial personal cost.
3) In cases of financial loss, if wrongdoing can be reported at no cost to the reporter, there is a positive obligation to do so. If wrongdoing would jeopardize the reporter's money or livelihood, there is no strict obligation to report wrongdoing. It is, however, appropriate to consider proportionality. It is appropriate to demur from reporting minor wrongdoing that would have a major cost to the reporter. On the other hand, in the event of

major wrongdoing, it is appropriate to go beyond the minimum requirement of the law, and report it even at substantial personal cost.[4]

Text 1.3. Weiss, "About Commercial Encroachment"

MINḤAT YITZḤAK, 2, NO. 90

Born in Poland, Rabbi Isaac Jacob Weiss (1902–89) became head of the yeshiva in Munkácz, at that time part of Hungary (later Czechoslovakia and now Ukraine) at age twenty.[5] Surviving the Holocaust in Romania, he later moved to Great Britain, where he served as the senior *dayyan* (rabbinic judge) of the *beit din* of Manchester. His reputation was such that the Chief Rabbi of the British Commonwealth, Rabbi Immanuel Jakobovits, himself a noted authority, consulted with him. In 1968 Rabbi Weiss moved to Israel, where he became chair of the official Haredi (Ultraorthodox) Beit Din of Jerusalem. His responsa appear in six volumes of *Minḥat Yitzḥak* (The afternoon offering of Isaac), which also include an account of his life in Hungary under Nazi oppression and his escape to Romania.

QUESTION

A *beit din* asks Rabbi Weiss for his opinion in a case where a broker (Simon) changed employer (Reuben) and is now selling the products of his new employer (Jacob) directly to the clients of his old employer, putting his old employer's business at risk. It is the custom to anonymize the parties to a dispute by replacing their names with Reuben, Simon, and Jacob. Rabbi Weiss formulates the question as follows:

> What is your opinion regarding this case? Simon was Reuben's broker and employee, and Reuben connected him with clients. Simon later left Reuben and became the broker and employee of Jacob, who was the principal supplier to Reuben. Simon went to all the clients of Reuben who knew him from before [when

Simon was working for Reuben] and sold them Jacob's merchandise. Jacob completely stopped selling to Reuben, claiming that Simon had other suppliers. Reuben claimed that there was a secret agreement between Jacob and Simon to end his business with that merchandise and that [the *beit din*] should forbid Jacob to sell [Simon] merchandise.... Simon will not obey the ruling [of the *beit din*]. But if it is clear that Simon is forbidden to take the clients from Reuben, then perhaps it is possible to forbid Jacob to sell to Simon [even though it is Simon who has wronged Reuben] ... because he would be facilitating those doing something wrong.

SECTION A: THE BASIC PRINCIPLES REGARDING COMPETITION IN BUSINESS[6]

Weighing a number of halakhic principles in a brief responsum, Rabbi Weiss observes that a competitor must respect an existing business's clients by not poaching them—all the more so when the competitor used to work for the existing business:

> It is clear from the words of the Talmud and rabbinic decisors that in general the rule of "a pauper examining an abandoned loaf of bread" [a case in which a second person comes and seizes it instead of allowing the pauper to take it, discussed in Babylonian Talmud *Kiddushin* 59a], the law is undecided as to who merits possession [even though] the second person is called wicked. But here [in the case of Reuben, Simon, and Jacob] where there is a burden, even a danger, to [Reuben's] livelihood, everyone agrees that it is forbidden, as it is explained in Babylonian Talmud *Bava Batra* 21b ... :
>
>> Rav Huna said: A certain resident of an alleyway set up a mill [in an alleyway] and earned his living by grinding [grain]. And [later] another resident of the alleyway came and set up

[a mill] next to his. The halakhah is that [the first one] may prevent [the second one from doing so], as he can say to him: You are endangering my livelihood [by competing with me and taking my customers]. [The anonymous voice in the Talmud suggests:] Let us say that a *baraita* supports his opinion: One must distance fish traps [from other fish traps], as far as fish travels, i.e., the distance from which the fish will travel. How much [is this distance]? Rabba bar Rav Huna says: Up to a parasang [about 3.5 miles or 5.6 kilometers]. [Therefore the proprietor of a specific business] must distance himself from the place where another has established [that specific business]. [The anonymous voice of the Talmud responds that this is no proof because perhaps] fish are different, as they look around [whereas the residents of an alleyway employ the miller in their alleyway].

Rashi [1040–1105, France] comments that [fish] look where they are accustomed to find food and therefore [the angler] is sure that he will catch them. This is analogous to [the case of Reuben] where a second person comes and endangers the livelihood of the first.

SECTION B: THE RULES FOR AN AGENT

Rabbi Weiss discusses whether the rules regarding the *ma'arufya*, a Jew serving as the non-Jew's supplier or financial agent, apply in this case. These rules would prevent another agent from encroaching on the original agent's livelihood. While the rules tend to be applied leniently, allowing others to do business with the client, Rabbi Weiss observes that, to the contrary, they should not be applied leniently in this case because Reuben's livelihood is severely affected. Simply put, Simon should refrain from doing business that affects Reuben. That said, because the *beit din* expects Simon not to follow this ruling, the court has called for Rabbi Weiss's advice.

PESAK DIN

Rabbi Weiss commends the rabbis who asked for his opinion because it is incumbent upon a *beit din* to remedy a situation. He gives his permission to the *beit din* to issue an order to Simon's new employer Jacob—someone who will heed the *beit din*—to stop competing with the old employer (Reuben) for a time:

> It is incumbent upon a *dayyan* to issue a decree as is appropriate.... If Simon will not heed the [*beit din*'s] ruling that it is forbidden for Jacob to sell him merchandise... then the seller [Jacob] must be forbidden from selling... at least for a time.[7]

This is an intriguing ruling, since there is no basis in halakhah for it. Rabbi Weiss rules this way because ethics dictate that the original employer needs the *beit din*'s help since his livelihood is at risk.

Text 1.4. Somekh and Al-Ḥakam, "On Commerce in the Markets of Malabar"[8]

ZIVḤEI TZEDEK, ḤOSHEN MISHPAṬ 2

Rabbi Abdallah Somekh (1813–89), born in Baghdad, studied with the esteemed *dayyan* (judge) Rabbi Jacob ben Joseph ha-Rofeh.[9] Rabbi Somekh combined commerce and study for a decade as a young man but decided to switch solely to rabbinic scholarship and teaching due to the weakness of Jewish learning among Baghdadi Jews. He went on to serve as the leading religious decisor for communities of Iraqi Jews across the Middle East and South Asia. With financial assistance from the famed philanthropist Ezekiel Menasseh and his sons, he established the famous yeshiva Midrash Beit Zilkhah and was widely praised for "restoring the crown of Torah to its ancient glory" in Iraq. He had a positive attitude toward modern technology and government—for example, permitting tram riding within the city limits on the Sabbath—but stringently ruled that those who performed ritual slaughter had to be professionalized (by formally receiving approval by a leading rabbi and fully observant of the mitzvot). He wrote *Zivḥei tzedek* (Righteous offerings), a book of responsa addressing many queries from Jews of Baghdadi origins living in India; a commentary on the Passover Haggadah that includes annotations by his brother-in-law Rabbi Joseph Ḥayyim Al-Ḥakam (see below); and a book on the Jewish calendar that contains explanations of the Islamic and Christian calendars as well as notes on natural phenomena.

Born in Baghdad, Rabbi Joseph Ḥayyim Al-Ḥakam (known as the Ben Ish Ḥai, 1835–1909) was recognized for his intellectual prowess from a young age. His brothers made him a silent partner in their business so he could devote himself to study and writing.[10] He never accepted a rabbinic post, but he delivered public talks that drew huge crowds and authored more than a hundred books. Rabbis and laypeople sent him many questions on halakhah, and after the death of his brother-in-law Rabbi Somekh, he became the leading *posek* of Iraqi Jews. Believing that *posekim* should study both Sefardic/Mizraḥi and Ashkenazic rulings and that creativity and innovation were the hallmarks of a great rabbinic decisor, he integrated into his responsa a wide range of arguments and considerations, including from Kabbalah and modern medicine. After experiencing a mystical transformation when visiting the grave of Benaiah ben Jehoiada, a biblical figure reputed to be among King David's leading warriors, he felt himself to be Benaiah's reincarnation. He titled his most important books after the way Benaiah is described in 2 Samuel 23:20, "*ben ish ḥai rav pe'alim*" ("son of a valiant man, performer of mighty deeds"): a two-volume edition of his sermons on halakhah, *Ben ish ḥai* (Son of a valiant man), and responsa in four volumes, *Rav pe'alim* (Mighty deeds).

QUESTION

Rabbi Somekh's nephew in Bombay, Ezekiel Gabbai, who married into the famous Sassoon family and is anonymously called Reuben here, asks his uncle whether he can continue to buy peppercorns through a non-Jewish broker when the broker's non-Jewish partner in Malabar pays bribes to the weighers of the peppercorns.[11] (The international trade in peppercorns was very competitive; native and colonial powers vied for control.) Ezekiel wonders whether a person removed from a misdeed by a number of intermediaries still bears responsibility:

> Reuben, a resident of Bombay, has a non-Jewish broker who regularly brings him peppercorns from Malabar [a region in India]. Reuben covers his expenses and gives him a commission. This middleman has a non-Jewish partner in Malabar, who there purchases the peppercorns for him [through a written request specifying that they are for Reuben].... In the city of Malabar... two or three specific persons weigh the peppercorns. They are appointed to that function, and except for them, the seller cannot have anyone else weigh the peppercorns. When this broker receives the peppercorns from the city of Malabar and gives them to Reuben, their weight is not constant; sometimes it is more, and sometimes less. However, Reuben has no choice but to take them as their weight is defined in the document from Malabar.... He cannot demand the difference from them. This is Reuben's practice, as he has been doing for many years.
>
> However, now Reuben has heard that when the non-Jew in Malabar purchases the peppercorns, he gives a bribe to those who weigh the peppercorns [so that] when they weigh a larger amount [they write that it is less] so that the buyer will profit. They steal from the seller and give to the buyer. This is the practice of all the buyers there. When Reuben heard that this is what they do, he said to the broker...: "According to our [laws], this is forbidden, for you are stealing and giving it to me." The broker replied: "We pay off the weighers, not so that they will weigh

PERSONAL AND BUSINESS ETHICS 23

more but so that they will not weigh less, only [that they] weigh honestly—so that you will not receive less. However, if I do not give them bribes, they will weigh much less.... Sometimes there are sellers who are very knowledgeable and violent and suspect the weighers, and they stand by the scales when they weigh the peppers and the weigher cannot steal anything from them." Finally [the broker argued:] "Are we taking from you the money we pay as bribes? What is it to you? We are doing this for our own business!" Reuben replied [that he still wanted the broker to write the non-Jew in Malabar to stop giving money to the weighers. The broker agreed to do so.]

But Reuben does not believe the broker, for the Torah testified "their mouth speaks in vain" (Ps. 144:8). It is likely that he will not so write to his partner.... So... [Reuben asks if he may] continue to import peppercorns from this broker, or not? For the Noahides [term for non-Jews referring to seven commandments incumbent upon them] are commanded against stealing, and [Reuben] is the cause of their stealing from the sellers. If so, is it forbidden or permitted?

SECTION A: PUTTING A STUMBLING BLOCK IN THE WAY[12]

Rabbi Somekh considers three halakhic principles in this responsum. He starts by analyzing whether the prohibition "do not put a stumbling block before the blind" applies: the non-Jewish partner in Malabar is committing a sin because Reuben asked him to purchase peppercorns on his behalf, but Rabbi Somekh notes that the sin would be committed anyway, since there are other buyers besides Reuben. Rabbi Somekh then notes that by making an order, Reuben is increasing sin, not an acceptable action:

> We have [a] prohibition that forbids Reuben to do this—the prohibition of "do not put a stumbling block before the blind," just as [it says in] Babylonian Talmud *Avodah Zarah* 6b:

From where is it derived that a person may not extend a cup of wine to a nazirite [who is prohibited from drinking wine] and that he may not extend a limb severed from a living animal to a Noahide [who is prohibited from consuming a limb severed from a living animal]? The verse states: "You shall not put a stumbling block before the blind" [Lev. 19:14]. But here, if they did not give it to him, [in either situation] he could take it himself, yet the one [who hands it] is guilty of placing a stumbling block before the blind.

The Tosafot [novellae on the commentaries on Babylonian Talmud, written in Ashkenaz during the twelfth through fourteenth centuries] there, s.v. "may not extend," [comments that] this is the case with regard to all other prohibitions, etc. . . . And if so, in our case, since the Noahides are commanded about theft, a Jew who asked him to bring peppercorns is causing [the broker's partner] to steal because it is known that it is the practice in Malabar that the buyer is the one who bribes the weigher through the scale, and the Jew is the one violating "You shall not put a stumbling block before the blind" because it is for him the non-Jew is stealing.

At first glance, we can find leniency [for Reuben] because even if Reuben did not ask his broker to bring peppercorns, there are otherwise many other buyers for that broker to bring peppercorns from Malabar, whether non-Jewish or Jewish. If so, Reuben is not responsible because if he doesn't ask him to bring peppercorns, there are other buyers who ask him to bring peppercorns [in the process of which] the non-Jewish [broker] will violate the prohibition of theft, and Reuben is not responsible at all. . . . In this case the non-Jewish [partner] would bring peppercorns to other people and [violate the prohibition of theft]. . . . [However,] this leniency is not so clear-cut because even if the non-Jewish [partner] violates the prohibition for other buyers, [Reuben] increases his sin and causes him to steal again [when he orders peppercorns repeatedly].... If so, this leniency "falls into the well" and is invalid.

SECTION B: CAUSING ANOTHER TO PUT A STUMBLING BLOCK

Rabbi Somekh considers the question of the chain of responsibility: If one person asks another person to make a purchase, and the second person asks a third person to make a purchase, and the third person is the one who commits a sin, should the first person be considered responsible?

We have found [another leniency]. Babylonian Talmud *Avodah Zarah* 14d [says]:

> A *tanna* [a rabbi of the period of the Mishnah] taught: But of any of these [items whose sale is prohibited to non-Jews because they could use it in idolatrous worship], one may sell to [non-Jews] a [large] package [because they intend to sell it, not use it themselves].... But should we be concerned lest [the non-Jew] goes and sells it to others who will offer it as a sacrifice [in idolatrous worship]? Abaye said: We are commanded to not [place a stumbling block] before [the blind], but we are not commanded to not place [a stumbling block] before one who may [then] place [a stumbling block] before the blind.
>
> The meaning [of this text] is that [the non-Jew who bought directly from a Jew] is the one who transgresses.... But if this person then goes and sells to another man ... [this person once removed] does not transgress. As for the second one who does this who is once removed [the non-Jew who then sells the prohibited item to another non-Jew who intends to use it in

idolatrous worship] — we do not consider this a transgression, just as Rashi explains. ... If so, in our case Reuben may order his broker to bring him peppercorns because it is not the broker himself who is committing the transgression, but rather he is commanding his partner who is in Malabar to buy the peppercorns. It is his emissary who is in Malabar who is committing the transgression. We are not concerned because it is "you shall not place a stumbling block before the blind" once removed. If so, Reuben can [order via his broker].

SECTION C: AIDING THOSE COMMITTING A SIN

Rabbi Somekh now addresses whether the prohibition against aiding those committing a sin applies to this transaction:

[There is yet a third halakhic principle to be taken into consideration] and that is the prohibition of aiding those committing a sin. ... The [broker] is worried that if he does not bribe the weighers of the peppercorns, it will weigh less, and Reuben will suffer a loss. Then Reuben may no longer buy peppercorns from him, and this will be the end of the non-Jew's livelihood. If so, this is not a matter of doubt, but [rather] it is certain that the broker did not write to his partner [as Reuben ordered]. And even if there is support to say that he did indeed write so to his partner, it is more likely that he did not. ... [Therefore,] Reuben is forbidden to [continue to order via his broker].

SECTION D: THE SELLERS WATCH THE WEIGHERS

Rabbi Somekh discusses whether selling someone something that might be sold to another for a sinful activity is prohibited. He notes that while directly aiding a non-Jew to sin is completely prohibited, allowing one to indirectly aid a non-Jew to commit a sin is ethically problematic as well. Furthermore, how can a clear distinction between direct and indirect aid be made? Ultimately, however, he concludes that Reuven is not responsible for what his broker's partner might do, since suspicious sellers do sometimes keep an eagle eye on the weighers to stop them from lying about the weight of the peppercorns and therefore no offense might be committed:

> After further analysis we see that we can give permission for this matter easily.... [Some rabbinic authorities hold that selling incense is permitted, even if the purchaser might use it for idolatrous worship] because it's possible that the non-Jew will sell it to another non-Jew and so on, but [in the case of] worn-out books that are suitable for prayer in houses of idolatrous worship, there is no doubt that the non-Jew will give them or sell them to the Christian priests: that would be as if a Jew sells them to the Christian priest himself [and is therefore forbidden]. However, we follow [the opinion of] the Tosafot ... that we are not concerned about a once removed violation of "you shall not put a stumbling block before the blind" except when a violation of a prohibited act will definitely [occur]. But if the violation is not certain, such as in the case of frankincense when we might be concerned that he will sell it to another non-Jew to offer up in idolatrous worship but it is also possible that he owns the frankincense for medicine, [it is permitted]....
>
> In our case ... it is very much [in] the realm of possibility that the non-Jews who sell [the peppercorns] do not believe those weighing them and they themselves stand next to them [so as] to not permit them to steal at all. Here the principle of aiding those who commit sins does not apply because it is possible that they will not commit the sin. If so, Reuben may order his non-Jewish broker to import peppercorns for him because [as we have analyzed] from all these considerations, there is no cause for concern.

SECTION E: RABBI JOSEPH ḤAYYIM AL-ḤAKAM'S OPINION

Rabbi Somekh sent his answer to his nephew, but he also asked his much younger colleague, Rabbi Joseph Ḥayyim Al-Ḥakam, for his opinion and included that opinion in his book. Rabbi Joseph Ḥayyim objects that it is obvious that an illegality is being committed when Reuben sees that he has received more peppercorns than he paid for, yet it is probably not a case of theft but rather swindling, since the scale is true and only the weighers are speaking deceitfully:

> Everything that is written above applies to outright theft or short weighing in which the scale has false weights . . . but here they weigh with a scale they call a *kabban*, in which there is no mendacity. Rather, it is the weigher who deceives the owner of the peppercorns by [intentionally] reading the sign [on the scale incorrectly], that is, the scale weighs ten measures, but the weigher says that the weight is eight measures. The weigher [not Reuben] is the one who misleads. . . .

Rabbi Joseph Ḥayyim goes on to urge Reuben to find out more about the specifics of the transaction. It is striking that both rabbis seek to find a leniency in halakhah in order to permit Reuben to continue doing business by ordering peppercorns from Malabar, probably because Reuben is not the one committing the sin.[13]

Text 1.5. Barmash, "Veal Calves"

COMMITTEE ON JEWISH LAW AND STANDARDS OF
THE RABBINICAL ASSEMBLY, EVEN HA-EZER 5:14

Rabbi Pamela Barmash is the chair of the Committee on Jewish Law and Standards of the Rabbinical Assembly and also a *dayyan* (judge) on the Joint Beit Din of the Conservative/Masorti movement. She earned a BA from Yale University, rabbinic ordination from the Jewish Theological Seminary, and a PhD from Harvard University. A professor of Hebrew Bible and Biblical Hebrew at Washington University in St. Louis, she has served as director of Jewish, Islamic, and Near Eastern Studies there. She was formerly the rabbi at Temple Shaare Tefilah, Norwood, Massachusetts, as well as a fellow at both the Hebrew University, Jerusalem, and the Institute for Advanced Study, Princeton. She has published five scholarly books. In her academic scholarship, she addresses issues of law and justice and highlights how ancient Israelite culture has been transformed to meet changing intellectual and religious concerns and shifting social structures. In her rabbinic writing, she wants to inspire more Jews to be mindful of God in the daily routines of life and to live deliberately ethical lives.

QUESTION

In a responsum approved by the Rabbinical Assembly's Committee on Jewish Law and Standards in 2007, Rabbi Barmash addresses the question:

> Considering the conditions in which veal calves are raised, do the halakhic prohibitions of *tza'ar ba'alei ḥayyim*, inflicting suffering on animals, and *akhzariyyut*, cruel behavior by human beings, make the raising of veal calves in such a manner and the selling, purchase, or consumption of veal from these animals no longer permissible?

SECTION A: INTRODUCTION

Rabbi Barmash starts by describing the practices of raising veal calves that have elicited concerns over their treatment:

> The manner in which veal calves are raised both in Israel and the United States has led to serious questions as to the halakhic permissibility of the raising of veal calves in such a manner and

of the selling, purchase, and consumption of veal from animals raised in this manner. Veal calves have been subjected to intensive confinement that prevents them from lying down or turning around and to inadequate nutrition, including an all-liquid milk replacer diet in place of a mixed diet with sufficient iron appropriate for young calves, among other problematic practices. Veterinarians and animal welfare groups have sought to draw attention to the plight of veal calves in order to ameliorate these conditions.

SECTION B: BIBLICAL CONSIDERATIONS

Rabbi Barmash analyzes the biblical rules about how to treat animals, in particular how human beings are permitted to use animals but still must treat them with compassion. She highlights that the Bible states explicitly in Genesis 3 that humanity is allowed to eat vegetation. Only in Genesis 9 is humanity allowed to eat animal flesh, and then solely under certain restrictions:

> Biblical passages demand that human beings treat animals with compassion:
>
>> If you see your fellow's donkey or ox fallen on the road, do not ignore it: you must help him raise it. (Deut. 22:4)
>>
>> You shall not plow with an ox and a donkey together. (Deut. 22:10)
>>
>> You shall not muzzle an ox when it is threshing. (Deut. 25:4)
>
> Sabbath rest is extended to animals:
>
>> Six days you shall do your work, but on the seventh day you shall cease from labor in order that your ox and your donkey may rest and your slave and resident alien may be refreshed. (Exod. 23:12)

Sabbath rest is required so that animals who toil for human beings may rest....

While human beings are portrayed as having a vegetarian diet initially, later generations are permitted to eat meat with restrictions. The first human beings are told: The LORD God commanded the man: "Of every tree of the garden you are free to eat" (Gen. 2:16).

However, after the Flood, the scope of what is acceptable as food is enlarged. Noah is instructed that the flesh of animals may be eaten as long as the blood is not consumed: "Every creature that lives shall be yours to eat; as with the green vegetation, I give you all these. You must not however eat flesh with its life-blood in it" (Gen. 9:3–4).

According to the regulations of the Torah ... human beings at first were disallowed from consuming animals, but then were permitted to do so under restrictions.

SECTION C: RABBINIC CONCERNS AND THE PARAMETERS OF *TZA'AR BA'ALEI ḤAYYIM*

Rabbi Barmash investigates two halakhic principles: one well-known, *tza'ar ba'alei ḥayyim*, the prohibition against cruelty to animals, and *akhzariyyut*, the less well-known prohibition against human beings behaving cruelly. She argues that while human needs can prevail over *tza'ar ba'alei ḥayyim*, the prohibition against *akhzariyyut* deters cruelty as normal human behavior:

> The classical rabbis coined the terminology *tza'ar ba'alei ḥayyim* as a way of expressing the requirement to avoid inflicting suffering on animals and to relieve the suffering of animals that is expressed in the biblical verses on compassion for animals.... It is forbidden to purchase a domestic or wild animal or bird if one does not have the means to feed it. According to Babylonian Talmud Berakhot 40a ... one may not sit down to eat

until one's animals are fed. Even if one has already uttered the blessing over bread, one may interrupt partaking of it to ask whether one's animals are fed. These concerns are reaffirmed and expanded in later halakhah.... Rabbi Judah Heḥasid [c. 1150–1217, Germany] writes:

> If one caused suffering to an animal without good cause, like putting too heavy a load upon an animal and beat[ing] it even though it could not walk, [he] would be liable because he caused an animal to suffer. Likewise, those who pull the ears of cats to make them scream are sinners. The sages expounded "On that day, declares the LORD, I will strike every horse with panic and its rider with madness" (Zech. 12:4) to mean that in the future God will requite the humiliation of horses by their riders who strike them with boots....

One may still ride a horse or have a beast of burden carry a load, but not in a cruel manner....

The prohibition of inflicting suffering on animals is linked to the requirements for *sheḥitah* [kosher slaughter of animals].... Maimonides writes in *The Guide for the Perplexed*:

> Now since the necessity to have good food requires that animals be killed, the aim was to kill them in the easiest manner, and it was forbidden to torment them through killing them by piercing the lower part of their throat or by cutting off one of their limbs....

Maimonides argues [there] that the purpose of this prohibition ... [was also] to inculcate habits of kindness in human beings and prevent human beings from behaving cruelly ... :

> As for their dictum: [To avoid causing] suffering to animals is [an injunction to be found] in the Torah, in which they refer to its dictum: "Why have you struck your she-donkey," it is

PERSONAL AND BUSINESS ETHICS 33

set down with a view to perfecting us so that we should not acquire moral habits of cruelty and should not inflict pain gratuitously without any utility, but that we should intend to be kind and merciful [with every animal], except in the case of need, "Because you wish to eat flesh," for we must not kill out of cruelty or for sport.

The need to train human beings not to act cruelly regulates human behavior beyond the prohibition of inflicting suffering on animals. . . .

Tza'ar ba'alei ḥayyim measures the pain suffered by an animal that can be negated by the benefit to human beings, whereas the prohibition of *akhzariyyut* prevents cruel behavior from becoming a normative form of behavior for a human being.

SECTION D: VEAL AND THE RAISING OF VEAL CALVES

Discussing the way veal calves are raised in Israel and the United States, Rabbi Barmash points to the differences between what the American Veal Association, the organization of veal producers, recommends in contrast to what a humane organization stipulates regarding the raising of veal calves for food:

> There are currently [in 2007] three farms in Israel on which veal calves are raised, and a number of complaints reached the Ministry of Agriculture and the police in Israel regarding the intensive confinement and extremely inadequate nutrition on these farms as well as the stereotypical stress behavior exhibited by the calves. . . . A special committee [in 2002] . . . issued its report on standards for the raising of veal calves in Israel in order to comply with . . . the law against cruelty to animals without destroying veal production in Israel. . . . They recommended that changes be made in veal husbandry . . . : 1) iron intake of veal calves should be increased in order to raise the level of hemoglobin in their blood; 2) isolation of calves should

be greatly limited; 3) calves should be given sufficient space that would allow them to lie down, rest, stand up, and lick themselves/groom themselves; 4) calves should not be limited to consuming milk, but should be allowed a mixed diet; 5) water for drinking should not be restricted; 6) the living quarters of the calves should have adequate ventilation; 7) the living quarters should be lit for at least as many hours of daylight as there are; 8) appropriate bedding should be made available....

Unlike [in] Israel... the law of the United States generally does not regulate the treatment of farm animals.... Federal laws... do not apply to farm animals while they are on the farm.... A few farms in the United States do allow veal calves to engage in natural behaviors.... However, animals from these farms are very rarely utilized by kosher producers, and fewer than 10% of veal calves are currently raised under these conditions.... Jews should pay as much attention to the way in which the animal is raised as we have to the way in which it meets its end....

Humane Farm Animal Care (HFAC) has established a set of high-level standards in the following categories... [in contrast] to the guidelines currently in effect recommended by the American Veal Association (AVA), a producer organization:

NUTRITION

> AVA: Calves may be fed an all-liquid milk replacer diet from birth until slaughter.
> HFAC: All calves must be fed a wholesome diet which satisfies their nutritional needs, including fiber and iron. Calves must have access to calf starter feed or appropriate grain by five weeks of age.

ENVIRONMENT

> AVA: Slatted floors are permitted.

HFAC: All animals must have access to a solid floored lying area and dry, clean bedding.

SPACE REQUIREMENTS

AVA: For calves up to 450 lbs, minimum space recommendations for individual stalls are 26 inches wide by 66–72 inches long (11.9–13 sq.ft.).

HFAC: For calves up to 180 lbs, pens must allow at least 16 sq.ft. per calf. For calves over 180 lbs, pens must allow 20 sq.ft. per calf. . . .

The HFAC's standards are clearly an advance over the AVA's standards in promoting a more humane level of raising veal calves.

As of the writing of this teshuvah, only a few farms are raising veal calves according to the HFAC's guidelines. . . .

However, the veal industry in the United States has started to recognize that it can no longer ignore the demands of consumers, retail and food service organizations, and animal welfare groups.

PESAK DIN

Rabbi Barmash rules that current practices mandate that Jews do not consume, sell, or buy veal products until humane practices are adopted:

> We rule that only veal from animals raised under humane standards can be sold, purchased, or consumed. Humane standards for the raising of veal calves include sufficient space for calves to lie down, stand up, turn around, and groom themselves; proper nutrition in a mixed diet appropriate for young calves with sufficient iron, dry, clean bedding; and limited isolation.[14]

Ritual 2

Observing rituals fosters a greater sense of closeness to God and deeper meaning. Whether performed in solitude by an individual or in a family or communal group, rituals also nurture a feeling of community with Jews throughout the ages and around the world. No wonder then that Jewish communities are generally organized through synagogues or that rituals, while occasionally sparking controversy, are cherished.

The first two responsa we discuss address conundrums of liturgy. Rabbi Moses Sofer responds negatively to the question of whether prayer may be recited in the vernacular because of his adamant belief that no changes in Judaism are permissible, even though rabbinic tradition holds that prayer may be recited in any language. Rabbi Ḥayyim David Halevi wrestles with the purpose of prayer: he avers that the true purpose of prayer is to inspire an experience of closeness to God, not to petition for personal needs.

The third responsum, issued by the Central Conference of American Rabbis (CCAR) Responsa Committee, confronts the question of sexual abuse in a particularly challenging case: may a minor who committed sexual abuse and then completed his sentence in juvenile detention be allowed to return to participate in the synagogue community? This question probes into what Jews believe about *teshuvah* (repentance) and our responsibility to protect our synagogue communities from harm.

Text 2.1. Sofer, "On Using the Vernacular in Prayer"[1]

HATAM SOFER, 6, LIKUTIM, NOS. 84 AND 86

Rabbi Moses Sofer (known as the Ḥatam Sofer, 1762–1839) was born in Frankfurt but left when his teacher, Rabbi Nathan Adler, was forced out because of opposition to Adler's innovations.[2] He was appointed rabbi in Pressburg (the leading Jewish community at that time in Hungary, now Bratislava in Slovakia), and he established an important yeshiva there, perhaps the largest since the mishnaic period. As one of the early advocates for ideological Orthodoxy, he fought vigorously against Reform Judaism and the Haskalah (a Jewish movement that sought to preserve Jewish identity, including the revival of Hebrew, as Jews integrated into surrounding societies), and sought to intensify the separation of Orthodox Jews from Jews who did not follow Orthodox Judaism. His energy, rhetorical ability, and writing skills prompted his rise to leadership in Orthodox circles, and his rulings and attitude toward halakhah ushered in the development of Ultraorthodox Judaism, for which he served as an authoritative figure. He famously reinterpreted the talmudic statement "Anything new is forbidden," originally meaning that new grain may not be consumed until the first crops offering is made on Shavuot (*Mishnah Orlah* 3:9), as a statement prohibiting all innovation in any area of Jewish life; and he advocated that loyalty to the Torah meant retaining the observances and life patterns that he ascribed to Jewish communities before modernity. He strongly supported the validity of customary practices, even against the rules of halakhah. After his death, his family published his responsa, entitled *Ḥatam sofer* (The seal of the scribe/*sofer*), in seven volumes, as well as his commentary on the Torah, two books of sermons, and many other writings.

Before reading Rabbi Sofer's responsa, it is helpful to understand both the historical context and rabbinic tradition on prayer in the vernacular. In the nineteenth century, a number of Jewish communities in Europe made changes to liturgical practice, including reciting statutory prayers, such as the *Shema* and the *Amidah*, in the vernacular. Traditional rabbinic texts permitted this. The Mishnah rules:

> These are recited in any language, not specifically Hebrew ... the *Shema*, the (*Amidah*) prayer, and Grace after Meals.[3]

The Babylonian Talmud *Sotah* 32b–33a derives this ruling from the wording of the *Shema*: the first word, *shema*, means "hear" or "understand" (in the imperative), indicating that the *Shema* must be comprehended by the one reciting it and, therefore, may be recited in a language one understands. The Talmud terms the *Amidah*, the prayer par excellence, as "*raḥamei*," meaning a deeply felt request for God's mercy—one that may also be recited in any language. The Shulḥan Arukh, the halakhic code deemed to be the most authoritative, affirms this ruling for the *Shema*:

> One may read [the *Shema*] in any language and should be careful to avoid mispronunciations in that language. One should be precise in it just as in Hebrew.[4]

However, the Shulḥan Arukh recalibrates this ruling for prayers not recited in community:

> One may pray [any prayer] in any language one wishes—this applies [when one is praying] with a congregation. But when [one is praying] alone, one should pray only in Hebrew. Some say that this [requirement to pray only in Hebrew] applies only when one is asking for one's own needs, such as one who is praying for someone who is ill or about some distress in one's household; however, in regard to the regular liturgy established for the congregation [outside of requests for one's own needs], even an individual may recite it in any language. Some say that even an individual requesting one's own personal needs may

request them in any language one wishes, except in the Aramaic language.[5]

Despite these rulings, Rabbi Sofer opposes prayer in the vernacular.

In 1818–21, a controversy arose over a Reform synagogue in Hamburg that modified the siddur text to use the vernacular in public worship—a dispute that marked a seminal turning point in European Jewry and the development of modern Jewish movements. Rabbi Sofer was drawn into this controversy when a leading rabbi in Hamburg made a public announcement in his synagogue condemning the use of the vernacular in prayer and forbidding anyone from praying in that Reform synagogue and then sent him two letters of inquiry on these matters.[6] Rabbi Sofer wrote two responsa in reply.

The most salient points of both responsa have been integrated into a single responsum that follows. As we will see, Rabbi Sofer makes many innovations in halakhic practice and principles in his two *teshuvot* on prayer in the vernacular. This is especially striking in light of his ideology that he is staunchly maintaining tradition.

OPENING REMARKS[7]

Rabbi Sofer begins by expressing in harsh terms his shock, whether real or rhetorical, at the changes in the text used by the Reform synagogue in Hamburg. With rhetorical and humorous flourish, he writes that the Reform synagogue, which apparently was open for prayer only on Shabbat, should also be closed on Shabbat as well:

> [When] your [letter] reached me, [the news] enfeebled and shocked me and with bitter herbs sated me by telling me the news that people who do not respect the yoke of heavenly sovereignty have set out to annul the covenant with plots for new religions that have arisen recently, with a [shared] plan that their synagogues are to be closed all week and open only on Shabbat.

Would that they would be closed on Shabbat as well since they have changed the text of prayer received from the members of the Great Assembly [the legendary council leading the Jewish people from the mid-fifth century to second century BCE], the sages of our Talmud, and our holy ancestors. They have added and subtracted from the texts based on their own imaginations, and they have rejected several of the morning blessings that are explicated in the ninth chapter of the Babylonian Talmud *Berakhot*, such as — it should not be mentioned! — the flowering anew of the sovereignty of King David the Messiah, and the complete rebuilding of Zion and Jerusalem the holy city . . . and most of their prayer is in German.

SECTION A: THE GLORY OF THE SECOND TEMPLE PERIOD IN CONTRAST TO CURRENT TIMES[8]

Glorifying the Second Temple period in which the text of Jewish liturgy developed, Rabbi Sofer castigates the Reformers of his time for their insolence in changing sacred text composed in the Second Temple period. He explains away differences between Ashkenazic and Sefardic/Mizraḥi liturgy by claiming that each group had its own text and no one dissented:

> It is known that during the Second Temple period [515 BCE–70 CE], Jews dwelled in their land and had a ruler governing in glory and honor for a number of those centuries. [During this period,] they had great sages whose complete attention was [devoted to] Torah, [with] the sages and their students in thousands and ten thousands, in *batei midrash* [religious academies] better than all of the universities of our day. They had a Sanhedrin [supreme rabbinic court] making fences [around the Torah] and issuing decrees, and [studying with them] were thousands and ten thousands of students and students' students, until Rabbi Judah Hanasi composed the Mishnah. Of those sages, only a

RITUAL 41

small number were mentioned in the Mishnah and the *baraitot*, as is explained in Maimonides' introduction to the Mishnah. From the words of those sages of those several centuries only a small number of statements from each one was mentioned.... And now, how could the words that left the mouths of the sages and wise people, whose hearts were as broad as the entrance to the Temple, whose words were refined repeatedly over hundreds of years by thousands of sages and were established in the heart of the nation for close to two thousand years without anyone uttering a word [of objection] or "waving a wing [in protest]"—how could small foxes, in the darkness of exile, arise to break their walls and destroy their fences and change the texts of their prayers and blessings and change the times they established for us? And if [they would base their changes] on legal principles, [our tradition holds that] no court can annul the words of another court unless it is greater in wisdom and number. Even if the reason [for an earlier court's enactment] has become void, the *takkanah* [enactment] is not void. This is especially true regarding prayer, which has spread in all of Israel, even in texts that vary from place to place; this is still considered to have "spread through all of Israel," since originally one text was established only for Ashkenazim and it spread among them without a dissenter, and another text [was established] for Sefardim and it spread among them without dissent.

SECTION B: PRAYER MUST BE IN HEBREW

Recognizing that both the Mishnah and Talmud rule that one may pray in any language, Rabbi Sofer qualifies this rule by introducing a nuance not found in either: praying in the vernacular is permitted only occasionally. He continues with an argument that public prayer must be in Hebrew, the language used by the Great Assembly for the text of the *Amidah* and other prayers. If people need to understand what they are praying, Rabbi Sofer asks, why did the members of the Great Assembly compose the *Amidah* in Hebrew, rather than Aramaic, the common language of the time? He argues that using Hebrew was necessary because just as one speaks to a king in his language, one must pray to God in Hebrew. Rabbi Sofer's proof for this is a rule ascribed to King Aḥashveirosh, perhaps a weak proof since Aḥashveirosh is generally viewed in negative tones. Rabbi Sofer offers three stronger proofs: (1) God is portrayed in the Bible as speaking to the prophets in Hebrew, (2) a famous midrash contends that Hebrew is the original language of humanity, and (3) the Torah is in Hebrew. Rabbi Sofer concludes his argument by emphasizing that those who follow tradition have a stronger position than those who seek to deviate:

> Regarding public prayer in a language other than the holy tongue, this is impossible in any form. While it is true that "these may be said in any tongue" [*Mishnah Sotah* 7:1], including the *Amidah* so that one may fulfill [the obligation to pray] the *Amidah* in any language—that refers to doing so occasionally. But to do this regularly and to appoint a *shaliaḥ tzibbur* in public to pray regularly in public in the language of the nations [this is a different matter]. If so, the Great Assembly would not have enacted prayer in the holy tongue as polished and clear. In their days, half the nation already spoke [another language]. See Maimonides, *Mishneh Torah*, Hilkhot Tefillah [Laws of the Prayer] 1:4. It would have been better for them to set [the prayers] in Aramaic, since it was the habitual language with which everyone was accustomed. About Ezra it says, "They read the scroll of the Torah of God, making it clear and giving the sense" [Neh. 8:8]. The sages explained that ["making it clear and giving the sense"] was translation [Babylonian Talmud *Megillah* 3a], indicating that the nation [at that time] did not understand the holy language and required a translator to explain the Torah. If so, why did they not enact prayer in translation? It must be that the sages

intentionally enacted [prayer in Hebrew], and it is not possible to hold that one may pray in any language and in any way....

[Regarding the concern that people will not understand what they say in Hebrew,] it would be easier to make sure that each person learns the meaning of the prayers and then prays in Hebrew than to enact prayer in a foreign language. Before mortal kings, they do not do so: one who speaks with the king must do so in the king's language, as is recorded regarding Aḥashveirosh, "speaking the language of his nation" [Esther 1:22], and one does not speak one's own language [before a king], even if the king understands it.

[Furthermore,] Naḥmanides [1194–1270, Spain, Israel] writes that [Hebrew] is the language with which God speaks to his prophets [beginning of Parashat Ki Tissa']. The sages say that the universe was created with this holy tongue since "[the Torah states in Gen. 2:23,] 'This one shall be called "woman [Hebrew *ishah*]" because she was taken from man [Hebrew *ish*].' From here we learn that Torah was given in Hebrew.... Just as the Torah was given in Hebrew, so too the world was created in Hebrew" [*Bereshit Rabbah* 18:4]. If so, this is God's language, with which He gave His Torah. One cannot speak before Him in our languages, with which we are accustomed, but only in His language, set aside for His holy words. This is why the Great Assembly set the text of prayers and blessings in the holy language. The one who would do differently has the lower hand, and one who holds onto the words of the sages and our ancestral custom has the upper hand.

SECTION C: IF THE TORAH READING IS IN
HEBREW, THEN PRAYER MUST BE IN HEBREW

In the second responsum on prayer in the vernacular, Rabbi Sofer augments his argument by asserting an unprecedented comparison: the public Torah reading serves as a model for prayer, and therefore just as the Torah reading has to be in Hebrew, so too does prayer.[9] Tradition holds that Ezra established the public Torah reading in Hebrew, and even though the Jews of Ezra's time had difficulty understanding the language and needed an Aramaic translation during his reading, Rabbi Sofer argues that Ezra intended the awkward process of Hebrew read aloud with Aramaic translation because the Hebrew text of the Torah possesses levels of meaning and significance that defy translation. A translation may succeed in uncovering one level of meaning but cannot possibly reveal all the levels of meaning of the Hebrew text of the Torah.

Rabbi Sofer then makes an analogy from the Torah reading to the liturgy devised by the members of the Great Assembly. Had they wanted the people to understand prayer completely, they would have written the *Amidah* in Aramaic. Rather, they wanted Jews to recite the specific words they selected, whether or not the words were understood. In making this argument, Rabbi Sofer transforms the concept of *kavvanah*, the intentionality requiring worshipers to pray in a language so that they understand and mean the words of their prayer, to refer to the unique meanings that the Hebrew text possesses that defy translation.

PESAK DIN

Rabbi Sofer rules:

> Therefore, regarding your announcement in your holy synagogue that it is forbidden to pray from their vernacular *siddurim* [prayer books] but only in the holy tongue and using the old texts printed before . . . , you have acted according to Torah, and your hands should be strengthened. May God be thus with you. There is no doubt that all the learned sages of this time will agree with this prohibition. The sages and I agree to forbid any Jew from changing a thing from what is mentioned above, and then they shall be saved from all evil and [punishments

invoked by the] curses in the Torah and will merit [seeing] the rebuilding of the Jerusalem Temple.[10]

Text 2.2. Halevi, "What Are the Chances That Our Prayers Are Answered by God?"

ASEH LEKHA RAV, 2, NO. 22

Born in Jerusalem to a Ladino-speaking family, Rabbi Ḥayyim David Halevi (1924–98) was educated in Yeshivat Porat Yosef and served in a yeshiva unit in the Israeli military during the 1948 War for Independence.[11] For almost fifty years, he was a major voice in halakhic discourse in Israel. Rabbi Halevi worked for two years as the private secretary to the Rishon Lezion Sefardic Chief Rabbi Ben-Zion Meir Ḥai Ouziel and then became the Sefardic rabbi of the city of Rishon Lezion. He served as the Sefardic Chief Rabbi of Tel Aviv from 1974 until his death in 1998. He was the Mizraḥi party (the long-standing Religious Zionist political party) candidate for the position of Rishon Lezion Sefardic Chief Rabbi of Israel in 1982 but was not selected because Rabbi Ovadia Yosef, a highly influential former Rishon Lezion Sefardic Chief Rabbi, wanted a rabbi affiliated with the Shas political party (a new Sefardic/Mizraḥi Israeli political party) to hold the position. A prolific author, Rabbi Halevi published numerous books and hosted a radio show for many years. His books of responsa, *Aseh lekha rav* (Make for yourself a rabbi, the name of his radio program and based on his talks there) and *Mayyim ḥayyim* (Living waters), address matters of theology as well as halakhic practice. Rabbi Halevi was innovative in how he composed *Aseh lekha rav*: rather than presenting detailed analyses of sources, he wrote in a lively, vivid manner, citing sources only as needed, and thereby making responsa literature more accessible to laypeople. He also wrote *Mekor ḥayyim* (Source of life), a code emphasizing the practices of Sefardic/Mizraḥi communities. He won the Israel Prize in 1997.

The following responsum is unusual because it discusses theological matters, whereas responsa generally address matters of practical law. Rabbi Halevi is one of the first rabbinic decisors to innovate writing responsa on theological questions.

QUESTION

Rabbi Halevi grapples with the theological dilemma of whether requests made during prayer will be answered positively by God. If the answer is yes, it appears that a person has caused God to change, but how can an omniscient, omnipotent, and perfect God possibly be induced by a mortal to fulfill that mortal's will?

> What are our chances of expecting that our requests and supplications will be fulfilled, if *ab initio* the will of God differs?

SECTION A: PETITIONARY PRAYER IS PART OF TRADITION[12]

Well aware that a significant part of prayer is devoted to requests for aid from God, Rabbi Halevi acknowledges—but does not belabor—the criticism that such prayer may be seen as problematic. Rather, he presents well-known examples of biblical characters making specific requests in prayer and then quotes from their general requests asking that their prayers be answered. In so doing, he affirms that petitioning God during prayer is acceptable—the clear evidence of biblical characters making requests in prayer is irrefutable:

> It is true that we cannot ignore that a considerable part of prayer is intended for entreaty and turning to God to fulfill our requests and our material and spiritual needs. One may claim that this isn't pure worship of God and is not worship of God at all. To this, we may say that this claim is in error, for the Torah itself tells of Abraham praying for the healing of Abimelekh, Eliezer praying by the well for the sake of a wife for Isaac, Moses praying

RITUAL 47

for Pharaoh, the Israelites praying for themselves at the time of peril near the Sea of Reeds, Moses praying for the Israelites a number of times in the wilderness and also for Aaron, and many of the prophets of Israel praying to God in times of peril—all of this explicit in the Torah. Solomon included this request of God [during the dedication of the Jerusalem Temple]: "May You hear in Your heavenly abode any prayer or supplication offered by any person among all Your people Israel—each of whom knows his own affliction—when he spreads his palms toward this House" [1 Kings 8:38].

Nehemiah prayed: "O LORD, God of Heaven, great and awesome God, who stays faithful to His covenant with those who love Him and keep His commandments, may Your ear be attentive and Your eyes open to receive the prayer of Your servant" [Neh. 1:5–6].

Supplication in prayer is one of its foundations, and it is therefore an important basic element in the worship of God, whether [the request] comes naturally or [in response to divine] judgment, as it is written in the Babylonian Talmud *Rosh Hashanah* 16a: "Crying [out to God] is favorable for a person both before [divine] judgment [has been decreed for that person] and after the judgment has been decreed."

SECTION B: THE TRUE NATURE OF PRAYER

Rabbi Halevi confronts two questions: (1) how is it possible to change God's will by making a request in prayer, and (2) if we are judged according to our deeds, and then rewarded or punished according to our good or bad deeds, how can we request a change in our situation through prayer? Rabbi Halevi argues that these questions are mistaken. What is positive in our lives is the result not of our good deeds, but of God's kindness toward human beings. Citing both a philosophical work and a halakhic code, Rabbi Halevi attests that the true purpose of prayer is not to change God but to change us—to inspire us to seek God and follow God's will rather than our material wants:

> Again the question must be asked—changing God's will is not possible and therefore what is the purpose of entreaty? Moreover, are not the conditions of our life, for good or for bad, derived in accordance with our deeds good or bad; if so, what is the power of prayer? But this is not the truth: only infrequently can we extrapolate our good situation directly from our good deeds. Many of the good circumstances of our life flow from [God's] loving-kindness, just as it says in Dan. 9:18: "Not because of any merit of ours do we lay our supplication before You but because of Your abundant mercies." . . .
>
> God's will is always for the good: "God values those who are in awe of Him" [Ps. 147:11]. Just as the light of the sun shines upon all earthly objects, and upon the entity most ready to receive [the light], it illumines more. Thus is the will of God: the person whose deeds are worthy is the one who is ready to absorb the loving-kindness of God and His mercy, which are the revelation of God's will. Therefore, the prayer that a person makes does not involve a change in God, may God be blessed, but rather a change in the human being who makes a shift in his spiritual preparation that causes him to let go of his will to return to God, who shines the light of God's superior will upon him. Therefore, the prayer that has a chance of being answered positively is that prayer that the worshiper thinks he is not worthy of receiving because his deeds prevent it, from the standpoint of "your iniquities have been a barrier between you and your God" [Isa. 49:2]. But that prayer whose purpose is drawing closer to God and divine worship, prayer that is in the heart, [and prayer seeking to] purify [one's] physical powers and transcend [one's material limitations] is the appropriate preparation to receive the outpouring of (God's) will and His

loving-kindness. This idea is based on the words of Rabbi Joseph Albo [c. 1380–1444, Spain] in his book *Ha'ikkarim*, 4.18, and see *Shulḥan Arukh Oraḥ Ḥayyim* 98:5.

SECTION C: THE TRUE GOAL OF PRAYER

Returning to the question of whether requests made during prayer will be answered, Rabbi Halevi issues the caution, bolstered by talmudic sources, that expecting answers is wrong-headed. While the traditional text of the siddur integrates both hymns and requests to God, he omits the possibility of modifying its text. Transcending the overt meaning of liturgical requests, he urges us toward modesty in prayer: we should use prayer as a means of drawing closer to God:

> And this is what our rabbis taught: "Anyone who prolongs his prayer and expects it [to be answered] will ultimately come to heartache" [Babylonian Talmud *Berakhot* 55a].

Rashi explains, the one who expects it says in his heart that his requests will be fulfilled because he prays in *kavvanah* will come to heartache because his request is not fulfilled. . . . If a person thinks that his prayer requests must be fulfilled because he is praying, his requests will never be granted.

Therefore if a person prays and is not answered he should pray again, as it is said in Babylonian Talmud *Berakhot* 32b:

> A person who prayed and saw that he was not answered, should pray again, as it is stated: "Hope in the LORD, strengthen yourself, let your heart take courage, and hope in the LORD" [Ps. 27:14].

For most of the time a person does not achieve the ultimate goal of prayer, which is drawing close to his Creator, the first time. Therefore, he must pray again, that is to say, he must continue preparing himself spiritually for his Creator, and in the end he shall be answered.[13]

Text 2.3. CCAR Responsa Committee, "A Sex Offender in the Synagogue"

CCAR RESPONSUM 5765.4

By the middle of the nineteenth century, the Reform movement stopped using responsa written by individual rabbis as a genre of literary expression. Instead, conferences of rabbis decided matters of religious practice by majority vote—a practice other rabbis across the movements would later adopt.

At the time, Reform rabbis consulted rabbinic texts not as guidance for their practice, but as examples of the historical development of Judaism, and generally did not define law as one of the facets of Judaism. Once the Reform rabbinic organization the Central Conference of American Rabbis (CCAR) was established in 1890, it tried to foster unity of practice by shared vision in subsequent decades, and a responsa committee was ultimately founded in 1906 in response to younger rabbis seeking guidance on how to conduct life-cycle rituals.[14] Rabbinic leaders thought that this responsa committee of rabbis writing as individuals or as members of a small committee would be a way of making their answers less authoritative than CCAR decisions as a whole.

The number of responsa published waxed and waned until Rabbi Solomon Freehof (1892–1990) became chair right after World War II. He gained much prestige and respect from his Reform colleagues for his work on the joint Committee on Responsa for American service personnel (see chapter 10), and he personally wrote most of the responsa. Initially, most of the questions concerned ritual matters, but in recent decades the CCAR Responsa Committee has addressed many more questions about ethical dilemmas, including the following one.

QUESTION

This English responsum, posted in 2005, tackles two questions regarding sexual abuse. What is to be done when a minor who has completed detention for his crime of sexual molestation then seeks access to the same synagogue attended by the victim? And what obligations does the synagogue have to uphold with regard to the perpetrator's mother, who chose not to inform synagogue authorities that her son had committed other such crimes before this one took place?

> A young man was sexually molested at a synagogue day camp program by a junior counselor, [who] was convicted, spent about a year in juvenile detention, and was recently released.... A restraining order ... prevents the perpetrator from being near the victim's home, school and synagogue.
>
> 1. If the judge had not ... included [the synagogue] in the restraining order, should we have allowed [the perpetrator, who also lives in our community] ... to attend services or religious school, and under what conditions? ...
>
> 2. It came out that the perpetrator's mother was aware that her son had previously molested other children and ... had not informed the Director of Education, who was in charge of the camp program.... Is there any reason to deny the mother access to the synagogue (especially since the mother of the child he abused cannot stand being anywhere near the abuser's mother)?

SECTION A: READMITTING THE OFFENDER?
THE MITZVAH OF REPENTANCE

The Responsa Committee begins by emphasizing that the offender's exclusion from the synagogue community is likely to send the message that the community does not truly believe in repentance:

> This [question] presents us with two separate cases. The first is a hypothetical one: should the synagogue have denied access to the perpetrator had the court not done so?

The perpetrator, who seeks access to the synagogue and to its programs, might argue that he has met the terms of the punishment administered for his crime. For the synagogue to deny him entry would be to add to his punishment, to make it more severe than required by law, and such a course ... does him an injustice. The wrong ... is compounded by the fact that he is a minor, whom the law does not hold totally responsible for his actions.... Expulsion from the synagogue ... would run counter to a fundamental goal ... of Judaism: the encouragement of repentance [Hebrew *teshuvah*[15]].... Our sources ... speak at length of the overriding importance of *teshuvah*.... *Teshuvah* ... expunges the record of our sins so that "even one who is wicked throughout his lifetime may do *teshuvah* at the very end, and not a single fact of all his evil will be remembered against him" [Babylonian Talmud *Kiddushin* 40b].... God ... does not desire the punishment of the sinner but rather that he or she turn away from wickedness....

In ancient times, the Temple and the sacrifices were the means by which Israel achieved atonement for sin. Today, when repentance is the only avenue remaining for atonement, it is the task of the synagogue ... to provide a locus for the work of *teshuvah*. To exclude this ... young man for whom rehabilitation is surely not yet an impossible dream would send the message that we do not truly believe in the possibility of *teshuvah* and that the synagogue is no longer a place in which those who truly seek to repent can work toward personal redemption.

SECTION B: READMITTING THE OFFENDER? THE
MITZVAH TO PROTECT OURSELVES FROM DANGER

Despite the serious concern that "the synagogue is no longer a place in which those who truly seek to repent can work toward personal redemption," the Responsa Committee holds that the possibility of the perpetrator's committing abuse again must prevail in the synagogue's decision:

> Those who would deny access to the perpetrator would argue that no individual possesses an unlimited right of membership in the community and of access to its institutions. Jewish tradition ... permits the community to exclude an individual from membership and participation for sufficient cause.
>
> Moreover ... all that we know about the etiology of sexual abuse suggests that this perpetrator ... may well pose a continued danger to the safety and well-being of ... children. And our tradition also teaches that we are obligated to remove from our property any factor that poses danger to the life, health, or property of others. Hence ... it is our duty to deny this young perpetrator access to our synagogue and that, should we allow him entry and should he repeat his abusive behavior, it is we who must do *teshuvah*.

SECTION C: THE COMMITTEE'S *PESAK DIN* ABOUT THE OFFENDER

The Responsa Committee rules:

> It is never an easy thing to decide between two moral or religious values that seem to pull us in opposite directions. In this case, however, it is clear to us that our first duty, the obligation that takes precedence over all others, is to ensure that our synagogues and schools are places of safety for those who enter them. While the convicted sex offender is right to look upon the synagogue as a place of spiritual healing, that right pertains to all of its members, its families and their children. ... In the case that prompted this inquiry, the court agreed that the danger was real and issued its restraining order. In the hypothetical case

posed by our [question], the danger might be no less real, and it is reasonable to presume that the offender's presence would be deeply disturbing to his victim as well as to others. It is their synagogue, too, and the congregation's leadership bears the overriding duty to reassure all its members that the synagogue is a safe place and that this safety extends to all congregational functions. The congregation is therefore under no Judaic religious obligation to admit this young person, a convicted and [hopefully] recovering sex offender, onto its grounds or into its ... activities.

SECTION D: THE OFFENDER'S MOTHER

The Responsa Committee censures the mother for her behavior. She is not a threat to the synagogue community, so she cannot be excluded from it, but she must do *teshuvah* and ask forgiveness.

> The second part of this (question) is not hypothetical: should the mother of the perpetrator, who did not inform the congregation of her son's history of sexual abuse, be denied access to the synagogue? ... The mother's failure to notify the synagogue ... is inexcusable. Unlike her son, she is an adult, and we hold her fully culpable for this shocking lapse of moral responsibility. Yet we think that it would be inappropriate for the congregation to deny her access. ... First, she poses no threat to the safety of congregants. Second, she, too, must do *teshuvah*, and she must do it in the synagogue, the very place where she committed her transgression. She must ask the forgiveness of those against whom she has sinned: her son's victim, the victim's family, and, for that matter, the entire congregation.

SECTION E: A PARTIAL DISSENT

A member of the Responsa Committee dissents:

One member of this Committee, though agreeing with the broad trend of the decision, believes that the congregation should be encouraged to find appropriate means of allowing those who have committed sexual offenses to participate in synagogue life.... A number of Christian churches... have developed protocols stipulating the precise conditions under which a sex offender might be allowed entry and participation in the community. These may include restricted access to the synagogue building(s) and grounds; a requirement that while on synagogue grounds the offender be accompanied at all times by a family member or by an individual designated by the synagogue; a prohibition of access to the school and nursery areas of the synagogue facility; and so forth. The synagogue might require that the offender and (if he/she is a minor) the offender's family sign an agreement expressly accepting these restrictions, and it might require them to report from time to time to an appropriate committee concerning their adherence to these guidelines. In addition, the synagogue might require the perpetrator to make a statement acknowledging the pain he or she has caused the victim. Such an open acknowledgment of responsibility, called a *vidui*, is perfectly consistent with our tradition's conception of repentance.... Should these protocols prove impractical to administer and enforce, or should they fail to reassure the congregants that they and their children are truly safe while at the synagogue, the congregation is entitled to deny access to the perpetrator, on the grounds that its overriding duty is to make the synagogue a safe place for all who make up its community.[16]

Personal Status 3

Knowing who we are as individuals and as members of a community is fundamental to every human being. Halakhah addresses a number of classic issues regarding personal status. In this chapter we explore two of them: the *mamzer* and "who is a Jew."

We begin with three responsa on the *mamzer*, a person of problematic family lineage whose status may impair relationships with other Jews whose family lineage is not an issue. This discussion illuminates how contemporary rabbis grapple with the injustice of a person doomed because of a parent's action. Rabbi Ephraim Oshry, famous for his responsa on the Holocaust, decrees that a young rabbi is a *mamzer* and therefore must divorce his wife and leave his rabbinic post; although Rabbi Oshry is deeply sympathetic to the young rabbi's plight, he does not seek ways to alleviate the situation. By contrast, other rabbis have sought to mitigate the status of a *mamzer*. We examine two more responsa in this light. One, by Rabbi Elie Spitz, presents a global solution that would apply across the board to all *mamzerim*: rabbis should refuse to hear any testimony that a person is a *mamzer*. The second, by Rabbi Shalom Mesas, is one of his many responsa that inspired the *batei din* of the official State Rabbinate of Israel to utilize halakhic principles in specific cases in order to prevent individuals from being declared a *mamzer*, even if applying those halakhic principles seems farfetched and contrary to reality.

We then move onto the issue of "who is a Jew?" Since the time of the Mishnah and the Talmud, Jewish status has been conferred either by being born to a Jewish mother, known as matrilineal descent, or by conversion to Judaism. In modernity, this status has prompted great debate. Among the many questions are: Should only Jews of matrilineal descent or by conversion through specific rituals under certain auspices be considered Jewish? How should one understand Jewish status in the State of Israel, given that according to the "who is a Jew" law (also known as the Law of Return), a person descending from a Jewish grandparent is entitled to Israeli citizenship upon arrival in Israel even though otherwise the State of Israel may not deem the immigrant Jewish on an Israeli identity card? What should be the Jewish status of far-flung Jewish communities, such as Ethiopian Jews, who have had little or no contact with the rest of the Jewish people?

As we will see, the Central Conference of American Rabbis Responsa Committee declares that those born of a Jewish father who engage in activities that confirm their Jewish identity are Jews (as well as those born of a Jewish mother). Rabbi Ovadiah Yosef rules that the Jews of Ethiopia are from the lost tribe of Dan and should be considered Jewish without conversion. Rabbi Pamela Barmash argues that the traditional categorization of the deaf as mentally incapacitated must be revoked and that sign language may be used in matters of personal status.

Text 3.1. Oshry, "The Case of a *Mamzer* Rabbi"

MIMA'AMAKIM, 3, NO. 98

Born in Lithuania, Rabbi Efraim Oshry (1914–2003) studied at the leading yeshivot of Slabodka and Ponevezh.[1] During the Holocaust, he became the rabbi of the Kovno ghetto, and the Nazis appointed him as caretaker of a warehouse that stored Jewish books, eventually to be displayed as part of a museum of the extinct Jewish people. This enabled him to answer halakhic questions raised by the terrible circumstances of the Holocaust, and he concealed written versions of his responsa. He managed to escape the deportation of the Kovno ghetto and was liberated by the Russians. After the war, he recovered his responsa and also retrieved Jewish children who had been hidden in monasteries or with non-Jewish families. In 1950 he moved to Montreal and then in 1952 to New York, where he served as the rabbi of the synagogue Beth Hamidrash Hagadol until his death in 2003. His responsa written during and after the Holocaust, published as a five-volume compilation titled *Mima'amakim* (From the depths), constitute the most comprehensive collection of responsa dealing with the Holocaust.[2]

Before we read his responsa on the *mamzer*, let's define the parameters of the *mamzer* and understand the quandary of the *mamzer*.

The Mishnah rules that a *mamzer* is the offspring of a forbidden union,[3] and the halakhic codes define the forbidden relationships that lead to *mamzerut* (the status of being a *mamzer*) as follows:

1. A child born of incest between relatives, as delineated in Leviticus 18.
2. A child born of sexual intercourse between a married woman and a man other than her husband.
3. A child of a woman who remarried believing incorrectly that her previous husband had died. When evidence that the previous husband is still alive is authenticated, the child from the later marriage is deemed a *mamzer*.[4]

It must be noted that a *mamzer* is not the same as "a bastard," an English term for an illegitimate child. This category does not exist in Judaism, and the Hebrew term *mamzer* should not be translated as such.

Deuteronomy 23:3, the only verse in the Torah about the *mamzer*, prohibits the *mamzer*'s participation in Jewish life as follows:

> A *mamzer* shall not enter into the congregation of the LORD; none of his descendants, even in the tenth generation, shall be admitted into the congregation of the LORD.

The Rabbis interpret the biblical clause "a *mamzer* shall not enter the congregation of the LORD" as prohibiting the marriage between a *mamzer* and a Jew who does not have the status of *mamzer*.[5] A *mamzer* may marry another *mamzer* or a convert.[6] The child of a *mamzer* is also a *mamzer*, with one exception—the child of a male *mamzer* and a non-Jewish woman is not Jewish and, therefore, does not have the status of *mamzer*.

Except for marriage, a *mamzer* is a full and equal member of the Jewish community and likewise required to observe the mitzvot. In the rules of inheritance, a *mamzer* is considered as any son and brother,[7] and Maimonides rules that a *mamzer* must uphold *kibbud av va'em* (respect toward parents).[8] A *mamzer* may serve in any public office, including as a judge in civil cases[9] and could even theoretically be a king.[10] The Mishnah emphasizes that a *mamzer* who was a scholar took precedence over an ignorant High Priest (*Mishnah Horayot* 3:8). However, a minority of rabbis rule against the full participation of *mamzerim* in communal life. For example, the extracanonical talmudic tractate *Soferim* (1:13) recounts that some hold that a Torah scroll written by a *mamzer* is unfit for use in the synagogue.

QUESTION

Rabbi Oshry addresses the case of a young rabbi whose mother, imprisoned in a ghetto, assumed erroneously that her first husband was no longer alive, remarried to save her own life, and gave birth to him, recounting the young rabbi's story as follows:

On 12 Tishrei 5702, October 3, 1941, the prisoners of the ghetto heard of a terrible edict [to be issued]. The German murderers had decided that since there were more women than men in the ghetto as a result of the previous acts in which more men, the heads of households, had been slaughtered and their widows were left without a man to support them and the number of women exceeded the number of men, [the Nazis] would equalize the numbers by putting all the bereaved women who had no means of support to death. Only women who had husbands to support them would be left alive. As a result . . . in order to save themselves from certain death, many of the single women began to search around for husbands. They married anyone willing to marry them. . . .

One woman, who no longer knew what happened to her husband after he was taken away by the accursed Germans—may their names be blotted out!—assumed that he had been killed, because otherwise he would have returned to her. Afraid for her life, she quickly found another man and married him and had a son. They managed to escape together from the ghetto, survived the war by hiding, and [thereby] saved their lives.

When the war ended, Rabbi Oshry continues, the mother and her second husband

> went to another country across the sea, like so many other Jews, and put down new roots and raised their son [who studied the Torah] in a yeshiva. He persevered in studying there [and] was ordained as a rabbi. . . . He eventually married and became the rabbi of a Jewish community.

Decades later, after the young rabbi's mother died, his mother's first husband located him and sought to destroy the young rabbi's marriage, family, and career:

One day, this young rabbi's world suddenly became dark. A man just appeared and told him that he was the [first] husband of the rabbi's mother, the husband whom she had assumed was dead, and explained that he had survived even though the Germans had detained him for a long time. Once he was liberated he had begun to search for his wife.... When he found out that she had married another man and had a son of extramarital relations with him, he was infuriated at the betrayal of the wife of his youth and decided to search for her and her *mamzer* son, to reveal their shame in public, and especially to expel her *mamzer* son out from among proper Jews.... In the meantime, however, his wife had died ... [and all his anger was aimed at the young rabbi]. [The first husband] sought not only to prevent him from raising a Jewish family as well as his children [from raising a Jewish family], but since [the son] was a rabbi and spiritual leader, [the husband] saw it as his duty to publicize the matter that [the young rabbi] was a *mamzer* and prevent him from marrying and serving as a rabbi [and force the young rabbi to divorce his wife, step down as rabbi, and have his children declared *mamzerim*].

The young rabbi fell down when he heard the terrible and bitter tale [of his birth], weeping and shouting at his grievous fate.... He was also very upset at the *ḥillul ha-Shem* [desecration of God's name caused by improper behavior of Jews] that would happen when it was publicly discovered that the rabbi of an important community was a *mamzer* and was forbidden to marry [almost all] Jewish women. He implored his mother's first husband tearfully not to make public the matter immediately but to wait until he could consult with rabbinic scholars to determine what should be done to prevent *ḥillul ha-Shem* [from being known] publicly.

The young rabbi then sought Rabbi Oshry's counsel:

> When the young rabbi came to me, I was shocked to see him. He looked devastated, bent over like an old man well on in years, and gray hairs had begun to appear in his beard and on his head. With flowing tears, he told me the story... and asked me to [rule on what must happen to him, his family, and his community] according to the laws of the Torah.

Surprisingly, neither rabbi seems to question or attempt to authenticate the identity of the man claiming to be the first husband of the young rabbi's mother.

SECTION A: MAY A *MAMZER* SERVE AS A RABBI?[11]

Rabbi Oshry does not address whether mitigating circumstances might be applied to prevent the young rabbi from being deemed a *mamzer*. Rather, he analyzes whether a *mamzer* may serve as a rabbi in modern times and may issue rulings on ritual matters and arbitrate civil disputes but not capital cases, as the Rabbis did in antiquity:

> In the Babylonian Talmud *Sanhedrin* 32b, we learn:
>
>> [The Mishnah teaches:] All are fit to judge cases of monetary law, but not all are fit to judge capital cases.
>
> And there in *Sanhedrin* 36b, [the question is asked]:
>
>> [What is added by the Mishnah's] employing [the expansive term] "all"? Rav Judah says: [It is employed] to include a *mamzer* [among those qualified to judge cases of monetary law].
>
> Accordingly, it is apparent that a *mamzer* is fit to be a rabbi or a judge, since in our time a rabbi rules on ritual law as well as on monetary cases. Therefore, the young rabbi is allowed to remain the rabbi of his community, even though he was a

mamzer. The only conundrum that needed to be addressed is ḥillul ha-Shem.

SECTION B: BUT WOULD IT BE A ḤILLUL HA-SHEM?

Yet Rabbi Oshry invokes the concept of *ḥillul ha-Shem*, the desecration of God's name as a result of improper Jewish behavior, as applying to the situation of a *mamzer* serving as a rabbi:

Rabbi Moses Sofer (*Ḥatam sofer*, Even ha-Ezer 2.94) writes:

> Even though it says that a *mamzer* who is a Torah scholar is superior to an ignoramus who is a *Kohen*, [that applies] only to honoring him. [But] he is not to be appointed as the rabbi of a community, because the common people will not listen to him. They will say "go and check your mother's abomination." Even more so in our generation, because of our many sins, in which respect is not given to the Torah, this is even more true. Even the most respected rabbis of impeccable lineage are subjected to indignities, even more so those of despised lineage. [A *mamzer* rabbi] should not take the position of rabbi if the community will not honor him appropriately.

PESAK DIN

Rabbi Oshry rules:

> So I ruled that this young rabbi must leave his holy office and resign from his exalted mission that was laid upon him to be a rabbi and spiritual leader in a Jewish congregation. I also made the arrangements necessary for him to divorce his wife, for halakhah forbids a *mamzer* to be married to a woman born Jewish [except if she herself is a *mamzeret* or a convert]. I also summoned his mother's first husband and attempted to convince him not to make public the matter because it would

create ḥillul ha-Shem. His goal he had already achieved when he caused [the young rabbi] to resign from his exalted mission and the destruction of [the rabbi's] family, his career, and his life. What more would he gain by humiliating him in public?... [The young rabbi] was certainly not responsible for [his mother's actions]. He did not know anything about his birth until this man [appeared and] told him....

May [God] require and cleanse from impurity all the poor of the community who confess their sin, and quickly may [God] have mercy upon His scattered sheep, to grant them salvation and to cast their sins into the deepest watery abyss,[12] speedily in our days, amen.[13]

Text 3.2. Spitz, "Mamzerut"

COMMITTEE ON JEWISH LAW AND STANDARDS OF THE RABBINICAL ASSEMBLY, EVEN HA-EZER 4.2000A

Rabbi Elie Kaplan Spitz graduated from Boston University Law School and was ordained by the Jewish Theological Seminary. He served one congregation, Congregation B'nai Israel of Tustin, California, from 1988 to 2021, and on the Rabbinical Assembly's Committee of Jewish Law and Standards for twenty years. He approaches Jewish law with respect for "tradition and change," based on understanding whether the goals of a law hold up in changed circumstances. Rabbi Spitz is also the author of three books on spirituality and Judaism: *Does the Soul Survive? A Jewish Journey to Belief in Afterlife, Past Lives & Living with Purpose*; *Healing from Despair: Choosing Wholeness in a Broken World*; and *Increasing Wholeness: Jewish Wisdom and Guided Meditations to Strengthen and Calm Body, Heart, Mind, and Spirit*. His responsum on *mamzerut* emerges from a legal curiosity as to the principles that underlie Jewish law, in line with how his spiritual writings focus on what is seen and what is beneath the surface.

QUESTION

In a responsum approved by the Committee on Jewish Law and Standards in 2000, Rabbi Spitz addresses the question: Is *mamzerut* operative in our community?

SECTION A: THE ETHICAL PROBLEM

Rabbi Spitz shows that the *mamzer*'s fate has been an ethical problem since the time of Talmud. He points out two conflicting streams of thought in the Torah about who is to be punished for committing a sin: (1) that only the sinner is punished and (2) that later generations may be punished for the sins of an earlier generation. He emphasizes that the possibility that a person may be a *mamzer* has increased in recent years because one of the parents may not have had a Jewish divorce with a *get* (document of Jewish divorce) before having a child with another person:

> A child is born a marital pariah due to no fault of his or her own, but rather for the sins of his or her parent. The unfair anguish inflicted by this [status] is already voiced in *Vayikra Rabbah* 32:8 as follows:
>
>> "I further observed all the oppression that goes on under the sun: the tears of the oppressed, with none to comfort them; and the power of their oppressors—with none to comfort them." (Eccles. 4:1)
>
> Daniel the Tailor interpreted this verse "all the oppression"—these are the *mamzerim*.
>
>> "The tears of the oppressed"—their parents committed a sin and these humiliated ones are removed?! This one's father had illicit sexual relations—what did [the child] do, and why should it make a difference for [the child]? "They had no comforter," but "from the hand of their persecutors

there is strength," this is the Great Assembly which comes against them with the power of the Torah and removes them based on "no *mamzer* shall enter the congregation of the Lord" (Deut. 23:3). Thus, God says that I will have to comfort them, because in this world they are refuse but in the messianic age . . . they are pure gold.

Daniel the Tailor's sympathy for the *mamzer* is reflected in a legal debate over whether the *mamzer* will be purified in the messianic era and be permitted to marry freely. . . . The Jerusalem and Babylonian Talmuds are split as to [which] opinion is correct. . . .

Daniel the Tailor's sympathy for the *mamzer* is linked to a Torah value emphasized by the prophets. The Torah says, "The fathers shall not be put to death for the [sins of their] children, nor children for [the sins of their parents]; every person shall be put to death for his [or her] sin" (Deut. 24:16). At the same time there is a second strand in Torah . . . which deals harshly with innocent children. We are told that God remembers wrongdoing until the third or fourth generation (Exod. 20:5). . . . We are commanded to wipe out the Amalekites in every generation, because of what their ancestors did to us (Exod. 17:14; Deut. 25:19). And there is the law of *mamzerut*, which would keep the child of an illicit relationship outside the community. . . .

The rule of *mamzerut* conflicts with the evolving moral challenge that each person is to be punished for his or her own acts. . . . There is an additional moral problem with *mamzerut*. . . . It deprecates the status of converts by permitting a *mamzer* to marry a convert, but not a native born Jew. . . .

In recent years, the numbers of people who qualify as *mamzerim* have proliferated. In America there are many who are married by a rabbi, receive a civil divorce but no *get*, and remarry a Jew—either with a justice of the peace or a Reform or Reconstructionist rabbi. The children of the subsequent marriage are technically *mamzerim*, although rarely was it the intent of the parents to knowingly violate the religious law.

SECTION B: THE LANGER CASE

Rabbi Spitz recounts the famous case of the Langer brother and sister. The official State Rabbinate in Israel had declared the two as *mamzerim* because their mother had not divorced her first husband, a convert to Judaism, when she married another man and had two children, a daughter and a son, with him. When the son wanted to marry in 1966, an official State Rabbinate *beit din* declared that the two now-adult children were *mamzerim*, and the Supreme Religious Court of Appeals confirmed the decree. The widely publicized decree was viewed as a travesty of justice because an Israeli who had served in the Israeli military and had celebrated his bar mitzvah was prohibited from marrying almost all Jewish women due to his mother's action.

Provoking both outrage and applause, Rabbi Shlomo Goren (see chapter 9), about to become Ashkenazic Chief Rabbi of Israel, devised a way to overturn this ruling and permit the Langers to marry other Jews whose family lineage is not problematic. He based his ruling on the argument that the first husband was an insincere convert; therefore, his Jewish marriage was invalidated, and hence the Langer brother and sister were not *mamzerim*.

For his part, Rabbi Spitz devotes space only to the well-founded objections to Rabbi Goren's ruling. He does not mention that prominent Orthodox and Ultraorthodox rabbis had called not only for rejecting Rabbi Goren's ruling in the Langer case, but for rejecting all of his rulings:

> Jewish legal authorities protested Goren's finding because of his violation of normal halakhic procedure. Among the irregularities were the following:

- Goren failed to give [the first husband] the opportunity to refute the charge that he had renounced his conversion to Judaism by having reverted to Christianity. In fact, there was much evidence that he had conducted himself as a practicing Jew.
- When there is "new evidence" the normal procedure is to remand the case to the original *beit din*, which was not done here.
- Goren refused to reveal the names of the other rabbis who issued the decree removing the stigma of *mamzerut* from the Langer children.

SECTION C: THE RATIONALES OF *MAMZERUT*

Exploring the reasons offered for the rules about *mamzerut*, Rabbi Spitz emphasizes that non-*mamzers* and *mamzers* have mixed matrimonially for generations:

> There are two reasons offered for the law of *mamzerut*: deterrence against illicit sex and the need to maintain the purity of Israel.
>
> 1. Deterrence Against Promiscuity: Jewish tradition emphasizes the sanctity of the marriage bond. Adultery is the seventh of the Ten Commandments....
>
> 2. Communal Purity: Communal purity is not mentioned in the Talmud as a justification for *mamzerut*, but it is advanced among medieval and even contemporary commentators.... [Rishon Lezion Sefardic Chief Rabbi] Ben Zion Meir Hai Ouziel [1880–1953]... asserts that the concept of communal purity is the underpinning of *mamzerut*. He writes, "A mamzer's base status should not be seen as a punishment for the sin of his parents, but is rather quasi-physical."... "Communal purity" rings false in our day.... We do not possess a record of pedigree.... In fact, *mamzerim* have mixed into the community for

generations ... (as) codified ... by [Rabbi] Moses Isserles [1525 or 1530–72, Poland] in his gloss to the Shulḥan Arukh *Even ha-Ezer* 2:5:

> It is forbidden to reveal the blemish of a family that is not public knowledge. If the family has been assimilated, it should be left with its presumption of validity, for all families are valid in the messianic age.

In sum, we as a people are mixed with *mamzerim*. We cannot justify punishing people for the sins of their parents because of the false assertion of purity.

SECTION D: MORALITY AND HALAKHAH

Rabbi Spitz turns to ways to alleviate *mamzerut* status. He argues that morality has always been a factor in halakhah, even when not articulated explicitly:

> Although *mamzerut* is morally reprehensible it has remained operative in Jewish law. . . .
>
> It is true that the rabbis in the past did not explicitly use morality as the basis for change or interpretation of a law. . . . Conservative Judaism would affirm that . . . the revelation at Sinai is seen as the beginning of a relationship [with God] and not the final word. Interpretation is understood as our communal attempt to understand the will of a compassionate divine partner. . . . If a law appears unconscionable, we would say that the shortcoming is either our previous understanding or that circumstances have so changed that the rule no longer meets its intended result. . . . In some cases changes are necessary to prevent or remove injustice, while in others they constitute a positive program to enhance the quality of Jewish life by elevating its moral standards or deepening its piety. . . . We affirm that the halakhic process has striven to embody the highest moral principles.

Mamzerut poses a moral problem.... *Mamzerut* is an opportunity to make explicit what was until now implicit: morality is at the center of the halakhic process.

SECTION E: A PROCEDURALLY INOPERATIVE LAW

Rabbi Spitz offers two examples of Torah laws that the talmudic Rabbis suspended by procedural decision in order to prevent injustice. Based on these examples, he rules that *mamzerut* should be prevented by using a procedural method: rabbis should refuse to hear any testimony about *mamzerut*:

> There are several examples cited in the Talmud of a biblical law that was made inoperative due to a procedural decision. In each of the cases a rationale for the change is offered, but no express claim is made that the ruling is an *uprooting* of a biblical law. Yet, the impact is the same. The following are ... examples of judicial discretion that prevented implementation of a biblical law:
>
> 1. According to Babylonian Talmud *Avodah Zarah* 8b, the Rabbis stopped imposing capital punishment, even though the Torah rules that execution was the just sentence for many crimes. They implemented the change procedurally ... by moving the twenty-three-person Sanhedrin from the Temple grounds, the only place that the Sanhedrin could issue execution decrees. Three reasons may have led to cessation of capital punishment: (a) it no longer served as a deterrent; (b) the increased case load might lead to incomplete examination of testimony and consequently unjust verdicts in specific cases; and (c) the increased case load might result in inequity as to who was tried for a capital crime.... The Rabbis explained the suspension of a biblical law for ethical reasons.
>
> 2. According to *Mishnah Sotah* 9:9; the *sotah*-water test for a wife accused of adultery by her husband was discontinued by

PERSONAL STATUS 71

the priests because the number of adulterers increased. The exact reasoning is left to speculation. Rabbinic decisors explain that the test was ineffective because the husbands committed adultery and were hypocrites in accusing their wives of adultery. The priests suspended a biblical law when it led to injustice.

As members of our community's law-making body [the Committee on Jewish Law and Standards] we are asked to reconsider whether *mamzerut* should have legal efficacy....

In our day, *mamzerut* is both unconscionable and ineffective as a deterrent against sexual misdeeds. When we say that children should not suffer for the sins of their parents, it is not a morality of the hour, but an ethical perspective firmly rooted in our tradition.... Our decision, then and now, is to refuse to consider evidence of *mamzerut*, because the law in our day does not serve as a deterrent to sexual misconduct and instead undermines respect for Torah.

PESAK DIN

Rabbi Spitz presents a global solution that will operate across the board, rather than a repertoire of halakhic principles that might be drawn upon in specific cases—in sharp contrast to Rabbi Shalom Mesas's subsequent *teshuvah* in this volume. Also striking is the road not taken: Rabbi Spitz does not call for a *takkanah* (formal enactment) to fully revoke *mamzerut* status:

> We render *mamzerut* inoperative, because we will not consider evidence of *mamzerut*. We will give permission to any Jew to marry and will perform the marriage of a Jew regardless of the possible sins of his or her parent.[14]

Text 3.3. Mesas, "A *Pesak Din* in a Matter of *Mamzerut*"

SHEMESH U-MAGEN, 3, NO. 12

The official State Rabbinate of Israel has jurisdiction over nonfinancial matters of personal status for Jews living in Israel, including marriage and divorce.[15] It maintains a list of *mamzerim*, and its *batei din* rule on cases about whether a person is a *mamzer*. In recent decades, the number of Israelis listed as *mamzerim* has decreased dramatically even though the population of Israel has increased significantly, largely because the *dayyanim* of the State Rabbinate courts are now applying specific halakhic principles (in ways that seem contrary to the facts of a situation) in order to avoid declaring a person as a *mamzer*, because of its terrible consequences and unfairness.[16] (Nonetheless, it must be noted that a case may entail years, even decades, of suffering and anxiety before the case is concluded and the person declared not to be a *mamzer*.) Rabbi Shalom Mesas championed the use of one of these halakhic principles—that a *beit din* can be sure that a person is the child of two people only if they were imprisoned together—and his long and well-argued record of employing this principle inspired the official State Rabbinate courts to adopt its use. Applying this principle means that a rabbinic decisor can point to doubt as to who a person's father is: if the father might not be Jewish, halakhah holds that the person is not a *mamzer*.[17]

Born in Meknes, Rabbi Shalom Mesas (1909–2003), a scion of two famous Moroccan rabbinic dynasties, the Mesas and Berdugo families, studied with his father and Rabbi Isaac Sebbag.[18] He moved to Casablanca to be its chief rabbi, then served as chief rabbi of Morocco for six years. After visiting with the two chief rabbis in Israel, Shlomo Goren (see chapter 9) and Ovadiah Yosef (see later in this chapter), who promised their support, he became Sefardic Chief Rabbi of Jerusalem in 1976 until his death. He tried to avoid the dissension in the Ultraorthodox communities and among the

Sefardic/Mizraḥi communities, although he upheld the customs of the Moroccan community against the mission of the Rishon Lezion Sefardic Chief Rabbi Ovadiah Yosef to promulgate a united Sefardic/Mizraḥi set of observances. He had good relations with King Hassan II of Morocco, who accompanied him to the airport when he left Morocco to serve as Sefardic Chief Rabbi of Jerusalem, and after his death, when Israel Post issued a stamp in his honor, King Mohammed VI sent a letter of appreciation to his son Rabbi David Mesas, chief Orthodox rabbi of Paris. He wrote a number of books of responsa, *Tevu'ot shemesh* (Products of the sun) and *Shemesh u-magen* (Sun and shield), as well as a book on Maimonides' *Mishneh Torah* and a book of sermons.[19]

Rabbi Mesas addresses a messy situation. A woman forced into an unwanted marriage in Tunis fled a few weeks into the marriage; divorced him civilly, without a *get*; remarried civilly; and apparently had a daughter with the second husband. That daughter now wants to marry in France but is accused of being a *mamzer* because her mother, having never obtained a Jewish divorce document, would still be considered married to her first husband when her daughter was born. Rabbi Mesas first thinks of nullifying the mother's original *kiddushin* (betrothal ceremony after which a couple is considered married) by holding that the witnesses were invalid; rabbinic decisors had long employed methods of invalidating witnesses to avoid designating a person as a *mamzer*. But there is a complication: in the Tunisian Jewish community it was customary to hold a private *kiddushin* ceremony in the office of the local chief rabbi with valid witnesses, and so this ceremony would be difficult to nullify. Rabbi Mesas must seek another way to avoid deeming the daughter a *mamzer*.

QUESTION

Rabbi Mesas begins to explain the situation:

The young woman L, daughter of F, came to be married under the auspices of the *beit din* of Paris.[20] A complaint was made against her that she was a *mamzeret*. Her mother was married in Tunis with *ketubbah* [Jewish marriage document] and *kiddushin* in 1964 to R. After a few weeks [of marriage], she fled from her husband's house because the marriage was not according to her liking. Moreover, she divorced her husband civilly, and he did not extend a *get*. Furthermore, she went and married civilly another man [and has been married to him] twenty-two years, and from this [marriage] the aforementioned daughter was born. Both the father and mother affirm that this [young woman] is truly their daughter. According to what is mentioned so far, the daughter is apparently a *mamzer* since her mother was not divorced with a *get*.

This matter was sent to me by my friend Rabbi Nissim Revivo, chair of the *beit din* of Paris, [requesting] my opinion. Concomitantly, the chief rabbi of Tunisia Rabbi Ḥayyim Madar [1933–2004, Tunisia; Maḍar according to the Arabic pronunciation] sent a letter [about this matter] in which he provided testimony about the marriage of the aforementioned couple. One of the witnesses for the *kiddushin* was the uncle of F,[21] and the other one violated the Sabbath in public and did not keep the laws of kashrut [kosher food regulations].[22] The rabbi also offers testimony about the pictures that were shown to him from the [wedding], in which the groom puts the ring for *kiddushin* on the bride's finger correctly according to halakhah and the *ḥazzan* appears with the cup for the blessings in one hand. . . . Next to him is the groom and the bride, with a tallit spread upon the head of the groom. . . . The sexton . . . with a pen in his hands is making a record into the record book in the synagogue. [Rabbi Madar] was astonished that this appears [to have taken place] in the absence of the chair of the *beit din*. . . . This [testimony] helps the aforementioned young woman because the *kiddushin* of her mother was invalid and never happened. Therefore, [her mother] was single, and her daughter is of completely proper [lineage].

SECTION A: COMPLICATING FACTORS[23]

Rabbi Mesas gets to the heart of the issue:

> Here lies the problem: At the end of the letter, the chief rabbi tells of the custom for marriage that was and still is practiced in Tunis till today. Before the day of the *ḥuppah* [wedding ceremony with marriage canopy], the couple has an appointment with the city scribes authorized by the rabbi and the secular authorities, and they perform the full *kiddushin* ceremony with the state currency. They write in the *ketubbah* "so-and-so performed *kiddushin* before us," etc., and the rest of the formula of the *ketubbah*. The groom and the bride and the two scribes sign below, and this is *erusin* [engagement]. Afterward they get a license as agreed from the rabbi, and then they hold in the synagogue the *ḥuppah* and *nisuin* [nuptials] ceremony, including the *berakhah* of *erusin* and repeat *kiddushin* a second time with a ring. The chief rabbi concludes [his letter] by saying that when the *beit din* was closed at the end of 1957, the couple would go to register their civil marriage and bring him the license number. They would go to the rabbi to deal with the *ketubbah*: [the groom] would do *kiddushin* with the bride before two witnesses and [in the *ketubbah*] they would write, "[The groom] did *kiddushin* before us," etc. At the end they would write that they did this after [the couple] effected civil marriage with the license number such and such. Afterward they would celebrate with a *ḥuppah* ceremony and *kiddushin* in the synagogue. This is the custom practiced until today.

According to what is mentioned above, "the bread has fallen into the pit [and disappeared and therefore is of no significance]" because, while the witnesses for *kiddushin* for the [ceremony in the synagogue were invalid], it appears that there were, according to the custom, other witnesses beforehand, and it's possible, indeed certain, that they were valid. If so, any doubt about the validity of the marriage is null.

Many letters were sent by private individuals from France [stating] that in this matter the woman was not willing to marry her husband and pretty much everything was done without her consent. They also said that there was no *kiddushin* prior to what happened in the synagogue. . . . The leader of the congregation of Tunis of that time, Mr. S, testified that she did not wish to sign beforehand, as was the custom in Tunis, and only with difficulty they forced her to go to the synagogue to receive the ring. . . . Also, the chair of the *beit din* of Paris mentioned above sent a letter that he received testimony that the bride did not wish to receive the ring, that they forced her to accept it, and that she fled from their joint home after a few weeks when she was still a virgin, according to a physician's certificate. The general sense is that she did not want this marriage.

Also, the chief rabbi of Tunis wrote in his letter that he was astonished that, having searched diligently in all the record books of the *ketubbot*, he did not find a record of the registration of their *ketubbah*. How is it possible that the rabbi would give a license without registering the *ketubbah*, [especially] when the husband and wife wrote that they don't remember [having] a *ketubbah*? . . . [The chief rabbi] also said that he went back [a] second time to search in [the archives of] the *beit din* of Tunis and saw that [the marriage] was not registered there at all.

All this raises great doubt upon doubt and supports the testimony of the people mentioned above that there was no *kiddushin* before [the invalid *kiddushin*] in the synagogue. And perhaps the reason is that [she did not want the marriage].

SECTION B: WHO IS THE FATHER?

Rabbi Mesas discusses whether the parents' statement that she is their daughter can be taken into evidence. According to halakhah, a mother's testimony is accepted *only* if she states that her child is *not* a *mamzer*; it is *not* accepted if she says her child *is* a *mamzer*. A father can validate that his child is a *mamzer*, according to a halakhic principle termed "[the father] shall acknowledge," but since the parents in question were not married in a Jewish ceremony, only in a civil one, and the mother did not receive a *get* for her first marriage, halakhah does not accept the father's status as a father, and his statement is considered invalid. Rabbi Mesas seals his argument by affirming that the principle of "[only] if [the parents] were imprisoned together in a jail, [only then is it certain] that [the child] is from him" applies in this situation. Her father might be someone else, and if the daughter's father was not Jewish, according to halakhah, she could not be a *mamzer*.

Rabbi Mesas was the first to apply this halakhic principle frequently and vigorously to prevent a person from being deemed a *mamzer*:

> First of all, we must clarify whether the daughter mentioned is definitely a *mamzer* and forbidden [to marry Jews of proper lineage] according to the Torah, even if the *kiddushin* was [attested] by valid witnesses, or whether she is a doubtful *mamzer* who is permitted [to marry Jews of proper lineage] according to the Torah.... It is only according to *de-rabbanan* law [Rabbinic law, not law ascribed to the Torah by the Rabbis] that they forbade a doubtful *mamzer* because of lineage.
>
> Just as I clarified in my book *Shemesh u-magen*, volume 1, *Even ha-Ezer*, section 3, [this case does not concern] a certain

mamzer, for even if the father and mother admit that the daughter is definitely theirs . . . , [their testimony] is deemed not completely reliable. For [halakhah holds that] the mother is believed when she validates [the pedigree of her child], but not when she impairs [the pedigree of her child], just as Maimonides writes in the Hilkhot Ishut [Laws of Marital Status], chapter 15 [halakhah 14]. A woman who says that [her child is] the child of so-and-so — if that so-and-so is a *mamzer*, she is not considered reliable in her testimony [to deem someone] a *mamzer* but [her child] will be a doubtful *mamzer*. The father is reliable to impair [the pedigree of] his child because of the halakhic rule [based on Deut. 21:17] of "[the father] shall acknowledge," [interpreted to mean] that the father is reliable to identify [his child] to others. Even though we hold that a person cannot render himself guilty, [in this case it is possible because] the text says that "[the father] shall acknowledge." So did our master [Rabbi Joseph Caro] rule in [Shulḥan Arukh] *Even ha-Ezer* 4:26. . . .

But this [case under discussion] is when he knows clearly that [the woman] is forbidden to him and he is with her without *nisuin*. [Therefore] he is not designated as the father, and the Torah does not give him permission to identify [his child], since she is not in a relationship with him through *ketubbah* and *kiddushin*. It is very possible that she was intimate with others [due to the halakhic principle] "from something doubtful we do not derive [a ruling]." So we learn explicitly from [the Shulḥan Arukh *Even ha-Ezer*] 156:9, "[In the case of a man] who has a sexual relationship with a woman, whether she is single or married, and she becomes pregnant — even if he says the baby is mine and she confirms him, this is [still in the category of] doubt. . . ." And there [Rabbi Moses Isserles writes] that [only] if they were imprisoned together in a jail, [then it is certain] that [the child] is from him. The reason for this reasoning is that because she is not in *nisuin* [and therefore has not fully completed the marriage ceremony and is not considered married], the law of "he shall identify" does not apply to him [because he is not identified as the father according to halakhah].

SECTION C: MANY DOUBTS

Rabbi Mesas argues that the principle of "only if they were imprisoned together in a jail is it certain that the child is from him" definitely applies in this situation because the couple knew that they did not have a Jewish marriage and the woman could easily have been sexually intimate with others, whether Jews or non-Jews. The case involves multiple doubts, he concludes, and the consequence of the multiplicity of doubt is that the daughter is not a *mamzer*:

> The consequences of this for the situation under discussion are: since there was no *nisuin* and they were together in extramarital relations since he knew that she had not been divorced with a *get* and she was [still] married, one can argue that since she was in extramarital relations with this one and she left her husband, she could have had extramarital relations with others, whether non-Jews or Jews. Even if they were in a relationship for a number of years and got married civilly, this is what Rabbi Moses Isserles wrote [about the principle of] "only if they were imprisoned together in a jail [can we be certain the child is his]," but without [imprisonment] there is a doubt.... See my book *Tevu'ot shemesh*, Even ha-Ezer no. 160.... Since she knows that she is unable to marry in *nisuin*, there is certainly nothing between them except extramarital love. She may [be sexually intimate] with other Jews, and all the more so it is a transgression easy [for her to commit] for her [to be sexually intimate] with non-Jews....
>
> Since there is no record of *kiddushin* in the register of the *beit din* of Tunis, this affirms the testimonies that were received that there was no *kiddushin* prior to the invalid [*kiddushin*] in

the synagogue. All the more so, we must place the matter [of *mamzerut*] in [the category of] doubt, whether or not [valid *kiddushin*] was conducted prior [to the invalid *kiddushin* in the synagogue]. Before us [is a case of] undeniable double doubt [that allows us] to release the young woman [from the taint of *mamzerut*]. [First] there was no [valid] *kiddushin* prior to the invalid one in the synagogue. [Second,] even if there was valid *kiddushin* [prior to the invalid *kiddushin* in the synagogue] and [therefore, the mother] was married, perhaps [the father of] the young woman is a non-Jew. Since there are two sets of doubt [in this scenario], she is easily deemed [of proper lineage]. Finally, whether [her father was] perhaps a non-Jew or perhaps, if you wish to claim, a Jew, perhaps there was no *kiddushin* other than the invalid ones and [therefore, the mother] was single and the young woman is [deemed to be of proper lineage].

PESAK DIN

Rabbi Mesas rules:

> The woman L daughter of F is permitted to marry Jews of proper lineage. Because this is a difficult matter, I require the affirmation of the Rishon Lezion Sefardic Chief Rabbi Ovadiah Yosef... my dear friend, who will confirm the truth for us. Amen.
>
> Signed in the holy city of Jerusalem, 5 Tammuz 1994.
>
> Shalom Mesas, may his end be good.[24]
>
> [followed by Rabbi Yosef's note of concurrence][25]

Text 3.4. CCAR Responsa Committee, "Patrilineal and Matrilineal Descent"

CONTEMPORARY AMERICAN REFORM RESPONSA, 61–68

In 1983, the Reform rabbinic organization the Central Conference of American Rabbis issued a resolution decreeing that Jewish status would be ascribed to children born to Jewish fathers as well as Jewish mothers (patrilineal as well as matrilineal descent)—provided that the children of Jewish fathers demonstrated their positive and exclusive Jewish identity through acts of identification.

The decision generated sensation throughout Jewish communities internationally, winning praise among Reform communities in the United States, resistance from Reform communities outside the United States, and criticism from those outside the Reform movement anticipating a future division between Reform Jews and the rest of the Jewish people. (As of this writing in 2024, only the Reform movement in the United States holds by this decision, although Reform rabbinic organizations outside the United States are considering changing their stance.) Later that year, the Central Conference of American Rabbis Responsa Committee (see chapter 2) decided to augment the CCAR declaration with a responsum showing the sources and reasoning on which it was based.

QUESTION

The Responsa Committee addresses the question:

> What halakhic justification is there for the recent Central Conference of American Rabbi's resolution on matrilineal and patrilineal descent, which also adds various requirements for the establishment of Jewish status?

SECTION A: HISTORY OF JEWISH STATUS[26]

The responsum starts by contrasting Judaism's long-held use of matrilineality (status according to whether a person's mother was Jewish at the time of that person's birth) to determine Jewish identity to the use of patrilineality (status according to whether a person's father was Jewish at the time of the person's birth) as the means to determine caste (*Kohen*, Levite, and commoner). In so doing it casts doubt on the reasons for establishing Jewish status based on the mother:

> It is clear that for the last two thousand years the Jewish identity of a child has been determined by matrilineal descent.... The child of a Jewish mother was Jewish irrespective of the father (Deut. 7:3, 4; *Mishnah Kiddushin* 3:12...).... The rabbinic decision that the child follow the religion of the mother solves the problem for offspring from illicit intercourse of unions which are not recognized, or in which paternity could not be established, or in which the father disappeared. This practice may have originated in the period of Ezra... and may parallel that of Pericles of Athens who sought to limit citizenship to descendants of Athenian mothers.... It may also have represented temporary, emergency legislation of that period. We hear nothing about such a permanent change till early rabbinic times, then the union between a Jew and a non-Jew was considered to have no legal status....
>
> We should contrast the rabbinic position to the view of the earlier biblical and post-biblical period. Patrilineal descent was the primary way of determining the status of children in this period. The biblical traditions... take it for granted that the paternal line was decisive in the tracing of descent, tribal identity, or priestly status....
>
> We should also recognize that later rabbinic tradition did not shift to the matrilineal line when conditions did not demand it.... It was and remains the male *kohen* who determines the status of his children. The child is a *kohen* even if the father married a Levite or an Israelite.

SECTION B: WHY WE ARE MAKING THIS CHANGE

The responsum highlights that times have changed and that mixed marriages between Jews and non-Jews have increased. Although it does not explicitly articulate this, the underlying premise may be that patrilineal descent is likely to help the children and grandchildren of Jewish fathers and non-Jewish mothers embrace their Jewish heritage and live more fully as Jews:

> Our tradition... changed the laws of descent to meet the problems of a specific age and if those problems persisted, then the changes remained in effect. The previous cited material has dealt with situations entirely different from those which have arisen in the last century and a half. Unions between Jews and non-Jews during earlier times remained rare....
>
> We in the twentieth century have been faced with an increasing number of mixed marriages, with changes in the structure of the family, and with the development of a new relationship between men and women....
>
> The Reform movement has espoused the equality of men and women, virtually since its inception.... As equality has been applied to every facet of Reform Jewish life, it should be applied in this instance....
>
> We are morally obliged to make provisions for the offsprings of such a union [of a Jew and a non-Jew] when either the father or mother seek to have their children recognized and educated as a Jew.
>
> We agree with the Israeli courts and their decisions on the matter of status for purposes of... the registration of the nationality of immigrants and the right to immigrate under the Law of Return. Such rulings are secular in nature and do not bind the Israeli rabbinic courts or us, yet they have far reaching implications for all Jews. In the Brother Daniel case of 1962, this apostate was not judged to be Jewish although he had a Jewish mother.[27]... The court decided that a Jew who practiced another religion would not be considered Jewish despite his descent from a Jewish mother. "Acts of religious identification"

were determinative for secular purposes of the State of Israel. The court recognized that this had no effect on the rabbinic courts; nonetheless, it marked a radical change which deals with new conditions....

The Law of Return included "the child and grandchild of a Jew, the spouse of a Jew and the spouse of the child and grandchild of a Jew—with the exception of a person who was a Jew and willingly changed his religion" (Law of Return Amendment #2, #4a, March, 1970). This meant that a dual definition (descendants from Jewish mothers or fathers) has remained operative for immigration into the State of Israel.

The decision of an Israeli court is a secular decision. It is, of course, not determinative for us as American Reform Jews, but we should note that their line of reasoning is somewhat similar to ours....

We have equated matrilineal and patrilineal descent in the determination of Jewish identity of a child of a mixed marriage.

SECTION C: ACTS OF IDENTIFICATION

The responsum stipulates that patrilineal Jewish identity be confirmed through affirmative acts. What is more, the Responsa Committee emphasizes, such mandated acts of identification for children born to Jewish fathers and non-Jewish mothers constitute far more stringent requirements for Jewish status than being born (passively) to a Jewish mother:

> Now let us turn to the section of the resolution which deals with "positive acts of identification." There are both traditional and modern considerations for requiring such acts and not relying on birth alone. The clause which deals with the "appropriate and timely acts of identification with the Jewish faith and people..." has gone beyond the traditional requirements for consideration as a Jew. Here we have become stricter than traditional Judaism.

We have done so as the normal life of Jews has changed during the last two centuries. . . .

We now require "appropriate and timely public and formal acts. . . ." The requirement has been worded to permit some flexibility for individual circumstances. With time and experience, custom will designate certain acts as appropriate and others not. It would be wrong, however, to set limits now at the beginning of the process.

We are aware that we have made more stringent requirements than our tradition. We believe that this will lead to a firmer commitment to Judaism on the part of these individuals and that it will enable them to become fully integrated into the Jewish community. We have taken this step for the following additional reasons:

1. We do not view birth as a determining factor in the religious identification of children of a mixed marriage.
2. We distinguish between descent and identification.
3. The mobility of American Jews has diminished the influence of the extended family upon such a child. This means that a significant informal bond with Judaism which played a role in the past does not exist for our generation.
4. Education has always been a strong factor in Jewish identity. In the recent past we could assume a minimal Jewish education for most children. In our time almost half the American Jewish community remains unaffiliated, and their children receive no Jewish education.

PESAK DIN

The responsum concludes:

The Central Conference of American Rabbis declares that the child of one Jewish parent is under the presumption of Jewish descent. This presumption of the Jewish status of the offspring of any mixed marriage is to be established through appropriate and timely public and formal acts of identification with the Jewish faith and people. The performance of these mitzvot serves to commit those who participate in them, both parents and child, to Jewish life.

Depending on circumstances, mitzvot leading toward a positive and exclusive Jewish identity will include entry into the covenant, acquisition of a Hebrew name, Torah study, Bar/Bat Mitzvah, and [Confirmation]. For those beyond childhood claiming Jewish identity, other public acts or declarations may be added or substituted after consultation with their rabbi.[28]

Text 3.5. Yosef, "On the Status of Ethiopian Jews"[29]
YABI'A OMER, 8, *EVEN HA-EZER*, NO. 11

Born in Baghdad under the name Abdallah Yusef, Rabbi Ovadiah Yosef (1920–2013) immigrated with his parents to Mandatory Palestine. Although his father wanted him to run the family grocery store, his teachers at Yeshivat Porat Yosef appealed to his father to allow him to continue in his studies, since he excelled in them. From 1947 to 1950 he served as deputy chief rabbi in Cairo. He later served on Israel's Supreme Rabbinical Court of Appeals, was appointed Sefardic Chief Rabbi of Tel Aviv, and was then elected as Rishon Lezion[30] Sefardic Chief Rabbi of Israel for two terms in 1973.[31]

Rabbi Yosef adamantly asserted Sefardic/Mizraḥi identity. Seeking "to restore the crown [of Sefardic Jews] to its former glory," he insisted upon Sefardic/Mizraḥi practice amid Ashkenazic religious hegemony. He tried to unify the halakhah of Sefardic/Mizraḥi communities by upholding the opinions of Rabbi Joseph Caro, the Sefardic author of the Shulḥan Arukh. He founded the Shas political party to help redress the prejudice and political and cultural marginalization of Sefardic/Mizraḥi Jews in Israel. He straddled the Ultraorthodox and Modern Orthodox boundary: by inclination, he was Ultraorthodox in the way he lived and the rulings he generally issued, but as an employee of the official State Rabbinate, he supported the institutions of the state. He did rule leniently in a number of significant areas, especially to prevent women from becoming *agunot* (unable to remarry because their husbands had not issued them a *get*). A prolific writer of halakhic works, most importantly *Yabi'a omer* (Speaking forth) and *Yeḥaveh da'at* (Revealing knowledge), he did not write commentary or *ḥiddushin* (novellae) on the Talmud, a genre thought to be the acme of Jewish intellectual creativity by Ashkenazic scholars. His funeral in 2013, attended by at least eight hundred thousand people, is thought to be the largest funeral in Jewish history.[32]

After vast waves of Jews moved from the Middle East and Europe to the State of Israel in the 1950s and 1960s, the question of whether Ethiopian Jews were Jews according to halakhah was hotly debated, especially given stark differences in their Jewish observance from halakhah. Among those striding into the fray was Rabbi Ovadiah Yosef.

SECTION A: THE ORIGIN OF ETHIOPIAN JEWS[33]

Rabbi Yosef begins by recounting public statements he made as Sefardic Chief Rabbi of Israel on the origin of Ethiopian Jewry. Basing his own views on those of earlier rabbinic decisors, he asserts that Ethiopian Jews are descendants of the tribe of Dan, a tribe from biblical times that would remain unaware of later rabbinic interpretations of the tradition. He defends the earlier rabbinic decisors he cites against Ashkenazic Chief Rabbi Isaac Herzog (see chapter 4), who casts doubts on the halakhic status of Ethiopian Jews based on academic research:[34]

> Regarding the immigrants from Ethiopia, the Falashas, what the Radbaz [Rabbi David ben Solomon ibn Abi Zimra, 1479–1573[35]] wrote in *Responsa divrei David*, no. 5, that the Ethiopians

who come from Ethiopia are from the tribe of Dan, is known without any doubt. Because they did not have in their past, sages who were aware of rabbinic tradition, they understood only the superficial meaning of Scripture, but if they had been teaching them [rabbinic tradition], they would not be heretics like the Karaites [who reject rabbinic interpretation]. . . . Therefore their religious status is like an infant who was taken in captivity among non-Jews [and knows nothing of Judaism], for whom it is a mitzvah to redeem them and sustain them. . . . Following him was his great student the Mahariqas [Rabbi Jacob Castro, 1525–1610 or 1612, Egypt].

I had already expressed my opinion on 7 Adar I 1973 [February 9, 1973] in a letter published publicly that the Falashas are Jews in every regard, relying on the Radbaz and on Rabbi Jacob Castro. I also saw this in a responsum of the pious gaon the Rishon Lezion Rabbi Rafael Meir Panigel [who served as chief rabbi of Palestine during the Ottoman Empire from 1880 to 1892] . . . , who wrote "Now, who would come after these two mighty kings [Radbaz and Rabbi Castro] to place a doubt about these Jews and not fear to be singed by the glowing coals [of the Radbaz and Rabbi Castro], since their words are like fiery coals and are established by the Lord of truth and justice. . . ."

When I served as Chief Rabbi of Israel, I replied to my questioners about the matter of the Falashas [relying on the authorities mentioned above] that the Falashas are without a doubt from the tribe of Dan. . . . I also found a number of [other] geonim [great rabbinic authorities] from the generation before us who agreed with this ruling . . . including Rabbi Azriel Hildesheimer [1820–99, Germany]. . . . Therefore, I came to my conclusion that the Falashas were members of a tribe of Israel who were driven southward to Ethiopia and without any doubt the geonim mentioned above who reached this conclusion did so through assiduous research through very reliable testimonies and proofs [as well as] through rabbinic tradition.... After the leaders of the Falashas turned to me requesting "to join with our brothers the Jews in the spirit of the Torah and the halakhah, the Written Torah as well as the Oral Torah without any restriction and to observe all the mitzvot of the holy Torah according to the instructions of our sages according to whose words we live," I thought to myself it is not a time to be silent. We must save them from assimilation, bring them quickly to the Land of Israel to educate them in the spirit of our sacred Torah and to join with them in the rebuilding of our sacred Land [in so doing fulfilling the scriptural verse Jer. 31:17,] "[Your] children shall return to their borders." In light of this, I turned to the government, the Jewish Agency, and all the organizations in Israel and in the Diaspora to do everything to bring them to the Land of Israel in order to educate them in religious schools so that none of them will go astray.... This ruling paved the way for the recognition of the Falasha community as Jews according to the Law of Return.... In a meeting on 16 Shevat 1975, an agreement was reached upon establishing an interagency team [of the Israeli government and the Jewish Agency] to investigate whether the Law of Return applies to Ethiopian Jews, and on the twentieth of the same month in 1975 they indeed decided to apply the Law of Return upon them, with the acknowledgment that "this is based upon the opinion of the Rishon Lezion Sefardic Chief Rabbi of Israel, Rabbi Ovadiah Yosef."...

However I shall not hide that I saw [a responsum of the Ashkenazic Chief Rabbi] Isaac Herzog [see chapter 4]..., who wrote about doubts regarding the Jewishness of the Falashas because he saw that rigorous academic researchers have concluded that the Falashas were of non-Jewish descent that had at some time converted, and if so, it is clear that they converted not on the condition that they observe our Judaism based on the Oral Law, but on Judaism that they invented from their [own] hearts.

> Their religious status is like one who converted on the condition to observe all the Torah except for one matter ascribed to the sages who are not accepted [for conversion] according to . . . Babylonian Talmud *Bekhorot* 30b. And if so, perhaps they are not Jews according to halakhic understanding. . . . I was shocked and very surprised to see [that Rabbi Herzog] rejected the words of the great authorities who determined with certainty [that the Ethiopian Jews are Jews according to halakhic understanding] . . . in place of [academic researchers] who have cast doubts on their Jewishness.

SECTION B: THE MARRIAGE PRACTICES OF ETHIOPIAN JEWS

Rabbi Yosef addresses the question of whether Ethiopian Jews may marry other Jews because of the halakhic status of their divorces. If their marriages are valid but their divorces are not, and then if a divorced Ethiopian man or woman has a child, that child is a *mamzer* because the parent would still be considered married to the original spouse:

> After studying the matter rigorously by consulting with the Ethiopian elders and *Kohanim* [plural of *Kohen*], it was clear [to me] that the Ethiopian community does not utilize *kiddushin* in any form at all as required by the Torah. Their marriages are generally done from about age fourteen for both the groom or the bride and sometimes even younger than this. They are done in this way: The parents of the young man visit the parents of the young woman, and if she finds favor in their eyes, they express their consent to the marriage. They set up a time for the marriage, and the groom and the bride do not see one another until the day of the *ḥuppah* ceremony. A day or two before the ceremony, the parents of the groom send jewelry and gifts to the parents of the bride, meant for the bride. Where the ceremony

is held, the groom sits among the men, and the bride among the women, and they don't go near one another. The father of the groom announces before those present and the bride's father that an agreement has been made between the groom and the bride. Neither [the groom's father] nor the groom give anything [to the bride]. The *Kohen* for the community says words of blessings only orally [signifying that no *ketubbah* has been signed] and nothing more. After the ceremony and the meal, the groom and the bride walk together and spend time alone with one another. They do not make any act of *kiddushin*, whether in words or action as required by Judaism because they have no knowledge that [*kiddushin*] is derived [from the hermeneutic method known as *gezerah shavah* that derives similar laws from similar words, as shown here] between the term "taking" stated with regard to betrothal [in Deut. 24:1] and . . . the term expressing "taking" with regard to the field of Ephron [in Gen. 23:13], according to Babylonian Talmud *Kiddushin* 2a. Even when they go and spend time together alone, [this does not fulfill the requirements of] *kiddushin* via sexual intimacy because [to do so], [the groom] must say to [the bride] in the presence of two witnesses, "You are sanctified to me through sexual intimacy," and [the groom and the bride] must be together with those witnesses [watching the room from outside], even though what the bride and groom are doing remains private, just as explained by Maimonides, Hilkhot Ishut [Laws of Marriage] 3:5, and *Arba'ah Ṭurim* [authoritative halakhic code of the fourteenth century] and Shulḥan Arukh *Even ha-Ezer* 33:1.

PESAK DIN

Rabbi Yosef concludes:

There is no reason to be concerned about marriage disqualifications among the Ethiopians. They are permitted to marry other

Jews without the need for conversion, not even conversion to allay doubt [*giyyur leḥumrah*]. May the blessed God preserve us from errors, and may he show us wonders from his Torah and enlighten our eyes with the light of the sacred Torah, amen.[36]

Text 3.6. Barmash, "The Status of the Ḥeresh [Deaf Mute] and of Sign Language"

COMMITTEE ON JEWISH LAW AND STANDARDS OF THE RABBINICAL ASSEMBLY, ḤOSHEN MISHPAṬ 35:11

Rabbinic tradition considers the deaf who do not speak to be mentally incapacitated, a category that greatly demeans the deaf, and exempts them from the mitzvot. Rabbi Pamela Barmash (see chapter 1) argues that the mental capacity of deaf people was misunderstood and it is now clear they are of sound mind. Therefore, deaf Jews are responsible for observing mitzvot.

QUESTION

In an English *teshuvah* approved by the Rabbinical Assembly's Committee on Jewish Law and Standards in 2011, Rabbi Barmash addresses:

> What is the status of the deaf, in particular those who communicate via sign language? May sign language be used in place of speech in liturgy and ... matters of personal status?

SECTION A: INTRODUCTION

Rabbi Barmash starts by emphasizing that while Jewish tradition has both been sensitive and insensitive to the *ḥeresh* (the deaf who do not speak),[37] the Jewish community of today must acknowledge the hurtful attitudes:

> Historically, the deaf have experienced great prejudice in human societies. Regrettably, they have suffered disdain and

oppression: they have been disenfranchised from education, religion, and commerce as well as excluded from regular interactions among individuals. Their opportunities for individual advancement and fulfillment have often been thwarted, and their intellectual abilities have been regarded with disdain. . . .

In our tradition, sensitivity to the disabled in general and to the deaf in particular is exhibited in certain laws. At the same time, certain regulations, stemming from a lack of knowledge about the cognitive abilities of the deaf, are seen by deaf Jews as reflecting indifference and callousness. . . .

While we may wish to cite only those elements of Jewish tradition that espouse sensitivity, we must not overlook the anguish of our deaf community members who read parts of our tradition with dismay and disappointment and who hope for a more . . . respectful response from us. It is especially the exclusion from communal activities that originated in a misunderstanding of the intellectual capacity of the deaf that is most hurtful and most in conflict with the currents of compassion . . . customary in our tradition.

SECTION B: CLASSICAL RABBINIC VIEWS OF THE DEAF

Rabbi Barmash discusses how the Rabbis came to categorize the *ḥeresh* with the *shoṭeh* (a mentally deranged person) and the minor — all of whom were exempted from the mitzvot. Since the Rabbis were unable to communicate effectively with the *ḥeresh*, they deemed the *ḥeresh* to be of impaired intelligence:

> The Babylonian Talmud in *Ḥagigah* 2b defines a *ḥeresh* as an individual who is placed alongside the categories of the *shoṭeh* (mentally confused) and the minor because [Rabbinic tradition holds] the *ḥeresh* himself is mentally incapacitated.
>
> [The Mishnah reads:] "Except the *ḥeresh*, the *shoṭeh* and the minor etc." [Our Mishnah] speaks of the *ḥeresh* similarly as of

the *shoteh* and minor: just as the *shoteh* and minor lack understanding, so *heresh* [means] one who lacks understanding.

[By holding this, the deaf who do not communicate via speech] are disqualified, excluded, and re-categorized as being unable to conduct themselves as equal to other human beings. It is their lack of speech alone that differentiates them and bars them from being considered lucid. . . .

Severe restrictions were placed upon a *heresh*. The most onerous was that a *heresh* was excluded from all the mitzvot. . . . The *heresh*, the *shoteh*, and the minor . . . were not required even to rejoice [on festivals, per Babylonian Talmud *Hagigah* 2b]:

> All are required to be seen [at the Temple in Jerusalem on the three pilgrimage festivals] and to rejoice. . . . Those who can neither hear nor speak, those who are *shoteh*, or those who are minors are exempt even from rejoicing since they are exempt from all the mitzvot of the Torah.

What is striking is that the only physical disability included among those exempted from the mitzvot is being a *heresh*. The rabbis associated mental impairment with the *heresh*; the rabbis did not impute any intellectual impairment to those with any other physical disability. . . . Those with other physical disabilities are restricted only when their particular physical limitation prevents them from participating in a particular act: their impairment hinders them from specific practices. A blind person cannot chant Scripture for the congregation because the person who does so must read the actual text. But outside of activities that require sight, the blind can participate. . . .

The bewilderment of the rabbis in determining the mental capacity of a *heresh* impelled them to rule that a *heresh* not only lacked hearing but also sound cognitive ability and to associate a *heresh* with the *shoteh*, marginalizing the *heresh*.

SECTION C: THE DEAF IN THE MODERN PERIOD

Rabbi Barmash notes that in the nineteenth century, rabbinic decisors began to doubt that the *ḥeresh* should be exempt from the mitzvot yet were hesitant to change the *ḥeresh*'s status in halakhah:

> Starting in the nineteenth century in western Europe, significant advances were made in the education of the deaf.... By the middle of the century, a number of Jewish communities had established schools for... deaf children....
>
> Rabbi Simḥah Bunim Sofer (1842–1907) reports in his book *Shevet Sofer*, Even ha-Ezer 21, that his father, Rabbi Abraham Samuel Benjamin Sofer, had visited the school for the deaf in Vienna and had been very impressed by the abilities of the students he saw there:
>
>> I heard a number of times from my father who would say that he was doubtful that they were not responsible for the mitzvot. When he was in Vienna, the teachers in a school for the deaf asked him to visit to see with his own eyes their wonderful training. He was so astonished by what he saw there in what they taught the deaf who do not speak that he began to doubt that the (deaf) were not of sound mind and (therefore they should deemed to) be responsible for the mitzvot.
>
> [Ashkenazic Chief Rabbi] Rabbi Isaac Herzog [observes]... in his collection of responsa *Heikhal Yitzhak*, Even ha-Ezer 2.47:
>
>> With this education that was not available in the days of the classical sages, (the *ḥeresh*) has exited from the category of one who is mentally deficient, and in any case, it is doubtful. There is no better proof than what (this deaf-mute) writes, from which it is apparent that his intelligence is totally sound. In fact, modern education is (equivalent to) complete healing (from his deafness).

In these responsa, these authorities recognize that the education that the deaf have received has enabled them to interact more fully with the hearing, demonstrating the soundness of their cognitive ability. However, while Sofer and Herzog were favorable toward conferring a change of status on the deaf, they hesitated to issue such a ruling. . . .

The presumption that deafness is a symptom of a flawed intelligence continued to prevail in the non-Jewish community. . . . Sign language was maligned as a broken version of a spoken language or a rude pantomime. . . . Only in 1960 did a professor of linguistics at Gallaudet University (then College), William C. Stokoe, Jr., publish the first analysis of a sign language as an ordered system governed by syntax, having invented a description system for sign language. Two linguists, Edward S. Klima and Ursula Bellugi, proved in 1979 that sign languages are as complex, abstract and systematic as spoken languages.

SECTION D: THE STATUS OF THE DEAF IN HALAKHAH IN CONTEMPORARY TIMES

Rabbi Barmash concludes that the deaf are now responsible for fulfilling the mitzvot and that sign language is appropriate for use in liturgy and rituals of personal status:

> We . . . are heirs of a tradition that at times exhibited sensitivity toward the disabled, but . . . the deaf in particular were stigmatized by being relegated with those lacking full cognitive ability. We must seek to redress this misconception and to re-educate ourselves and our communities.
>
> The Committee on Jewish Law and Standards . . . rules that the prior record of discrimination against the deaf be reversed due to the increased understanding and awareness of the cognitive ability of the deaf among the hearing and due to the advancements in the education of the deaf. The categorization

of the deaf as mentally incapacitated is to be revoked, and they are to be considered completely lucid.

It is impossible to find precedents for the use of sign language in classical rabbinic literature or in later halakhic literature since sign language did not exist during most of the time period during which this literature was composed....

Sign language and speech... both involve abstraction and generalization. Both speech and sign language utilize basic units... to which meaning is attached arbitrarily....

Sign language... is a means of communication equal to speech. It fulfills all the communicative functions that (an oral) language does. It meets what halakhah needs in a means of communication used in halakhic proceedings: sign language imparts that the signer comprehends and acquiesces to an act and does so in a manner that can clearly be... discerned by witnesses. It can be used in matters of personal status, such as marriage and divorce, and it can be used in rituals such as *brit milah* [circumcision ritual for male infants] or *brit kodesh* [naming ritual for female infants] by the parents or *mohel* [ritual circumciser] and *kehillah* [congregation] and *pidyon ha-ben* [ceremony of the redemption of the firstborn] by the parents or *kohen*.

Can sign language be used liturgically?... The Shema can be recited in any language but the recitation must be done in a specific way [per *Mishnah Berakhot* 2:3]:

> The one who recites the Shema but not loudly enough for him to hear, he has fulfilled his obligation. Rabbi Yose says: he has not fulfilled it. If he recited it without clearly pronouncing the letters, Rabbi Yose says: he has fulfilled his obligation. Rabbi Judah says: he has not fulfilled his obligation.

The rishonim [medieval rabbis] defined the requirement as "articulated with his lips" or "uttered with his lips."... The mouth must move, but it is not necessary for the words to be loud enough to hear or pronounced clearly....

Articulating the Shema (or other liturgy) with the movement of the mouth is more than simply embodying the physical act of speech. By following the halakhic requirement to recite prayers aloud, even if too softly to hear ... we are ... concentrating in a way distinct from reading a fixed text quietly and internally to ourselves. The physical gestures of speech impress us to concentrate. If the physical act of moving our mouths in speech does so, the gestures of sign language do so even more. Sign language is, therefore, a perfect substitute for oral articulation in prayer and may be used to fulfill the requirement for the physical articulation of the words of the Shema.

Sign language may ... be used in liturgy. A deaf person called to the Torah who does not speak may recite the *berakhot* via sign language.... A deaf person may serve as *shaliah tzibbur* in sign language in a minyan whose medium of communication is sign language....

The sound of the shofar must be of a certain tone and rhythm and, therefore, an individual who cannot hear cannot blow it on behalf of others. However, listening to the sounding of the shofar is not limited to hearing the pitch: the sounding of the shofar can be sensed through its vibrations. A deaf person who senses the sounding of the shofar through other senses is having an authentic experience of the mitzvah....

A final thought: The Torah states ..., "Do not curse the deaf nor put a stumbling-block before the blind" (Lev. 19:14). It is the responsibility of our communities, synagogues, schools, and camps to draw on the essence of this mitzvah in making our communities welcoming and inclusive of the deaf.

PESAK DIN

Rabbi Barmash rules:

> The Committee on Jewish Law and Standards rules that the deaf who communicate via sign language and do not speak are no longer to be considered mentally incapacitated:
>
> 1. Jews who are deaf are responsible for the mitzvot.
> 2. Our communities, synagogues, schools, and camps must strive to be welcoming, accessible, and inclusive.
> 3. Sign language may be used in matters of personal status ... and may be used in rituals. ...
> 4. Sign language may be used in liturgy.[38]

Women 4

The status of women has been one of the most controversial issues in Jewish communities in the modern period. Women's roles in all areas of Jewish life have changed significantly across all the movements, especially in the last one hundred years. These developments raise questions about the interrelationship between halakhic principles, ethics, and sociological change. To what extent do principles and ethics drive the reassessment of women's roles in Judaism? Or is it the reverse: to what extent does societal change prompt the reshaping of halakhah and ethics concerning women? Or is it a combination thereof?

The five responsa in this chapter manifest this profound transformation. In 1922, Rabbi Jacob Lauterbach (Reform) avers that allowing women to be ordained as rabbis in the Reform movement is a step too far—a stance his Reform colleagues soundly reject. In 1950, Rabbi Isaac Herzog, first Ashkenazic Chief Rabbi of the modern State of Israel, gains the support of his counterpart, the Rishon Lezion Sefardic Chief Rabbi Ben-Zion Meir Ḥai Ouziel, as well as a council of rabbis, to issue a *takkanah* (a type of responsum that serves as a formal halakhic decree) forbidding a number of traditional halakhic practices affecting women practiced in some Jewish communities. While this *takkanah* helped women in Israel, male rabbis are making the decisions for women. Among the transformations of women's status in recent times, women from across the movements have started to serve as halakhic decisors. The striking development of *yo'atzot halakhah* (halakhic advisors), Orthodox Jewish women serving as rabbinic decisors in everything but name, merits the inclusion of one of their responsa in this chapter.

The next two *teshuvot* address other fundamental transformations: one in liturgy and the other in the overall status of women. In 1990, Rabbi Joel Rembaum (Conservative/Masorti) argues for including the Matriarchs in Jewish liturgy as a way of recognizing women's partnership in the covenant with God. And in 2014, Rabbi Pamela Barmash (Conservative/Masorti) argues that in light of transformations in women's self-perception as well as their perception by others along with changes in social behavior, women are as obligated as men to observe the mitzvot.

Text 4.1. Lauterbach, "Shall Women Be Ordained Rabbis?"
YEARBOOK OF THE CENTRAL CONFERENCE OF AMERICA RABBIS, 32:156–77

Rabbi Jacob Lauterbach (1873–1942), born in Galicia, studied at the University of Berlin and the University of Göttingen and received his ordination from the Orthodox Rabbiner-Seminar in Berlin.[1] His critical edition and translation of the midrash *Mekhilta de-Rabbi Ishmael* won acclamation as a model work of modern scholarship.[2] He served as the rabbi of two Orthodox synagogues in Illinois and upstate New York before leading a Reform synagogue in Huntsville, Alabama (a not uncommon shift at that time, far more rare today). He became professor of Talmud at the Reform seminary Hebrew Union College in Cincinnati, and as chair of the CCAR Responsa Committee, he wrote responsa highlighting the continuity of Reform legal decisions with Jewish tradition, even if these decisions differed greatly from Jewish tradition.

In 1921, the Board of Governors of Hebrew Union College discussed the issue of ordaining women as rabbis when a female student in the preparatory division asked to be assigned a High

Holy Day pulpit, a first in HUC history. The board decided to refer the matter to the Central Conference of American Rabbis (CCAR).[3] As a result, Rabbi Lauterbach wrote this responsum and presented it at a CCAR plenary session in 1922.

QUESTION

Rabbi Lauterbach acknowledges that the precedent of women entering many professions in recent decades prior to his writing inspires the question of whether women should be ordained as rabbis:

> The very raising of this question is due... to the great changes in the general position of women, brought about during the last half century or so. Women have been admitted to other professions, formerly practiced by men only, and have proven themselves successful as regards personal achievement as well as raising the standards or furthering the interests of the professions. Hence the question suggested itself, why not admit women also to the rabbinical profession?

SECTION A: WOMEN IN JEWISH TRADITION[4]

Rabbi Lauterbach analyzes whether Jewish tradition would permit women as rabbis. First, he argues, the rabbinic profession is the only one that traditional Judaism demands be held by men only.[5] Additionally, he contends, even as many talmudic and midrashic texts express high regard for women, these texts assume a traditional social structure in which women take care of the home and the men oversee other activities. In light of this point, his reference to the prophet Deborah follows a midrashic tradition upheld by the Rabbis that she was just teaching the law, rather than serving as a judge, as the biblical text clearly states she did:

> The question resolves itself into the following two parts: first, the attitude of traditional Judaism on this point, and

second, whether Reform Judaism should follow tradition in this regard.... From the point of view of traditional Judaism there is an important distinction between the rabbinate and the other professions.... In the case of the other professions there is nothing inherent in their teachings or principles which might limit their practice to men exclusively. In the case of the rabbinate, on the other hand, there are ... definite teachings and principles in traditional Judaism ... which demand that its official representatives and functionaries be men only. To admit women to the rabbinate is, therefore, not merely a question of liberalism; it is contrary to the very spirit of traditional Judaism which the rabbinate seeks to uphold and preserve....

The rabbis of old entertained a high opinion of womanhood and frequently expressed their admiration for [a] woman's ability and appreciated her great usefulness in religious work.... They say, "God has endowed woman with a finer appreciation and a better understanding than man" [Babylonian Talmud *Niddah* 45b].... "It was due to the pious women of that generation that the Israelites were redeemed from Egypt" [Babylonian Talmud *Sotah* 11b]; and "The women were the first ones to receive and accept the Torah" [*Tanḥuma*, Buber, Metsora' 18, 27a].... These and many other sayings could be cited from Rabbinic literature in praise of woman, her equality to man and, in some respects, superiority to him. So we may safely conclude that their excluding of women from the rabbinate does not at all imply depreciation on their part of [a] woman's worth.

But with all their appreciation of [a] woman's fine talents and noble qualities, the Rabbis of old have also recognized that man and woman have each been assigned by the Torah certain spheres of activity.... The main sphere of [a] woman's activity and her duties centered in the house. Since she has her own duties to perform, and since especially in her position as wife and mother she would often be prevented from carrying on many of the regular activities imposed upon man, the law frees her from many religious obligations incumbent upon men, and especially exempts her from such positive duties the performance of which must take place at certain fixed times, like reciting the "Shema" or at prescribed seasons, like Sukkot [*Mishnah Kiddushin* 1:7].... This fact, that she was exempt from certain obligations and religious duties, necessarily excluded her from the privilege of acting as the religious leader or representative of the congregation [*shaliah tzibbur*]. She could not represent the congregation in the performing of certain religious functions, since, according to the Rabbinic principle, one who is not personally obliged to perform a certain duty, cannot perform that duty on behalf of others and certainly cannot represent the congregation in the performance of such duties [*Mishnah Rosh Hashanah* 3:8]....

On the same principle, she was expressly disqualified from writing Torah scrolls. Since she could not perform for the congregation the duty of reading from the Torah, the text prepared by her was also not qualified for use in connection with the performance of that duty [Babylonian Talmud *Gittin* 45b; *Massekhet Soferim* 1:14]. Women were also considered exempt from the obligation to study the Torah [Babylonian Talmud *Eruvin* 27a; *Kiddushin* 29b–30a]....

This law, that women cannot be rabbis, was always taken for granted in the Talmud. It was considered to be so generally known and unanimously agreed upon that it was not even deemed necessary to make it a special subject of discussion. The very idea of a woman becoming a rabbi never even entered the mind of the Rabbis of old. It is for this reason that we find only few direct and definite statements to the effect that women cannot be rabbis. Only occasionally ... reference — direct or indirect — is made to the established law that women cannot act as judges or be rabbis. Thus, in a *baraita* [Palestinian Talmud

Shevuot 4:1, 35b, and *Sanhedrin* 4:10, 21c] it is stated: "We have learned that a woman cannot act as judge," i.e., cannot render decisions of law....

These Talmudic principles have been accepted by all medieval Jewish authorities.... To be sure, the rabbis do permit the women to be religious teachers, like ... Deborah, whom the Rabbis believed to have been merely teaching the law.

SECTION B: REFORM RABBIS VIS-À-VIS TRADITIONAL RABBIS

Rabbi Lauterbach argues that while Reform Judaism has deviated in many ways from traditional Judaism, ordaining women would unalterably create a breach between the traditional and the Reform rabbinate that all other changes in observance and belief promulgated or approved by Reform rabbis to date have not. Why he believes that allowing women into the rabbinate is *the* breaking point is not clear. In the nineteenth and twentieth centuries, rabbis opposed to Reform Judaism issued many responsa and declarations expressing that because of "non-traditional" Reform practices such as playing an organ during services or including non-Jews in a synagogue choir, Reform Jews were not even to be considered Jews. Often by this time (as we will see in chapter 8), traditional rabbis did whatever they could to separate themselves and their communities from Reform communities:

> This is the attitude of traditional Judaism towards the question of women rabbis, a view strictly adhered to by all Jewry all over the world throughout all generations, even unto this day.
>
> Now we come to the second part of our question; that is, shall we adhere to this tradition, or shall we separate ourselves ... and introduce radical innovation which would necessarily create a distinction between the title Rabbi as held by a Reform rabbi and the title Rabbi in general? I believe that hitherto no

distinction could . . . be drawn between the ordination of our modern rabbis and the ordination of all the rabbis of preceding generations. We are still carrying on the activity of the Rabbis of old who traced their authority through a chain of tradition to Moses . . . though in many points we interpret our Judaism in a manner quite different from theirs. . . . For our time we have the same standing as they had. . . .

We should therefore not jeopardize the hitherto indisputable authoritative character of our ordination. We should not make our ordination entirely different in character from the traditional ordination, and thereby give the larger group of Jewry that follows traditional Judaism a good reason to question our authority and to doubt whether we are rabbis in the sense in which this honored title was always understood.

SECTION C: WOMEN CANNOT SERVE EFFECTIVELY AS RABBIS

Rabbi Lauterbach argues that women rabbis would not be as effective as male rabbis. Since married women must serve as helper to their husbands, they could not serve a congregation wholeheartedly. Nor would a man deign to serve as a helper to his rabbinic wife:

> Nor is there, to my mind, any actual need for making such a radical departure from this established Jewish law and time-honored practice. The supposed lack of a sufficient number of rabbis will not be made up by this radical innovation. There are other and better means of meeting this emergency. This could be accomplished if our rabbis would follow the advice of the men of the Great Synagogue, to raise many disciples and thus encourage more men to enter the ministry. And the standard of the rabbinate in America, while no doubt it could be improved in many directions, is certainly not so low as to need a new and refining influence such as the influence brought by women to

any profession they enter. Neither could women, with all due respect to their talents and abilities, raise the standard of the rabbinate.... Women could not even raise it to the high standard reached by men, in this particular calling. If there is any calling which requires a wholehearted devotion to the exclusion of all other things and the determination to make it one's whole life work, it is the rabbinate. It is not to be considered merely as a profession by which one earns a livelihood. Nor is it to be entered upon as a temporary occupation. One must choose it for his life work and be prepared to give to it all his energies and to devote to it all the years of his life, constantly learning and improving and thus growing in it. It has been rightly said that the woman who enters a profession must make her choice between following her chosen profession or the calling of mother and home-maker. She cannot do both well at the same time. This certainly would hold true in the case of the rabbinical profession.... For in all likelihood she could not continue it as a married woman. For, one holding the rabbinical office must teach by precept and example, and must give an example of Jewish family and home life where all the traditional Jewish virtues are cultivated. The rabbi can do so all the better when he is married and has a home and a family of his own. The wife whom God has made as helpmate to him can be, and in most cases is, of great assistance to him in making his home a Jewish home, a model for the congregation to follow. In this important activity of the rabbi, exercising a wholesome influence upon the congregation, the woman rabbi would be deficient. The woman in the rabbinical office could not expect the man to whom she was married to be merely a helpmate to her, assisting her in her rabbinical activities. And even if she could find such a man willing to take a subordinate position in the family, the influence upon the families in the congregation of such an arrangement in the home and in the family life of the rabbi would not be very wholesome. Not to mention the fact that if she is to be a mother, she could not go on with her regular activities in the congregation. And there is, to my mind, no injustice done to woman by excluding her from this office. There are many avenues open to her if she chooses to do religious or educational work. I can see no reason why we should make this radical departure from traditional practice except the specious argument that we are modern men and we recognize the full equality of women to men, hence we should be thoroughly consistent. But I would not class the rabbis with those people whose main characteristic is consistency.

SECTION D: OTHER REFORM RABBIS RESPOND

Rabbi Lauterbach presented his responsum as his own opinion, per CCAR Responsa Committee procedures whereby responsa were offered presented as the opinion of an individual rabbi and not voted upon. The rabbis attending the 1922 CCAR plenary session responded with mostly negative comments about Rabbi Lauterbach's responsum. The CCAR president appointed a committee headed by Henry Cohen, a prominent rabbi from Galveston, Texas, to formulate a statement (excerpted here) reflecting the CCAR's broader views:

> The Central Conference of American Rabbis has repeatedly made pronouncements urging the fullest measures of self-expression for woman, as well as the fullest utilization of her gifts, in the service of the Most High, and... it gratefully acknowledges the enrichments and enlargement of congregational life which has resulted therefrom. Whatever may have been the specific legal status of the Jewish woman regarding certain religious function, her general position in Jewish religious life has ever been an exalted one. She has been the priestess in the home, and our sages have always recognized her as the preserver of Israel. In

view of the Jewish teachings and in keeping with the spirit of our age and the traditions of our conference, we declare that woman cannot be justly denied the privilege of ordination.[6]

This declaration contradicting Rabbi Lauterbach's responsum—the only responsum the CCAR would issue on women rabbis—was approved by a vote of fifty-six in favor, eleven against.

Yet the board of Hebrew Union College voted down women's ordination, and it would take another half century, until 1972, for HUC to ordain its first woman rabbi, Sally Priesand. Helen Levinthal, a student at the Jewish Institute of Religion (JIR), another liberal seminary independent of Hebrew Union College until the HUC-JIR merger, did complete the rabbinic program in the 1930s but was not ordained as a rabbi when she graduated in 1939.[7] Only by the late 1960s and early 1970s, a time of worldwide social and political ferment, was the Hebrew Union College–Jewish Institute of Religion leadership ready to ordain women.

Text 4.2. Herzog, "*Takkanot* on Marriage and *Yibbum*"[8]
TEḤUKAH LE-YISRAEL AL PI HA-TORAH, 3:168–69

Born in Poland, Rabbi Isaac Herzog (1888–1959) moved as a young boy to Leeds, England, when his father became the rabbi of a congregation there.[9] He rose to the highest levels of traditional rabbinic scholarship, even though he never attended a yeshiva but was taught by his father, and gained the attention of continental rabbinic authorities by sending them essays demonstrating his traditional Jewish learning. After studying at the Sorbonne and earning a doctorate at the University of London, he served as rabbi of Belfast, then of Dublin, and held the title of Chief Rabbi of Ireland. As a staunch supporter of Irish independence, he became friends with the Irish prime minister, Eamon de Valera, and he frustrated a threatened ban on kosher slaughter. Widely respected for his brilliance and personal charisma, he succeeded Rabbi Abraham Isaac Kook as

Ashkenazic Chief Rabbi of Israel over Rabbi Jacob Harlap, a close friend and student of Rabbi Kook and his expected successor. In a famous episode, Rabbi Herzog stood before a crowd at the Hurva Synagogue in Jerusalem's Old City in 1939 with a copy of the British White Paper (a decree restricting Jewish immigration to Palestine) in his hands and stated that he could not support it and would rip it in half just as the biblical prophets did, and then did so.[10] Starting in 1938 he convened rabbinic conferences trying to prepare halakhah for the reality of a modern Jewish state, of which the *takkanah* in this chapter is one example. He engaged energetically in public affairs and diplomacy, trying to save Jews arrested in Mandatory Palestine from the death penalty, meeting with President Roosevelt and others during World War II, and searching for Jewish children who had been hidden during the Holocaust after the war. He established an institute that has been publishing an encyclopedia of the Talmud. His son Chaim Herzog and grandson Isaac Herzog are the first father-son pair to serve as president of the State of Israel. Rabbi Herzog wrote two volumes of responsa, *Heikhal Yitzḥak* (The sanctuary of Isaac); three volumes on halakhah in a Jewish state, *Teḥukah le-Yisrael al pi ha-Torah* (A constitution for Israel according to the Torah); and the first two volumes of the English-language work *Main Institutions of Jewish Law*.

A genre of responsum, a *takkanah* (plural, *takkanot*) is a formal edict issued to rule decisively on a contested matter for the sake of the common good. Only a group of rabbis or a rabbi with an unusually high level of personal authority can issue *takkanot*.

A *takkanah* may also have a formal literary style, with a grandiose introduction bespeaking the momentousness of the decree. Such is the case with the following *takkanah* written by Ashkenazic Chief Rabbi Isaac Herzog, affirmed by his counterpart Rishon Lezion Sefardic Chief Rabbi Ben-Zion Meir Ḥai Ouziel, and accepted unanimously by a national gathering of rabbis in Jerusalem in 1950.

SECTION A. PREAMBLE

Intending to institute major changes in Jewish marriage practices, Rabbi Herzog starts with a poetic introduction emphasizing that the different Jewish communities that have immigrated to Israel must set aside their time-honored customs and agree on a single set of marriage and divorce procedures. The lofty ruling begins:

> With God's help, in light of the bringing together of those from all diaspora communities, from the ends of the earth and distant islands, who are making *aliyah* in their thousands and tens of thousands, and settling in the Land of Israel through the great loving-kindness of God upon us and who are bringing with them ancient customs that do not cohere with the *takkanot* of the sages of the Land of Israel who are in the holy city of Jerusalem and with the *takkanot* of the rabbis of the communities of Israel in the matters of betrothal marriage and in the matters of *gittin* and divorce, *yibbum*, and *halitzah*, phenomena that are liable to raise controversy in Israel and destroy the peace of the house of Israel, we have seen fit to obligate ourselves anew to the *takkanot* of our ancient Rabbis, may their memories be for a blessing, and to add other *takkanot* such as the hour requires for the sake of *darkhei shalom* [peace between communities] and the peace of the house of Israel that hold the basis for all the *takkanot* of our ancient Rabbis from the days of Moses our teacher until the most recent generations of their communities.
>
> With the permission of the Holy One, blessed be He, and His divine presence, and with the permission of the *beit din* above and the *beit din* below, and with the permission of the earlier rabbis of the Land of Israel, and with the agreement of the great geonim [highest-level rabbis], members of the Supreme Council of the Chief Rabbinate of Israel issuing *gezerot* [interdictions] and *takkanot* through the authority of the holy Torah, just like

all the *takkanot* of the Jewish people that were issued among the Jewish people in their communities throughout the generations.

SECTION B: PROVISIONS[11]

The four parts of this *takkanah* are articulated in categorical style, with little or no citation of sources and argumentation. The first part prevents civil marriage without a religious marriage, as well as a religious marriage without a civil license, and makes the Chief Rabbinate the authority for matters of personal status for all Jews resident in the Land of Israel. The second part establishes sixteen as the minimum age females can marry. In certain diaspora communities, men customarily married girls as young as twelve years old or even younger. Notably Rabbi Herzog does not explain this restriction by saying it no longer seems ethical for girls of such tender age to marry; rather he argues that people in modernity are physically weaker than those of earlier generations and hence need to wait until they are best prepared for childbearing. The third part disallows polygyny, except by permission of both chief rabbis — presumably a permission that would be very difficult to obtain. The fourth and arguably the most controversial part bans *yibbum* (levirate marriage, a marriage between a widow whose husband had no children and his brother, who may already be married). Because a number of Sefardic/Mizraḥi communities were still practicing *yibbum*, both the Ashkenazic and Sefardic chief rabbis need to issue this joint ruling demanding that the widow and brother perform *ḥalitzah*, a ceremony in which the widow repudiates the brother and *yibbum* does not occur.

For his part, Rabbi Herzog feels compelled to provide two explanations for this ban: first, to foster peace and unity in the State of Israel and among the Jewish people; and second, to prevent the practice of *yibbum* by men who are not doing so for the sake of fulfilling the mitzvah but for other unstated reasons, perhaps for the sake of gaining a sexual outlet or having access to the deceased brother's property. The first reason is definitely true, but the second is arguable: why does he assume nefarious reasons? Here, too, Rabbi Herzog does not articulate the rationale from a woman's point of view; he does not say it is unethical to force a widow into a marriage for the sake of providing offspring in her late husband's name, although it could be argued that this is what prompts the joint ruling:

> 1. It is forbidden for any Jew, man or woman, to enter into an engagement or marriage without a *ḥuppah* and a minyan of ten after the marriage has been registered in the local offices of the State Rabbinate. This prohibition is based on a weighty *ḥerem* [ban] upon all Jewish men who are required to have proper witnesses for engagement and marriage, and [whoever violates this prohibition] is to be considered a criminal subject to punishment. Any man who marries a woman outside of *ḥuppah* and *kiddushin* . . . shall be required to divorce her through a *get*. . . . After paying damages that a *beit din* authorized by the Chief Rabbinate of Israel shall determine, he will be required to support her sustenance as imposed upon him by the *beit din* until he divorces [her] and pays the damages mentioned above.
>
> 2. It is forbidden for any man to marry a woman who is younger than sixteen years old and a day, since the health of a younger girl may be in danger because of a pregnancy, whether to the mother or to the fetus, in our time due to the diminution of the physical strength of our generation. . . . [This is also the case because] marriages [of a girl younger than sixteen years old and a day] are liable to problems, just as has been proved in many instances. This prohibition also applies to the father of a young woman [so that] he shall not enter his daughter into betrothal [*kiddushin*] when she is younger than the age mentioned above.

3. It is forbidden for any Jew, man or woman, to enter into marriage when [the woman] would be a second wife in a [continuing marriage] with the first wife, unless [they receive] formal permission to marry signed by [both] chief rabbis of Israel.

4. Most Jewish communities, especially the Ashkenazic communities in the Land of Israel, accepted in practice that *halitzah* precedes *yibbum*: even if both the man and the woman involved desired *yibbum*, they were not permitted to do *yibbum*. And if the man was already married, every community did not permit them to do *yibbum*. In our time it is clear that the majority of the men who would do *yibbum* are not intending to do so for the sake of the mitzvah, and [therefore] so that the Torah will not become two torahs, for the sake of *darkhei shalom* and the unity of the State of Israel, we now issue an injunction upon the inhabitants of the Land of Israel and upon those who would make *aliyah* and settle here from now on prohibiting them from the mitzvah of *yibbum* completely and requiring them to do *halitzah*. They are required to provide the [woman's] sustenance as a *beit din* decrees until they release [the woman with *halitzah*].

Informed by modern social conventions and customs, this *takkanah* that concerns women is mostly addressed to men, threatening them (not the women) if they do not comply.

Text 4.3. Roness, "When Staining Renders a Woman *Niddah*"
NISHMAT HA-BAYIT: CONTEMPORARY QUESTIONS ON WOMEN'S REPRODUCTIVE HEALTH, NO. 42

In 1997, a program to train Orthodox women to answer questions about *taharat ha-mishpahah* (family purity), sexual activity, and reproductive health opened in Israel at Nishmat, a school offering women higher-level traditional Jewish education, under the auspices of Chana Henkin, her husband Rabbi Yehuda Henkin, and Rabbi Yaakov Warhaftig. Chana Henkin was inspired to initiate this program due to her experience as a rabbi's wife answering women's questions, and the two rabbis joined her in the project because they realized that women were reluctant to address their questions to them. They deliberately called the graduates *yo'atzot halakhah* (halakhic advisors) rather than *posekot* (halakhic decisors) to signal that the trained women would work with (male) rabbis and have the modesty not to seek authority to decide matters of Jewish law on their own.

Within twenty years, more than 150 women enrolled in the program and were certified: most serve in Israel, while dozens work in Orthodox communities outside Israel. The hotline and website established through Nishmat and the *yo'atzot halakhah* themselves have received a flood of questions. In 2017, *Nishmat Ha-Bayit* (The soul of the house), a book of answers written by the *yo'atzot halakhah*, was published in Hebrew, and an English translation followed in 2021. Even though the introduction avers that the volume is not intended to be "a book purporting to innovate halakhah but [a book] organizing issues,"[12] the chapters are termed "responsa." That there exists an entire educational enterprise (in this case for Orthodox women) to facilitate the answering of halakhic questions, that the answers are written in the traditional format of a responsum, and that their publication is intended to educate and persuade is entirely in line with the responsa tradition.

The *teshuvah* included here was written by *yo'etzet halakhah* Michal Roness, coordinator both of Nishmat's Yoatzot Halacha Fertility Counselor Project and of the research institute that published the first *Nishmat Ha-Bayit* volume. A native of Australia, she holds a BA in political science and communication from Bar Ilan University and an MA in conflict resolution from Hebrew University. She served as coordinator of the Conflict Management and Negotiation Program at Bar Ilan University for fifteen years.

This responsum follows the usual three-part format of the genre: (1) question followed by (2) an answer citing halakhic and other sources, analyzing, and arguing for a particular ruling, (3) concluding in a formal articulation of a *pesak din*. Yet the formatting of the answer is distinct. It appears in two parts: the first part is a clear, concise exposition of the halakhic and medical factors involved in answering the question, and the second part delves in greater detail into the halakhic sources and opinions. This unique format offers readers with different levels of Jewish knowledge the content most appropriate for them: those with a basic level of Jewish education can comprehend the first exposition, and those more educated in Jewish textual sources can understand the second part. This dual format manifests both the change and lack of change in the education of Jewish women: some are educated only at a basic level of knowledge, while others have acquired deeper learning.

The responsum discusses *niddah*, defined in this volume's glossary as "the halakhic status of a woman who experiences uterine bleeding not due to trauma." While the most common cause of *niddah* is menstruation, *niddah* and menstruation are not considered synonymous (*niddah* is defined by halakhic criteria, whereas menstruation is a medical condition characterized by physiological phenomena). At the time of *niddah*, the woman herself is referred to as a *niddah*; her status is *teme'ah*, "ritually impure"; and physical contact between husband and wife is prohibited, according to Orthodox halakhah.

QUESTION

Yo'etzet Roness responds to the question:

> I am nursing and taking the mini-pill (progestogen-only pills). Recently I've been finding numerous bloodstains, and I can no longer differentiate between staining and actual menstruation. I do not feel anything internally during the discharge, but the discharge is red, and sometimes due to the amount of discharge, I have to change the panty liner several times a day. Does the situation I described make me *niddah*?

SECTION A: A CONCISE ANSWER[13]

Roness begins by explaining that what her questioner is experiencing is not *niddah*:

> As long as you have not experienced a halakhic *hargashah* [physical sensation accompanying the onset of uterine bleeding that has halakhic significance] accompanying the bloody discharge from your body, halakhah relates to the discharge according to the laws of *ketamim* [stains that render a woman *niddah* only under certain criteria]. If you find these *ketamim* on a panty liner or a colored undergarment, you are not *niddah*, even if the condition persists.
>
> Nevertheless, it is worthwhile to refrain from marital relations during these days, lest you find blood that renders you *teme'ah* right after intercourse, thus raising the very difficult question of bleeding experienced as a result of marital relations. While refraining, you will also be able to ascertain whether this bleeding will develop into actual menstrual bleeding.
>
> If the stains continue to appear for a prolonged period of time, it is worthwhile for you to perform an external wiping with toilet paper before marital relations, to confirm that you are not staining. It is recommended that you wipe yourselves after intercourse using colored towels [which obscure spotting], and that you do not look at the towels, because when a woman is *tehorah*, and it is not a time when she must anticipate the onset of menses, she should not look for possible *ketamim*. However, once the discharge accumulates to a quantity of blood that approximates menstruation, you are *teme'ah*.
>
> If the staining continues even after a long time, we recommend you consult a gynecologist about the possibility of switching to a different contraceptive.

SECTION B: HALAKHIC ELABORATION

Yo'etzet Roness explains that the pills the questioner is taking may have the side effect of causing spotting between periods. She elaborates on the basic question as to when menstrual discharge signals that a woman has become becomes *teme'ah de-oraita* (ritually impure per the law ascribed to the Torah by the Rabbis): does the woman need to feel a *hargashah* (physical sensation) during the flow of blood? The Shulhan Arukh requires it, according to the opinion of a prominent Babylonian talmudic authority, but a prominent early modern *posek*, Rabbi Elhanan Ashkenazi (1713–80, Poland, Germany) disagrees, basing his view on Rashi and Tosafot (both do not require *hargashah*). Roness then presents three contemporary—and disputing—halakhic opinions on what renders a woman *teme'ah*:

1. [Rabbi Eliezer Waldenberg (see chapter 6)] maintains that premenstrual sensations ... that accompany the onset of menses are considered [the *hargashah* recognized by halakhah]. ... The sensations of menstruation render the woman *teme'ah*.

2. [Rabbi Mordechai I. Willig (b. 1947, United States) holds] that even if we accept that women nowadays do not experience any *hargashah* whatsoever, they still become [*teme'ah*] at the onset of menses. ... The timing is what actually determines. ...

3. [Rabbi Yekutiel Yehudah Halberstam (1905–94, Israel, *Teshuvot divrei yatziv*, Yoreh De'ah, no. 85) holds that] ... when [a woman] experiences bleeding in large quantities [without a *hargashah*], we presume that it was accompanied by *hargashah*. ... The quantity of blood is what determines.

PESAK DIN

Yo'etzet Roness decides to follow the third of the modern views, perhaps because she is addressing a question about whether stains constitute enough blood to indicate menstruation, and concludes:

> Where the [questioner] finds numerous, non-periodic *ketamim* without the *hargashot* that accompany menstruation, she is not *ṭeme'ah de-oraita*, but it is proper to observe the third view cited above.... Therefore, as long as the woman is uncertain whether the onset of menses has arrived, she maintains her presumption of *ṭaharah* [ritual purity], and the stains are judged according to the laws of *ketamim*, even according to those opinions who maintain that a woman becomes *ṭeme'ah de-oraita* at the onset of menstruation, even if there is no *hargashah*. If the bleeding intensifies, one should observe the opinion that a woman becomes *niddah* when she experiences bleeding in a quantity similar to menstruation.[14]

Text 4.4. Rembaum, "Regarding the Inclusion of the Names of the Matriarchs in the First Blessing of the *Amidah*"

COMMITTEE ON JEWISH LAW AND STANDARDS OF THE RABBINICAL ASSEMBLY, ORAḤ ḤAYYIM 112.1990

Rabbi Joel Rembaum, a native of Los Angeles, earned a bachelor's, master's, and PhD from UCLA and received rabbinic ordination from the Jewish Theological Seminary. He served for fifteen years as a professor and administrator at the American Jewish University and then for twenty-five years as the senior rabbi of Temple Beth Am, Los Angeles. He has also taught at the Zacharias Frankel College, a Conservative/Masorti rabbinical school in Potsdam, Germany. Greatly involved with Camp Ramah California, he has also served as president of the Board of Rabbis of Southern California, chair of the Middle East Commission of the Jewish Community Relations Committee of the Los Angeles Jewish Federation, chair of the Los Angeles Israel Bonds Rabbinic Cabinet, and chair of the Executive Committee of the National Rabbinic Cabinet of Israel Bonds. He follows this approach to halakhah: For three thousand years—from the most ancient of the Pentateuchal law codes to the most recent Conservative movement responsa—Torah has been an evolving tradition that allows the words of the Eternal One to speak meaningfully to each successive generation of the people of Israel. Today's Conservative/Masorti halakhic decisions must ensure that the evolution of the *masoret* (tradition) keeps moving forward into the future.

Rabbi Rembaum was inspired to write this responsum after a minyan that meets at his congregation asked him whether they could add the names of the Matriarchs to the liturgy. He then sent this responsum to the Committee on Jewish Law and Standards, which approved it in 1990.

QUESTION

Rabbi Rembaum explains how he came to answer this question:

> The Library Minyan of Temple Beth Am, a participatory and egalitarian congregation of observant Jews affiliated with the synagogue I serve, has been studying and discussing the possibility of including the names of the Matriarchs in the *Avot* blessing [the first blessing of the *Amidah*].... As *mara de-atra* [rabbinic decisor for a local community] of the synagogue, I was asked to render an opinion.

SECTION A: THE LITURGY IS FLEXIBLE

Discussing the feasibility of the technical issues in modifying liturgy, Rabbi Rembaum discusses the theological motivation for it at the conclusion of his responsum. He emphasizes that historically, there *have* been modest modifications in Jewish liturgy, as demonstrated by utilizing the work of academic scholars studying the texts found in the Cairo Genizah and disagreements between two outstanding rabbis of the gaonic period (650–1050 CE). In suggesting new liturgical changes herewith, he follows the pattern of other Conservative/Masorti rabbis in incorporating academic historical research in a responsum:

> While remaining within a framework established in Talmudic times, Jewish liturgy has retained a flexibility that has allowed it to be adjusted and adapted to the spiritual needs of different generations of Jews. A survey of various versions of the *Amidah* reveals that in the early post-Talmudic period the wording of a number of [its] blessings was considerably different from the language that eventually became standardized in the later Geonic period. The reader is referred to a fragment from the Cairo *Genizah*. Especially striking is the language of the thirteenth blessing, with its emphasis on the righteous converts and the absence of references to the other categories of righteous individuals found in the later texts. And, an examination of the fourteenth blessing indicates that the tradition of the Palestinian Talmud is retained, and the splitting of the blessing into [the prayers beginning] "the one who rebuilds Jerusalem" and "the one who causes the dynasty of David to flourish," reflecting the Babylonian Talmud version, is ignored or not known.... The subsequent versions of the *Amidah* reflect considerable change, change that corresponded to the theological needs of later generations.

While it could be argued that this early text represents a transitional version that is too ancient to be considered in a discussion of later twentieth-century liturgical change, I hasten to add that we commonly refer to Talmudic precedents which are even older than these traditions. Furthermore, the Conservative/Masorti movement's addition of the term "in the world" to the *Sim Shalom* prayer harks back to the *Amidah* of Rabbi Sa'adia

[Gaon]'s *Siddur*, itself an early text which often differs from the later "standard" versions.[15]

A good example of the impact on liturgy of a significant theological development is Rabbi Sa'adia [Gaon]'s reaction to the reference to the light that shines on Zion, "may a new light shine upon Zion," in the conclusion to the *Yotzer* prayer. Rabbi Sa'adia [Gaon] [882–942 CE] argued that since the prayer refers to the light of creation and not the light of the Messianic age, such an allusion is unacceptable. Rabbi Sherira [Gaon] [906–1006 CE], in his response to Rabbi Sa'adia [Gaon]'s comment, noted that the reference has always been accepted in the academies and is appropriate for the prayer. It appears as if the people's hopes for redemption overruled Rabbi Sa'adia [Gaon]'s plea for ideological consistency. Saadiah Gaon's opinion did carry the day, however, in certain [Sefardic/Mizraḥi] communities where [that] phrase is still absent from the standard morning liturgy. This indicates that Jewish liturgical tradition can, indeed, tolerate variations in the basic structure of communal prayer.

SECTION B: DEVIATIONS FROM FIXED LANGUAGE

Still, Rabbi Rembaum must answer the question of whether it is appropriate to modify liturgical wording that has been fixed for a millennium. He presents the rules Maimonides [Rambam] proposes for modifying liturgy, points out Maimonides' inconsistent approach to liturgical revisions, and shares the resolution Rabbi Joseph Caro offers. Ultimately, Rabbi Rembaum concludes that Maimonides and his commentators accept liturgical change within normative parameters:

> Regarding the matter of deviating from the authorized wording of blessings ... [Maimonides'] *Mishneh Torah, Hilkhot Berakhot* [Laws of Blessings] 1:6 indicates that should the worshiper deviate from the fixed language of a blessing (the *maṭbe'a*),

the religious obligation associated with the blessing *has been fulfilled* as long as the blessing includes reference to God's ineffable name and his kingship and its wording ["Adonai, king of the universe"] remains consistent with the established theme of the prayer. This principle is set forth in the same paragraph in which Rambam [Maimonides] allows for the recitation of blessings in all languages....

Rambam [Maimonides] is ambiguous with regard to the matter of changing the established liturgy. Although in *Hilkhot Berakhot* 1:6 he allows for the possibility of modifying the language of the prayers, in the preceding paragraph he states that one should not deviate from the versions of the blessings established by Ezra and his court; nor should one add to them or delete anything from them. One who changes the established version is in error. He expresses an even stronger negative opinion in *Hilkhot Keri'at Shema* [Laws of Reciting the *Shema*], where he concludes that one who deviates from the *matbe'a* must repeat the prayer. [Rabbi Joseph Caro's commentary on the *Mishneh Torah*] the *Kesef Mishneh* on *Hilkhot Berakhot* 1:5–6 offers the following resolution of these inconsistencies in Maimonides' thinking ... and distinguishes among four kinds of deviations to which Maimonides alludes:

1) The clause in [*Mishneh Torah, Hilkhot Berakhot*] 1:5 beginning "and it is not appropriate" refers to a change which *fulfills* the religious obligation associated with the prayer but which is not recommended because it still is an unwarranted change, [and Rabbi Caro] designates two kinds of changes which fall into this category:
   a) One recites a blessing that conveys the essential concept of intent of the established blessing but does so in words different from those of the authorized version.

b) One recites a blessing according to the version established by the sages but adds to it or deletes something from it.
2) When one changes a blessing to the degree that a specific reference to a divine act [such as the creation of bread] is replaced by a general reference to God's creation and no references to God's kingship are included in the blessing, the religious obligation has not been fulfilled.
3) When a general reference has replaced a specific reference, but God's ineffable name and his kingship [that is, "the Lord . . . the king of the universe"] are included, though this can be considered an error . . . , the religious obligation is, nevertheless, fulfilled.
4) The statement in *Hilkhot Keri'at Shema* 1:7 refers to a case where one deviated from the established rules regarding when [an opening formula] or a [closing formula] is used with a given blessing. In such a case, the religious obligation has not been fulfilled, and the blessing must be repeated. [Rabbi Caro] concludes his comment on *Hilkhot Berakhot* 1:6 by emphasizing that the permissive statement of Maimonides in that paragraph is in a case where one has changed the wording of the blessing while retaining the basic theme and not altering its opening or closing structure. . . .

Maimonides and his commentators are tolerant of liturgical change as long as it takes place within certain normative parameters. The change that is being recommended in this paper falls within these parameters.

SECTION C: RABBINICAL ASSEMBLY LITURGICAL INNOVATIONS

Rabbi Rembaum highlights a number of liturgical changes already instituted by the Conservative/Masorti movement that are more radical than what is being proposed here:

> The Rabbinical Assembly has ... instituted changes in the liturgy that are more radical than the additions to the *Amidah* prayer suggested above. Rabbi Morris Silverman's removal of the term "and the sacrificial offerings" from the *Avodah* blessing of the *Amidah* in his *Sabbath and Festival Prayer Book* and the parallel shift in the *Siddur* from the future tense to the past tense in the language of the *Musaf Amidah* references to sacrifices represent significant textural and ideological changes in the expression of Judaism's hopes for the messianic future. These are far more extreme than the addition of references to the Matriarchs to the *Amidah*, since the latter do not negate the intent of the prayer, but rather reinforce it. . . . It should be noted that the Silverman *Siddur* anticipates the issue under discussion in this paper with its change in the Morning Blessings [*Birkat ha-Shahar* section of the liturgy] to "who has made me in his image."[16] Given these changes, it would be hard to imagine how the modifications suggested in this paper could be considered objectionable.

SECTION D: *SIDDUR SIM SHALOM*

Rabbi Rembaum identifies liturgical changes already made within what is (at that time) the most recent Conservative/Masorti siddur, *Siddur Sim Shalom*:

> *Siddur Sim Shalom* has continued in the Conservative/Masorti movement's tradition of evolutionary liturgical change. The additions to the "You have established" paragraph of the Sabbath *Amidah*, for example, reinforce Judaism's historical Zionist

yearnings and, at the same time, recognize the legitimacy of the worship of God wherever Jews may find themselves.[17] Indeed, *Siddur Sim Shalom* begins to address the issue under discussion in this paper by including references to the Matriarchs in an English alternative to the weekday *Amidah* and in the *Mi Sheberakh* prayers recited when the Torah is read and with the inclusion of the term "free woman" in the Morning Blessings.[18]

The inclusion of the names of the Matriarchs in the *Avot* blessing is consistent with the traditions of the Bible, normative Jewish theology and the theme of the first paragraph of the *Amidah*. In the Genesis accounts the Matriarchs function as significant factors in the unfolding of the covenant between God and the Israelite nation. The *Avot* blessing functions as an affirmation of the covenantal bond between God and his people, and, given the Matriarchs' role in the development of that relationship, allusion to them in this blessing is most appropriate. Jewish tradition already has recognized within the liturgy the significance of this matriarchal role in the selection of the account of God's remembering Sarah as the Torah reading for the first day of Rosh Hashanah. Continuing in this vein, the addition of the term "the one who remembers Sarah" to the conclusion of the *Avot* blessing is an important reinforcement to a prayer that highlights this unique covenantal bond.

PESAK DIN

Rabbi Rembaum rules:

> Because the *Siddur*, perhaps more than any other compilation of Jewish religious expression, has embodied the ideas that have both shaped and reflected the deepest beliefs and concerns of our people, significant ideological and communal developments and trends have always been represented in our prayers. In a generation when women are assuming a more significant role

in the religious life of the Conservative Jewish community, it is appropriate that the prayer that expresses the unity, commitment and lofty aspirations of the Jewish people, the *Amidah*, be modified so that it can speak to all members of our congregations, male and female alike. The inclusion of the names of the Matriarchs in the *Avot* blessing of the *Amidah* is permissible and recommended [as follows:] to the blessing: after "the God of Jacob," add the words "the God of Sarah, the God of Rebecca, the God of Rachel, the God of Leah"; after the term "king who helps," add the word, "and who remembers"; and in the [closing] of the *Avot* blessing, after "the shield of Abraham," add "and the one who remembers Sarah."[19]

Text 4.5. Barmash, "Women and Mitzvot"

COMMITTEE ON JEWISH LAW AND STANDARDS OF THE RABBINICAL ASSEMBLY, YOREH DE'AH 246:6.2014A

The first bat mitzvah was conducted by a professor from the Conservative movement's Jewish Theological Seminary in 1922, and starting in the 1950s the Conservative/Masorti Committee on Jewish Law and Standards began to approve responsa transforming the role of women in halakhah: *aliyot* for women in 1955; counting women in the minyan in 1973; women taking the first two *aliyot* historically reserved for a male *Kohen* or Levite in 1989; *pidyon ha-ben* (ceremony of redemption for firstborn males) for female firstborn babies in 1993; women reciting the Priestly Benediction in 1994; and women serving as witnesses in 2001. In light of these decisions, Rabbi Pamela Barmash (see chapter 1) addresses another essential question: are men and women equally obligated to observe mitzvot?

QUESTION

In a responsum approved in 2014 by the Committee on Jewish Law and Standards, Rabbi Barmash addresses the question:

Are Jewish women responsible for observing the mitzvot from which they have traditionally been exempted?

SECTION A: REFLECTIONS ON MITZVOT, SPIRITUALITY, AND WOMEN

Rabbi Barmash begins with a theological discussion of the spiritual significance of mitzvot and how egalitarianism embodies Conservative/Masorti Judaism. She concludes with the argument that making Jewish women as responsible as men for observing all the mitzvot demonstrates the movement's profound love for tradition by encouraging more Jews to observe more mitzvot:

> This teshuvah is both retrospective and prospective. It is breathtaking to see the vast advances in the participation of women in the Conservative movement in the past century, especially accelerated in recent decades. Who would have imagined the developments that have occurred since the first declarations and decisions of the Committee on Jewish Law and Standards on the role of women in 1955? At the same time, we must take a prospective view toward the future: how do we envision the spiritual life of the communities we are aspiring to build and nurture? Egalitarianism, the equality of women in the observance of mitzvot, is not just about the participation of women: it is about fostering the fulfillment of mitzvot by all Jews.
>
> Observing mitzvot is the primary way Jews live a religious life. We express our search for God and our quest to live in holiness through the observance of mitzvot. The mitzvot inspire us by focusing our thoughts and elevating our feelings: they guide us toward behavior imbued with certain values and goals. The observance of mitzvot shapes our actions and sanctifies our behavior. We make ourselves open to the spirit through the act of fulfilling mitzvot.

Women have always been responsible to observe mitzvot, but women were exempted from many ritual mitzvot that men were required to observe.... Women were exempted from the study of Torah and, thereby, played a greatly limited role in the process of transmitting and interpreting Torah....

In the past century, accelerated in recent decades, women have sought to suffuse their lives with greater Torah and more mitzvot. By integrating more mitzvot to their lives, women have enriched themselves by the daily routines of Torah and of seeking God both in public and private. At the same time, cultural attitudes have shifted dramatically in society in general, and doors into business and the professions formerly closed to women are now open. Women participate in public life in ways unimaginable a century or two ago, or even a few decades ago. This is not just a change in external behavior but an intellectual and psychological transformation in how women perceive themselves and are perceived by others. Women are now seen as equal to men, in social status, in political and legal rights, and in intellectual ability by both men and women.

For many Jewish women, the pathway of observance that Judaism has traditionally assigned to women is no longer sufficient. They want to observe more mitzvot and participate equally in the public life of Jewish liturgy and community. They want to study Torah in the same depth and breadth that Jewish men have enjoyed. Jewish women are seeking to grow in their religious lives....

This development has happened in most, if not all, Jewish communities, and the Conservative movement has been at the forefront of this development....

Egalitarianism, the equality of women in the observance of mitzvot, reflects how our view of Judaism is distinct. We are both traditional and innovative. We adhere to preserving halakhah, and we are creative in the process of preserving it. Women observing more mitzvot is at once both deeply conservative and profoundly innovative. While extending women's observance to include the mitzvot from which they have traditionally been exempted (and often excluded) may seem radical to some, it demonstrates our profound love for tradition: we want more Jews to observe more mitzvot.

SECTION B: THE CATEGORY OF TIME-BOUND POSITIVE MITZVOT

Turning to halakhic sources, Rabbi Barmash investigates the category of mitzvot from which women were traditionally exempted: time-bound positive mitzvot, meaning deeds to be actively performed at a certain set time. She argues that the rule exempting women from time-bound positive mitzvot makes little sense: women are only excluded from certain time-bound positive mitzvot and expected to perform others, and many of the exempted mitzvot do not truly have to be performed within a narrow window of time. Even the Babylonian Talmud sensed and tried to grapple with such problems:

> The rabbinic text that often serves as the initial entry into the issue of women and mitzvot is Mishnah Kiddushin 1:7:
>
>> The observance of all time-bound positive mitzvot is obligatory for men but not for women, and the observance of all positive mitzvot that are not time-bound is obligatory for men and women. The observance of all the negative mitzvot, whether they are time-bound or not, is incumbent on both men and women.
>
> This mishnah presents the category of being time-bound and positive as the principle that determines whether women are to be exempted from particular mitzvot. These mitzvot are deeds to be actively performed; hence they are termed "positive," in

contrast to mitzvot of refraining from an action, usually termed "negative mitzvot." These mitzvot are "time-bound" in that they are performed at a certain time of the day, week or year....

The *time-bound positive mitzvot from which women were exempted* are: reciting the *Shema*, wearing *tzitzit* and donning *tefillin*, residing in a *sukkah*, taking up the *lulav*, hearing the *shofar*, and counting the *omer*. However, there are *time-bound positive mitzvot that were considered incumbent on women*: eating matzah on Passover, drinking the four cups of wine on Passover, rejoicing on festivals, ... lighting the Hanukkah candles, reading the Megillah on Purim, reciting kiddush, lighting Shabbat candles, reciting the *Amidah*, observing *niddah*, fasting on Yom Kippur, and reciting *Birkat ha-Mazon*. Furthermore, rabbinic tradition specifically *exempts women from the obligation to perform specific positive mitzvot that are not time-bound*: women are not obligated to procreate, to study Torah, to circumcise their sons, to redeem their first-born children.... Rabbinic tradition also designated *communal ceremonies from which women were excluded from participation*.... They could not be honored with an aliyah to the Torah. They could not be counted in the minyan necessary for the recitation of *Barkhu*, the reader's repetition of the *Amidah*, the *Kedushah* and the Kaddish, and therefore they could not serve as *shlihat tzibbur* [leader of public prayer]....

The exemption of women based on whether a mitzvah is positive and time-bound is problematic:

- First, many mitzvot from which women were exempted do not have to be performed in a narrow window of time. There is ... a very wide window of time in which they can be fulfilled.... They can be performed at home, and a number of them require only a slight amount of time to fulfill. The mitzvah of *lulav* ... could be performed at any point in time during the day. Women were exempted ... from hearing the *shofar*,

another mitzvah that could be completed at any point during the day....
- Second, there were many time-bound positive mitzvot that were incumbent on women.... Lastly, it must be also noted that women were put into the same category as minors and slaves with an essential difference: minors could grow up and slaves could be emancipated, but women always remained with limited capacity....

The Babylonian Talmud is well aware that the category is deeply problematic:

> "*All time-bound positive mitzvot* . . ." Our rabbis taught: Which are the time-bound positive mitzvot? *Sukkah, lulav, shofar, tzitzit,* and *tefillin.* And what are affirmative precepts not limited to time? Mezuzah, installing a parapet on a flat roof, returning lost property, and the shooing of a bird away from a nest. Now, is this a general principle? But matzah, rejoicing on Festivals . . . are time-bound positive mitzvot that are incumbent upon women. Furthermore, study of the Torah, procreation, and the redemption of the firstborn are not time-bound positive mitzvot, and yet women are exempt. Rabbi Yohanan answered: We cannot learn from general principles, even where exceptions are stated....[20]

The Babylonian Talmud acknowledges that this category does not hold up well and that the distinction is not a determinative principle.... What, then, caused women to be exempted from certain mitzvot?

SECTION C: IF THE CATEGORY OF TIME-BOUND POSITIVE MITZVOT WAS NOT A GENERATIVE PRINCIPLE, WHY WERE WOMEN EXEMPTED FROM CERTAIN MITZVOT?

Rabbi Barmash argues that women's place in social structure precipitated the exemption, even though Rabbinic literature does not articulate the rationale in those terms:

> The Tosefta ... [explains]:
>
>> What is the obligation of the son to the father? He must feed him, give him drink, clothe him, help him out and in, and wash his face, hands and feet. [It should be that] the same obligation applies to both men and women, except that a man has the means at his disposal (to perform these tasks) but a woman does not because she is under the control of others (and therefore she is exempted). . . .
>
> The Tosefta explains that a woman is exempt from caring for a parent because she and her financial resources are under the jurisdiction of others (presumably her husband). . . . Her time, activity, and financial resources are not in her power. . . .
>
> The Babylonian Talmud [*Kiddushin* 30b] in its analysis of the Tosefta provides an ... opinion about the opposite case, one in which a woman is *not* exempted from her obligation to care for her parents:
>
>> Said Rav Iddi ben Abin, said Rav: If she gets divorced, the two of them [the son and the daughter] are equal.
>
> A married woman is exempted from caring for her parents, but a divorcee, who is no longer under the control of a man, is obligated. . . .
>
> The reason for women's exemption [from time-bound positive mitzvot] is that women are under the authority of another. . . . The essential ritual acts should be performed only by those of

the highest social standing, those who are independent, not subordinate to anyone else.... The acts of those who are subordinate... honor God in a lesser way.

It must be emphasized that the subordination of women is about their social status, about their place in the hierarchy of family and society, not about the demands on their time by domestic duties. This is... reflected in the socio-economic reality of the rabbinic period.... The women in the household shared domestic responsibilities.... The chores and requirements of earning a living sufficient for the daily needs of food and shelter were very time-consuming. Both men and women were hard-pressed to fulfill ritual mitzvot if they lacked servants to assist them. The mitzvah that arguably takes up the most time is that of the daily recitation of the Amidah... and it was obligatory on men and... on women....

Women could not fulfill the responsibilities of men to perform specific mitzvot.... Rabbinic sources suggest that social standing matters and that those of higher social standing would lose their dignity if some of lower social standing functioned on their behalf. In the case of the public reading of Scripture:

> A minor may translate for an adult [who is chanting from Scripture in public] but it is beneath his dignity for an adult to translate for a minor.[21]

The reader's social status matters: a woman or a minor... cannot represent the congregation, and to do so would infringe on the dignity of the congregation.

SECTION D: LATER REASONING ABOUT THE
CATEGORY OF TIME-BOUND POSITIVE MITZVOT

Rabbi Barmash discusses how thinkers in the Middle Ages and modernity understand the exemption of women. She holds that their justifications didn't apply even to their own times, when there were unmarried women and many Ashkenazic Jewish women ran businesses:

> Rabbi David Abudraham (14th century, Spain) argues that women were freed from time-bound positive mitzvot because they needed to take care of their husbands.... Abudraham's claim that women must drop everything to attend to their husband's needs may have been satisfactory in the past.... It is unacceptable that such a consideration would apply to current society when women are now seen as equal to men (nor to women even in his own time who were widowed or not married)....
>
> One of the (most) distinguished rabbis of the 19th century already recognized the impossibility of defending a subservience theory like Abudraham's.... Rabbi Samson Raphael Hirsch (1808–1888, Germany) contends that women are more spiritual and that since women were less involved in business and the professions, they did not need to have as many periodic infusions of religious inspiration as men, whose occupations made them more subject to the snares of dishonesty and fraud....
>
> It is debatable whether women were, or are, more spiritual, and if they are, should they not perform the mitzvot to inspire others, especially those who are less spiritual (in Hirsch's opinion, men), to a higher spiritual plane?... Hirsch's second reason does not work in modern times: as the role of women has changed and they have become more involved in public life, commerce, and politics, they too require the daily infusions of ritual that Hirsch argued are necessary to prevent men from lapsing into sin.

SECTION E: THE EXEMPTION FROM MITZVOT AND THE STUDY OF TORAH

Exploring how the Rabbis arrive at women's exemption from Torah study, Rabbi Barmash characterizes the ruling as deeply subjective. The midrash makes the assumption that only men are included from a biblical verse (Deuteronomy 11:19) that could have just as easily been interpreted to include both men and women:

> Inextricably linked with all mitzvot is . . . the study of Torah. . . . The study of Torah constitutes the central project of rabbinic Judaism. . . .
>
> It is deeply instructive to see how a tannaitic midrash [midrash from the period of the Mishnah] links women's exemption from the family pattern of Torah study to a biblical verse (Deut. 11:19). . . . :
>
> > *Teach them (the words of God) to your sons* (beneikhem) — your sons and not your daughters. These are the words of Rabbi Yose ben Akiva.[22]
>
> The exemption of women from the mitzvah of studying Torah is based on a reading of Deuteronomy 11:19, a reading that understands the word "beneikhem" to mean "your sons," not "your children." This reading is deeply subjective: the noun is a masculine plural, often used as a common plural. The phrase could easily have been understood as "your children" — there is nothing in the context that restrict it to "sons." Yet it was obvious to the rabbis that this was the case. . . . It simply was not conceivable to them that women were required to study Torah. The rabbis lived in a male-dominated world, where the model in all legal discussions is the adult free Jewish man. . . .
>
> How do we relate to the exclusion of women from Torah study? . . . The study of Torah is the highest spiritual activity, and at the heart of our communities is a culture of Torah study.

To obligate women to study Torah is to make women equal members of the central project of rabbinic Judaism.... Women's role in the transmission and creation of Torah is needed and expected in order to sustain our communities....

We can return to the verse in Deuteronomy... and understand it differently, *Teach them to your children*, both your sons and your daughters.

PESAK DIN
Rabbi Barmash rules:

We aim to guide our people into lives suffused with more Torah and more holiness... with seeking God both in public and private. Therefore, we rule that women and men are equally obligated to observe the mitzvot.[23]

LGBTQIA+   5

Perhaps few other issues in recent years have been so hotly debated as that of sexual orientation. Society in general and Jewish communities in particular have shifted their stance greatly or not at all. Those who feel that the question has been settled for all time and those who advocate for change in halakhic rulings are equally adamant.

The four responsa in this chapter embody how Jewish understandings of LGBTQIA+ lives have developed. Three responsa address gay and lesbian Jews, and the fourth, transgender Jews. Rabbi Joel Roth holds that "homosexual love for homosexuals is as potentially beautiful, fulfilling, rewarding and meaningful for homosexuals as heterosexual love is for heterosexuals," but writes with anguish and sadness that for halakhic reasons, homosexuals must choose celibacy. Rabbis Elliot Dorff, Daniel Nevins, and Avram Reisner "favor the establishment of committed and loving relationships for gay and lesbian Jews" in large part because "the rabbinic restrictions upon gay men and lesbian women that result in a total ban on all sexual expression throughout life are in direct conflict with the ability of these Jews to live in dignity as members of the people of Israel," but do not consider such marriages *kiddushin*. By contrast, the CCAR Responsa Committee rules that "same-sex marriages . . . meet the long-standing Reform definition of *kiddushin* as a mutual and egalitarian marital covenant between two Jews." Rabbi Leonard Sharzer, a physician, says that gender identity needs to be self-determined by transgender Jews and then addresses appropriate conversion rituals, among other issues.

Text 5.1. Roth, "Homosexuality"

COMMITTEE ON JEWISH LAW AND STANDARDS OF THE RABBINICAL ASSEMBLY, EVEN HA-EZER 24.1992B

Rabbi Joel Roth, born in Detroit, earned his ordination at the Jewish Theological Seminary. Officially appointed to the faculty in 1968 after receiving his PhD, he remained on the faculty until retiring in 2021. He served as dean of the rabbinical school as well as the chair of the Talmud and the Hebrew Language departments. Rabbi Roth was also the rosh yeshiva of the Conservative Yeshiva in Jerusalem and visiting professor at the Seminario Rabinico Latinoamericano in Buenos Aires. He has served as the primary teacher for several Rabbinical Assembly programs, training doctors to serve as *mohalim* and training rabbis to serve as kashrut supervisors. A member of the Committee on Jewish Law and Standards from 1978 until 2006, he served as its chair from 1984 to 1992. His traditionalist philosophy of halakhah is spelled out in detail in his book *The Halakhic Process: A Systemic Analysis*.

SECTION A: INTRODUCTION

In a *teshuvah* on whether halakhah permits same-sex relationships, approved in 1992, Rabbi Roth starts by justifying why he is writing a *teshuvah* on a question that for some is settled without a doubt and whose ruling will be unsatisfying for others:

> We must assert that there is no question which cannot be on the agenda of the Law Committee. Each age may have its... questions which seem unlikely ever to require serious discussion, yet subsequent ages may find it necessary to discuss those very questions.... However, willingness to discuss a question in no way predetermines what the answer will be.... It must

be remembered that those who are questioning the precedent are offering what they believe to be compelling reason for overturning it. One who wishes to reaffirm the precedent must now respond to the claim that there is compelling reason to overturn it....

[*Posekim*] are duty-bound to listen carefully and attentively to the claims and contentions of those who address questions to them.... [Rabbinic decisors] can be sensitive, understanding, and caring—and still disagree with the claim of the constituent....

We must assert from the outset that the question of homosexuality cannot be excluded from halakhic discourse on the grounds that halakhah stops at the bedroom door. While it may be possible to claim that a secular legal system should say nothing about the legality or morality of private acts between consenting adults, that could hardly be a tenable claim for a religious legal system. Not only are there myriad areas where halakhah does already have something to say about what goes on between consenting adults and behind closed doors, it seems unthinkable to claim that private behavior could or should be of no concern to God.

SECTION B: BIBLICAL RULINGS

Rabbi Roth focuses on the biblical texts that serve as the prooftexts that shape halakhah on homosexuality, analyzing in detail the use of the term *to'evah*, "abhorrence." His emphasis that the characteristic *to'evah* is ascribed, not inherent, in homosexual behavior is prompted by his understanding that homosexuality is natural, not an aberration:

Leviticus 18:22 reads: "Do not lie with a man as one lies with a woman: it is an abhorrence [*to'evah*]."... The term *to'evah* is applied specifically only in verse 22, though verses 26, 29, and

30 apply the term *to'evah* to all of the forbidden relationships. Leviticus 20:13 reads: "If a man lies with a male as one lies with a woman, the two of them have done an abhorrent thing [*to'evah*]; they shall be put to death—their bloodguilt is upon them." ...

Referring to an act as *to'evah* surely is a term of opprobrium. ... The term, as it appears in Leviticus 18 and 20, seems to connote some universally recognized inherent quality called *to'evah*. That is, it could be read to imply that anyone who looks at the acts described in those chapters would recognize them as acts of *to'evah* even if they had not been called *to'evah* by the Torah. ...

Upon closer analysis, however, it seems to me that the opposite is the case. The term *to'evah* in the Torah does not refer to an inherent quality of an act. Acts are *to'evah* because the Torah calls them *to'evah*. "Abhorrence" is not an inherent quality of the act, it is an attributed quality. The most telling evidence that *to'evah* is an attributed, rather than an inherent, quality can be found in ... Genesis 43:32 [where] the Torah says, "The Egyptians could not dine with the Hebrews, since that would be abhorrent to the Egyptians." Mixed eating is not inherently abhorrent. ... It is abhorrent to Egyptians for whatever reason they consider it abhorrent. It is *to'evah to the Egyptians*—not inherently. ... The Torah recognizes *to'evah* as an attributed quality for matters that are abhorrent to Jews, too. It is not contending that foreigners might mistakenly think certain things to be abhorrent, while Jews consider abhorrent only those things that are inherently abhorrent.

There are four cases that make this abundantly clear, in my opinion. Regarding the sacrifice of a blemished animal the Torah says: "For it is a *to'evah* for the LORD your God" (Deut. 17:1). Regarding cross-dressing it says: "For all who do this are *to'evah* to the LORD your God" (Deut. 22:5). Regarding the prohibition against remarrying one's divorced wife the Torah says, "For it is a *to'evah* before the LORD" (Deut. 24:4), and regarding the use of unjust weights and measures the Torah says, "For all who do this, who deal dishonestly are *to'evah* before the LORD your God" (Deut. 25:16).... We consider these acts abhorrent because the Torah informs us that God considers them abhorrent, not because they are inherently or objectively abhorrent....

Legally speaking, the Torah defines homosexuality as *to'evah*. It does not define why it is to be considered *to'evah*....

The legal liability about which the Torah speaks is incurred by the act of intercourse, not by any thought or fantasy of homosexual intercourse.

SECTION C: LESBIAN INTIMACY

Rabbi Roth analyzes the prohibition on lesbianism:

> The two explicit biblical verses refer to male homosexuality, not to female homosexuality.... The Sages, however, have forbidden female homosexuality.... The primary difference between male and female homosexuality in halakhah is that one is forbidden *de-oraita* [law ascribed to the Torah by the Rabbis] and the other is forbidden *de-rabbanan* [law promulgated by the Rabbis]....
>
> It is important ... to make clear why lesbianism is forbidden *de-rabbanan* rather than *de-oraita* from a legal point of view. Let us, therefore, look first ... in Sifra [Aḥarei Mot 9.5]:
>
>> "You should not follow the acts of the land of Egypt ... or the acts of the land of Canaan (Lev. 18:3)"—Is it conceivable that [the Israelites] should not build buildings or plant plantings as they [i.e., the Egyptians and Canaanites] do? The Torah states: "You should not follow their practices"—[implying] "I [God] have declared prohibited only the practices which they and their ancestors established." And what did they do? A man would marry a man and a woman [marry] a woman, a

man would marry a woman and her daughter, and a woman would be married to two men. Regarding these it is said: "You shall not follow their practices." ...

Male homosexuality is forbidden by a specific prohibition of the Torah, female homosexuality by implication of the Torah. Both are equally forbidden.

SECTION D: PSYCHOLOGICAL THEORIES

Rabbi Roth turns to modern views of homosexuality. He starts by addressing the argument that homosexuality is unnatural because of the anatomical unfitness of non-vaginal sex. He notes that (a) homosexuals have no trouble making their organs fit in other orifices, (b) there is a long history of acceptable non-vaginal sexual intimacies among heterosexuals, and (c) there is a long rabbinic history of recognition of non-vaginal intercourse. Then he disproves the contention that same-sex relations are unnatural because they are not procreative by arguing that because of technological advances, homosexuals and lesbians need not be prevented from procreating and, if procreativity is a sine qua non, many heterosexual unions would be equally forbidden.

He then weighs whether modern theories of homosexuality should have halakhic significance:

> It is not inherently immoral to esteem the values and principles embodied in the prohibition against homosexuality so greatly that we recognize the morality of the mandate even in the hardest of cases—the obligatory homosexual or the homosexual for whom therapy has failed. We may understand when one cannot fulfill the mandate that the law imposes, but that does not lead us to the conclusion that the mandate was itself immoral. We asked whether a moral God could prohibit homosexual behavior even in the hardest of cases. We have answered that God could,

and did.... We [have discussed that God could ask us to make a great sacrifice as part of [one's] service to God with the example of a kohen who is prohibited from service in the Temple because of physical deformity]....

We humans pride ourselves on our having transcended nature in many ways. The development of human culture, with language, science, and religion often both seems to and does, in fact, elevate us above pure biological determinism. On the other hand, human culture is comparatively young from an evolutionary perspective. For the vast part of the history of life (not restricted to human life) on earth, evolution has been the primary factor.... Homosexuality is not abnormal or aberrational; it is part of the natural selection process of evolution. It is not some type of error in God's creation (as hormonal imbalance might be); it is an integral part of the evolutionary process. And, for a believing Jew, evolution is not free and independent from God's providence.

SECTION E: TO THE HETEROSEXUAL COMMUNITY

Rabbi Roth sends a strong warning to heterosexuals against oppressing homosexuals:

> Much of the heterosexual community reacts to homosexuality as if it were inherently ugly, inherently immoral and inherently repulsive. None of these claims is true.
>
> Homosexuality, from a halakhic perspective, is *to'evah*, but it is the Jewish legal tradition that attributes that characteristic to it.... Homosexuality is neither inherently immoral, ugly, or repulsive; the perceived justification for the vilification of the class of homosexuals no longer exists.... Homosexual behavior is to homosexuals as heterosexual behavior is to heterosexuals. Just as the latter engage in intercourse because they find it beautiful, fulfilling, rewarding and meaningful, so, too, do

the former. Homosexual love for homosexuals is as potentially beautiful, fulfilling, rewarding and meaningful for homosexuals as heterosexual love is for heterosexuals. . . .

Homosexuals are no less members of the Jewish community though they may flout its commitments. . . . The heterosexual community must remember that the halakhic demand being made upon homosexuals—celibacy—is far more severe and difficult a demand than any that is made by halakhah on heterosexuals. Homosexuals must observe all of the same mitzvot as heterosexuals, and are denied the pleasure and fulfillment of sexual relations.

SECTION F: TO THE HOMOSEXUAL COMMUNITY

Rabbi Roth gives an equally strong admonition to gays and lesbians:

> Jewish law is a religious legal system. In the final analysis, it seeks to determine what God wishes. God's wishes clearly impinge with great frequency on the behavior of individuals. . . . Jewish law dictates what one may eat, drink, and wear; it posits restrictions and obligations on the relationship between a person and the person's spouse. . . . The law obligates Jews and they are expected to submit themselves to its authority, even when it mandates or forbids actions that are wholly personal or consensual.
>
> Members of the homosexual community must recognize that saying no to a request for halakhic validation of homosexuality does not imply rejection of homosexuals or their exclusion from the greater community. Rather, the halakhic community is more than merely entitled to stand by its commitment to the authority of halakhah; it is obligated to do so. . . . It is possible for a decisor to be understanding, empathic, sensitive, caring and without irrational fears and yet conclude that the halakhic precedents are defensible, warranted and compelling.

PESAK DIN

Rabbi Roth issues his ruling:

> In the opinion of this author, the clarity of the halakhic position on homosexual behavior is not open to any real doubt.... The halakhically committed Jewish community... ought not take any act which can reasonably be understood to imply the halakhic co-equality, validation, or acceptability of a homosexual lifestyle....
>
> Where there can be no halakhic legitimacy to the union, no matter how loving and caring, there can be no marriage. The halakhic community, therefore, should not legitimate such unions by performing or recognizing affirmation ceremonies.... We do understand that homosexual couples can be loving and caring, we must reach out to them, and we must do our best to make them feel comfortable in our midst—but the line must be drawn at performing the marriages or recognizing them as halakhically valid....
>
> If a person were to consult a rabbi on this matter, one might conjure up a scene in which a young man might say, "Rabbi, I am deeply confused, I am having trouble sorting out my sexual identity and my sexual behavior.... It is clear to me that most of my arousals are homosexual, though some are heterosexual.... Can you possibly tell me what Jewish law would have me do?..." [We must] answer the questioner by telling him that Jewish law would have him act on his heterosexual urges, and not on his homosexual urges.... "Jewish law would have you be celibate."
>
> Nobody should misunderstand the dispassionate sound of the answer as an absence of feeling on the part of the *posek* who gives it. It is given with anguish, tears, and a heavy heart. It is given only after being convinced that the values implied by the prohibition are of such importance that they warrant asking

an individual to suppress acting on his or her sexuality.... We disapprove of the behaviors, not of the people....

Finally, I wish to make as clear as I possibly can that... nothing I have written forbids or discourages anyone from offering interpretations of the legal texts of the halakhic system to support the conclusion opposite from mine.[1]

Text 5.2. Dorff, Nevins, and Reisner, "Homosexuality, Human Dignity and Halakhah"

COMMITTEE ON JEWISH LAW AND STANDARDS OF THE RABBINICAL ASSEMBLY, EVEN HA-EZER 24.2006B

Rabbi Elliot Dorff, born in Milwaukee, earned his rabbinic ordination at the Jewish Theological Seminary of America and his PhD in philosophy from Columbia University. He is Rector and Distinguished Service Professor of Philosophy at American Jewish University and visiting professor at UCLA School of Law. He has served on three U.S. federal government commissions—on access to health care, reducing the spread of sexually transmitted diseases, and research on human subjects—and currently serves on the State of California's commission to govern stem cell research within the state. A member of the Conservative movement's Committee on Jewish Law and Standards (CJLS) since 1984, he served as its chair from 2007 to 2022. He has written fourteen books, edited or co-edited fourteen more, developed or co-developed twenty-nine responsa approved by the committee, and published over two hundred articles on Jewish thought, law, and ethics. His responsa and other works on halakhah follow the conviction that Jewish law is an important part of the organic whole of the Jewish tradition and people. As such, it influences and is influenced by Jewish moral and theological convictions as well as the contexts in which Jews live, including their social, political, economic, technological, and medical circumstances. No factor automatically supersedes any other in any given legal decision; every decision requires judgment and, hopefully, wisdom as to how to interpret and apply the received law in light of all the parts of this organic, Jewish whole.[2]

Rabbi Daniel Nevins grew up in northern New Jersey and studied in Jerusalem at Yeshivat Hamivtar before earning a BA at Harvard University and rabbinic ordination at the Jewish Theological Seminary (JTS). He has been a rabbi at Adat Shalom Synagogue, Farmington Hills, Michigan, and the rabbinical school dean at JTS, and he is currently the head of school at Golda Och Academy in New Jersey. The author of many CJLS responsa, Rabbi Nevins approaches halakhic interpretation by seeking grounding in the formal precedents found in halakhic sources as well as the theological and ethical ideas expressed in diverse Jewish sources, including midrash and Kabbalah. His broad purpose is to expand the range of people and topics addressed by Jewish law so that more of life may be invested with sanctity and understanding. Rabbi Nevins has written responsa on issues of inclusion and environmentalism as well as a series of responsa dealing with technology.

For a short biography of Rabbi Avram Reisner, the third coauthor, see chapter 1.

QUESTION

In a *teshuvah* approved by the Committee on Jewish Law and Standards in 2006, Rabbis Dorff, Nevins, and Reisner integrated their individual drafts into one addressing the question:

> What guidance does halakhah offer to Jews who are homosexual? Which intimate activities are permitted to them, and which are forbidden?

SECTION A: INTRODUCTION

The three rabbis start by emphasizing their commitment to stay within the boundaries of traditional halakhah when evaluating the questions at hand:

This responsum works within the limits of traditional halakhic discourse. To do otherwise would compromise the integrity of the halakhah and would accomplish nothing for those gay and lesbian people who strive to live as observant Jews. People who are not Torah observant have no particular need for a traditional halakhic responsum. But people who are observant and are also gay or lesbian are caught in a terrible dilemma, with no halakhic guidance about the integration of their Jewish identity and their sexual orientation. Our core conviction is that dignity for gay and lesbian Jews—as for heterosexual Jews—results neither from blanket permission nor from blanket prohibition of all sexual activity, but rather from situating it within the matrix of *issur veheter*, permission and prohibition, which permeates all of Jewish life. . . .

The Committee on Jewish Law and Standards has a long and proud history of addressing weighty issues of ritual and social practice as our community wrestles with the challenges of observing Jewish law in a modern context. We are motivated always by our tradition's mandate that rabbis in every generation apply Jewish law sensitively and effectively to the new circumstances of their time, drawing upon not only the precedents of our tradition but also its fundamental concepts and values. . . .

We . . . believe that those motivated to live within the framework of halakhah are necessarily willing to accept limits on personal autonomy . . . for the sake of pursuing a life of holiness. . . . We approach this challenging subject with reverence for God, humility, and with respect for the dignity of humans, all of whom are created in the divine image.

SECTION B: CONTEMPORARY THEORIES
OF SEXUAL ORIENTATION

The rabbis assert that halakhic precedents for gay and lesbian Jews have led to discrimination against them, as well as devastation within their families, and ultimately undermine their human dignity:

> There remains much to be learned regarding the psycho-social construction of sexual orientation, yet this much is absolutely clear to ... leading scientific authorities ... : homosexual orientation is not a form of mental illness; it is not inherently harmful to individuals or to their children or families. ... Social acceptance of gay relationships will not "convince" children to become homosexual who would otherwise be heterosexual; current research indicates that sexual orientation is set in a person at an early age, long before sexual experimentation takes place. What social acceptance will do, however, is reduce the amount of discrimination against gays and lesbians and their need to remain in the closet, with all the suffering, indignity, and the increased risk of suicide that this entails. ...
> There is also an emergent literature on the damage caused to married couples and their children when one spouse "comes out" as gay. Such revelations often result in divorce, leaving the heterosexual spouse devastated. ...
> We will argue that the permanent social and sexual loneliness mandated by halakhic precedent for homosexuals undermines their human dignity. However, we reject attempts to distort this argument by claiming that, if so, every human desire deserves to be satisfied. In fact, Judaism teaches us constantly to bend individual desire to fulfill the will of God. Some sexual desires must be delayed, and some must be permanently suppressed. What distinguishes the situation of gay and lesbian Jews from others who experience forbidden sexual desires is that heretofore, gay and lesbian Jews have had absolutely no permitted avenue for sexual expression or for the creation of a committed romantic relationship. It is this situation of absolute and permanent isolation that undermines their human dignity.

SECTION C: HALAKHIC SOURCES REGARDING HOMOSEXUAL INTIMACY

They argue, against Rabbi Roth's 1992 opinion,[3] that the biblical prohibition of homosexuality solely pertains to anal sex between men:

> The standard codes of Jewish law establish all-encompassing prohibitions on homosexual contact. However, only one act is explicitly prohibited in the Torah: anal sex between men.... Lev. 18:22 states: "Do not lie with a man the lyings of a woman; it is abhorrent." Lev. 20:13 restates the law, adding a severe punishment for both partners: "If a man lies with a male the lyings of a woman, the two of them have done an abhorrent thing; they shall be put to death—their bloodguilt is upon them." ...
>
> The Talmud derives from this plural construct ["lyings of a woman"] that there are two forms of sexual intercourse between a man and a woman, vaginal and anal (Babylonian Talmud Sanhedrin 54a). The Sages understand these verses to prohibit anal sex between men without any exception, even as the other sexual behaviors on this list are forbidden without exception.
>
> Ancient authors employed euphemism when describing sex, making it difficult to prove exactly what activities they understood to be included within these verses. Is it possible that the biblical prohibition called *mishkevei ishah* ["intimate relations with a woman"] and later, by the Rabbis, *mishkav zakhur* ["intimate relations with a man"], includes actions other than anal intercourse? These verses have been variously translated, but almost all readers conclude that they prohibit anal sex between men.... Our colleague, Rabbi Joel Roth, has argued that the rabbinic expression for heterosexual anal sex may possibly include not only homosexual anal sex, but even oral sex between men. Rabbi Roth is *sui generis* in this reading, which is rejected by other contemporary halakhic interpreters....

Moreover, the definition of *mishkav zakhur* is made abundantly clear at Babylonian Talmud Yevamot 83b, which discusses the prohibition of homosexual relations with an *androginus*. An *androginus* is defined as a person with both male and female external genitalia, but is considered legally male. The Talmud states that such an *androginus* has the potential to transgress *mishkav zakhur* in two places. If, as Rabbi Roth argues, oral sex is to be included in the transgression of *mishkav zakhur*, then any male has two potential orifices about which one may be liable. Why does the Talmud specify an *androginus*? Clearly only of the *androginus* is this true, for oral sex is not considered *mishkav zakhur*....

To strike this law from the Torah is a radical step. On the other hand, to expand the biblical prohibition beyond what is actually written is unnecessarily harsh. The Torah forbids anal sex between men, nothing more, and nothing less.

SECTION D: RABBINIC PROHIBITIONS ON HOMOSEXUAL APPROACH

They contend that the Rabbis alone forbid other forms of gay and lesbian sexuality—and, moreover, that the Rabbis chose to expand upon the original biblical prohibition against anal sex between men in order to impede transgression of this fundamental biblical rule:

> The Torah prohibits anal sex between men, while remaining silent regarding other forms of sexual intimacy between men and between women. Nevertheless rabbinic codes describe a much broader prohibition of all male and female homosexual intimacy. Rabbi Joseph Caro writes in *Shulḥan Arukh, Even haEzer* 20:1:
>
>> Whoever copulates with one of the forbidden relations nongenitally, or hugged and kissed [that relation] or enjoyed

skin-to-skin contact—such a person is lashed, and is suspected of *arayot* [forbidden intercourse].

We do not hold, as a matter of fact, that the laws of "approach" are biblically mandated, but rather that they are in the category of rabbinic fences and borders that are all ultimately intended to protect against transgression of the fundamental biblical rules about sexual conduct.

SECTION E: DIGNITY

They argue that the halakhic principle of upholding human dignity establishes permitting same-sex couples to have a halakhically sanctioned relationship:

> Observant Jews who are gay or lesbian are caught in an impossible dilemma, unable to fulfill the traditional Jewish norm of heterosexual marriage, usually incapable of practicing life-long celibacy, and yet unwilling to abandon a life of Torah and mitzvot. In those rare occasions in which we consider modifying or even reversing a rabbinic precedent, we look for guidance and support from within the rabbinic tradition itself....
>
> There is a ... halakhic principle that is undermined by our current policy: human dignity. The halakhic status quo is deeply degrading to gay and lesbian Jews ... and as such it evokes the principle stated dramatically and repeatedly in the Talmud (Babylonian Talmud Berakhot 19b) ... :
>
>> Come and learn: So great is human dignity that it supersedes a negative commandment of the Torah. And why? Don't we say, "there is no wisdom, nor comprehension nor counsel against the Lord" (Prov. 21:30)? Rav bar Sheba interpreted it thus before Rav Kahana: "[this principle applies only] to the negative commandment of 'do not stray'" (Deut. 17:11). They [i.e., his colleagues] laughed at him, saying, "'Do not

stray' is itself from the Torah!" But Rav Kahana said to them, "When a great man states a matter, do not laugh at it. For all of the words of the Sages are supported by the negative commandment of 'do not stray,' but for his dignity, the Rabbis permitted him [to ignore their ruling]."

This passage establishes that the Sages waived their own dignity (i.e., the power of their precedents), but not the dignity of the Torah, in deference to the dignity of other people.... They still distinguished between the stature of their rulings and those of the Torah itself....

We are concerned for the dignity of gay and lesbian Jews not only because we are sympathetic to their dilemma, but also because their humiliation is our humiliation. We wish to welcome them, but we do so in such a forbidding fashion that they are repeatedly humiliated. Looking at our own congregations, we too are embarrassed by our cold welcome.... When gay and lesbian Jews are finally welcomed to take their rightful places in our community, then we will have safeguarded their dignity as individuals, and our dignity as a community.

PESAK DIN

The rabbis rule:

It is not possible to set aside the explicit biblical prohibition on anal sex that is stated twice in Leviticus and frequently reaffirmed by the Rabbis.... The rabbinic restrictions upon gay men and lesbian women that result in a total ban on all sexual expression throughout life are in direct conflict with the ability of these Jews to live in dignity as members of the people of Israel. For this reason, the halakhic principle of [human dignity] must be invoked by the CJLS to relieve their intolerable humiliation. We must make open and rigorous efforts to include gay and lesbian Jews in our communities, to provide a proper welcome and a legal framework for the normalization of their status in our congregations.

We are aware that the continued biblical ban on anal sex may be extremely difficult for some gay men to observe.... However, this responsum provides gay men with other options for sexual intimacy, with full social acceptance in the observant Jewish community, and with a feasible path to a life of Torah observance.... We favor the establishment of committed and loving relationships for gay and lesbian Jews....

Some have maintained that once we permit homosexual Jews to create unions that are celebrated in some form of Jewish ceremony and to be students and ultimately graduates of our professional schools, all other sexual prohibitions of the Jewish tradition will soon fall as well. This kind of "slippery slope" argument is faulty on several grounds. First, the very essence of moral and legal sophistication is the increasing ability that one learns to distinguish cases. Second, the arguments that we have mustered to permit homosexual unions and ordination simply do not apply to adultery, incest, bestiality, rape, or any of the other prohibitions of sexual acts in the Torah. On the contrary, we insist that the Jewish values and norms that apply to heterosexual sex be observed by homosexuals as well, including fidelity, safety, respect for one's sexual partner, modesty, and love. Far from undermining Judaism's sexual norms, this responsum seeks to extend them to homosexual sex.[4]

This 2006 ruling did not override Rabbi Joel Roth's responsum, which the Committee on Jewish Law and Standards also accepted at the same time. Both responsa coexist alongside one another as valid options for the Conservative/Masorti movement.

Nonetheless, shortly after the Dorff/Nevins/Reisner decision in 2006, the rabbinical schools at the Jewish Theological Seminary and

American Jewish University in Los Angeles began welcoming gay and lesbian students. In 2012, Rabbis Dorff, Nevins, and Reisner went on to create ceremonies and documents for same-sex unions (subsequently integrated into their original 2006 responsum as an appendix), but they did not employ the traditional term for Jewish marriage, *kiddushin*.

Text 5.3. CCAR Responsa Committee, "Same-Sex Marriage as *Kiddushin*"

CCAR RESPONSUM 5774.4

The Reform movement's CCAR Responsa Committee (see chapter 1) approaches the *kiddushin* question for same-sex couples very differently.

QUESTION

In 2014, the CCAR Responsa Committee asks:

> In states where same-sex marriage and civil unions are legal by civil law, is it appropriate for Reform rabbis to officiate at a ceremony of marriage of two Jews of the same sex, and to consider the union *kiddushin*? Is it appropriate for Reform rabbis in states that have not yet legalized same-sex marriage to officiate at a ceremony of marriage of two Jews of the same sex, and to consider the union *kiddushin*?

SECTION A: HISTORICAL SUMMARY OF THE CCAR'S STANCE

The Responsa Committee starts by reviewing past CCAR responsa on same-sex relationships, because society's understanding of same-sex relationships has developed since they were written:

> Our stance on officiation has changed sharply during the last quarter century. In 1990, the majority of an ad hoc committee of the Conference declared that only heterosexual relationships

qualify as *kiddushin* and that special ceremonies solemnizing same-sex unions "are matters of continuing discussion and differences of opinion." ... In 1996, the Responsa Committee issued a responsum that explored the question of whether a "Reform rabbi [may] officiate at a wedding or 'commitment' ceremony between two homosexuals" and whether such a union may be considered *kiddushin* from a Reform perspective. The responsum was unusually long, encompassing two extensively argued opinions, one speaking for the majority and one speaking for the minority.... In the end, the majority held that "we do not understand Jewish marriage apart from the concept of *kiddushin*, and our interpretation of rabbinic authority does not embrace the power to 'sanctify' any relationship that cannot be *kiddushin* as its functional equivalent," while the minority expressed the view that "a Reform rabbi may officiate at a wedding or 'commitment' ceremony for two homosexuals, although for important historical and theological reasons, that ceremony should perhaps not be called *kiddushin*." ... Now in 2013, it is time to revisit this question.

SECTION B: SAME-SEX MARRIAGE AS *KIDDUSHIN*

The Responsa Committee completely rejects the biblical text's view that homosexual sexual relationships are sinful and *to'evah*. This outright rejection of a text for reasons of justice and ethics is characteristic of Reform halakhah. All the more, because same-sex couples demonstrate the same love and commitments in their relationships as do heterosexual couples, their union is equally worthy of being called *kiddushin*, the tradition's term for Jewish marriage:

> Our question pertains to two individuals of the same sex. Both are Jews, both members of the covenant of Israel, and they wish to be joined in marriage in a ceremony—specifically

kiddushin—in which a rabbi serves as officiant. Our starting point is the recognition that homosexuality is neither a sin nor a *to'evah* (abomination), as was long a prevailing opinion. There is abundant scientific and psychological evidence that homosexuality is an inherent sexual orientation (and not a "lifestyle choice," as has often been erroneously claimed). Our tradition is grounded in justice and ethics, and both demand that we recognize not only the full humanity and equality of homosexuals, but that their love and commitments are no less than those of heterosexuals.... A union of marriage between two Jews deserves to be called *kiddushin*, the tradition's term for Jewish marriage. We agree....

At the core of this legal contract [employed in Jewish marriage] lie the underlying Jewish values that characterize *kiddushin*. These flow, we believe, from the verse "It is not good for a person to be alone" (Gen. 2:18), by which we understand that Torah supports loving and committed marital relationship as a natural state of human existence. We would hope that such relationships are a source of joy for the two people involved, and a blessing to family members, friends, and the Jewish community....

Our tradition understands such a partnership contracted between two Jews as *kiddushin*. What are the salient and defining values of this institution? We hold that they include three essential commitments:

- The commitment of two Jews to establish a Jewish home together.
- Their commitment to support and nurture one another physically, financially, emotionally, psychologically, and spiritually.
- Their commitment, should their union be blessed with children, to raise those children together as Jews.

The union of a same-sex Jewish couple, no less than that of an opposite-sex couple, can be defined by these commitments.... Same-sex Jewish couples who forge a loving and devoted union and who commit themselves to establishing a Jewish home and raising a Jewish family should not be denied the rites that define marital status in the Jewish tradition.

SECTION C: *KIDDUSHIN* AND REFORM JUDAISM

The Responsa Committee stresses that it is not offering a novel definition of *kiddushin* here that would accommodate same-sex unions. Rather, in contrast to the traditional halakhic definition, a long-standing Reform definition holds that *kiddushin* is a mutual and egalitarian marital covenant between two Jews. What is new is solely the recognition that same-sex unions are an equivalent form of mutual and egalitarian marriage to heterosexual relationships:

> The above, obviously, stands at odds with our traditional literature, which never applies the term *kiddushin* to same-sex unions. Yet it is quite consistent with our own Reform Jewish tradition, in which the understanding of *kiddushin* has long diverged from the way that institution was originally defined and structured in our sources.
>
> In its most original formulation, *kiddushin* is non-egalitarian.... Reform Judaism, by contrast, has always defined *kiddushin* as an egalitarian and therefore mutual institution....
>
> These aspects of Reform Jewish marriage underscore a critical point. We are not now suddenly "changing" the traditional definition of *kiddushin* in order to accommodate same-sex marriage.... What has changed... is our recognition that same-sex unions, no less than opposite-sex unions, are a form of marriage.... Same-sex marriages therefore meet the long-standing Reform definition of *kiddushin* as a mutual and egalitarian marital covenant between two Jews.

SECTION D: SAME-SEX WEDDINGS IN JURISDICTIONS THAT DO NOT YET RECOGNIZE SUCH UNIONS AS LEGAL MARRIAGE

The Responsa Committee provides guidance for rabbinic officiants in U.S. states that do not permit same-sex marriages:

> It is CCAR policy that Reform rabbis should not officiate at weddings in the absence of a valid civil marriage license. This does not prevent a rabbi from officiating at a ceremony of union for a same-sex couple in a state that does not recognize such unions as legal marriage, provided that the rabbi make[s] clear to the couple that the ceremony as a matter of law is not a legally-binding marriage. Still, the situation is ripe for confusion. The current state of civil law in the United States is similarly confusing. Since June 26, 2013, when the Supreme Court struck down DOMA (the "Defense of Marriage Act"), same-sex couples who marry in states that legally recognize and register same-sex marriages are guaranteed equal protection under the law with respect to federal marriage benefits, including Social Security survivors' benefits, insurance benefits, immigration, and tax filing. However, there are important rights and protections not assured by the Federal Government in the realms of inheritance, medical care, and children. While couples who marry in states that recognize same-sex marriage enjoy these protections, couples in states that do not recognize same-sex marriage do not.
>
> In response to this situation, we strongly encourage Reform rabbis who live in such states to advise same-sex couples who seek a wedding to contract a civil marriage, prior to the *chupah*, in a jurisdiction that recognizes the legality of same-sex marriage. This will remove any objection that the rabbi is officiating at a wedding for a couple that lacks a valid civil marriage license. It will also insure that the couple will be entitled to federal benefits even should they choose to live in a state that does not

recognize same-sex marriage. We also encourage Reform rabbis who officiate at same-sex marriages in states that do not provide for civil same-sex marriage to advise same-sex couples to seek legal advice and services in order to set in place legal mechanisms including estate planning, durable power of attorney, health care proxy, wills, and anything else required to protect the couple, as well as children the couple has or plans to have.

PESAK DIN

The Responsa Committee rules:

1. Since 2000, Reform rabbis in North America have officiated with the full support of the CCAR at the marriage ceremonies of Jews of the same sex.
2. We now affirm that, in light of the underlying purpose and values of Jewish marriage, as well as of our historic Reform Jewish understanding of the concept of *kiddushin*, Reform rabbis may consider these same-sex marriages to be *kiddushin*, utilizing in the marriage ceremony the Jewish forms and rites that are most appropriate to the Jewish partners involved.
3. Couples who marry in jurisdictions that grant legal recognition to same-sex marriages are entitled to, and protected by, both federal and state laws. In jurisdictions that do not grant such recognition, rabbis should advise couples who request their officiation to first seek civil marriage in a state that recognizes same-sex marriage.[5]

Text 5.4. Sharzer, "Transgender Jews and Halakhah"

COMMITTEE ON JEWISH LAW AND STANDARDS OF THE RABBINICAL ASSEMBLY, EVEN HA-EZER 5:11.2017B

Rabbi Leonard A. Sharzer, a native of Boston, graduated from Boston University School of Medicine, earning a master's degree in surgery for organ preservation for transplantation, completed training in plastic and reconstructive surgery at the Eastern Virginia Medical School, and joined the faculty of the Albert Einstein College of Medicine of Yeshiva University. After retiring from medical practice, he entered rabbinical school and received ordination from the Jewish Theological Seminary. He remained there, serving as associate director of the Finkelstein Institute for Religious and Social Studies and teaching bioethics and organized public programming in the field. Rabbi Sharzer's work emphasizes the importance of developing a thorough and detailed understanding of the medical science underlying the ethical issue at hand.

QUESTION

Rabbi Sharzer poses multiple questions:

> What are the appropriate rituals for conversion to Judaism of transgender individuals? What are the appropriate rituals for solemnizing a marriage in which one or both parties are transgender? How is the marriage of a transgender person (which was entered into before transition) to be dissolved (after transition)? ... Are hormonal therapy and gender confirming surgery permissible for people with gender dysphoria? ... Who should prepare the body of a transgender person for burial? At what point in the process of transition is the person recognized as the new gender?

SECTION A: INTRODUCTION

Rabbi Sharzer begins by discussing how the medical understanding of gender identity has changed over time. A person's self-identity appears to be constant over a lifetime and is not changed by surgery, hormonal therapy, or psychotherapy. One challenge in welcoming transgender Jews into Jewish communities with dignity and respect involves discussing gender identity when a given language complicates that conversation:

There has been a sea change in our understanding as a society at large, and no less so in the Jewish community, of the meaning of gender and gender identity. This has in large part been the result of more and more transgender people being open about themselves in their daily lives as well as in books and as part of online discussion and advocacy groups.... In the Jewish world, the ordination of transgender rabbis and the lived experience of transgender Jews, their parents, their spouses, their children, have also helped... to give a human face to those living out this life experience....

Within the Jewish community and the larger culture, too often transgender people have been excluded, marginalized, harassed, or worse. The Jewish community... must be committed to the proposition that all people be treated with dignity and respect and that our institutions, culture, and practices be welcoming and accommodating to the needs of transgender Jews as well as trans people who wish to become Jewish, and to doing so in an authentically Jewish way.

Among the challenges we face in accomplishing this goal is that we often do not have adequate language to discuss it.... Language poses a... problem in Hebrew and other gendered languages.... Hebrew... is Judaism's universal language. It is the language of ritual and prayer. It is the language we turn to at times of our greatest joy and our greatest sorrow, our greatest satisfaction and our greatest fear....

A second problem we face from a language standpoint is a result of the way we have tended to use the word "change." We have talked about "sex change surgery," or "a man changing to a woman," or vice versa. This is more than a language problem, however, because our conceptual understanding has been molded by the language. We are beginning to understand that a transgender man, for example, has very likely had a male gender identity, certainly from a very early age and very likely from birth—even though he may not have been aware of it, or had the vocabulary to speak about it, or have acted on it until much later. In many instances, the person's identity has not and is not changed—not by surgery, not by hormonal therapy, not by psychotherapy. It is possible to change the body's internal hormonal milieu pharmacologically, and the body's anatomic appearance surgically to conform to the individual's identity but identity appears to be constant. Attempts to change gender identity by so-called "conversion therapy" have been discredited as ineffective, dangerous and cruel.

In addressing the questions that arise regarding transgender people in Jewish life, we must keep in mind that although halakhah deals with categories, rabbis and *posekim* deal with people, and that the transgender community is a large and diverse group of people.

SECTION B: STRATEGIES IN CLASSIC AND CONTEMPORARY HALAKHIC DISCOURSE

Rabbi Sharzer notes that the Rabbis of the Mishnah and the Talmud recognize the existence of individuals who do not fit the female/male gender binary. Yet he critiques classic (and contemporary) halakhic sources as not being particularly helpful on questions of *changing* gender. He avers that he is going to move from status based on anatomy to status based on self-assessed gender identity:

> The Rabbis . . . recognized several types of people who did not fit the male/female binary. The two most often mentioned are the *tumtum* [person with unrecognizable genitalia] and the *androgynos* [person with ambiguous sexual characteristics], but the Rabbis also refer to the *saris ḥammah* [congenital eunuch] and the *aylonit* [not entirely clear, perhaps a person born female who develops male characteristics]. . . . For a given individual some laws and restrictions were applied as they would be for a man

and some laws and restrictions as they would be for a woman. Thus chapter 4 of *Mishnah Bikkurim* enumerates the ways in which an *androgynos* is treated for some halakhic purposes like a man, for some like a woman, for others like both men and women, and for still others like neither men nor women but rather like a unique being *sui generis*. . . .

Gender is a binary social construct related to but not identical with various dimensions of human sexual biology which exist along multiple non-congruent axes. In modern times, there is an ongoing debate as to which of these dimensions or axes is the best determinant of gender: . . . genital anatomy . . . genetic make-up . . . hormonal makeup . . . gender identity [as distinct from gender expression]. . . .

Classic and contemporary halakhic sources are not particularly helpful on the question of changing gender. Those that do discuss the issue raise it regarding the question of divorce and usually formulate . . . a situation in which for no apparent reason, as if by magic, a woman becomes a man in all respects. There is no mention of her role in affecting this transformation or even her desiring it. . . . In the real world, there are not people who one day are magically transformed to the other side of the binary in all respects. Rather there are people in whom there is an incongruity between their most deeply held sense of themselves as gendered individuals and the gender assigned to them at birth, people who demand and deserve to live fully and authentically in a Jewish context. . . .

I have chosen to frame the questions differently . . . [by] examining the specific halakhic questions that actually do arise (and they are arising with increasing frequency) in relation to trans people based on their gender identity rather than their [physiological] status.

SECTION C: MEDICAL ISSUES

Rabbi Sharzer addresses the halakhic acceptability of gender confirming surgery:

> The questions raised by surgery for gender dysphoria [discomfort or distress that a person may have because of a mismatch between their biological sex and their gender identity] fall into two distinct categories. The first set of questions relate to all the many types of surgery transgender people may choose to undergo and are similar to those raised by cosmetic surgery: Is the surgery medically necessary? Does it violate the prohibition against self-wounding? Does it violate the prohibition against placing oneself in a dangerous situation? . . .
>
> The second set of questions relates specifically to genital surgery and asks whether this is a violation of the prohibition against castration . . . (Lev. 22:24) in the case of trans women . . . and men.
>
> When the first set of questions has been raised in relation to cosmetic surgery, most rabbinic decisors have been permissive. If the surgery is done to alleviate pain, and with the consent of the patient, then the wounding does not violate the prohibition of self-wounding. . . . Relief of psychological pain or embarrassment is as valid a justification for surgery as relief of physical pain. Similarly with the issue of risk, no human activity is risk free, and as long as the risk is mitigated by using expert surgeons and properly equipped hospitals, then the risk is allowable and justified by the anticipated relief of pain or distress.
>
> Extrapolating from conditions that produce psychological pain or distress even in the absence of a recognized psychological diagnosis, in which surgery is permitted, to gender dysphoria, which is not only a recognized, diagnosable condition, but one that can cause distress severe enough to lead to suicide, gender confirming surgery should be permitted.

As to whether genital surgery violates the specific prohibition against castration, one need only look at conditions like testicular or ovarian cancer. If the best hope for survival is removal of the testicles or ovaries, surely no one would argue for avoiding this treatment because of the biblical or rabbinic prohibition of castration.... Since in the case of gender confirming surgery, the removal of the gonads is being done to treat a medical condition, and may in some cases be lifesaving, it should be permitted as well....

Many of the issues discussed in relation to surgery, apply to hormonal therapy as well.

SECTION D: ISSUES IN PRACTICAL RABBINICS

Rabbi Sharzer addresses pastoral issues:

1. An often raised question relates to the appropriate conversion ritual for transgender men and women (already a binary shorthand for the variety of transgender people) who seek to convert to Judaism. In the case of cisgender people, all converts require immersion in a *mikveh*. In addition, the vast majority of cis men require either ritual circumcision or, if they have previously been circumcised, *hatafat dam brit* [ritual drawing of a drop of blood]....

The questions we face with respect to transgender conversion candidates, especially trans men who have undergone some form of genital surgery and trans women who have not, are often emotionally fraught and require the utmost sensitivity and compassion. There are often issues of shame and embarrassment that we must pay attention to and we must recognize that these discussions may make us as rabbis as uncomfortable as they make the potential convert. Some rabbis have even questioned whether it is appropriate even to ask questions of a trans woman conversion candidate that they would never ask of a cis woman.

In proposing rituals for transgender converts, I would make an analogy to the medical setting. If a physician is to examine a trans woman, she should be treated like any woman patient.... But if she has a prostate, the physician would be remiss not to examine it or do a PSA test if indicated. Similarly, a trans man should be treated like all male patients, but if he needs a pap smear, the physician must do it....

In the case of non-binary or gender non-confirming individuals, the schema above has the advantage of being based solely on anatomy. A person who has a penis, whatever their gender identity, requires circumcision or *hatafat dam brit* [ritual for those already circumcised]; a person who does not have a penis, does not....

2. It is ... incumbent upon the rabbi solemnizing a Jewish marriage to be aware of the laws that may apply in the particular jurisdiction in which the ceremony is taking place....

3. For marriages entered into prior to transition, in which the couple desires to remain married after the transition of one of the partners, the marriage remains valid and there is no requirement for any ritual....

4. If the couple is certain they want to divorce, they should be encouraged to do so before the transition process is complete. In this situation, the usual laws and procedures of *gittin* will apply....

5. When a transgender Jew dies, a not infrequently raised question is which members of the *ḥevra kadisha* (burial society) should take on the task of preparing the body for burial. Should it be members of the same sexual identity or of the sex assigned at birth? Does it matter whether or not the deceased has undergone gender confirming surgery?...

The *Ṭur* and the *Shulḥan Arukh* [read:]

> A man may not prepare [the body of] a woman [for burial], but a woman may prepare [the body of] a man.

Commentators suggest two reasons for this prohibition:

> [Commenting on why a man may take care of a man who is ill but not a woman, but a woman may take care of a man or woman who is ill] ... therefore it seems to me that the reason is because of degradation and lewdness which are greater when a man takes care of a woman with regard to cleaning her up and the like, than when a woman takes care of a man, because a man's lust is greater than that of a woman....[6]

We must categorically reject these underlying premises.... There is no evidence that men who are not otherwise psychologically impaired experience these types of thoughts from seeing or washing and dressing a female corpse. How much more is this true in the case of members of the *hevra kadisha*, people of high moral character, acting out of the highest degree of *hesed* [loving-kindness]!

We conclude that there is no valid halakhic prohibition for either men or women, cis or trans, gay or straight, or non-binary, helping to prepare the body of any Jew for burial. That notwithstanding, the decision as to which *hevra kadisha* members should perform the taharah of any body must take into account values such as *kevod hamet* (honoring the deceased), *kevod beriyot* (personal dignity) and *tzeni'ut* (modesty) as they relate to both the deceased and the members of the *hevra kadisha*. We should therefore adhere to the traditional practice that the body of a transgender person should be prepared by members of the *hevra kadisha* of the same gender identity as the deceased....

6. In the case of trans men or non-binary persons who menstruate, the laws of *niddah* apply. We would then be faced with the problem that the "women's area" of many *mikvaot* is individual and private while the "men's area" is more communal and public. This situation could become awkward for both trans and cis men using the "men's area" of the *mikveh*, and although

private immersion can be arranged in unusual circumstances, it may be worthwhile for planners of community *mikvaot* to design them with greater degrees of privacy for everyone. A greater degree of privacy might enhance and encourage use of the *mikveh* for many people, regardless of their gender identity or expression.

7. Is *brit milah* [ritual circumcision] required of transgender women? *Brit milah* is performed at 8 days of age, unless there is a medical reason to delay.... Unlike the conversion situation discussed above, this person's status as Jewish is not in doubt. The question boils down to this: To whom does the mitzvah of [*brit*] *milah* apply? The Torah says:

> This is my covenant between me and your descendants after you which you must preserve, circumcise every *zakhar*. (Gen. 17:10)

Our ancestors ... understood the word *zakhar* to refer to someone with male genitalia.... The mitzvah of *brit milah* is based on anatomy rather than gender and applies to any person with a penis....

We may teach publicly about the requirement of *brit milah* for anyone with male genitalia, and if specifically asked by a trans woman if she were obligated for *brit milah*, answer in the affirmative....

8. A frequently asked question is when transition is considered complete, or when the transgender person is considered to be the new gender.... The thesis of this *teshuvah* is that gender identity is an intrinsic part of a person's being, no less than that person's genetic makeup or anatomy.... Hormonal treatment does not change that identity, psychotherapy does not change that identity, surgery does not change that identity; and that identity should be determinative for interpersonal relationships as well as matters of halakhah.

That said, once a transgender person makes the decision to transition, the process takes some time. There is a process of becoming.... There may be situations where an individual who transitions desires a ceremony to mark that transition and be recognized in the eyes of the community as the new gender.

PESAK DIN

Rabbi Sharzer concludes:

1. A transgender person is to be recognized as their publicly declared gender and to be addressed by their publicly declared name and pronouns. This change takes place when that person has gone through a process of transition, which may or may not include any medical procedures or treatments, and asserts and publicly declares their gender identity.
2. All conversion candidates require immersion in a *mikveh*.... Transgender women who have not undergone genital surgery do require either circumcision or *hatafat dam brit*....
3. Obligation for *brit milah* applies to people of any gender who have a penis and a foreskin. This includes some transgender women and some non-binary people. This must be conveyed with care and sensitivity, and does not invalidate or contradict the gender identity of that person.
4. Transgender people who marry do so according to their publicly lived gender identities through the rituals established by the CJLS for same sex and opposite sex marriages....
5. The marriage of couples who choose to remain married after the transition of one partner remains valid and no ritual is required....

6. All medical treatments intended to alleviate the symptoms of people with gender dysphoria by more closely aligning their body with their gender identity, including pharmacological, surgical, and psychological treatments, are permissible. . . .
7. Preparation for burial (*taharah*) should be performed by members of the *ḥevra kadisha* of the same gender identity as the deceased. However, in unusual or extenuating circumstances, *taharah* may be performed by people of any gender identity.
8. Laws of *tohorat ha-mishpaḥah* [family purity] apply to people of any gender who menstruate, including some transgender men and some non-binary people.
9. Rituals and ceremonies should be created to recognize and commemorate a person's transition, but they do not affect the transition and are not required.[7]

Medical Ethics 6

Life and death, sexuality and reproduction, illness and healing, relationships of control and care: all these and more plumb the depths of what it means to be a human being. Medical ethics touches on the fundamentals of human existence, and as medicine and technology have evolved, rabbinic decisors have sought to respond to medical dilemmas and offer guidance on how to navigate through them.

In this chapter, Rabbi Moses Sternbuch addresses whether a man whose first wife suffers from Alzheimer's disease may divorce her and marry another while still attending to his first wife's personal needs and medical care. Rabbi Tomer Mevorakh analyzes the case of a person suffering from anorexia whose medical team believes must eat (or be fed through tubal feeding) on Yom Kippur, otherwise a fast day.

Three responsa on the controversial issue of abortion follow. Notably, as the responsum by Rabbi Eliezer Waldenberg on abortion in general indicates, rabbinic decisors almost universally advocated for a much more permissive stance toward abortion than the societies they lived in before restrictions lifted in Western societies in the 1970s. Other issues arose: whether and which kinds of previously undetectable fetal abnormalities might be considered accepting criteria for performing an abortion. The politics of abortion in American society also prompted Rabbi Susan Grossman to consider whether the dilation and extraction procedure known as "partial birth abortion" is halakhically acceptable.

Text 6.1. Sternbuch, "A Woman Suffering from Alzheimer's Disease Whose Husband Wishes to Divorce Her"

TESHUVOT VE-HANHAGOT, 5, NO. 316

Rabbi Moshe Sternbuch, born in London, won acclaim as a child prodigy. His family fled London during the Blitz, and after the war he traveled to Israel to study in the Hebron Yeshiva. He established an upper-level yeshiva in Rosh Ha'ayin after he was advised to strengthen the Yemenite community there. In 1960 he moved to Johannesburg to serve as the rabbi of the Ultraorthodox community there and returned after the death of Rabbi Isaac Jacob Weiss (see chapter 1) to serve as vice president of the Haredi (Ultraorthodox non-Hasidic) Beit Din in Jerusalem. He is strongly anti-Zionist. He has published seven volumes of responsa to date, as well as books on specific aspects of halakhah.

In the following responsum, Rabbi Sternbuch addresses a troubling situation in which a man who was given a *heiter* (rabbinic permission) to divorce his wife because she has Alzheimer's now wants to check whether he may care for her personal needs. Should this man have even been allowed to divorce his wife because she has Alzheimer's?

QUESTION

Rabbi Sternbuch presents background on the question he was asked:

> I was asked about a case of a woman who was sick with Alzheimer's disease and her husband claimed that he needed a woman's company. Even though he had children, he could not live without a woman. He was allowed to marry another woman after he issued a *get* through the trustee for his wife and set up financial support [for her]. But since he had compassionate feelings for his first wife, he asked his second wife for permission to take care of his first wife as needed and to involve himself

with her medical care. His question is, since he married a second woman and he is not permitted to be sexually intimate with his first wife, may he be alone with her and touch her?

SECTION A: THE FIRST WIFE'S DAILY NEEDS AND MEDICAL CARE[1]

Rabbi Sternbuch discusses whether a ruling from the Shulḥan Arukh forbidding touching one's wife on Yom Kippur is pertinent:

> At first glance, since he is forbidden to be married to two women and he is not allowed to be sexually intimate with his first wife, he should not touch her, just as it is explained in the Shulḥan Arukh *Oraḥ Ḥayyim* 715:1 that on Yom Kippur one is forbidden both to be sexually intimate and to touch one's wife as if she is in *niddah*. But here a distinction should be made, since on Yom Kippur one should be concerned about sexual arousal [since sexual intimacy is forbidden on Yom Kippur]. If he comes close to her, he is liable [to be enticed into sexual intimacy], but here because of her health situation, intimacy is out of the question. Since he has another wife on whom he is focused, there is no reason to be concerned [and he is allowed to touch his first wife].

SECTION B: CAN HE BE ALONE WITH HIS FIRST WIFE?

Rabbi Sternbuch analyzes how the man in this case ought to interact with his first wife. Among Ultraorthodox Jews, a man cannot touch (or be alone in private with) any women except his (current) wife, mother, daughters, and possibly other close relatives. Sternbuch cites a famous *takkanah* of Rabbenu Gershom (c. 960–1028, Germany) forbidding a man to be married to more than one woman in order to see whether it would allow the man in this case to be alone with his first wife to oversee her care even as he is forbidden from being sexually intimate with her:

> Rabbi Akiva Eiger [1761–1867, Germany] ... thinks that since his first wife became mentally ill and he married a second wife with a *heiter* [rabbinic permission], he should be able [to be married to] both of them since Rabbenu Gershom did not rule in this particular matter and [therefore] he is permitted to have two wives [responsa of Rabbi Akiva Eiger, 2nd edition, no. 44]. ... It seems that the reason ... is that Rabbenu Gershom issued [his *takkanah*] to prevent acrimony and the second wife could claim that he is sexually focused on his first wife and not on her. Therefore Rabbenu Gershom's ruling applies to her in that he is forbidden to be married to two women.
>
> Therefore, according to the [ruling] of Rabbenu Gershom, he is forbidden to be sexually intimate with his ill first wife, but he is allowed to be alone with her. Regarding hugging and kissing, I believe that it is best to be stringent [and not do this] ... because he is liable to be aroused, and sinful thoughts are more difficult than sin itself. The husband must make an agreement with his second wife that he is allowed to visit his first wife and to take care of her when needed and to involve himself with her medical care. But if his first wife is in *niddah*, we cannot permit him [to take care of her] except if there is no one else.

PESAK DIN

Rabbi Sternbuch expresses discontent with the basis of the original question—the permission granted to the man to divorce his wife and marry another. He concludes his responsum on an ambivalent note. At first, he states, it could be *ḥillul ha-Shem* (desecration of God's name caused by inappropriate human behavior) for the man to divorce his first wife when she becomes ill:

> The husband is already sixty years old and [his wife] is at ease with him at home, but she cannot fulfill her role because her mind is elsewhere. Therefore he wishes to divorce her and marry

another woman who will be able to be sexually intimate with him. . . . I believe that one should be concerned with *hillul ha-Shem* because people will say that she was with him and was intimate with him and now that she has grown old and has become ill and can no longer [be sexually intimate] with him, he casts her aside and marries another. I am also concerned that the *heter* to marry another woman is liable to be a breach of the essence [of Rabbenu Gershom's ruling], and the great rabbinic decisors need to discuss this. I would not have joined into granting [permission for him to divorce his first wife and marry his second wife]. But one must judge each case on its own. Perhaps if he is granted this permission and [marries a second wife], maybe there is no *hillul ha-Shem*. All this requires deeper thought.[2]

Inasmuch as this ruling sheds light on the situation, it also isn't clear why Rabbi Sternbuch thinks "the *heter* to marry another woman is liable to be a breach of the essence" of Rabbenu Gershom's ruling. Possibly he means that (1) the first wife could not be properly divorced since her mental state does not allow her to accept a divorce (the *beit din* would accept it on her behalf), and therefore he is really married to two women simultaneously; (2) casting the first wife aside when she is ill is not an acceptable reason for divorce; or (3) another reason.

Text 6.2. Mevorakh, "Eating on Yom Kippur When a Person Is Suffering from an Eating Disorder (Anorexia)"

TEHUMIN 38 (2018): 75–84

An Israeli, Rabbi Tomer Mevorakh studied at Yeshivat Gush Etzion with Rabbi Aaron Lichtenstein and received rabbinic ordination from the State Rabbinate of Israel. He earned his medical degree at Hebrew University and did his residency in child psychiatry at Schneider Child's Hospital in Israel. He taught at the Beit Midrash at Hebrew University, and he currently teaches at Midreshet Lindenbaum in Lod and serves as a marriage officiant for Tzohar. He writes on questions intersecting child psychiatry and halakhah.

In an article published in the halakhic journal *Teḥumin* in 2018, Rabbi Mevorakh addresses the question of whether a person ill with anorexia must eat on Yom Kippur, a fast day. On the one hand, eating on Yom Kippur is required if someone is ill and needs to eat; on the other hand, having to eat on Yom Kippur may cause spiritual and psychological distress. Rabbi Mevorakh analyzes whether two halakhic principles, *pikku'aḥ nefesh* (mortal danger to human life) and the status of *shoṭeh* (mental derangement), apply to those suffering with anorexia.

QUESTION

Rabbi Mevorakh explains:

> An eating disorder of the type anorexia nervosa is a mental illness characterized by a reduction in the consumption of food that affects body weight, a fear of gaining weight, and an excessive focus on body weight. This illness appears most often in girls at the age of adolescence and is considered a difficult illness to treat and, at times, is even fatal. The question that must be asked is whether and under which conditions is it permitted for someone suffering from this illness to transgress the mitzvah of fasting on Yom Kippur.

SECTION A: INTRODUCTION

Rabbi Mevorakh explains what anorexia is and explains how its stages of treatment move from an initial focus on physiological danger to psychological treatment:

> According to current medical definitions, in order to diagnose anorexia three criteria must be present: (1) a restriction in energy

intake that leads to body weight less than minimally expected, (2) an intense fear of gaining weight or behavior preventing weight gain in the case of low body weight, and (3) psychological disturbance in relation to body image, an exaggerated influence of weight upon self-image, or the lack of recognition of the seriousness of low body weight.

The treatment for this Illness has two main levels. The first concentrates intensively on the physiological problems of underfeeding: the concentration of sodium in the blood, absence of menstruation, low pulse, hair loss, weakness, low bone density, etc. In this level, feeding through medical intervention and a close watch on the physiological manifestations of the illness are required. After the patients reach a certain weight, showing a moderation in the physiological severity of the illness, the focus of treatment changes. In the second level, the patient goes through psychological treatment so that she is able to eat the appropriate amount of food for her bodily needs on her own. Even in this level, a continued increase in bodily weight to the appropriate weight is required: this is not the exclusive goal of treatment but represents a sign of mental healing.

If there is physiological danger, the first level takes place at a hospital, usually in a regular department (whether pediatric or internal medicine depends on the age). The second level may take place in a closed or open psychiatric unit, a specialized clinic, or other treatment center, depending on the patient's ability to deal with the treatment and her need to be closely watched.

SECTION B: THE FIRST LEVEL OF
TREATMENT—*PIKKU'AḤ NEFESH*

Rabbi Mevorakh establishes that halakhah holds that eating on Yom Kippur is permitted without question for a pregnant woman or ill person. The only consideration is the amount of food: should it be limited to less than the minimum amount considered to be food consumption on the holiday, or may it be more?

Mishnah Yoma 8:4 says:

> A pregnant woman who smelled food [and feels a craving for it] is fed [on Yom Kippur] until she recovers. An ill person is fed [on Yom Kippur] according to the advice of medical experts, and if there are no experts there, one feeds him according to his own instructions, until he says that he has eaten enough.

The Babylonian Talmud *Yoma* 82a comments:

> There is nothing that stands in the way of saving a life from mortal danger [*pikku'aḥ nefesh*] except for the prohibitions against idol worship [*avodah zarah*], forbidden sexual relationships [*arayot*], and bloodshed.

It is clear that if we are dealing with a situation in which fasting constitutes a danger to life—that is to say, the early levels of medical treatment in which the physiological state is unstable—it is permitted, and indeed required, to eat and drink as necessary. Nevertheless, when it is permitted to eat because of a danger to life, it is at the level of food consumption less than the amount that would involve the punishment of *karet* [the punishment for eating on Yom Kippur], as the Shulḥan Arukh rules in *Oraḥ Ḥayyim* 618:7:

> When one feeds a pregnant woman or sick person, we feed that person little by little so that (the food) will not combine to the prescribed amount of food which is prohibited to eat.

The source for this is the Rabbi Asher ben Jehiel, *Yoma* 8.13:

> Naḥmanides wrote that it is clear that inserting a straw [into the liquid of a food] is [permitted] for a pregnant woman for

whom we do not have an estimate as to when her craving will ease: perhaps it will be enough for [her to have nourishment from the liquid], or perhaps she will need the fat [solid food] itself. But in regard to an ill person who is fed in accordance with medical experts, [that ill person] is fed with what he needs and how much he needs according to what the physicians say, and we do not limit him to the liquid but feed him the minimal amount. We learn from Babylonian Talmud *Keritot* 13a that they permitted a pregnant woman to eat less than an olive's amount[3] because of danger, yet the anonymous voice of the Talmud objects that since her eating is due to danger, let her eat more. Rav Pappa responded that this is what is meant—they permitted a pregnant woman to eat less than an olive's amount in the time that it would take to eat a half loaf of bread so that it would not add up [to what would be considered normal eating].... It would seem that this would be the case for an ill person as well.... One should do this for an ill person only on a physician's orders if [the physician] says that it would be sufficient to feed him slowly. [Otherwise, he should be fed more.]

Halakhic opinion... holds that if a slow rate of feeding is insufficient, a higher rate is permitted to save [the individual] from danger.

It must be emphasized that in patients suffering from anorexia in the first stage [of treatment] in which underfeeding is great, often there are clear signs that there is critical danger to life.... In anorexia there is considerable difficulty in eating a sufficient amount in a small amount of time, and one of the outstanding characteristics in treating this illness is the attempt of the patient to lengthen the time it takes to eat out of fear.... What must be considered carefully [is] if eating in small amounts is practical and effective for those suffering from this illness.

SECTION C: THE MIDDLE STAGES OF
TREATMENT: *SEFEIK PIKKU'AḤ NEFESH*

Rabbi Mevorakh considers who should decide matters of food consumption by an ill person on Yom Kippur:

> Already in the Babylonian Talmud, the question arises as to how and who is authorized to measure the amount of danger. The Talmud suggests two possibilities, eating according to expert opinion ... and eating according to the patient in the case where the patient believes that he must eat. The Talmud continues its discussion to deal with the case in which the experts and the patient disagree or in which the experts disagree. The medieval authorities enlarge the discussion by inquiring as to the identity and authority of the experts. ... The [continuing] discussion [among the authorities] is based on the principle that in the case of *sefeik pikku'aḥ nefesh* [possible mortal danger to human life], it is permitted for the ill person to eat on Yom Kippur.

SECTION D: ADVANCED STAGES OF
TREATMENT: DANGEROUS ILLNESS WITHOUT
IMMEDIATE DANGER (TO LIFE)

Rabbi Mevorakh argues for food consumption in cases of serious illness unaccompanied by immediate danger:

> In the situation of immediate danger to life and doubtful danger to life there is clear permission to eat on Yom Kippur. But what about serious illness without immediate danger? ...
> Shulḥan Arukh *Oraḥ Ḥayyim* 618 rules:
>
> [Regarding] a sick person who needs to eat, if there is an expert physician there, even if he is a non-Jew, who says that if this person is not fed, it is possible that his illness will worsen

and he will be in danger, they feed him on the physician's orders, and he does not have to say that he will die.

SECTION E: AN ILL PERSON'S RESPONSIBILITY FOR OBSERVING THE MITZVOT

Rabbi Mevorakh now turns to the halakhic category of *shoteh*, a mentally deranged person who is considered not responsible for observing the mitzvot. Does this apply to a person with anorexia?

> Rabbi Ezekiel Landau [1713–93, Poland, Bohemia, known after his most famous book *Noda bihudah*] is of the opinion that one can define a partially deranged person, a partial *shoteh*, whose mental problems are limited to a specific area and not others. He explains: It is only to this matter that his mind is always unhinged, and therefore it is only for this matter that he can be considered a *shoteh*. He is not responsible for all the mitzvot that are connected with this matter, but he is responsible for all other matters for which he is mentally fit.
>
> As to what we are discussing, an eating disorder constitutes a specific case among the mental illnesses ... because those who are ill are clear minded in general ... except for their body image. Their judgment and thought patterns are not injured except that their self-image is impaired greatly, and they have no recognition that their body weight is too low and that there is an essential need to gain weight for health reasons. ... This is a clear example of a limited mental problem that does not affect other areas. It would be difficult to exempt them from all the mitzvot. ... But in regard to eating and perhaps other activities that deal with ... self-image, there is a reason to be permissive according to the approach of Rabbi Landau.

PESAK DIN

Rabbi Mevorakh concludes:

> One must note that eating on Yom Kippur may involve a personal cost because of the sanctity and importance of the day. Yet one must be careful of [mental disorder] in which the patient deems his situation as less dangerous than it is, especially when eating is enforced by others and not from internal desire.[4]

In summary, people with anorexia are expected to observe all the mitzvot except those that affect their self-image. Like people with a physical illness, they are likely to need to eat (more or less) on Yom Kippur to improve their health. In these particular cases, one must be careful not to take patients at their word if they say they do not want or need to eat when they should.

Text 6.3. Waldenberg, "On Abortion in General"

TZITZ ELIEZER, 9, NO. 51.3

Born in Jerusalem, Rabbi Eliezer Waldenberg (1915–2006) studied in the Etz Ḥayyim Yeshiva and served as the rabbi of a small synagogue near Shaare Zedek Hospital in Jerusalem, where many physicians would pray and discuss medical issues with him (although he was never the official rabbi of the hospital). He taught a weekly class at the hospital for the physicians and nurses, and in his twenty-one volumes of responsa, entitled *Tzitz Eliezer* (The diadem of Eliezer), he published many responsa on medical ethics. He also published responsa on political issues and maritime law and was awarded the Israel Prize.

We will study two of his seven responsa on abortion, beginning with the general question of when abortion is and is not permitted and by which means. It is helpful to start by explaining some basic features of halakhah on abortion. The biblical text that serves as the foundational text shaping halakhah on abortion, Exodus 21:22–25, makes a distinction between the lives of the mother and the fetus:

> If men brawl and knock against a pregnant woman so that a miscarriage results but an *ason* does not ensue, [the offender] shall surely be obliged according to whatever the husband may exact from him and pay according to the assessment. But if an *ason* ensues, it shall be a life for a life—an eye for an eye, a tooth for a tooth, a hand for a hand, a leg for a leg, a burn for a burn, wound for a wound, bruise for a bruise.

While there are many interpretive puzzles in this passage,[5] the main stream in rabbinic interpretation takes *ason* to refer to the death of the mother; therefore, anything that happens to a fetus is not deemed homicide but a lesser offense.

In the course of the development of halakhah in the Middle Ages, two major viewpoints on this distinction emerge based on a passage in the Babylonian Talmud *Sanhedrin* 72b:

> Rav Huna says: [In the case of] a minor who was a *rodef* [a pursuer], the pursued may be saved [by taking the pursuer's] life. [Rav Huna] holds that a pursuer does not require forewarning, and there is no difference [with regard to this matter] between an adult and a minor. Rav Hisda raised an objection to Rav Huna: [If a woman was giving birth and her life was being endangered by the fetus, the fetus may be aborted in order to save the mother. But] once his head has emerged, he may not be harmed in order to save the mother, because one *nefesh* [a living being] may not be cast aside for another *nefesh*. Why is this so? [Shouldn't the fetus be also considered] a *rodef*? [The anonymous voice in the Talmud answers:] There is a difference [between the two cases: in the case of the birth, once the fetus has emerged, the danger to her is not caused by the fetus but by heaven].

MEDICAL ETHICS 187

Rashi, the noted eleventh-century commentator on the Bible and the Babylonian Talmud, remarks:

> [In regard to] a woman who is experiencing difficulty giving birth and is in danger, it is taught in the first section [of this unit], "The midwife extends her hand and cuts it up and extracts the pieces," for as long as [the fetus] did not come out into the world, it is not a *nefesh* [a living being], and it is permitted to kill it and save its mother. But once the head has emerged, it may not be harmed, because it is considered as fully born, and one may not cast aside the life of one *nefesh* in favor of another.

Rashi's understanding supports the possibility that an abortion may be performed for reasons other than a direct threat to the mother's life. By contrast, Maimonides reinterprets the passage in the Babylonian Talmud restrictively in *Mishneh Torah* Hilkhot Rotze'aḥ (Laws of Murderers) 1.9:

> [This rule] is a negative commandment: not to have compassion on the life of a *rodef*. Therefore, the sages instructed us that when a woman has difficulty in labor, it is permitted to dismember the fetus within her by either medications or surgery, because the fetus is like a *rodef* [trying] to kill her. But once the head has emerged, [the child] may not be harmed, for we do not cast aside one *nefesh* in favor of another. This is the natural course of the world.

Maimonides deems the fetus to be like a *rodef*, a pursuer when the mother's life is in danger. Surprisingly, the passage in *Sanhedrin* 72b rejects that idea: rather, it assumes that before the fetus has emerged, it cannot be a *rodef*. As a consequence of Maimonides' reinterpretation, if the fetus is not posing a threat to the mother, presumably it cannot be aborted: abortions could be performed only if there is an imminent threat to the mother's life. Why Maimonides sees fit to contradict the Talmud is also bewildering. Even more perplexing is the fact that the status of *rodef* would continue to apply to the baby: once the head emerges, if the threat to the mother's life continues, the baby would still be deemed a *rodef* and therefore is liable to be killed. Rabbinic decisors have sought to make sense of the divergent viewpoints of Rashi and Maimonides.

With this background in mind, let's turn to Rabbi Waldenberg's responsum on abortion in general.

SECTION A: A BASIC DISTINCTION ON ABORTION[6]

Rabbi Waldenberg addresses whether there are different rules in halakhah for Jews and non-Jews performing an abortion. He terms non-Jews Noahides because Rabbinic tradition holds that the covenant God made with Noah in Genesis 8:20–9:17 includes seven laws for non-Jews to follow, one of which is the prohibition against bloodshed (the killing of a human being).[7] He quotes a talmudic passage that prohibits Noahides from performing an abortion:

> Babylonian Talmud *Sanhedrin* 47b [reads]:
>
>> It is said in the name of Rabbi Ishmael that a Noahide is liable to the death penalty even for killing fetuses. What is the reason for the opinion of Rabbi Ishmael? It is derived from that which is written: "One who sheds the blood of a person, by a person [*ba-adam*] his blood shall be shed" [Gen. 9:6]. The word *ba-adam* means: In a person, and is interpreted homiletically: What is a person that is in a person? You must say: This is a fetus that is in its mother's womb.
>
> Accordingly, a Noahide is liable [for the death penalty] for killing a fetus....
>
> We derive from the meaning of the Talmud that it is obvious, and a principle that no one disputes, that a Jew is not put to death for killing a fetus [but is still forbidden from doing so except in special circumstances].... [The Rabbis] debated

only whether a Noahide is liable or not [for the death penalty and ruled that a Noahide is punished with the death penalty].

Rabbi Waldenberg then explains the contrasting interpretations of Rashi and Maimonides in addressing in which situations Jews are allowed to perform abortions:

> Rashi explains that the fetus can be killed as long as it has not emerged into the air in order to save its mother because as long as it does not go out into the air, it is not a living being. This is also the reason why a Jew is not liable to execution for aborting a fetus because it is not a living being, and so it appears to me.
> However, Maimonides provides a different reason ... for why it is permitted to kill [the fetus] before it emerges.... He explains ... that [the fetus] is like a *rodef*, and this means that outside of this, it is forbidden to abort it, because apparently [Maimonides thinks] it is designated a living being, and if [Maimonides' interpretation is correct, this leads to the question of] ... why a Jew is not liable to execution for aborting a fetus.... In addition to this, Maimonides' words do not make sense, since what difference does it make that [the baby's] head has emerged, why isn't it still deemed a *rodef*, and if it is the natural course of the world before [it emerges that it is a *rodef*], then it is the nature of the world afterward....
> Great rabbinic scholars have labored to understand the words of Maimonides, and they have also tried to fathom why Jews are not included in the verse "the one who spills the blood of a person by a person his blood shall be spilled" [Gen. 9:6].

Rabbi Waldenberg concludes that once the laws of the Torah are given at Sinai, notably among them the passage in Exodus from which the halakhah on abortion is derived, Jews are to follow these laws, whereas Genesis 9:6 remains the law for Noahides. As a result, Jews may perform abortions when non-Jews may not.

Note, however, that holding that Jews are allowed to do something not permitted for non-Jews is hotly debated among rabbinic decisors.

SECTION B: THE OPINION OF RABBI JOSEPH TRANI

Rabbi Waldenberg then highlights the opinions of two early modern rabbinic decisors. Since their cases and arguments might otherwise seem perplexing,[8] their stances are mostly paraphrased rather than excerpted throughout this responsum.

First, Rabbi Waldenberg cites Rabbi Joseph Trani (1568–1639, chief rabbi of Turkey), known by his acronym Maharit. Addressing the question of whether a Jewish physician or midwife is permitted to perform an abortion for a non-Jewish woman, Rabbi Trani argues that abortion is not considered murder when it is performed by Jews; he derives this from a source in Babylonian Talmud *Arakhin* 7a that prescribes the speedy execution of a pregnant woman condemned to death, because the delay would cause the woman suffering and disgrace. The anonymous voice in the Talmud comments that it is obvious that this is the case and then asks, if that is so, why does anyone need to state that the woman should be put to death without delay? The answer is that without this rule, one might think to delay the execution on the basis on Exodus 21:22–25, where one who causes a miscarriage must pay compensation because it is still an offense to kill a fetus and, therefore, the execution must wait until the child is born. But Rabbinic tradition holds that the disgrace to the woman caused by a delay is of far greater weight. If her execution is to be carried out promptly, how much the more so would an abortion for the sake of the mother's need.

Rabbi Trani rules that a Jew may perform an abortion only for the mother's need. In general, abortion is forbidden, because it violates the prohibition against *ḥabbalah*, wounding the body. Because the body of a human being is God's possession, it may not be damaged. This understanding fits the rule about a pregnant woman sentenced to the death penalty since the prohibition of wounding the body does not apply in her case. Therefore, Rabbi Trani rules that a non-Jew is banned from abortion and a Jew may not assist in such an abortion lest one transgress the prohibition of putting a stumbling block before the blind (Lev. 19:14). However, a Jew may perform an abortion for the need of the mother.

It should be noted that Trani follows Rashi's viewpoint. He does not mention Maimonides; nor does he imply that an abortion may be performed only if the woman's life is at stake. Only abortion without sufficient reason is forbidden.

Rabbi Waldenberg comments:

> We learn that it is obvious to Rabbi Trani's intention that the permission to have an abortion applies even when there is no danger to the life of the mother [when] her medical status [is such that] the continuation of the pregnancy will harm her health.... The Jewish physician who was asked to perform the abortion should do so.

SECTION C: THE OPINION OF RABBI JAIR ḤAYYIM BACHARACH

Rabbi Waldenberg then discusses the responsum of Rabbi Jair Ḥayyim Bacharach (1638–1702, Germany), known by the name of his book, *Ḥavvot Ya'ir* (The opinions of Jair). Addressing whether a woman who became pregnant through an adulterous relationship and is now repentant would be permitted to have an abortion, Rabbi Bacharach states there is no difference between a *mamzer* (a person whose family lineage is problematic) and a person whose family lineage is not problematic except that the *mamzer* may not marry a non-*mamzer* nor serve on a court dealing with capital cases.

He argues against some rabbinic decisors who make a distinction between three stages—the first forty days of pregnancy, the end of three months when the fetus is sensed, and the time later on when movement of the fetus is perceived—and who place more restrictions on abortion as the fetus develops. Rabbi Bacharach argues that abortion should not be considered murder since only someone who kills a day-old baby, and not someone who kills a fetus, would be considered guilty of murder. The implication is that one can abort a fetus until the onset of labor because the fetus becomes a *nefesh* only at birth. Still, that does not mean that abortion should be allowed.

Rabbi Bacharach offers a new basis for why abortion forbidden in general: performing an abortion violates the prohibition against wanton spilling of semen. He argues that women are included in this prohibition and that the ban on abortion applies to all stages of pregnancy. He concludes that although in principle a repentant adulterous woman should be allowed to have an abortion, nonetheless we follow the widespread custom among Jews to forbid abortion in such situations in order to prevent the spread of sexual immorality.

Rabbi Waldenberg then notes Rabbi Bacharach's argument that

> there is no distinction between before forty days, three months of pregnancy, or when she feels the movement of the fetus inside her [but Rabbi Waldenberg disagrees]. . . . Rabbi Bacharach believes that the prohibition of abortion originates in the prohibition of the wanton spilling of semen [but Rabbi Waldenberg argues that] this prohibition applies from the onset . . . and in time of need, even if it does not reach the level of *pikku'aḥ nefesh* [mortal danger], there is room to permit it since ex post facto [transgressing it] is permitted. . . . [Rabbi Waldenberg argues that] the prohibition [of spilling seed] does not apply to the woman [and women in general]. . . . The significance of this is

that it is best when there is a need to perform an abortion to have a female physician rather than a male physician perform it.

SECTION D: AN IMPORTANT CONSEQUENCE OF THE MORE RESTRICTIVE POINT OF VIEW

Rabbi Waldenberg concludes that an abortion is permitted when harm may occur to the mother even when there is no danger to her life, yet he notes that the more restrictive opinions may be helpful in certain situations, such as when a pregnant woman with cancer wants to leave a child behind her if she dies. He writes:

> There is room to permit [an abortion] even when there is no danger to the life of the mother [as long as there is sufficient reason].... There are times that the stringency of a number of rabbinic decisors can bring help in certain halakhic problems. An example: the case of a woman who is ill with cancer who wants to continue with her pregnancy and leave behind a child. If we follow the approaches of those who believe that the prohibition of abortion does not stem from the prohibition of loss of life and ... who are lenient to permit an abortion for the sake of the mother's health or her emotional state, then one should not listen to the pleas of the mother and should cast aside the life of the fetus in order to lengthen her life. For the principle of *pikku'aḥ nefesh* [mortal danger] applies to prolonging life even for an hour, even transgressing all the prohibitions in the Torah [to do so]. But if we want to rely in this rare and tragic incident upon those who are stringent to not undertake an abortion even when there is danger to life of the mother, we can rule that the plea of the woman should be heeded and that we should follow *shev ve'al ta'aseh* [the halakhic principle of not doing anything in certain situations rather than act] in order to rely upon the mercy of heaven and allow her to complete the pregnancy.

PESAK DIN

Rabbi Waldenberg concludes:

1. When there is a need, and the law determines that it is permitted to arrange for an abortion, it is preferable to have it done by a Jewish doctor.... When there is a need to arrange for an abortion for a non-Jew, a Jewish doctor should perform it....

2. When there is a danger to the mother in continuing the pregnancy, an abortion can be allowed easily. Even when there is no danger, but the mother's health is very delicate, and for the sake of her health or to relieve her of severe pain, it is advised to perform an abortion, even though there is no real risk to life, even here one can allow this, according to the judgment of the decisor, as he sees the case. One can also allow this when the woman is nursing.

3. A married woman who committed adultery or was raped and became pregnant, even from a non-Jew, where the child would not be a *mamzer*, and she has now repented [in the case of adultery], a number of great decisors are inclined to allow for an abortion....

4. [Permitting] an abortion before forty days from conception, as well as earlier than three months from conception, is much more allowable than to do so after these periods. It is thus preferable to arrange for the abortion prior to these periods, while the fetus has not begun to stir, when there is a well-based concern that the fetus that will be born deformed and beset by afflictions. At the other extreme, it is permitted to abort a fetus once the woman is in the process of giving birth and the fetus is moving to emerge ... when there is a direct threat to the mother's life....

> 5. It is also preferable to have an abortion by drinking a medicine than by direct surgical means.
> 6. All Jews are commanded ... not to deal lightly regarding ending a pregnancy, and great responsibility [devolves] in such a case, both on the one asking to have the abortion and on the rabbinic decisor being asked.... Even the nations of the world have made laws regarding this ... and Jews are a holy people.[9]

Text 6.4. Waldenberg, "On the Abortion of a Fetus with Tay-Sachs Disease"

TZITZ ELIEZER, 13, NO. 102

After writing the responsum above, Rabbi Waldenberg devotes two later responsa addressing specific cases. In the following responsum, he weighs whether it is permitted to abort a fetus with a fatal illness, in this case Tay-Sachs disease, when the fetus's diagnosis is only ascertained far along in the pregnancy.

QUESTION

Rabbi Waldenberg recounts:

> The question [submitted by Dr. David Meir, director of Shaare Zedek Hospital] is regarding terminating a pregnancy because of Tay-Sachs disease.... The technology of today that allows testing for this disease cannot give reliable results prior to three months into the pregnancy. Thus the question is whether one can deem such a disease with such severe and certain consequences of sufficient severity to allow for an abortion even after three months, or whether the period of three months is absolute, and there is no justification, short of direct risk to the life to the mother, that would allow for an abortion after three months.

SECTION A: A FETUS WITH TAY-SACHS DISEASE[10]

Rabbi Waldenberg analyzes whether the child's suffering and the mother's suffering after the child is born would permit an abortion to be performed:

> Now ... it seems in my humble opinion, on the basis of the analysis that I wrote in my previous responsum, 9.51.3 ... that in a case such as this, in which the consequences are so grave ... it is permissible to terminate the pregnancy until seven months have elapsed.... Beyond seven months the issue is more serious ... since at the end of seven months the fetus is often fully developed ... [Regarding a ruling to allow an abortion,] where is there a greater need regarding pain and more suffering than in our case [where pain and suffering] will be inflicted upon [the mother]—if she gives birth to such a creature whose very being is one of pain and suffering and whose death is certain within a few years ... and added to that is the pain and suffering of the infant, this would seem to be the classic case in which abortion may be permitted. It does not matter what type of pain and suffering is endured, physical or emotional, as emotional pain and suffering are to a large extent much greater than physical pain and suffering.

PESAK DIN

Rabbi Waldenberg concludes:

> Permission is granted to end the pregnancy immediately upon [receiving] the clear and certain information that [the fetus] will be born [with Tay-Sachs disease] even in the seventh month [of pregnancy]. [The abortion] is to be performed in the method least dangerous to the mother.[11]

That Rabbi Waldenberg rules that abortion is permitted in a case when there is no immediate physical danger to the mother is very striking. He increases the scope of what is considered to be *pikku'aḥ nefesh*, mortal danger to the life of the mother, to include the child's suffering after being born and the mother's psychological suffering as she witnesses her child's suffering.

In a later responsum, he addresses the distressing situation in which one fetus needs to be aborted so other fetuses can be safely carried to term, ruling to abort this fetus, thus increasing the scope of permitted abortions to include danger within the womb.[12]

Text 6.5. Grossman, "'Partial Birth Abortion' and the Question of When Human Life Begins"

COMMITTEE ON JEWISH LAW AND STANDARDS OF THE RABBINICAL ASSEMBLY, ḤOSHEN MISHPAṬ 425:2.2003

Rabbi Susan Grossman grew up in New York, studied at SUNY-Binghamton, and worked as a Jewish journalist before she received ordination from the Jewish Theological Seminary. She served Beth Shalom Congregation in Columbia, Maryland, for twenty-five years. In 1992 she became one of the first women to serve on the Conservative movement's Committee on Jewish Law and Standards.

Rabbi Grossman's approach to halakhah focuses on how understanding the textual and sociohistorical context of talmudic and later halakhic literature allows rabbis to revise entrenched practices, particularly when these originated from misunderstandings and when socioeconomic, medical, and/or scientific conditions have now changed, particularly when inconsistent with the metahalakhic values enshrined in Scripture, such as *pikku'aḥ nefesh* (mortal danger) and *be-tzelem Elohim* (respecting the dignity of every human being because every human being is created in the image of God).

In a responsum approved by the CJLS in 2003, Rabbi Grossman addresses a form of abortion that has become politically controversial in the United States and has been termed "partial birth abortion" by its critics. She concludes that halakhah permits the procedure, because it is less harmful to a woman endangered by her pregnancy.

QUESTION

Rabbi Grossman addresses the question:

> When is an intact dilation and extraction procedure, popularly referred to as a "partial-birth abortion," permitted to be performed?

SECTION A: DEFINING HUMAN LIFE

Analyzing the Rabbis' legal and theological concepts about the significance of human life, Rabbi Grossman notes that Rabbinic law considers a fetus part of a woman's body. Even as Judaism affirms the sacred potential for a human life, Rabbinic law does not grant the fetus the status of *nefesh*, a living being independent of the mother, until birth, defined as the head or majority of the body having exited the mother's body:

> Judaism is a life affirming religion. The biblical statement *v'hai bahem* ["you shall live through (the commandments)"] (Lev. 18:5) was interpreted by the Rabbis as a commandment to affirm life, placing the value of human life above almost all other commandments.... Rabbinic law established the time of ensoulment as taking place on the 40th day, irrespective of the sex of the fetus. Before the 40th day, the fetus is considered merely liquid by the Rabbis and, if miscarried before that time, does not affect the status as first born of any future offspring.
>
> If the fetus is not human life, what is it? Rabbinic law views the fetus as part of its mother's body, *ubar yerekh imo* (the fetus is [like] the thigh of its mother), and it is to be treated as such....

> Humility, awe and reverence surround our appreciation for the miracle and preciousness of life and the desire to see human life come to fruition with birth. Therefore Judaism, as a rule, does not warrant the destruction of a fetus without cause. Recognizing the sacred potential for human life vested in the fetus, as a work in progress by the Holy One, rabbinic law nevertheless did not grant the fetus the status of human life. . . .
>
> The fetus does not become a *nefesh*, a living being independent of the mother, until birth. Birth is defined as once its head or the majority of its body has exited her body. At this point the fetus becomes a child, its legal status changes from a fetus to a *nefesh* (a living being), an independent human being, with the right to the full protections due human beings under Jewish law.

SECTION B: UNDER WHAT CONDITIONS IS A LATE TERM ABORTION PERMITTED UNDER JEWISH LAW?

Rabbi Grossman argues that abortion is permitted for the mother's physical well-being and to forestall extreme emotional distress:

> When is a late term abortion permitted under Conservative Jewish law? A late term abortion is never permitted for the mere convenience of the mother or as a form of birth control. However, an abortion even in the latest stages of pregnancy is permitted under Jewish law for maternal cause, when continuation of the pregnancy poses a significant risk to the mother's physical well being, as determined by her physician, or in the face of maternal emotional distress, for example as when faced with a fetus with severe abnormalities.

SECTION C: UNDER WHAT CONDITIONS WOULD AN INTACT D AND X PROCEDURE, POPULARLY LABELED "PARTIAL BIRTH ABORTION," BE PERMISSIBLE UNDER JEWISH LAW?

Rabbi Grossman explains the medical problems that prompted the development of the intact d and x and how it safeguards both the mother's health and her ability to bear children in the future:

> Late term abortions are often the result of heart-rending decisions made by the mother and her family, upon learning late in the pregnancy that the fetus has severe abnormalities, has little or no chance of surviving, or that continuing to carry would endanger the mother's life or her physical health. Lacking definitive information earlier in the pregnancy and/or in an attempt to bring a much wanted fetus to term, the mother and her doctor could not have made the painful decision to abort any earlier in the term of the pregnancy....
>
> Physicians rely on the intact dilation and extraction procedure (henceforth to be referred to as an intact d and x) when, in their medical opinion, they have determined it provides the safest procedure to protect the short and long term health of the mother under such conditions.
>
> The procedure is as follows: The cervix is chemically and manually dilated, the body of the fetus is manually extracted from the womb feet first.... The majority of the fetus remains within the woman's body, usually only the feet, and sometimes also the legs possibly extend outside her body. (In other words, at no time is the majority of the fetal body external to the mother.) The head remains within the womb and its intracranial contents are extracted. The fetus is therefore terminated before its head leaves the womb and before the majority of its body is external to the mother's body. Following extraction of its intracranial contents, the head is compressed, which permits it to be withdrawn through the vagina without the necessity of performing

surgery on the mother. The terminated fetus and womb lining are evacuated manually and/or, as necessary, with the help of suction through the vagina.

An intact d and x is one of a number of procedures available to a physician to terminate a late term pregnancy.... One option, when time and the health of the mother allows, is for an intact d and e (dilation and evacuation), which allows the physician to dissect the fetus while still wholly within the mother's womb.... High risk obstetrics specialists at Johns Hopkins University assure me that the intact d and e is no longer a viable procedure for the latest term abortions, at which point the bones of the fetus are already formed and the danger exists that bone chips could rip the mother's uterus. The d and x procedure does not pose the same dangers because the fetal body is withdrawn intact into the vaginal canal....

The alternative to an intact d and x is not a caesarean section but the much more risky hysterotomy. A hysterotomy requires a much larger and vertical incision of the uterus. More tissue is cut and more bleeding occurs than with a normal caesarean section. Infections are much more likely. The danger of adhesions is great, and with it future fertility is often affected.... Statistics on morbidity rates of hysterotomies are so high that medical practitioners generally stopped performing them once the intact d and e and, for late term abortions, the intact d and x procedures became available....

The doctor should be free to choose the medical procedure which has the best chance of protecting his or her patient's health and well being.

SECTION D: THE LARGER CONTEXT OF THE DEBATE
Rabbi Grossman explains how a medical procedure became drawn into American civil politics:

[Intact d and x] has generated much controversy in the public arena. Opponents of abortion have labeled it "partial birth abortion" in their effort to elicit sympathy for their cause. Under pressure from the anti-abortion forces, the American Medical Association (AMA) recommended that the intact d and x procedure not be used unless other procedures pose greater maternal risk. This position seemed to put into question the necessity of ever needing to rely on the intact d and x procedure, according to both those who supported and opposed the decision, thereby influencing public debate on this issue. A number of specialists in the field of high risk obstetrics subsequently resigned their AMA membership in protest that the AMA had turned away from the best interests of their patients since the intact d and x is, at times and without doubt, the safest procedure for their patients.

Though the number of women for whom the intact d and x would be the safest treatment may be low in raw numbers statistically, there nevertheless exists a significant number of women whose health would be endangered or compromised if the intact d and x were not an available option upon which the physician could rely.

PESAK DIN

Rabbi Grossman rules:

> It is permissible under Jewish law for an intact d and x procedure to be performed whenever the patient's doctor deems it the preferable procedure in the best interests of the woman's health and well being.[13]

The COVID-19 Pandemic   7

By the first week of March 2020 most people were aware a global pandemic was happening. Jewish communities especially had to figure out how to deal with it posthaste because of the timing—Purim was less than a week away, Passover a month away. Much was unclear about how the coronavirus was transmitted and how contagious it was.

Rabbinic authorities needed to provide halakhic guidance as expeditiously as they could in the light of what was known and unknown. Fortunately, technology enabled them to post decisions in texts and/or videos on websites and apps and to email listservs and multiple recipients relatively easily.

The five responsa in this chapter, all posted within the first few months of the pandemic, illuminate how halakhah deals with pressing, unprecedented challenges.[1] Strikingly, yet not so surprisingly, rabbinic decisors across the movements offer similar rulings, because they base them on the principle of *pikku'aḥ nefesh*, human life must be protected from mortal danger. Where they diverge emerges from their prior disagreements over halakhah.

Among the first responsa, if not the first, to be issued was by the co-chairs of the Committee on Jewish Law and Standards (Conservative) offering halakhic guidance on the coronavirus (March 4, 2020). Subsequently, the CCAR Responsa Committee (Reform) addressed whether a minyan may be constituted via Zoom (March 28, 2020); Rabbi Herschel (Tzvi) Schachter, a Modern Orthodox rabbinic decisor in the United States, weighed (among other issues) whether washing for hygienic purpose is permitted on Tisha b'Av, a fast day on which washing is generally forbidden (July 21 and 29, 2020), and Rabbi Pamela Barmash wrote a responsum for the Conservative/Masorti movement in preparation for the High Holy Days when only a fraction of the community is present (July 22, 2020). The *teshuvah* that induced the most controversy was by Iggud Ḥakhmei ha-Ma'arav be-Eretz Yisrael, a group of rabbis of Moroccan descent who permitted videoconferencing for a Pesaḥ seder (March 24, 2020). The hullaballoo that ensued induced many of the decisors to withdraw their support or claim they never meant to support it to begin with.

Text 7.1. Co-chairs, Committee on Jewish Law and Standards, "Halakhic Guidance from CJLS about Coronavirus"

Written just as the world became aware of the pandemic and just a few days before Shabbat Zakhor and Purim, this responsum in letter form tackled many questions pouring into the Committee on Jewish Law and Standards (CJLS) and the Rabbinical Assembly offices from rabbis nationwide. In real time, Conservative rabbis sought the guidance of CJLS rabbinic decisors, so as not to have to make halakhic decisions solely on their own.

Technically, this responsum is not considered an official CJLS responsa, because it was not formally approved by vote during a meeting of the full CJLS, as is the protocol for CJLS responsa, but rather issued on the committee co-chairs' authority in order to respond expeditiously to pressing needs. Guidance on navigating ritual observances and the upcoming holidays in community needed to be sent and posted quickly, and it was—on Wednesday, March 4, 2020.

SECTION A: *PIKKU'AḤ NEFESH*

The committee emphasizes that *pikku'aḥ nefesh* is the overriding principle guiding Jewish life in a pandemic:

> We urge those who are ill to stay home, and those whom medical authorities have recommended for quarantine or self-quarantine to follow medical advice and stay in quarantine. *Pikku'aḥ nefesh*, protecting human life, overrides almost every other Jewish value.

SECTION B: GENERAL PRACTICES

The committee addresses practical matters of weekday and Shabbat rituals at a time when the means of coronavirus transmission remained unclear:

> A. All should follow advice regarding hygiene and handwashing. In particular:
>
> 1. Congregations should discourage handshaking and other direct physical contact.
> 2. It is advisable to refrain from kissing ritual objects (*sifrei torah* [Torah scrolls], communal *tallitot*, *siddurim* [prayer books], *mezuzot*) that are also kissed or touched directly by other individuals.
>
> B. In some communities, it may be medically advisable, or mandated by health authorities, for people to stay away from congregational worship. In such cases we recommend the following:
>
> 1. Those who wish to be part of a weekday minyan to recite prayers requiring a minyan, including mourner's *Kaddish*, may connect virtually (through audio or video) with a minyan (whether of their own congregation or another) whose members are meeting in person,

preferably in their time zone. They may recite *Kaddish, Kedushah, Barkhu* [all of these are prayers that may only be recited with a minyan], etc., and hear Torah reading along with that minyan....

2. Congregational leadership should provide guidance for home davenning and Torah study for those not able to attend Shabbat or Yom Tov services.
3. Our committee has not made a formal ruling on livestreaming on Shabbat and Yom Tov... but for the current *sha'at hadeḥak* (pressing circumstances), those congregations that are already offering streaming and that are still able to hold services with a minyan, should encourage members whose health may be at risk, or whose presence may be a risk to others, to stay home and make use of this option if the alternative would be to risk their own health or the health of others by attending services. Every attempt should be made to reduce potential violations of Shabbat (for example, activating the stream before Shabbat or holiday... or by someone who is not of the Jewish faith).
4. If a congregation is in quarantine and not able to bring together a minyan for services, the leadership should provide guidance for home davenning and Torah study.

SECTION C: PURIM

In discussing new procedures for Purim, less than a week away, the rabbinic decisors deal with two debatable issues: one of long-standing dispute—whether listening to the Megillah via amplification fulfills the mitzvah of "hearing the Megillah"; and one rarely receiving attention but now at issue—whether one may fulfill the mitzvah of a special Torah reading for Purim at another time:

> Some poskim [rabbinic decisors] have expressed concern about whether one fulfills one's obligation to hear the Megillah

reading by doing so via amplification or electronic reproduction, declaring it to be similar to shofar, where the mitzvah is to "hear" the shofar, so the actual sound must be heard.... Hearing the Megillah being read via telephone or live streaming is permitted when necessary, so long as the sound is undistorted, live and not a recording. Regarding Parashat Zakhor [the special Torah reading for the Shabbat before Purim], which has a higher level of obligation...—if one cannot hear Zakhor read from a Torah scroll, then one is advised to read it at home and to hear the Torah reading on Purim day (if possible), or to hear the same verses when they are read again for Parashat Ki Tetze' during the yearly Torah reading cycle.

SECTION D: A PRAYER

The rabbinic decisors offer a prayer from the Babylonian Talmud originally concerned with the welfare of Jews and extend its focus to the welfare of all people:

> The Babylonian Talmud Ketubbot 8b records the prayer of Reish Lakish "Master of the worlds, redeem and save, rescue and deliver Your people, Israel, from the pestilence and from the sword... and from all types of afflictions that suddenly erupt and come to the world. Before we call You are already responding. Blessed are You, Adonai, Who halts the plague."
>
> We pray for healing for those who are ill and for health and wellness for us, our communities, and all people.[2]

Text 7.2. CCAR Responsa Committee, "Virtual Minyan in Time of COVID-19 Emergency"

CCAR RESPONSUM 5780.2

On March 18, 2020, the Reform movement's CCAR Responsa Committee (see chapter 1) posted this responsum addressing whether a minyan may be constituted virtually.³ As was true in the Conservative movement, many Reform rabbis had sought the guidance of their respective responsa committee. Even though praying privately as an individual is permitted and the mitzvah of prayer is an individual's responsibility according to halakhah, prayers of major importance may only be recited in the presence of a minyan, and communal prayer had long been viewed as desirable to the point of being a necessity[4] — and hence modern medical protocols of physical distancing and quarantine for societal protection during a pandemic posed new challenges. Communal prayer might violate the principle of *pikku'aḥ nefesh*.

QUESTION

The CCAR Responsa Committee addresses multiple intersecting questions:

> May we rely on technology to create a virtual minyan in a time of crisis when we cannot gather in our synagogues? If so, what are the criteria for constituting a valid virtual minyan? How does one recite [Mourners'] Kaddish in a virtual minyan? At what point do we know it is appropriate to discontinue the virtual minyan and return to a physical minyan?

SECTION A: THE MINYAN AND PARTICIPATION "OUTSIDE" THE MINYAN

This Responsa Committee acknowledges that the same committee had previously rejected constituting a minyan via videoconferencing in 2012[5] but accentuates that a holy community must continue to operate in an emergency. Relying on the precedent that a person outside a synagogue seen through a window by those in the synagogue may be included in a minyan,[6] the Responsa Committee rules that those on videoconferencing but not those joining in via livestreaming may be included in the number of people needed for a minyan:

> Although we have a recent decision that rejects the virtual minyan, we are now in an emergency situation. In an emergency situation, a *bet din* is responsible for taking action for the welfare of the community and may issue a temporary ruling (*hora'at sha'ah*) to prevent the *kahal* from going astray. People will certainly "go astray" by turning to all sorts of sources of comfort if we do not ensure that the *kehillah kedoshah*, the holy community, can continue to function.
>
> The essence of the minyan is the reciprocity of the social contract—the shared obligation that binds all ten individuals to one another, transforming them from a number of individuals into a community.... The halakhah translated that conceptual essence into a physical one by mapping it onto a space, requiring the members of a minyan to be in one room together. The majority view in the halakhah is that the individuals who constitute the minyan must be in one room, though some authorities hold that it is sufficient for them to be able to see each other, thus including the individual who is visible through the window of the synagogue.
>
> Now, however, we are in a situation where people may not gather in one room. Therefore, for the duration of this emergency, we permit the convening of a minyan by means of *interactive technology*, i.e., technology that enables all members of the minyan to see and hear each other.... As always, and especially in this time of economic distress, we presume our congregations and all of our people will adhere to all intellectual property and copyright laws as they obtain software.
>
> As long as there are ten people connected in an *interactive* manner, any number of additional people may also be "present"

passively, via live streaming. In accordance with the precedent of 5772.1, we do not count these individuals in the minyan. In our current context, the obstacle to counting the livestream viewer in the minyan is that s/he cannot be seen or heard, and therefore cannot be an equal participant in the minyan's underlying social contract. Additionally, there is no way for the service leader to know how many people, if any, are watching a live stream, and therefore no way of knowing whether a minyan is "present" in the absence of ten interconnected members.

We affirm that one who is viewing a live stream should still respond to all the prayers; this is considered the same as having recited them. The same is true for the livestream viewer who recites the words of the Mourners' Kaddish along with the service leader.

PESAK DIN

The responsum concludes with the emphasis that permission to constitute a minyan via videoconferencing will be withdrawn when the health crisis subsides:

> The duration of these temporary procedures: Finally, at some point in the future, we know that this health crisis will end. When the authorities stop restricting attendance at public functions, this *hora'at sha'ah* should be set aside. People should return to the synagogue and the practice of interactive virtual *minyanim* should cease.[7]

Text 7.3. Iggud Ḥakhmei ha-Ma'arav be-Eretz Yisrael, "On a Seder via Zoom"[8]

A group of Sefardic/Mizraḥi rabbis of Moroccan background calling themselves Iggud Ḥakhmei ha-Ma'arav be-Eretz Yisrael (the Association of North African Rabbis in the Land of Israel) issued this ruling in a brief public letter on March 24, 2020, in time for

Passover 2020. Rabbi Elijah Abergil, chair of the Sefardic *beit din* in Jerusalem; Rabbi Shlomo Benhamu, Sephardic chief rabbi of Kiryat Gat; and Rabbi Daniel Bouskila, rabbi of Westwood Village Synagogue in Los Angeles were among the fifteen signatories. A protocol of strict physical isolation was in force in Israel, and the rabbis sought to bring families together for the holiday in another way: elderly people who would be forced to celebrate Passover alone without their families would be permitted to link in to their family's celebration by Zoom. A hullaballoo ensued in Orthodox circles, and many, if not most, of the signatories withdrew their signature or claimed they never signed it to begin with.

QUESTION

The rabbis present the question they have been asked:

> We have been asked by a learned Jew whether it is permissible to utilize the Zoom app (and other videoconferencing means) for seder night, to connect elderly people to their family members, as they are unable to be with them due to the ongoing coronavirus epidemic, so that they can all do the seder together via the app.
>
> One screen would be in the home of the elderly person and another screen in the home of their family, and [using Zoom] they would be able to see each other, speak to each other, and hear one another. The [Zoom] program and the computer would already be on before the festival begins, and nobody will have to do anything at all on the festival itself. The question is this: can one use this app for the purposes of making the seder [in the way that we have described] as a leniency to be used only in this time of great emergency?

SECTION A: THE RELEVANT ISSUES[9]

The rabbis base their ruling on their rulings of many Sefardic/Mizrahi decisors, especially those of Moroccan descent, that permit electricity to be turned on during a festival because certain activities prohibited on Shabbat, such as cooking food, are permitted on a festival.[10] Usually Sefardic/Mizrahi Jews living in Israel do not abide by this ruling, for two reasons: (1) they decided not to deviate from the common practice in the Land of Israel to not turn on electricity on a festival (*yom tov*); and (2) they decided not to contest the prestige and authority of Rabbi Ovadiah Yosef, who banned turning on electricity on a festival and who aimed to create a unified Sefardic/Mizrahi *minhag* (set of ritual practices). However, in light of the extreme situation of the pandemic, the rabbis of Iggud Ḥakhmei ha-Ma'arav be-Eretz Yisrael call upon the prior rulings of the Sefardic/Mizrahi decisors to support their stance that it is permitted to hold a seder by Zoom, even if a person will have to turn on the screen again if it goes dark during the festival.

They introduce other considerations, more ethical than granular law: everyone understands that the pandemic is an extreme situation, and without the impetus of celebrating with their family, some young people might not participate in a seder at all. This is a surprising argument—is there truly a worry that without their grandparents, a significant number of young Jews of Sefardic/Mizrahi origin might not attend a seder?

There are three central issues relevant to this question:

1. Operating the device on a festival
2. Weekday-type behavior
3. The concern that people will use this leniency in the future when it is not called for

1. Concerning the permissibility of turning on electricity on a holiday, it is well-known that the Sefardic rabbinic scholars

and North African rabbinic scholars were divided on the matter, but almost all of them permitted it, including the Rishon Lezion Chief Rabbi Ben-Zion Meir Ḥai Ouziel, Rabbi Raphael Aharon ben Shimon, Rabbis Joseph and Shalom Mesas, Rabbi Moshe Malka, Rabbi David Chelouche (may the memory of the righteous be a blessing), among others. Many Ashkenazic rabbinic scholars prohibited it *de-rabbanan*, that is, only as a rabbinic-level prohibition.

However, in our situation there is no need to operate the device, as it will be on already before the holiday starts, although there is a slight concern that perhaps [the screen] will go dark and someone will have to turn it on again. Regarding this concern it would appear that we can rely on those who have permitted [turning on an electric device on a festival] *lekhathilah* [ab initio].

2. As to the question of whether this is [the kind of] weekday-type behavior that will lead the festival to be treated like a weekday, it would appear that it is possible to be lenient in order to fulfill a mitzvah, as the talmudic sages permitted *shevut de-shevut* [two degrees of Rabbinic prohibition regarding resting on Shabbat] when a mitzvah is involved, such as measuring the volume of a *mikveh* [ritual bath] on a festival, in order to permit that mitzvah to be upheld.

3. As to whether the concern that people will end up using this app on other holidays when there is no urgent need, it is clear to everyone that this entire leniency is only here due to the current emergency. Furthermore, the holiday of Pesaḥ is unique, especially seder night, which everyone sees as a special event marking the covenant between God and Israel. Additionally, for many young Jews, if not for the connection between them and their grandfather and grandmother, it is possible they would not even attend the seder, and it is this connection with the grandparents in particular that prompts them to join in the

mitzvah of telling the story of the Exodus and of eating matzah. And for this generation, it is a matter of extreme urgency to turn the hearts and minds of the youth toward their forebears.

Additionally, there is another relevant issue: the need to lift the sadness from adults and elders, to motivate them to continue and go on with their lives, and to remove from them depression and weariness, which could result in a feeling of total desperation.

PESAK DIN
They conclude:

> Therefore, we think it is appropriate to permit this, emphasizing that [our lenient ruling in this regard] is only due to the extreme circumstances and is only for the purpose of seder night this year (5780/2020) for those who are need of such a solution. And in the same way as we permit healing the sick on Shabbat even if they are not fatally ill, [the situation of the elderly during the coronavirus pandemic] is a similar situation.[11]

Text 7.4. Schachter, "Washing on Tisha b'Av" and "Regarding the Rule of 'God Protects the Simple'"

Rabbi Hershel (Tzvi) Schachter studied at Yeshiva University, earning a BA, an MA, and rabbinic ordination. He was appointed assistant to the renowned Modern Orthodox leader Rabbi Joseph B. Soloveitchik, and he joined Yeshiva University's Rabbi Isaac Elchanan Theological Seminary in 1967 as the youngest *rosh yeshiva* (highest rank for a teacher at a yeshiva). A prolific author of responsa, he has also written seven books, several of them on Rabbi Soloveitchik's teachings, and more than one hundred articles for rabbinic journals.

Rabbi Schachter wrote a number of responsa on issues arising from the pandemic, among them his two responsa on washing on Tisha b'Av, posted on July 21 and 29, 2020, which have been integrated into one responsum below. The format is worthy of note. Both original responsa appear in Hebrew and in English, but the English is a summary without the sources rather than a translation of the Hebrew. (Possibly Rabbi Schachter believes that those interested in reading rabbinic sources are able to read Hebrew and those who read only English are seeking the ruling, not the reasoning.) Also, the Hebrew is not printed in the usual Hebrew script, but in Rashi script, a script of Hebrew employed in many rabbinic works. (Perhaps a responsum seemed more authoritative in Rashi script, perhaps the ruling was meant to continue in the line of rabbinic writing, or perhaps whoever posted Rabbi Schachter's responsa chose the Rashi script, or a bit of all three reasons.)

SECTION A: HEBREW VERSION[12]

Rabbi Schachter investigates the prohibition of washing on Tisha b'Av to see how it might apply during the pandemic. He draws a distinction based on the subjective instinct of each individual: those who feel they are in danger and demonstrate this by wearing a mask are permitted to wash their hands, while those who feel that there is no need to distance themselves are not permitted to do so. He contends that those who feel they are not in danger are proceeding based on the principle of "God protects the simple," generally not a positive evaluation of a person's intelligence:

> We hold that, according to Shulḥan Arukh *Oraḥ Ḥayyim* 554:7, even dipping one's fingers into water, whether hot or cold, is forbidden [on Tisha b'Av], except if one's fingers are filthy with dirt or excrement (554:9). Even so, one is not permitted [to wash] one's entire hand, but only as needed, and one may wash one's hands in the morning because of *ru'aḥ ra'ah* [an evil spirit], just as Tosafot wrote that this is if one's hands are dirty (see 554:10 and *Mishnah Berurah* 554:21). During this current period of the pandemic, we have already adduced from Rabbi

Moses Isserles in the name of the responsa of Maharil [Rabbi Jacob ben Moses Levi Moellin, c. 1360–1427, Germany, Austria, Bohemia] that certainly one can rule permissibly according to need—see what I wrote about this on 25 Nisan regarding during the *sefirah* [the counting of the Omer leading up to the festival of Shavuot] and on 17 Tammuz on mourning during the Nine Days [leading up to Tisha b'Av]—for those who are concerned and wear a mask on their mouth and nose, for in their regard this is considered as possible danger. But as for those who are not concerned and who are lenient regarding the distancing that the government has ordered because of the law [derived from] "God protects the simple" (Ps. 116:6), the law for them is clearly [based on] their lack of concern about washing their hands, and the prohibition of washing hands remains in effect. For those who are concerned [about possible danger], the law is that they are permitted to clean their hands with disinfectant, because of possible danger, [which is] considered as if their hands are filthy with dirt and [washing hands] is permitted. But for those who are not concerned and are not careful about all the distancing and other matters of carefulness because they believe that they are covered under the rule of "God protects the simple," it is obvious that they are not allowed to clean their hands with disinfectant.

SECTION B: ENGLISH VERSION

He summarizes his ruling succinctly in English:

It is rabbinically forbidden to wash oneself with either hot or cold water on Tisha B'Av, unless it is for the purpose of removing dirt from one's body (which includes washing hands when waking up in the morning). Individuals who have been vigilant in following the updated CDC recommendations would be allowed to wash or sanitize their hands on Tisha B'Av as they otherwise would. There is no allowance for those who have disregarded the CDC recommendations as this would be categorized as [washing] which is Rabbinically prohibited on Tisha B'Av.[13]

SECTION C: REGARDING THE RULE OF "GOD PROTECTS THE SIMPLE"

Rabbi Schachter subsequently issues a second responsum, in Hebrew only, analyzing the principle of "God protects the simple." First he justifies the practice of those refraining from health measures based on a midrash about whether the Israelite tribes practiced circumcision while in the wilderness. Then he walks back his justification by noting that a person whose actions may endanger others must follow medical guidelines:

> On the verse "your covenant they kept" (Deut. 33:9), Rashi cites the words of the Babylonian Talmud that for the entire forty years that the Israelites were in the wilderness, the rest of the tribes did not circumcise their children, for the climate was such that there was a bit of possible danger in circumcision and that only the tribe of Levi practiced circumcision. Already Rabbi Moses Sofer [see chapter 2] in his responsa discussed what was the opinion of Moses our rabbi about this, for if there truly was possible danger, he should have forbidden the Levites from circumcising their sons, and if there was no possible danger, he should have forced the other tribes to circumcise, just like the tribe of Levi. According to the contextual meaning [of the verse], it seems appropriate to explain that the threat of danger was very minute. In every case, the law depends upon a specific ill individual, so that for those who are fearful about danger, [that individual's] law is based on possible danger, while for those who are not fearful, we say [that they follow the rule of] "God protects the simple" and [their situation] is not considered [one of] possible danger, just as it is explained in Rabbi Ḥayyim

Ozer Grodzinski [1863–1940, Lithuania] in *Responsa Aḥiezer* in the name of a number of *aḥaronim* [modern rabbinic decisors].... Both [the other tribes and the tribe of Levi] behaved properly because the tribe of Levi had more faithful people and they didn't worry about possible danger, so for them [the situation] was not of possible danger, while [the members of] the other tribes were worried, so for them [the situation] was that of possible danger. Even though no human being is the possessor of his/her own life [for God is the one who gives human beings life], as it is written "but for your own lifeblood [I will require a reckoning]" [Gen. 9:5], and we hold that a person may not hurt himself/herself (Babylonian Talmud *Bava Kamma* 90b), in this situation the human being is considered the possessor of his/her life and may determine whether [a situation] is [one of] possible danger, even if the chance of danger is one in a billion. Rabbi Sofer wrote that [in this case] we say that confusion has taken hold [of a person] (Babylonian Talmud *Yoma* 83a). [Even though individuals may deem the situation as one of danger,] this is not considered to be possible danger in general.

The matter of "God protects the simple" depends on each individual: for one who is afraid of the possibility of danger, the rule [for that person] is according to possible danger, but Reuben may not determine for Simon that there is no possible danger. In any case it is clear that cleaning hands with disinfectant pertains only to the health of Reuben; he is the possessor of his own life [following the principle] of "God protects the simple," and he does not have to be concerned; therefore it is forbidden to him to clean his hands on Tisha B'Av. But if the matter pertains to [the health of] others, and others are concerned, it is obvious that he is required to clean his hands. [This is analogous to the case of] a completely healthy mother who does not have to eat on Yom Kippur but her baby will be in danger if he does not suckle from his mother. If the mother does not eat on Yom Kippur, she will not have enough milk for the baby. Therefore the mother is required to eat, even though she is healthy and is not in any danger, and so it is explained in the responsa of Rabbi Sofer. Even though a decision is made not by the ill person but by the parents, it is clear that it is necessary, for [we hold that] every ill person is not able to make a decision [because of his youth, in the case of circumcision, or because of his dotage, if he is in a coma]. Then it is understood that whoever is responsible for [the ill person's] health, whether parents for a baby, his wife or children for an elderly man in a coma, is the one responsible to make this decision.... It is clear that for a medical worker, like a physician or nurse, who is not concerned and relies upon "God protects the simple" [in personal behavior outside of medical work] but according to the rules of the hospital must clean his/her hands with disinfectant because of possible danger for all the other people who are there, it is certainly permitted [to wash] and [indeed] required to clean one's hands because of danger to others, analogous to [the ruling in] the responsa of Rabbi Sofer mentioned above regarding a lactating mother on Yom Kippur because of danger to a baby.[14]

Text 7.5. Barmash, "Ethics of Gathering When Not All of Us May Attend in Person"

COMMITTEE ON JEWISH LAW AND STANDARDS
OF THE RABBINICAL ASSEMBLY

In a responsum posted on July 22, 2020, Rabbi Pamela Barmash (see chapter 1) analyzes the particular challenge posed by the High Holy Days during the pandemic. As a highlight of the Jewish ritual year, how well a synagogue community feels about itself is often appraised by what transpires in the synagogue during the High Holy Days. Since Conservative/Masorti synagogue communities across the globe were experiencing the pandemic at different rates, Rabbi Barmash presents criteria for rabbis and lay leaders to consider in deciding how to celebrate the High Holy Days in their respective communities.

Once again, this is not considered an official CJLS responsum. Posting a responsum speedily was paramount, and in contrast to the usual extensive CJLS approval process, this responsum required and received approval on the authority of the CJLS committee co-chairs.

QUESTION

Rabbi Barmash presents the challenge:

> A quandary lies before us as rabbis, *hazzanim*, and lay leaders. Should our congregations offer in-person davenning for the High Holidays 5781/2020 when not all of us may attend in person? The transmission through aerosolization of COVID-19 means that physical distancing and risk will limit the number of people able to be present and that those at greater risk may be advised not to attend or even [be] forbidden from attending. This quandary applies in general, but the High Holidays 5781/2020 present a special challenge because of the sense that they are a high point of our spiritual year, the greater number of participants, and our intuition that through them, we can estimate how well our communities are doing, whether in terms of religious identity, spiritual fulfillment, or financial viability....
>
> The contexts in which we find ourselves as rabbis, *hazzanim*, and lay leaders are as diverse as we are. As a result, in deciding whether and how to hold in-person davenning for the High Holidays 5781/2020, the factors that need to be weighed, and the balance that will be struck, will vary considerably. Our congregations in the United States, Canada, Central and Latin America, Israel, Europe, Japan, Uganda, Australia, and elsewhere face different trajectories of COVID-19. The curve of infection and fatality due to COVID-19 has flattened in some areas and not

in others, and some localities with currently low rates are wary of a flare-up or have experienced a resurgence.

Rabbis and communities have chosen to remain offline or go online on Shabbat and *yom tov* and are thinking through what to do for the High Holidays. Some of us avoid technology and/or electricity on Shabbat and *yom tov*, and others of us feel we can make use of them in certain restricted ways during Shabbat and *yom tov*. . . .

Moreover, because medical science and guidelines are developing and changing, rabbis, hazzanim, and lay leaders are advised to consult with the congregation's medical advisors (medical scientists and medical doctors currently practicing medicine in appropriate specialties), as well as their national and local medical authorities, for guidance as it is updated and revised.

SECTION A: IS IT ETHICAL TO EXCLUDE?

She presents three questions to consider. The first addresses the ethics of holding communal prayer when some congregants would have to be excluded based on risk or limited seating capacity:

> Here are three questions with halakhic resources to help us navigate specific practical considerations:
>
> 1. *Is it ethical to open given the need to exclude based on risk or limited seating capacity?*
>
> The ethics of opening given the need to exclude some people demands balancing a number of factors.
>
> Among the values and factors to be considered:
>
> > a. Fulfilling the halakhic obligation to pray on the High Holy Days. One factor to be considered is the community's obligation to assist its members in fulfilling their prayer obligations on the High Holy Days.

    b. Fulfilling spiritual, emotional and communal needs on the High Holy Days. . . . For individuals these days nurture the work of teshuvah and character development, help people to repair damaged relationships, deepen the connection with God, inspire deeds of *gemilut ḥasadim* [kind deeds] and *tikkun olam* [perfecting the world]. . . . Communally, the High Holy Days reinforce Jewish identity and commitment and strengthen institutional ties and communal belonging.

    c. Honoring God through an assembly and *kevod habriyyot* [human dignity]. The principle of "when many people assemble together, a king is glorified" (Proverbs 14:28), that the glorification of God and our sense of divine presence are heightened when we are together as a community in prayer (Babylonian Talmud Berakhot 53a), and the principle of human dignity, that respect needs to be shown toward each and every person (Babylonian Talmud Berakhot 19b), are both at play in determining whether and how we resume davenning in person.

In weighing these factors, some of us may conclude that in-person services in which significant groups of people cannot attend are ethically impermissible. Options to fulfill prayer obligations while safeguarding life exist: by praying individually or creating a liturgical connection and/or Torah study through technology. . . .

Some of us—perhaps many of us—will extrapolate from the democracy and number of participants of the minyan that having smaller gatherings is appropriate, whether outdoors or indoors, even if not everyone can attend who would otherwise be able to as in previous years. Options do exist for us to safeguard life by physical distancing and other protective actions. Some communities may hold many small in-person gatherings, either simultaneously with different leadership, or shorter sequential services. If presence at those services is allocated among community members fairly (see below), this is an ethical option. Indeed, complete accessibility for everyone is a moving target....

Some communities may conclude that limited in-person davenning counted as a minyan, with live-stream or videoconferencing for everyone else, is the best way to fulfill everyone's obligations. This, too, is an ethical option, provided that the leadership makes an effort to ensure that neither the group watching by livestream, nor the group constituting the minyan in person, is offered a "second best" experience. Every effort should be made to create an experience that is equally engaging, inclusive, and inspiring for both groups.

Finally, for those communities offering virtual services as all or part of their High Holy Day worship, participants' financial means and technological skills (or the lack thereof) must also be considered.

SECTION B: HOW TO ALLOT FAIRLY

Rabbi Barmash addresses how to allot seats via lottery based on an early nineteenth-century precedent:

> If a congregation decides to open with limited in-person davenning, what is the most ethical way to assign limited spots when there are more people than places?
>
> A lottery was seen in biblical times as a fair way of distributing resources. The tribes are depicted as receiving their land through a lottery held at Shiloh by Joshua (Josh. 18:8–10; Num. 26:55–56)....
>
> In modernity, Rabbi Akiva Eiger [1761–1867, Germany] ... cognizant of physical distancing, advised Jewish communities to hold small minyanim during an epidemic and to use a lottery to distribute seats for the High Holidays:

It is true that gathering in a small space is inappropriate, but it is possible to pray in groups, each one very small, about 15 people. They should begin with the first light of day and then have another group, and each one should have a designated time to come pray there. The same for minhah . . . and they should be careful not to be crowded from the number mentioned above in coming to the synagogue.[15] . . .

In every synagogue, whether in the men's section or the women's section, it is permitted only to fill half of the seats on Rosh Hashanah and Yom Kippur, such that next to every person there will be an empty seat. Therefore, only half of the seats will be available on the High Holidays. Since everyone has equal right to a seat, half will get their seats on the two days of Rosh Hashanah and the other half will get their seat on Yom Kippur, day and night.[16]

Eiger also suggested that those invited to a particular service should receive a card in special shape and that only those who have the appropriate ticket for each day should be let in. Otherwise, he noted, those without invitations should pray in private house minyanim with physical distancing. (For his service during the 1831 epidemic, Eiger received a royal message of thanks from Frederick William III, the king of Prussia. . . .)

With the biblical and modern examples of lottery in mind, the most ethical way for us to assign seats is by having a lottery through which seats for in-person davenning is distributed to households, whether a household consists of one or many individuals. Each congregation is urged to figure out a fair way to allot seats by lottery, even if not everyone will receive the slot they wish. . . .

Clergy, *shelihei tzibbur*, Torah readers, and others with responsibilities for managing davenning may be excluded from the lottery since their presence is necessary. . . .

Because accessibility of services is sometimes a function of need rather than choice or preference, treating everyone equally does not necessarily mean treating everyone the same. For this reason, in determining who will attend which service, some provision ought to be made to accommodate individual needs. For example, services at night might be impossible for some people to attend for reasons of health, age, or care for young children. It would not be equitable for such people to be assigned Kol Nidrei by lottery; rather, effort should be made to match them with a service that would in fact be accessible to them. Similarly, in communities offering multiple simultaneous or sequential services, there would be an ethical obligation to structure some of those services in order to make them safer for those who wish to attend who have a disability.

SECTION C: THE DISABLED IN A TIME OF CRISIS

Rabbi Barmash addresses an often overlooked concern in times of crisis: access to communal worship for individuals with disabilities:

> The focus during this time of pandemic has been on those at greater risk for COVID-19. What about the general issue of inclusion for those of us with disability, whether of mobility, hearing, sight, or sensory processing, among other concerns?
>
> In this time of pandemic, we must continue to strive to be inclusive of all, not just those at risk of COVID-19. This issue for us is nuanced and multifaceted because inclusivity is not only an issue for the High Holidays 2020/5781 in a time of pandemic, nor is it just about those who are at greater risk of COVID-19....
>
> Issues of inclusion are as relevant in this unusual time as ever, and they should not be swept under the rug. For example:
>
> > a. A congregation meeting in person or online should provide for access, whether davenning on the usual synagogue premises or in private homes or backyards

or other places. For example, one backyard may be handicapped accessible while another is not, and our communal buildings are a mixed bag of accessibility.
b. As set forth above, a purely random lottery is not necessarily fair and may not meet everyone's needs.
c. If multiple in-person simultaneous or sequential services will be held, perhaps one or more of them should be specifically designed for those with [a] specific disability, whether of mobility, hearing, sight, or sensory processing (e.g. a service for those with mobility issues may have people stationed in certain spots to provide assistance)....

SECTION D: PLACING THESE ETHICAL CONSIDERATIONS IN A BROADER CONTEXT[17]

Rabbi Barmash concludes:

> Meaningful prayer and Torah study come in different forms. Our regular in-person davenning, for example, has options for those for whom the entire davenning is spiritually meaningful as well as those for whom a brief period is enough, and for those with varieties of spiritual needs in between. And there are options for those who want congregational singing, those who seek to listen to solo hazzanut, and those seeking a balance in varying degrees in between.
>
> One useful way of thinking is to conceive of our High Holiday davenning and Torah study as a retreat, with sessions in community and sessions in private, time slots in person, and time slots live streaming.[18]

Relationships with the Other   8

Since antiquity, Jews have molded their identity through a combination of relationships both within and outside the Jewish community. Often these relationships proved contentious.

Ancient Israelites, composed of different tribes and living in two kingdoms, north and south, had to integrate their differences to create communal identity. A similar challenge faces Jews today as different Jewish religious and ideological movements have developed in modern times.

Beyond their community, the Israelites' belief that their religion was distinct from the religions practiced around them presented them with a dilemma: what could they adopt and what did they have to reject as they interacted with other peoples? This challenge persists in modern times, and then some: as Jews participate more freely with others in multiple societies in which they reside, they have had to navigate their relationships with others in more complex ways.

The five responsa presented here address the interrelationships between Jews belonging to various streams of Judaism as well as their interactions with non-Jews. Rabbi Hayyim Eleazar Shapira, a prominent Hasidic rabbi in Hungary, refuses to participate in a public fast with other Jews in solidarity with German Jews as the Nazi regime begins to unleash atrocities upon them; instead, he vehemently criticizes them and other Jewish leaders. Rabbi Jehiel Jacob Weinberg (Orthodox) rules that Orthodox Jews should be buried eight cubits away from the grave of a person who converted under Reform auspices and vehemently urges Orthodox rabbis to oppose "the liberals." Rabbi Ḥayyim David Halevi (Orthodox) analyzes whether Transcendental Meditation is *avodah zarah* (idolatry), and Rabbis Liz P.G. Hirsch and Yael Rooks Rapport (Reform) do the same for yoga. Rabbi Reuven Hammer (Conservative) examines modern expressions of Jewish hatred and violence toward non-Jews.

Text 8.1. Shapira, "Engaging in a Public Fast in Sympathy with German Jews"

MINḤAT ELEAZAR, LIKUTIM, ORAḤ ḤAYYIM, NO. 36

A prominent leader among the Ultraorthodox rabbis of Hungary, Rabbi Hayyim Eleazar Shapira (known as the Munkáczer Rebbe, 1872–1937) exerted great influence upon them, even after Munkácz became part of Czechoslovakia after World War I.[1] He expressed harsh and acerbic criticism of other Jewish leaders and organizations, including the Belzer rebbe, another Hasidic rebbe who was forced to relocate to Munkácz due to the Russian invasion of Belz during World War I. Rabbi Shapira's followers were awed when his curse of the tzar during the High Holy Days in 1917 was followed by a coup and the execution of the tzar and his family. Similarly, his curse of the princes of the earth during the High Holy Days in 1918 was followed a few months later by the abdication of the kaiser and the Austro-Hungarian emperor. That his curse on the British Empire during the High Holy Days in 1919 did not have immediate results did not seem to affect his followers' steadfast loyalty to him.

Rabbi Shapira staunchly followed the viewpoint of Rabbi Moses Sofer (see chapter 2), opposing any and all innovation in Jewish life, whether in education, culture, medicine, or technology. Strongly anti-Zionist, he rejected the British government's 1917 Balfour Declaration, maintaining that only a miraculous redemption would permit Jews to resettle the Land of Israel. He opposed the migration of European Jews to America and warned those who immigrated to the Land of Israel that they would die a violent death. He authored over twenty volumes, including five volumes of responsa, *Minḥat Eleazar* (The afternoon offering of Eleazar).

Following a Nazi boycott of Jewish businesses on April 1, 1933, Rabbi Shapira was asked to sign a proclamation endorsing a public fast on an agreed-upon day for all Jews worldwide in solidarity with German Jews. In a brief responsum, he rejects that request with harsh and strident language.

SECTION A: THE TRUE REASON FOR TRIBULATION[2]

Rabbi Shapira strongly rebukes Jews for failing to comprehend that Nazi persecution is merely a part of the global calamities and upheavals that will usher in the Messianic Age. He also harshly criticizes other Jewish leaders, including other Hasidic leaders, as accomplices of the demonic world:

> About your requesting my consent to ordain a public fast on account of the murders and oppression that have occurred to our fellow Jews in Germany due to our many sins.... [Our fellow Jews'] thoughts have until now been confused. They have yet to see the truth, for I think the war is just the period of tribulation preceding the coming of the Messiah: when Jews return to God [by observing the commandments], [only] then we will be redeemed through the coming of the righteous Messiah, may it soon be in our days....
>
> However, the legions of the *siṭra aḥra* [the realm of evil], including the hypocritical leaders, among them many Hasidic rebbes ... have led all Israel astray. For their main action is just to pray for the welfare of the nations and other foolishness. They have turned the things upside down, as in the destruction of Sodom and Gomorrah, but [in their case] against the Torah. They flatter [the non-Jews], give them large amounts

RELATIONSHIPS WITH THE OTHER 231

of money, etc. At the same time, I have cried aloud at the risk of my life from the day the war began until now—every day is worse than the previous day—that their despicable peace... will be worse for all Israel, especially for [observant Jews] than the war in every way.

SECTION B: NO FAST IN SOLIDARITY WITH SINNERS

Dismissing other Jews with even greater disdain,[3] Rabbi Shapira renounces any solidarity with German Jews, whose stores have generally been open on Shabbat and now are forced to close during the week. He urges them to repent, but he doubts they will:

> I thought that when [the Nazis] imposed the boycott in Germany against Jewish businesses, this was definitely not a reason to authorize a fast because the overwhelming majority of [the Jews] in Germany violate the Sabbath publicly [by keeping their stores open] on the Sabbath. They are now being paid back measure for measure [through] the closing of their stores for the rest of the week! If the German Jews do not repent for their sin of violating the Sabbath, how can we reinforce their practice of profaning the Sabbath [through authorizing a public fast]? It is better to warn our fellow Jews from the beginning, for even though they have sinned, they will see and understand that it is the finger of God[4] [punishing them] for violating the Sabbath, and they will return to God by closing their stores and ceasing from their work on the Sabbath. Then we will pray for them and authorize a public fast for their rescue and welfare together with all Israel....
>
> I cannot agree to sign my name to this proclamation. For who would agree [to join in this fast] in this generation of apostasy? Will the Zionists, the adherents of Mizrahi,[5] the members of Agudat Yisrael,[6] and the like, return to God and Judaism?

SECTION C: MOST OF THOSE WHO FAST MUST BE RIGHTEOUS

Rabbi Shapira cites the talmudic ruling that sinners must participate in a public fast, a ruling that may signify that the German Jews whom he criticizes for violating the Sabbath are worthy of a public fast, but then adduces the opinion of the Maharsha (Rabbi Samuel Eidels, 1555–1631, Poland), who limits their number to a tenth of those fasting:

> Our sages say in the Babylonian Talmud *Keritot* 6b: Any fast that does not include the participation of the sinners of the Jewish people is not a fast.
>
> They learned this from the galbanum [a substance whose smell is foul and which was one of the ingredients of] the incense [in the Temple]. This means that the sinners may comprise only 1/10 [of those who fast], as understood by the Maharsha in *Hiddushei Aggadot*, [who taught] that the essential matter is that ten righteous [Jews participate in the fast], then they combine with the eleventh part [the sinners], as in [the addition of] the galbanum [to the incense]. It also appears that the Maharsha means sinners who have not separated from the way of life of [their] community. . . . But our situation does not warrant a worldwide fast, for those wicked Jews [in Germany] are nearly as numerous as we are, and almost all of them separate themselves from the [Orthodox] community's way of life.

PESAK DIN

Since he deems the majority of German Jews to be sinners, he concludes:

> Therefore it is definitely not appropriate, in my humble opinion, to authorize a general worldwide public fast. May God have mercy on the remnant of His people with salvation and redemption.[7]

Text 8.2. Weinberg, "On the Burial of a Person Converted by Liberal Rabbis"[8]

SERIDEI ESH, 3, NO. 100 (NEW EDITION 2, NO. 99)

Born to a humble family in a midsized town in Poland, Rabbi Jehiel Jacob Weinberg (1884–1966) received his education at the Slobodka Yeshiva. Its emphasis on the study of both *musar* (Jewish ethical teachings) and Talmud made a profound impact upon him.[9] He went on to study at the Mir Yeshiva and also read the secular Hebrew literature of the Haskalah. In order to be appointed in his first job as rabbi, he agreed to marry the sixteen-year-old daughter of the deceased rabbi, a relationship that contributed to an unhappiness that pervaded him for the rest of his life. During a trip to Germany at the onset of World War I, he remained there, unable to return to Lithuania. Rabbi Abraham Isaac Kook (later the first Ashkenazic chief rabbi in Israel), attending a convention in Germany at the time, connected with him and proceeded to help him financially and personally. He gradually became enamored with Modern Orthodox Jewish culture and went on to earn a PhD at the University of Giessen, studying with the renowned Christian scholar of the Bible and Semitic languages Paul Kahle. In 1924 he was appointed to the faculty of the Orthodox Rabbiner-Seminar in Berlin and thrived in his position there until Kristallnacht triggered a mental breakdown. He survived the war in a detention camp in Germany. His biographers deem his final decades as tragic: the culture in which he had flourished, German Orthodoxy of the early twentieth century, no longer existed, and he lived in a small town in Switzerland with few Jewish residents.

Most of Rabbi Weinberg's responsa along with his doctoral dissertation and three book manuscripts were lost when he left Germany. He reconstructed them, assisted by students and rabbinic colleagues, and added new ones written after the war, publishing them in volumes entitled *Seridei esh* (The remnants saved from the fire).

Here in a brief responsum he addresses a question from Rabbi Max Warschawski, a rabbi in Strasbourg, about the potential burial of a female convert by Reform auspices in a Jewish cemetery. He heaps scorn upon conversions conducted by liberal rabbis, whom he does not consider to be rabbis and therefore never refers to them as such; instead he calls them "the liberals" and insists that all Orthodox rabbis take a resolute stance against them. In his use of militaristic language and emphasis on a sharp distinction between Orthodox and Reform Jews, he aligns himself with an early nineteenth-century movement to delegitimize non-Orthodox Judaism.

QUESTION

Rabbi Weinberg considers:

> Is it permissible to bury a female convert who was converted by the liberals in a Jewish cemetery?

SECTION A: DISTANCING A GRAVE FROM THOSE CONVERTED UNDER LIBERAL AUSPICES[10]

Rabbi Weinberg draws an analogy between individuals converted under the auspices of "the liberals" and those whose conversion process is incomplete or those whose mother is Jewish but whose father is not:

> This question has already been brought in the writings of the *aharonim* [the rabbinic authorities of recent centuries]. They speak of a conversion that is incomplete, such as a boy who was circumcised and not immersed [in a *mikveh*], or the son of Jewish woman whose father is a gentile, [in whose case] although the law is that he is a Jew, several *rishonim* [medieval

rabbinic authorities] rule that he requires conversion. While it is permissible to bury him in a Jewish cemetery, it is nevertheless necessary to distance his grave eight cubits from that of other Jewish graves. See . . . [Rabbi Gedalia Felder, 1921/2–91, Canada], *Naḥalat Tzvi*, 138.

About a conversion conducted by [the liberals], the opinion of Rabbi Moses Feinstein in *Iggerot Moshe*, Yoreh De'ah 1:160, is that the conversion is nothing, as [those performing conversions] are not scrupulous in insisting upon "the acceptance of the commandments" or upon [the requirement] that immersion [in a *mikveh*] be during the day and before three [witnesses]. At the end of his responsum, [he ruled that] that it was necessary to distance [the person] eight cubits [from other Jews], and [if this ruling] would erupt into a major controversy when it is possible that the community would not heed him, then one is not obligated to engage in an argument. He only needs to warn God-fearing Jews [in his opinion, only Orthodox Jews] to distance [their graves] eight cubits from these false converts.

Indeed, I know that in a community like that of greater Strasbourg, where the great majority [of Jews] are secular, [such a stance] on this matter would stir up a major controversy. Nevertheless, my opinion is that you should stand in the breach[11] and propose that converts of this type, who were converted by the liberals, be buried in a special row, eight cubits distant from the graves of proper Jews.

SECTION B: IF THERE IS EVEN A MODEST DOUBT
ABOUT A CONVERT, DISTANCING IS REQUIRED

Rabbi Weinberg mentions that a number of liberal officiants at conversions in Germany fulfill the requirements that Rabbi Feinstein assumed they would not, but he casts doubt on those conversions anyway:

In Germany, there were several liberal [officiants] who were scrupulous to perform conversions in a halakhically correct manner [with] acceptance of the commandments and immersion before [a *beit din* of] three, and it is possible that there are liberals in France [where Strasbourg is located] who act in this way. Even so, it remains doubtful that the conversions were conducted in accord with Torah law.... The *aharonim* decided that if there was a doubt as to whether a conversion was conducted in accord with Torah law, then it is permissible to bury [such a convert] in a Jewish cemetery but distancing [from the graves of proper Jews] is required.

PESAK DIN

Rabbi Weinberg concludes:

This is a completely unpleasant assignment. However, in our generation, it is impossible to sustain Judaism except through war and stoutheartedness. There are boundaries that one cannot transgress with indifference. Conversion conducted by the liberals is truly only a joke lacking any meaning, and it elicits scorn from the best of Christians. One who marries a convert of this type knows in his soul that his deed throws dirt in the eyes of his fellow creatures.[12]

Text 8.3. Halevi, "Transcendental Meditation"

ASEH LEKHA RAV, 2, NO. 47

On his call-in radio show, Rabbi Ḥayyim David Halevi (see chapter 2) is asked by a yeshiva student whether halakhah permits Transcendental Meditation (TM). His subsequent responsum explains if any aspects of TM are permitted.

QUESTION

Rabbi Halevi explains why he is examining this question:

> Recently articles were published in newspapers describing the benefits of Transcendental Meditation, a practical technique for relaxing psychological tension.... Whether this matter is forbidden according to halakhah was asked to me [by a yeshiva student] during my call-in radio program *Aseh lekha rav*, "Select for yourself a rabbi."[13]

SECTION A: THE RITUAL

Rabbi Halevi deems the initiation ritual of Transcendental Meditation to be *avodah zarah* (the worship of polytheistic deities, considered to be idolatry and contrary to the monotheistic worship of God in Judaism) but starts to develop an argument that will eventually lead to a different conclusion about other aspects of Transcendental Meditation. He presents a distinction between religious actions and non-religious ones: religious actions have no logic to them, whereas non-religious ones make sense. Whether that is the case is debatable; his example of blowing the shofar on Rosh Hashanah as having no meaning except for divine command seems to be contradicted by the many reasons offered in Jewish tradition for it (or perhaps the many reasons show that no one is sure of the real reason the shofar is blown!):

> First, we must clarify the true nature of [the initiation ceremony and the mantra].... One student recounts the ritual: "I approached the reception room and brought with me six flowers, three ripe sweet fruits, and a new unwashed white cloth, with everything arranged on a platter. I entered the private chamber and presented the platter to the teacher. The teacher arranged the presentation on a table before the picture

of Guru Dev. On the table candles were lit, and there was a small bowl with incense and a few other things, like salt and rice. The teacher prayed in Sanskrit about eight minutes, during which he bowed toward the picture and lit the incense in the small bowl, while scattering rice grains and salt near the picture. Finally he turned to the student, whispering to him [the mantra], requiring him not to reveal the incantation word. He had him sit on a chair, secluding himself for the first time with the word that has been transmitted to him...."

In my opinion, there is enough in these things to definitely forbid Transcendental Meditation. For it is clear that any distinctly human-centered action is based on the tenets of logic and has an explanation and meaning. In contrast, any action that has no meaning or logic originates without doubt in religious faith, [such as]—to make a distinction [between two very different matters]—the blowing of the shofar on Rosh Hashanah, which is a religious mitzvah, whose origin is in a divine command for which we have no explanation. The flowers and fruit presented on a new cloth that has never been washed, ... the prayer ... in a language that the student does not understand, the lit candles opposite a particular picture, and especially the incense burned during the prayer—there is no doubt that these actions have no meaning or logic but whose source is religious faith deriving from *avodah zarah* that was practiced in the past and is still partially practiced till today in the Far East, from where Transcendental Meditation originates....

It is clear without any doubt that this is a traditional ceremony ... that contains remnants of ancient worship that is completely tied into the worship of the gods. Therefore since [the initiation ritual contains] remnants of worship that is *avodah zarah*, all of the ceremony mentioned above is completely forbidden.

SECTION B: THE MANTRA

Rabbi Halevi argues that since a mantra is derived from prayer or is the name of a polytheistic god, it is forbidden to use one. However, he notes that scientists believe that other words can be used in place of the mantras employed in Transcendental Meditation to achieve the same goals of releasing the mind from stress:

> The mantra, an incantation word for meditation that is repeated twice a day for twenty minutes, is an issue of itself.... One expert with whom I discussed [this matter] explained that [mantras] have much meaning and are anchored in divine terms and are repeated both in meditation and in prayer.... Another expert found in an encyclopedia that every mantra is the name of a god. Therefore, these [mantras] ... are certainly forbidden in daily repetition. An explicit biblical verse, Exodus 23:13, [states], "The names of other gods you shall not mention; they shall not be heard on your lips."... [Rabbi Joseph Caro] made in the Shulḥan Arukh a clear-cut ruling: "It is forbidden to mention [the names of the gods] whether for a good reason or not" (*Yoreh De'ah* 147:1).
>
> Furthermore, it is unquestionable that there is no need for those specific [mantras] in order to achieve the technical outcome of meditation. Many scientists have expressed their opinion that any use of a particular note or word with a certain monotone rhythm is able to achieve the same results. If so, the question must be asked, why were these words necessarily taken from the conceptual world of *avodah zarah*? ... There is no doubt that the intention was to use the name of the gods in order to induce this technical result out of honoring [the gods] or that the ancient world truly believed that these outcomes were achieved through the power of those gods whose names were uttered.

SECTION C: THE ORIGINS OF THE GODS OF MEDITATION

Rabbi Halevi analyzes whether the religious aspects of Transcendental Meditation are forbidden:

> The roots of this technique are in antiquity.... Maharishi received the knowledge of this technique from his teacher, Guru Dev. The tradition of monks tells that twenty-five hundred years ago a learned genius revived this very ancient wisdom (H. H. Bloomfield, *Transcendental Meditation*, 72).... It is very clear that a tradition preserved by monks in the ancient world is entirely based on religious values. There is no doubt that all the technique of meditation is accompanied by the names, symbols, and worship taken from the false belief of the *avodah zarah* of ancient India. Is it not true that until this very day India is full of *avodah zarah* with [an abundance of] evidence? Therefore, it is clear above all doubt that the worship that accompanies [Transcendental] Meditation originates in *avodah zarah* and is completely forbidden.

SECTION D: THE PURPOSE OF MEDITATION

Rabbi Halevi explains the purpose of Transcendental Meditation:

> What does the person who meditates achieve?.... The Maharishi explains that the source of thought is in the most tranquil depths of awareness.... The one who meditates allows his listening to dive deep from the active level of his awareness into the tranquil depths of consciousness ... in order to sever gently the consciousness from intellectual activity that burdens it normally ... so that finally his consciousness completely settles and without any effort is beyond any thought and merits pure consciousness.
>
> Let us translate this complicated technique into simple language. At first they try to concentrate thought into a single

point lacking meaning, a mantra. Through this, they empty the vessels of thought from routine day-to-day problems by forgetting everything that surrounds a human being. Finally, they reach the depths of the awareness of tranquility.

SECTION E: JEWISH PRAYER AND MEDITATION

Rabbi Halevi contrasts Transcendental Meditation with Jewish prayer, prayer that seeks the same goal of release from the tumult of everyday life by filling a person with holiness. Focusing on the tranquility of the Sabbath and its activities, even offering grudging leeway for reading the literary section of a newspaper during Shabbat, he wonders why Jews, especially yeshiva students, are ignoring the Jewish meditative practices of prayer and Shabbat:

> The inner life of a human being is positive: it is a divine creation. The negative, which is the externality of a person, comes in when a person enters the world. . . . Therefore, just as a person can concentrate to forget everything that surrounds him, all the evil that encircles him . . . as he settles internally into the goodness of his soul and, therefore, feels sweetness—that is a pleasant experience. And just as one does this twice a day . . . one may achieve positive results. Therefore, I answered the question of that yeshiva student [as follows]: in and of itself, this technique is not forbidden, if one does it without the initiation, the ritual, and the mantra, if one can find for oneself an incantation word of some form or just concentrate in quietness. But a Jew does not need meditation in order to achieve the yearned-for tranquility. The mitzvot of the Torah affect a person just like the meditation described above very effectively. The first prayer of a person every morning is:
>
>> My God, the soul You have placed in me is pure,
>> You created it,
>> You formed it,

> You breathed it into me....
> As long as the soul is within me, I thank You....
> Blessed are You, who restores the soul to the lifeless form.

This opening prayer, entering the very depths of a person ... achieves concentration of thought ... The same prayer casts aside materiality ... and the routine thoughts of every day, just as [Rabbi Joseph Caro wrote in] the Shulḥan Arukh, Laws of Prayer, *Oraḥ Ḥayyim* 98:1:

> The one who prays must remove distracting thoughts until his thoughts and attention merit prayer.... Pious ones and the men of action used to seclude themselves and concentrate in prayer until they could remove [the imperfections of] materiality and strengthen the power of the intellect. Then, they could draw close to the exalted level of prophecy. And if another [extraneous] thought came upon them in the midst of prayer, they would be quiet until the thought dissipated.

1) If a person can focus in his prayer properly, he will arrive at the final level that meditation, so it seems, is supposed to bring him, going deep into the depths of consciousness, the innermost part of the soul, the purity and beauty of creation that the Holy One breathes into human beings....

2) How great is the difference between prayer, Jewish meditation, to the technique of Transcendental Meditation. The latter seeks to empty a human being from his thoughts, the routine of every day ... that is, emptiness within emptiness. But Judaism achieving the same goal, emptying a human being from the thoughts that trouble him but in such a manner filling him with feelings of holiness of divine reality by turning toward God, not concentrating toward emptiness but concentrating full of the essence of holiness, just as David, the sweet singer of Israel [said], "As for me, nearness to God is good" (Ps. 73:28).

And if this were not enough, when Shabbat comes, so does tranquility. The Shabbat of a Jew who observes the Torah and mitzvot is a type of meditation that continues for an entire day (and) for which there is none other better than it. This is not the place to describe the greatness of Shabbat and the depth of its importance, but it is clear that a Jew who observes the Torah and mitzvot lets go completely of everything [stressful]. . . . The Shabbat is another world, a world that is entirely good, that is entirely repose and calm. [The Jew who observes Shabbat] engages in the pleasant prayers of Shabbat, the delicious meals of Shabbat, in studying the [Torah] and commentators, or in a section of the Talmud, all of which together are a world that is entirely good. And even reading the literary section of a respectable paper, perhaps not so desirable in and of itself on Shabbat, still preserves the tranquility of the soul and complete repose. This is wonderful meditation. Not the emptiness of a mantra lacking meaning, but a world that is all beauty and purity, a world that is all Shabbat and repose, that only those who observe Shabbat and sanctify the Sabbath day sense it in all its beauty and glory. They achieve disengagement from the stress that is borne all the days of the week, deep concentration in the spiritual world, tranquility, and calm. Do Jews who observe the mitzvot, and all the more so, yeshiva students who are busy in [the study of] Torah, need Transcendental Meditation? It is unfortunate that our generation abandons all the beauty and wonder of God's Torah with its system of eternal values in order to dig leaky wells that will not hold water.[14]

PESAK DIN

Rabbi Halevi concludes:

The initiation ritual of transcendental meditation as well as the mantra . . . have clear signs of *avodah zarah* and are completely and totally forbidden. The technique of Transcendental Meditation of itself is not forbidden if a person uses it without the ritual mentioned above and without the supervision of those teachers. A Jew who observes Torah and mitzvot does not feel a need for Transcendental Meditation. A Jew who feels emptiness in his life and the need for calm and tranquility will find it when he returns to Jewish values in sincere repentance [*teshuvah*] by [living a life of] Torah and mitzvot.[15]

Text 8.4. Hirsch and Rapport, "Yoga as a Jewish Worship Practice: *Chukat Hagoyim* or Spiritual Innovation?"

CCAR JOURNAL: A REFORM JEWISH
QUARTERLY, SPRING 2020

Rabbi Liz P.G. Hirsch serves Temple Anshe Amunim, Pittsfield, Massachusetts. She completed her undergraduate education at Brown University and was ordained by the Reform seminary Hebrew Union College–Jewish Institute of Religion (HUC-JIR) with a Wexner Graduate Fellowship and Tisch Fellowship. She is also the founding co-chair of the Religious Action Center of Massachusetts and was a key leader in the 2020 campaign to pass the ROE Act safeguarding reproductive rights in Massachusetts. She writes frequently for the CCAR *Journal* and other publications.

Rabbi Yael Rooks Rapport is director of the Gottesman Center for Jewish Living at the Marlene Meyerson JCC of Manhattan. She graduated from Brandeis University, received ordination from HUC-JIR, and became certified as a yoga teacher through Yoga Vida NYC. She served as a chaplain resident at Mount Sinai Beth Israel and as a rabbi at New York's Congregation Beit Simchat Torah, the largest LGBTQ+ synagogue in the world, where she created the Yoga/Meditation Minyan. Rabbi Rapport contributes articles to major Jewish publications and practices and teaches yoga.

Just as Rabbi Halevi analyzed whether and which aspects of Transcendental Meditation are acceptable halakhically, so too Rabbis

Hirsch and Rapport address the issue of whether yoga is permissible. But they emphasize their own dilemma in doing and teaching yoga, a non-Jewish ritual practice.

QUESTION

Rabbis Hirsch and Rapport frame their questions:

> As two rabbis who are quite public about the importance of our own personal yoga practice and who sought to adapt it into worship modes for our communities, we initially struggled to determine our level of comfort promoting and participating in a spiritual system that is appropriated or borrowed originally from a non-Jewish source. We wondered, can we create a yoga practice that is also a Jewish practice? What might we learn from halakhah as we seek to integrate spiritual practices from outside of Jewish tradition? Should yoga by Jewish practitioners only be approached in its physical but not its spiritual aspects? ... Finally, how as Jews and how as rabbis would we integrate yoga and prayer in a way that is holistic, current, halakhically sound, and intellectually honest about its strengths and limitations?

SECTION A: THE CHALLENGE OF NON-JEWISH PRACTICES

Setting the bases for their analysis, Rabbis Hirsch and Rapport cite biblical and halakhic prohibition against following non-Jewish ways and highlight Jewish communities' struggles in adopting and rejecting non-Jewish practices:

> Our starting point, which provided both a resonant halakhic super-structure as well as a breadth and depth of interpretations and commentaries across Jewish sources, was the biblical edict ... against following non-Jewish practices. Leviticus 18:3

reads, "As is done of the land of Egypt, where you dwelt, you shall not do; and after the doings of the land of Canaan, where I will bring you, you shall not do; you shall not walk in their ways." ... This remains a relevant red-line in the Reform Movement; authors of a CCAR responsum ... from 1991 address this legal stricture ... :

> The biblical phrase, "you shall not walk in their ways" was understood as one of the negative commandments and was seen to reinforce the distinctiveness and separateness of the Jews, who are set apart from the nations (Leviticus 20:26): "And you shall be holy unto Me; for I the Eternal am holy, and have set you apart from the peoples, that you should be Mine." While the principle of the prohibition was never in doubt, it was understood that it had limits, but just what these were was a subject of frequent debate. ...

Stretching across time and throughout the Jewish world, communities have struggled with and sometimes adopted practices of their cultural context to their Jewish practice. Proponents of such incorporation hail them as innovations; detractors describe them as assimilation or heresy.

SECTION B: STRATEGIES FOR ABSORBING NON-JEWISH PRACTICES

Rabbis Hirsch and Rapport employ the distinction made by an academic scholar between nativizing a non-Jewish practice by identifying as a Jewish practice as well and neutralizing a non-Jewish practice by deeming it non-religious. Claims that yoga practice is Jewish in origin are disingenuous; even though medieval Jewish mystics did use chant and motion in their prayers, contemporary Jews are basing their use of chant and motion on yoga, not on medieval Jewish practice:

Throughout Jewish history, we observe two main strategies that Beth A. Berkowitz... in her book *Defining Jewish Difference* categorizes [as "nativization" and "neutralization"] based on two separate episodes in the Babylonian Talmud that describe two different viewpoints on the practice of burning funeral pyres at the death of an Israelite king.... [Babylonian] Talmud, at Sanhedrin 52b, employs the strategy of "nativization."... When faced with the prevalence of what is considered an "outside practice"... this talmudic *sugya* puts forward the etiology of the practice as an inherently Jewish one by connecting it to a reference in... Jeremiah... making this a "native" Jewish practice. The Talmud does not attempt to deny that funeral pyres are *also* an outside practice; rather, its primary objective is to create convincing "concentric circles, so that the practice can remain a part of both cultural clusters."

As Berkowitz categorizes it, a "nativized" approach to yoga would be to prove that its etiology is inherent to Jewish cultural practice. The benefits that many practitioners derive from yoga can be traced to the physical, mental, and spiritual well-being that come from its system of flexibility in stretching and holding postures, its concentrated attention on breath control, and its meditative approach to mindfulness and feeling present in the current moment, rather than being focused on past or future. These practices at their core are quite universal in nature.... The medieval mystics... were in the habit of accompanying their traditional prayers with chant and motion. However, if we designate the core benefits and approaches of yoga as *exclusively* "native" to Judaism, we would be guilty of not giving credit where it is due. Our ancient mystics and modern congregants do find that these practices enhance their enjoyment and engagement in Judaism, but when we are honest with ourselves, we cannot purport that our inspiration for this current type of exercise and worship comes straight from [Jewish mystics]....

As progressive Jews, we recognize and celebrate that no one person or institution has a complete monopoly on truth, and that beauty and meaning can come from many different sources to enrich understanding and experience. Therefore, we do not recommend adopting a completely nativized approach.... It is only appropriate and respectful to give credit... to those from whom we draw inspiration....

The second strategy employed by the Talmud in response to the widespread practice of burning funeral pyres [views them] as "neutralization." At [Babylonian Talmud] Avodah Zarah 11a, the rabbis do not consider the practice of funeral pyres to be a... gentile practice that is explicitly religious...:

> Everyone agrees that the public burning itself is not an idolatrous custom. It is performed due to the great importance of the king who passed away....

Therefore, we understand public burning of funeral pyres to be a permitted cultural practice for Jewish funerals, despite the fact that gentiles *also* light funeral pyres.... The Sanhedrin *sugya* claims that burning is a Torah practice but does not deny that it is also a gentile practice. The Avodah Zarah *sugya*, on the other hand, negates the presence of its religious, and therefore idolatrous, intent, demonstrating the effectiveness of the neutralization strategy in this particular example.

SECTION C: TRADITIONAL CRITERIA FOR PERMITTING
NON-JEWISH PRACTICE INTO JEWISH ONES

It would seem that the two rabbis are going to advocate on behalf of neutralizing a non-Jewish practice by deeming it non-religious. But before they do so, they present the traditional criteria of Rabbi Moses Isserles for determining whether a non-Jewish practice is acceptable or not and concur with his criteria as applicable to yoga, although they leave it to the reader to reflect on how these criteria apply:

In his glosses to Rabbi Joseph Caro's *Shulchan Aruch*, Rabbi Moses Isserles ... establishes three qualifications for acceptable gentile practices that are allowed ... into Jewish practice: (1) those that are not done for the sake of licentiousness ... ; (2) those that are done for a useful purpose, such as identifying a doctor by his garb; or (3) those that are done out of respect, such as burning a fire for a deceased king. We value and concur with these principles today. ... We see his parameters as an historic and helpful set of boundaries ... that can help to focus respect for both Judaism and for the non-Jewish culture from which we borrow this yoga practice.

SECTION D: MODERN YOGA

Rabbis Hirsch and Rapport call attention to the historical setting popularizing yoga practice. Yoga emerged as a homegrown form of local resistance to oppression when the British occupied India. The rabbis urge Jewish practitioners of yoga to be sensitive to how this history resonates with Jewish history:

> Since our earliest days as a people, we Jews have faced the question of how to meaningfully and authentically process outside cultural influence. Some of these outside practices were reviled and decried, but some of them were integrated by these means of nativization or neutralization. ... However, with yoga specifically, we feel particularly conscious of the dynamics of the identity politics at play. ...
>
> We encourage every practitioner of yoga, Jewish or not, to take responsibility as an admirer or consumer and learn more about the fullness of its roots and history. What we typically think of as yoga was only one part of a substantial Eastern Ayurvedic system that encompassed many streams of practice as it was originally conceived. The pathway of *asana*, the physical component in which the practitioner holds postural poses, is the

most widely practiced in our North American context, sometimes in concert with *dhyana*, the pathway of meditation.... Our modern posturally-centered yoga practice, with its focus on health benefits rather than metaphysical attainments, bears little resemblance to the 5,000 year old system from which it was derived. It retains the clear imprints of a major cultural shift that occurred in India with the rise of British imperialism a mere hundred years ago, where it gained widespread popularity as a resistance movement. Where Western colonial definitions of power determined the ideal to be those who could exert the maximum amount of external force, as in the military subjugation of an entire people, yoga practice was a home-grown movement, emphasizing internal power through awareness, integration, flexibility, and self control.... We must empathize with an ancient system of belief that has been marginalized by an oppressive majority culture. The story of yoga and the story of Judaism share many common themes.

PESAK DIN

Rabbis Hirsch and Rapport conclude:

> We are supportive of the thoughtful and intentional inclusion of yoga-inspired *asana* practice within a Jewish framework.... We invite and celebrate incorporating [it] into Jewish worship within these respectful boundaries proposed by Isserles...: (1) examine your intention: does your practice have a stated thoughtful aim and *kavannah*?; (2) is it done for a "useful purpose," in an accessible way that brings others towards greater engagement and fulfillment?; and (3) is it done out of respect, with transparency and credit offered to the teachers ancient and new who have influenced it and you as the next generation of teacher and leader?[16]

Text 8.5. Hammer, "The Status of Non-Jews in Jewish Law and Lore Today"

COMMITTEE ON JEWISH LAW AND STANDARDS OF THE RABBINICAL ASSEMBLY, ḤOSHEN MISHPAṬ 359:1.2016

Rabbi Reuven Hammer (1933–2019), born in Syracuse, New York, graduated from Yeshiva University and went on to receive rabbinic ordination from the Jewish Theological Seminary (JTS) and a PhD in special education from Northwestern University. After a tour of duty as a United States Air Force chaplain, he served congregations in Denver, Akron, and the Chicago suburb of Wilmette. Making *aliyah* with his family in 1973, he worked in special education, establishing the first diagnostic clinic in Israel at David Yellen College and serving as an advisor to the Ministry of Education. He was instrumental in founding institutions of Conservative/Masorti Judaism in Israel, including the Schechter Institute of Jewish Studies, where he served as founding director and taught rabbinics. For eighteen years he headed JTS's Israel programs in Jerusalem.

He also served on the Va'ad Halakhah for Conservative/Masorti Judaism, as a member of the Committee on Jewish Law and Standards, and as the head of the Conservative/Masorti Beit Din for conversion in Israel. He was a prolific author of both scholarly and more popular works. In his responsa, he sought to probe deeply into Jewish tradition and highlight how its values remain eternally fruitful in finding solutions to contemporary questions.

In a *teshuvah* approved by the Committee on Jewish Law and Standards in 2016, Rabbi Hammer addresses how Jews ought to respond to extremist rabbis' vitriolic teachings about non-Jews.

QUESTION

Rabbi Hammer formulates his question:

What is the status of gentiles in Jewish law today? How should we deal with statements in traditional Jewish literature that are negative or discriminatory regarding non-Jews?

SECTION A: BACKGROUND

Rabbi Hammer starts by articulating that Jewish tradition contains both positive and negative appraisals of non-Jews. He emphasizes the importance of acknowledging and intentionally discerning which aspects of the tradition to accept and which to disregard, especially when modern extremists advocating for very negative beliefs about non-Jews also support attacking and killing them *ab initio*:

> The Torah [and rabbinic literature] teach the equality of all human beings created in the image of God and is positive toward non-Israelites.... Nevertheless it cannot be denied that there are passages in rabbinic literature, kabbalah and medieval philosophical works that depict Gentiles in negative terms....
>
> Dealing with discriminatory laws and negative texts when teaching our tradition to youth and adults can be problematic.... Unfortunately in Israel, an extremely serious situation has arisen in recent times because of the publication of radical books ... lauded by a small number of well-known extremist rabbis in which non-Jews are depicted as being of a lesser species than Jews and in which slaying Arabs, including young children, is deemed permissible and even commanded. The so-called halakhic positions of these rabbis have influenced fanatical groups of extremists and have led to acts of destruction, injury and death.... For the first time in thousands of years, a Jewish state governs the lives of non-Jews. Jews constitute the majority and must deal with the status of the non-Jewish minority. Even though [halakhah] is not the civil law of Israel, it is influential.... What was once a theoretical problem or a merely a matter of

embarrassment has now become a practical matter of great importance.

It will be necessary to deal honestly with the sources, to admit that different attitudes existed over the course of the development of Judaism and to candidly criticize and reject certain parts of the tradition while embracing others as representing ... the true core of Jewish belief.... Our movement is uniquely qualified to understand that both laws and concepts change in accord with differing times and conditions.... It is our responsibility to define what is appropriate for us in our time, basing it upon those teachings within the tradition that represent the highest ideals of Judaism.

SECTION B: NON-JEWS IN SCRIPTURE

Rabbi Hammer emphasizes the Bible's teachings on human equality: all human beings are created in the image of God, righteous non-Jews merit praise, and sinful human beings, whether Israelite or not, draw criticism. The laws about fighting the Canaanites applied only to the period of the Israelite conquest of the Land of Israel and cannot be used to justify attacks on non-Jews today:

> The Torah's attitude toward non-Israelites is overwhelmingly positive ... based on the concept that all human beings are created in the image of the Divine. The verses of the Torah that form the very basis of its attitude toward humanity as a whole are found in the stories of the creation of human beings.... These verses ... designate humans as ... created in the image of God and ... depict the creation of humans as the pinnacle of creation (Gen. 5:1–2).... No differentiation is made among groups of human beings....
>
> Since there is a basic equality among all humans ... it is not surprising that non-Israelites are depicted in biblical books as moral and God-fearing.... Noah is a righteous man (Gen.

6:8–9).... Job, not an Israelite, is called "blameless and upright; he feared God and shunned evil" (Job 1:1).... That some [of the other nations] are depicted as evil does not diminish their humanity.... Israelites are also frequently depicted as sinners....

In what way then, are Israelites differentiated from others? ... [In] the Covenant at Sinai ... they take upon themselves the task of being God's holy people, a priestly people who will therefore be devoted to and minister to the one true God and demonstrate God's ways to the entire world (Exod. 19:5).... Israel is not depicted as superior to [other nations] nor is it to rule over them (Deut. 9:4–6).

Whatever one may think about the concept of the chosen people in the Bible, it is clear that it does not imply racial superiority of Israelites over others. All human beings are judged on the basis of their deeds and held responsible for breaches of morality.... Idolatry is a sin for Israel alone....

In prophetic literature the doctrine is taught that the time will come when all nations will learn what Israel knows and teaches about God and, while not becoming Israelites, will worship the one God and thus become God's people as well ... (Isa. 19:24–25)....

There are specific laws regarding the Canaanite nations, such as "They shall not dwell in your land" (Exod. 23:33), and even calling for their destruction (Deut. 20:17), but the reason is stated there as well—"lest they cause you to sin against Me (ibid)."... The biblical verse is not a general command concerning either killing or robbing of all enemies but referred specifically [to] the Canaanite nations [the Israelites] fought in order to attain possession of the Land of Canaan. These and similar laws referred only to the Canaanites.... The laws concerning [the Canaanites] were restricted to them alone at that particular time and ... could never be used as a reason to similarly eliminate any group today.

SECTION C: ATTITUDES TOWARD GENTILES IN RABBINIC LITERATURE

Highlighting rabbinic texts that alternately express positive and negative attitudes toward non-Jews, Rabbi Hammer argues that the negative attitudes stem from Jews' historic oppression under Greek and Roman foreign rule. Today, Jews need to decide which beliefs to encourage and which to oppose:

> Based upon... the creation of Adam, the Sages taught, "Only one human being was created in the world... in order to create harmony among humans so that one cannot say to another, 'My father is greater than your father...'" (Babylonian Talmud Sanhedrin 4:4).... Only one human being was created in order to teach that "if one destroys one person it is accounted to him as if he had destroyed an entire world and if one sustains one life it is accounted to him as if he had sustained an entire world" (Babylonian Talmud Sanhedrin 4:6).... There are numerous rabbinic sayings (as well as halakhic decisions) advocating fair and just treatment of non-Jews and making no differentiation between Jews and Gentiles...
>
> Other teachings... contradict the [positive ones]. How then are we to understand the negative attitudes toward non-Jews...? It is well known that there are laws in the Mishnah and the Talmud as well as in Medieval Codes that differentiate between Jews and Gentiles and single out non-Jews for special [negative] treatment. Some of these laws simply delineate what parts of Jewish religious practices are restricted to Jews alone.... Yet there are also laws that are discriminatory and contradict our concepts of justice and fairness, therefore presenting us with a serious dilemma.
>
> Many negative statements reflect the intense suffering of Jews under foreign rule, Greek and Roman.... It is obvious, then, that Rabbinic literature... is a vast collection of writings

gathered from hundreds of years of teachings by myriads of sages. By its very nature, then, it includes a variety of opinions on all subjects.... Honesty demands that we confront all of these opinions and make a decision as to which represent the beliefs we wish to encourage and which we oppose.

SECTION D: ATTITUDES TOWARD GENTILES
IN MEDIEVAL LITERATURE

Rabbi Hammer describes the striking development of the idea that Jews are innately superior. Rabbi Judah Halevi and the kabbalists (practitioners of esoteric Jewish mysticism) advanced a radically different concept of chosenness than the Torah's view:

> In the Middle Ages, Jews often had to deal with accusations against Judaism ... as well as misrepresentations of Jewish law.... The general opinion among Ashkenazim and ... Sefardim echoes the Torah's words and those of the Rabbinic Sages: the Jews were chosen not because of their own merits, but because of the merits of their ancestors. The purpose of chosenness was so that they would accept the Torah and perform the mitzvot and thus serve God and set an example for others.... Jews are not endowed with a special soul or innate superiority, only with a special task.
>
> The other view posited something inherently superior in the Jew as opposed to the Gentile. Influenced by mystical thinking ... this view stressed totally different ideas that are not to be found in Scripture ... although it was attributed to Scripture in various interpretation(s). The idea that there is something inherently different about the Jew and the non-Jew, that there is a distinct Jewish soul as opposed to a non-Jewish soul, became widespread in kabbalistic works and was popularized through the writings of the ... Spanish poet and polemicist Judah Halevi (c. 1075–1140, Spain).... The Zohar [the major text of kabbalah,

esoteric Jewish mysticism] became a primary source of these concepts of Jewish inherent superiority over other humans.... It taught that... the sin of the golden calf was caused not by the Israelites but by the "mixed multitude" that left Egypt with them....

This concept of chosenness, radically different from the Torah's view, was influential in many circles, including mystics and Hassidut.... This became a basic teaching of some Hassidic sects in the 18th century, especially through the writings of Shneur Zalman of Lyady [1745–1813, Belorussia, Russia], the founder of the Lubavitch sect [also known as Chabad]... [who wrote that] the Jew possesses two souls [including] a divine soul, which no other [human] group has... while the soul of the non-Jew derives from impure kelipot which are totally evil. This view continued to be influential in Hasidic circles.... In our time some have drawn that conclusion and used these teachings as a justification for far reaching and dangerous doctrines....

If there is any lesson that the [Holocaust] can teach us, it is that any doctrine that reflects belief in racial superiority or inferiority is evil, no matter who teaches it.

SECTION E: THE NON-JEW IN RABBINIC AND MEDIEVAL HALAKHAH

By contrast, Rabbi Hammer points out, rabbinic decisors in the Middle Ages ruled that Christians and Moslems are not idolaters or pagans but monotheists who act like Jews in following religious and ethical norms:

> The relations between Jews and non-Jews in medieval times in Europe were very different from those in the Rabbinic period. Jews were not only in exile, but were a small minority dependent for their very existence upon the good will of Christian rulers....

An important innovation was created by Rabbi Menahem ben Solomon of Provence Meiri [1249–1316] which has remained influential until today. He coined the phrase "nations who are bound by religious law" and ruled that all statements in the Mishnah, Talmud and other rabbinic works referring to non-Jews in a negative way did not apply to Gentiles of his day who are not idolaters but follow religious and ethical norms. . . . On financial matters [he rules], "They [non-Jews of the current time] are like complete Israelites concerning these matters of loss, mistake and all other matters" (Beit Habehirah to Bava Kamma, 330). Other medieval works take this same position. . . .

Turning to the Jews in Islamic lands, Maimonides . . . specifically excludes Islam from the definition of paganism ([*Mishneh Torah*], Ma'akhalot Asurot [Laws of Forbidden Foods] 11:7). . . .

Following these rulings, any assertions concerning non-Jews found in the Mishnah or Talmud are not applicable to the non-Jews among whom we live today. We do not hold that either Christianity or Islam is paganism, even though neither is identical with our beliefs and indeed often contradict[s] them.

SECTION F: DIFFERENTIAL LAWS AND DISCRIMINATORY LAWS

Rabbi Hammer contrasts differential laws (societal laws for citizens versus those for non-citizens), which he deems legitimate, with discriminatory laws, in this instance those that violate the Torah's essential principle of common humanity:

> The laws . . . which set non-Jews apart from Jews can be categorized as either differential or discriminatory. By "differential laws" we mean those laws that exclude non-Jews in ways that reflect common usage in all legal systems distinguishing between members of the group (or citizens of the nation) and

non-members. Members and citizens commonly have some privileges that others do not enjoy.... Every religious group has similar regulations on such matters and it is legitimate for certain ceremonies to be open only to those who are members of that religious group....

Our movement continues to believe in integration into society and not in ghettoization. Our attitude toward non-Jews today is positive and we do not aspire to be a "people that lives apart," but we do desire... to preserve our identity as a covenanted people. We believe that Judaism has contributed to humanity and continues to have vital ideas that are valuable....

On the other hand,... discriminatory laws... treat non-Jews differently from Jews in ethical and civil matters and can be seen as departing from the Torah's basic principle of the common humanity of all human beings....

Differential laws are not intrinsically invalid while discriminatory laws violate that principle.

SECTION G: CURRENT APPROACHES

Rabbi Hammer argues that the extremist ideology that non-Jews, even infants, may be killed because eventually these non-Jews will kill Jews completely misconstrues Jewish tradition:

> Since the emancipation the attitude toward gentiles in western lands changed radically. As Jews were accepted as citizens with equal rights, Jews reciprocated by attempting to break down barriers between themselves and non-Jews.... The positive attitude toward gentiles in Western Europe was... generally accepted by the late 1800s.... Prominent authorities such as Rabbi Samson Raphael Hirsch took it for granted that "Love your neighbor (as yourself)" (Lev. 19:18) applied to gentiles....
> In the early days of the settlement of the Land of Israel the same tendency could be found.... Unfortunately this was not

true in more recent times when ... in certain Religious Zionist circles, conditions of life in Israel, the enmity between Jews and Arabs, including terrorist activities ... helped to revive a general attitude of hatred toward Arabs. An increasingly negative attitude arose against both Islam and Christianity, seeing them as idolatrous religions.... All too often radical rabbinical authorities added fuel to the fire by voicing opinions that discriminate against non-Jews, including feelings that non-Jews were intrinsically inferior.

The most extreme example of anti-Gentile rulings is the book ... *Torat Hamelekh*.... The introductory endorsement [is] by Rabbi Yitzhak Ginzburg whose ideas and works, according to the authors ... are the basis for (the) volume. Ginzburg, a Habad [Lubavitch rabbi] of considerable influence in the Israeli religious-extreme right ... writes that his basic beliefs are:

a. Israel must conquer the entire Land and subjugate all non-Jews who live there;
b. The people of Israel preceded the creation, the Torah and even the thought of creating the world;
c. Non-Jews are inferior to Jews.

The book ... declares the inherent superiority of Jews over non-Jews.... Arabs are all to be considered as those who are coming to kill a Jew—a *rodef*—and if one is attacking you, you may kill that person first. They apply this ruling to every Arab and specifically include young children whom Jews are permitted to kill since when they grow up they will kill Jews (page 205). This also includes infants because of the certainty that they will either participate in injuring Jews or aid in doing so when they grow up (pages 206–7).... The authors of *Torat Hamelekh* make an attempt to apply the law of *rodef* to all Arabs.... (They claim that) in self-defense it is permitted to kill anyone who is intending to kill you, Jew or non-Jew. However *din rodef* applies only to one who is actively pursuing another with the intention of killing them. The conclusion that you may kill an Arab child, even an infant ... has no basis in Jewish Law or ethics. ...

The rulings found in *Torat Hamelekh* are a distortion of traditional Jewish beliefs which do not consider Jews to be superior to non-Jews, do not claim that the Jewish soul is superior to that of the non-Jew, and would never claim that all Arabs can be killed because they are all "pursuers." These beliefs are clearly based on teachings from the Zohar and the Tanya ... while ignoring the myriad other teachings that emphasize the equality of all human beings and require fair treatment of the non-Jew.

PESAK DIN

Rabbi Hammer rules:

1. [We] specifically reject the teachings of such works as *Torat Hamelekh*. ... Living in an interconnected world when enlightened religious leaders of all faiths are seeking ways of reconciliation, we as Jews, whether living in the diaspora with equal rights, or in Israel where we have the responsibility of caring for ... our fellow citizens of minority groups, cannot allow ourselves to be influenced by teachings that disseminate hatred and disdain for human beings of whatever nation or faith. ... We declare that all rules discriminating against Gentiles in matters of a civil nature and moral actions are no longer to be considered authoritative in Judaism ... because they are intrinsically immoral and deter us from attaining the honest virtues to which we aspire as Jews. ...

2. We declare that any rulings concerning matters of financial or civil law in the Mishnah and Talmud that discriminate against Gentiles are not to be considered official operative Jewish Law in our day. ... Only those rulings regarding ritual differences between Jews and non-Jews ... remain in effect.[17]

The Modern State of Israel 9

The State of Israel's establishment in 1948 brought to the forefront the question of whether halakhah should guide the conduct of a modern state. In the past, issues related to the state—such as conducting war or negotiating diplomatic treaties—were not practical concerns in halakhah, but in the context of the new nation these issues became crucial. Should halakhah be used as a source of law for a modern state founded as a Jewish homeland, and if so, in which areas and types of cases? Should halakhah shape the conduct of government institutions and individuals, and if so, how?

Five responsa that discuss state-related issues represent significant trends in the halakhic discourse regarding Israeli statecraft. Rabbi Shlomo Goren argues that the pertinent operational principles for the Israeli military must be taken from the halakhic laws pertaining to monarchy and warfare, even if these have not been operative for almost two millennia, and sometimes even if they do not make tactical or strategic sense. Rabbi Ḥayyim David Halevi, by contrast, draws from halakhic rules for personal behavior and common sense as the bases for his ruling. Rabbi Theodore Friedman analyzes a concept accepted as authoritative in a number of Jewish political circles, that of the greater Land of Israel, to show that it has changed dramatically over time and therefore should not be relied upon in determining the modern state's borders. Rabbi Ovadiah Yosef and Rabbi Shaul Yisraeli present differing views on the ceding of territory for peace based on many of the same halakhic principles.

Text 9.1. Goren, "The Siege on Beirut in Light of Halakhah"

TORAT HA-MEDINAH, 402–23

Rabbi Shlomo Goren (born Shlomo Gorontschik in Poland, 1917–94) served as the first Chief Rabbi of the Israel Defense Forces. His parents moved to Mandatory Palestine in 1925 to work in agriculture. The youngest student at the Hebron Yeshiva, he later studied at the Hebrew University (shying away from academic Jewish studies), joined the Haganah (predecessor to the Israel Defense Forces) in 1935, and saw combat in the Jerusalem area during the 1948 War for Independence. He was subsequently designated as the chief rabbi of the army with the rank of *aluf* (defined at the time of his retirement as major general). Trained as a paratrooper, he went into the field with troops in the 1956 and 1967 wars. He was noted for his valor under fire and his dedication to retrieving fallen comrades in combat from enemy territory.

Rabbi Goren aimed to create a Jewish military rather than a military of Jews. Seeking to enable observant and non-observant Jews to serve together in the same unit, he developed new halakhic concepts applicable to a Jewish military and established protocols to allow observant service members to maintain their religious observance while on active duty, without withdrawing from field duties during the Sabbath and festivals and having non-observant personnel take their place. He published a unified Ashkenazic-Sefardic siddur as well as a Passover Haggadah for use in the Israeli military.[1]

He was elected Ashkenazic Chief Rabbi of Tel Aviv in 1968 and Ashkenazic Chief Rabbi of Israel in 1972. He made many innovative halakhic rulings, a number of which garnered much hostility and opposition. (In the famous case of the Langer brother and sister who had been deemed as *mamzerim*, Jews with questionable family lineage, he devised a way for a *beit din* that he convened to free them from that status, which prompted great animosity.)[2] As a result of opposition to his innovative rulings, his blunt personality, and public bickering with the Rishon Lezion Sefardic Chief Rabbi Ovadiah Yosef, the Knesset did not change the law approved in 1972 setting a ten-year term limit for chief rabbis.[3] Rabbi Goren won the Israel Prize in 1961 for the first volume of his commentary on the Talmud of the Land of Israel, and he published many books of responsa addressing military issues as well as medical dilemmas.

In the introduction to the first volume of his responsa concerning military law, Rabbi Goren articulates his goal:

> This book is different from all other books of responsa in that the topics in this book do not have an ongoing tradition of rulings from generation to generation. There is nothing parallel in the Shulḥan Arukh [the most important code of Jewish law, written in the sixteenth century] or in the books written by *posekim*. From the time of Bar Kokhba [leader of third Jewish revolt against Rome in 132–135 CE], about sixty-five years after the destruction of the Second Temple, there were no laws of the military, war, and national security that had a real connection to the lives of the people. For nearly two thousand years, these issues appeared as "laws for the Messiah." Even Maimonides' Hilkhot Melakhim [Laws of Kings and Their Wars] is not capable of guiding the establishment of military procedure for the modern day State of Israel, since they are also directed to messianic times.... I am happy to point out that these rulings ... have become established standards not only for the religious soldier but for the Israel Defense Forces in total. Orders of the senior command and regulations in matters of religion that have been publicized in our time have been based on halakhic foundations that are established in this book, which is intended to be a military Shulḥan Arukh.[4]

In 1982, the Israeli military besieged Lebanon's capital city of Beirut during a military campaign called Operation Peace for Galilee because the PLO had its headquarters there. Rabbi Goren, then Ashkenazic Chief Rabbi of Israel, issued a responsum discussing the question of whether halakhah required that a side of the besieged area must be left unblocked so that those trying to flee the city could escape unimpeded.[5]

SECTION A: THE LAW OF SIEGE[6]

Rabbi Goren believes that state affairs should be conducted according to halakhic rules specific to states, and not rules meant for individuals. As a result, he cites Maimonides' *Mishneh Torah*, a work that deals with both practical halakhah and halakhah meant for a Jewish state under the rule of a Jewish monarch, even though there has been no Jewish monarch from the first century CE onward, a scope shared by very few halakhic works.

Rabbi Goren focuses on Maimonides' understanding of the regulation: that in a war of conquest, one side must be left open. In other words, during a siege, one must surround the besieged territory on three rather than four sides. This may seem surprising and counterintuitive: one might question whether a siege that leaves one side open without a hermetic seal on a city could be effective, but Rabbi Goren stresses that the primary purpose of the open-siege rule is to teach Jews to be compassionate toward their enemies. He cites two possible tactical advantages to the rule as well but considers these of secondary importance.

Rabbi Goren buttresses the authority of this rule by noting that both an ancient translation of the Bible, *Targum Pseudo-Jonathan*, and a tannaitic midrash, *Sifrei*, cite the ruling, signifying it is not something Maimonides invented but possesses the authority typically accorded to rabbinic sources from the mishnaic period. Additionally, a later midrash includes a different quote from *Sifrei* that supports the open-siege rule and confirms that the anonymous main voice in *Sifrei* holds the same opinion:

There is a specific law in the laws of siege and warfare from which we can learn about the high level of humanitarianism and ethics of the Torah of warfare and of the value of human life, including that of an enemy who fights us.

Maimonides in the *Mishneh Torah*, Hilkhot Melakhim [Laws of Kings and Their Wars] 6:7 writes:

> When we besiege a city to capture it, we do not surround it on all four sides but only from three sides. We leave a place open for escapees. Anyone who wishes to escape with their life may do so, as it is written in Numbers 30:7, "They deployed against Midian just as God commanded Moses." We learn from tradition that God commanded Moses thus [to leave one side open].

This [understanding of the biblical verse] is also the rendering in the *Targum Pseudo-Jonathan*.

This law in Maimonides is based on the approach of Rabbi Nathan in *Sifrei* Matot section 157, who interprets "they deployed against Midian" as Moses allowed [the Midianites] to flee from the fourth side, just as Maimonides wrote. It would seem that the writer of *Sifrei* disagreed with Rabbi Nathan because the anonymous main voice of *Sifrei* [who Rabbi Goren believes is Rabbi Simon bar Yoḥai] holds to this interpretation: "they deployed against Midian" means that they surrounded Midian from all four sides. However, *Yalkut Shimoni* Matot [a later midrash] preserves [what Rabbi Goren believes is] the original reading of *Sifrei*, showing that the anonymous main voice of *Sifrei* also agrees that Moses was commanded to besiege Midian only on three sides. Rabbi Nathan then came to give a reason for this ruling [not disagreeing with the anonymous main voice]: its purpose was to give a besieged enemy a fourth open side so that the enemy may flee and escape with his life, just as Maimonides wrote. Therefore it appears that the reason for this law is humanitarian: the Torah has compassion upon the enemies of Israel to save them from being killed, allowing them to escape with their lives.

It appears from the words of Maimonides that what is being discussed [in Num. 30:7] is a war of conquest.... In a siege like this, this law achieves two additional military goals, besides the humanitarian goal: (1) giving an enemy the possibility of escape may weaken the will of the besieged to continue to fight so that they will not fight until the bitter end; (2) opening a way of escape may result in clearing the population from the city, a goal of a war of conquest.

SECTION B: DOES THE RULE OF LEAVING A FOURTH SIDE OPEN APPLY TO OBLIGATORY WARS?

Rabbi Goren weighs whether Operation Peace for Galilee constitutes an obligatory war (*milḥemet mitzvah*) or an optional war for the sake of conquest or to glorify a king (*milḥemet reshut*), the two main types of war according to halakhah. Different rules apply to each type, such as who may declare a war and who may be drafted to fight.

Rabbi Goren argues that Operation Peace for Galilee was an obligatory war. He then points to what he characterizes as the obligatory war with Midian in Numbers 31 to bolster his claim that the open-siege rule should operate in both obligatory and optional wars:

> The siege ... [of Beirut] ..., however, is not for the purpose of conquering the city but rather to defend Israel from an enemy and to destroy that enemy. [This type of war is an obligatory war, termed in Hebrew *milḥemet mitzvah*, not an optional war taken just for the sake of conquest.] ...
>
> A Jewish military force undertaking a siege must leave one side open so that the people of a besieged city may escape with

their lives. This is because the essential aspect of this law is learned from the war with Midian, a war that was not a war of conquest but a war of retribution against enemies of Israel [an obligatory war], just as it is defined twice in the Torah: in Numbers 25:16–17, "The LORD spoke to Moses, saying, 'Attack the Midianites and defeat them because they attacked you by trickery,'" and in Numbers 31:1–2, "The LORD spoke to Moses, 'Avenge the Israelites on the Midianites.'" . . .

Despite this, Moses is commanded not to surround Midian on all four sides but only on three sides in order to give an opportunity to one who wishes to escape and save his life. According to this law, in any kind of warfare, no matter its goal, it is forbidden to close off a besieged city from all sides. Since this rule is operative even in a war of retribution with Midian, the Israelites are commanded to give an opportunity to anyone who wishes to flee and save his life [in any kind of war].

Nonetheless, we have the right to prevent the besieged from receiving reinforcements or the means to break the siege, such as food, water, and armaments, through the open fourth side. The obligation to leave a side open in a siege is to allow movement in one direction only, from the city outward, not from the outside to the city.

SECTION C: IS THIS LAW OBLIGATORY FOR WARS IN OUR TIME?

Rabbi Goren analyzes whether the halakhic rules for war operate only in the times of the Messiah; or in the past, when a Jewish king with political authority had the authority to decree and conduct an optional war according to halakhah; or at any time, including our own, for a Jewish military:

> Now we must consider whether this law recounted in Maimonides is obligatory for us today in Operation Peace for Galilee in

regard to the siege that we are undertaking on Beirut, if we are to be faithful to the Torah and our laws of war....

Perhaps [it is] intended just for the time in which the Jerusalem Temple was standing, when wars were conducted according to Jewish law, or in the future, when wars will be conducted according to Jewish law, but not today. Wars are not conducted by a Jewish military today according to Jewish law [because of the following requirement stated by] Maimonides at the end of root 14 in *Sefer ha-mitzvot* (Book of mitzvot):

> It is known that war and the conquest of cities can only be waged by the authority of a king and with the consent of the Great Sanhedrin and High Priest, just as it is written, "And before Eleazar the priest shall he stand" (Num. 27:21).

It seems from the printed text of Maimonides that we have that he is speaking about an optional war, not in an obligatory war, whose rules are applicable at all times. However, in the manuscript text ... Maimonides understands this as applying even in an obligatory war.... We have determined that Operation Peace for Galilee is an obligatory war, whose purpose is to defend Israel from an enemy coming to attack. Just as it is clear that the war with Midian was determined to be an obligatory war commanded by God, when even then we were commanded not to surround [the Midianites] on all four sides but rather to allow them to escape, it is the law with regard to Operation Peace for Galilee.

SECTION D: IS MAIMONIDES' UNDERSTANDING OF THIS RULE HUMANITARIAN OR TACTICAL?

Rabbi Goren discusses whether Maimonides' rationale for the original law to leave one side open during a siege was humanitarian or tactical. If the original intent of the open-siege rule was humanitarian, to allow civilians to escape, then this law would apply in all obligatory wars, including Operation Peace for Galilee. However, he argues, if the original intent was tactical, to give the Jewish military strategic advantage, then perhaps today's Israeli military should evaluate its own best tactical approach and not necessarily apply the open-siege rule:

> Are the reasons for [this law of leaving open the fourth side in a siege] ethical and humanitarian, originating from the Torah's compassion upon human life, including that of our enemies? ... If this is the case, then it is clear that it applies to us at all times and under all conditions.
>
> But perhaps the reasons for this commandment are not humanitarian at all but rather military and tactical. If the besieged are allowed the opportunity to escape, the intensity of their opposition will weaken; they will cease to fight, and they will prefer to flee. This would make victory in war easier for us. We are, then, not obligated to behave in such a way in all sieges but only if military tactical considerations warrant it. If the evaluation of the military situation demands a hermetic seal of a besieged city, [then it should be done so] just as in the case of the siege on Jericho, about which it is written: "Jericho was completely sealed up: no one went out and no one came in" (Josh. 10:1). . . . According to this approach, we should conduct the siege on Beirut only according to military evaluation of the necessary tactical approach without taking into consideration the law of siege.

SECTION E: RABBI SIMḤAH HACOHEN'S VIEW OF THE RATIONALE FOR THE OPEN-SIEGE RULE

Then Rabbi Goren turns to discuss the famous opinion of Rabbi Simḥah Hacohen of Dvinsk (1843–1926, Russia), who holds in his book *Meshekh ha-ḥokhmah* (Continuum of wisdom)[7] that Nahmanides thought the basis of the open-siege rule was both humanitarian (first reason) and tactical (second reason), whereas Maimonides thought it was tactical, contrary to Rabbi Goren's own reading of Maimonides:

> Rabbi Simḥah Hacohen argues: Maimonides did not include this in his *Sefer ha-mitzvot*, even though he included it in his *Mishneh Torah*, while by contrast, Naḥmanides includes this among the 613 commandments. Naḥmanides writes in his critique of *Sefer ha-mitzvot* of Maimonides that we are commanded to leave one side open in a siege so that those who wish to flee will have a means of escape. We are, according to Naḥmanides, to do this so that we will learn to behave with compassion even upon our enemies during war. Furthermore, they will be able to flee and not continue to oppose us. This is not a commandment just for the war with Midian, but rather it is a commandment for all generations in all optional wars. According to Naḥmanides, then, the reason for the commandment is humanitarian, just as when the Torah commands: "When you draw near a city to fight against it, you shall offer it terms of peace" (Deut. 20:10). This is done in compassion for the lives of the enemy. We are commanded to be compassionate to the inhabitants of a city that we have besieged and allow them a side open so that they can escape and save their lives. However, Maimonides [according to Rabbi Simḥah Hacohen] thinks that the reason for this commandment is not humanitarian. Rather, it derives from the tactics of war: if we encircle them from all sides and do not allow them to flee, they will continue to fight. They will protect their lives with all of their power, and they may achieve victory because it is well known from history that in a number of occasions, victory came from great desperation. Therefore this law is not to be counted among the commandments of the Torah. Rather, the Torah offers us good advice on how to achieve victory in a siege [and, therefore, this applies only to optional wars, not obligatory wars].

From here, Rabbi Goren argues against Rabbi Hacohen's view:

> First, while Naḥmanides includes both reasons, he thinks it obvious to include this law among the 613 commandments because of the first reason. His language regarding the second reason is "and there is an additional enactment"—this is obviously an additional matter of support for the law, but the first reason is the essential one.[8] Second, Maimonides does not limit this law of leaving the fourth side open in a siege to optional wars exclusively [because] he believes ... that this law operated in the same way as the law requiring that an enemy be offered peace, whether in an optional war or in an obligatory war, just as he ruled in Hilkhot Melakhim 6:1.

PESAK DIN

Goren ultimately concludes that the humanitarian rule of offering an enemy the option of peace signals that a similar humanitarian goal serves as the basis for the open-siege rule that one side be left open in a siege, and therefore one side must be left open in both obligatory and optional wars:

> According to Maimonides, this law operates in our time—if we besiege an enemy city whether in an obligatory war or in an optional war, whether within the borders of the Land of Israel or outside, we are forbidden to encircle a city from all sides. We must allow one side to remain open in order to offer an opportunity to those who wish to flee from the besieged city and save their life, as long as they do not take advantage of this [open] side in order to bring in reinforcements, whether soldiers, armaments, or food....
>
> May peace come to our soldiers and tranquility arrive within our borders.[9]

Text 9.2. Halevi, "The Law of 'the One Who Comes Forth to Kill You, Kill Him First' in Our State Affairs"

ASEH LEKHA RAV, 4, NO. 2

Unlike Rabbi Goren, Rabbi Ḥayyim David Halevi (see chapter 2) believes that halakhah of individual self-defense, norms that have been applicable throughout the millennia, can be utilized in public policy—yet, he stresses, the government, rather than individual members of society, must be responsible for deciding whether these norms should be employed. This is a striking transformation: heretofore, an individual decides on the spot whether using deadly force is justified. A government, by contrast, must go through its procedures of consultation and approval, which preclude an on-the-spot decision.

His responsum on how to treat members of a hostile population, written in response to a letter of inquiry he received in 1979, was first published in 1980. Halevi does not indicate who asked the question or why.

In other writings, Rabbi Halevi emphasizes that the call for equal citizenship for people of all faiths as stated in the Declaration of the Establishment of the State of Israel, a secular document, and not the halakhic principle of *darkhei shalom*, "peaceful relations (between communities)," should serve as the guiding principle for relations between Jewish and Arab citizens in Israel. The principle of equal citizenship denotes that all Israeli citizens, regardless of their religion, are entitled to equal rights within Israel's borders. By contrast, the halakhic principle of *darkhei shalom* calls on Jews to avoid conflict with non-Jews.

QUESTION

The questioner asks Rabbi Halevi how to apply two major halakhic principles: (1) "one who breaks in through a tunnel," a principle derived from Exodus 22:1 that if a burglar breaks in through a tunnel, he may be killed under certain circumstances; and (2) "the one who comes forth to kill you, kill him first," a principle that gives a person about to be assaulted mortally the right, and indeed the responsibility, to kill the would-be assassin first:

> The principle of "the one who comes forth to kill you, kill him first" gives permission, in the eyes of many, to view any Arab as "one who breaks in through a tunnel" because he belongs to a public that is hostile to us, and therefore it is permitted, or even required, to suspect that an Arab is always in the status of "the one who comes forth to kill you, kill him first." In connection with this point of view, a number of halakhic questions of great import arise in the public sphere:
>
> 1. Does the halakhic norm of "the one who comes forth to kill you, kill him first" apply only to a person who endangers or is about to endanger my life? Or is it applicable [only] in specific circumstances [when there is an immediate danger to my life], and only the combination of these two factors, a person in danger and a dangerous situation, fulfills the requirements that permit the application of this norm?
> 2. Does the hostility of a given community or the extreme hostility of a segment of that community justify the application of this principle ["the one who comes forth to kill you, kill him first"] upon every person who belongs to that community?
> 3. Is this norm dependent also on specific circumstances? Is there a definition of the circumstances in which it is permissible, or even required, to apply this principle?
> 4. The Torah says, "There is no bloodguilt for him" (Exod. 22:1). [Based on this text] in Babylonian Talmud *Sanhedrin* 72a, Rashi explains that [the burglar] is like a person who has no blood or soul, and therefore he may

be killed. May we learn from Rashi's explanation that this principle comes to teach us the laws of [individual] self-defense [only] and is not a principle that [can be extended to] permit the killing of people who belong to a hostile population [as a principle of public affairs]? [How can people claim that] belonging to a hostile population is sufficient in order to apply this principle? . . .

5. Is this principle applicable to our political situation? There are those who claim that the recognition of our right to exist as a free nation in our land is identical to the right of an individual to protect his/her life, and therefore we must apply this principle when a person is determined to kill us in order to preserve our right to be a free nation in our land.

6. Perhaps another question arises: since the laws of this country that apply to everyone establish rules for when [individual] self-defense is permitted, should these rules limit this principle?

SECTION A: THE PRINCIPLE "THE ONE WHO COMES FORTH TO KILL YOU, KILL HIM FIRST"

Rabbi Halevi expresses his revulsion that anyone might think that the halakhic principles of "the one who comes forth to kill you, kill him first" and "one who breaks in through a tunnel" could serve as the basis for killing Arabs in general because of a small minority of Arabs who try to kill Jews:

> You begin with the statement that the principle of "the one who comes forth to kill, you kill him first" gives permission, in the eyes of many, to view any Arab as "one who breaks in through a tunnel" because he belongs to a public that is hostile to us, and therefore it is permitted, or even required, to suspect that an Arab is always in the status of "the one who comes forth to kill you, kill him first." First and foremost, I must take issue with

"this opinion of many" that you refer to. It is very astonishing to me that [such a view is taken of] a million and a half Arabs, the overwhelming majority of whom live peacefully and quietly, even though they see Israelis as occupiers. Without a doubt, it is only an extremely small minority who attack us and try to kill us. I would be astonished if, due to this small minority, a death warrant be issued for a million and a half human beings.

SECTION B: THE SOURCE OF THE PRINCIPLE OF "THE ONE WHO COMES FORTH TO KILL YOU, KILL HIM FIRST"

Rabbi Halevi contrasts the interpretations of Rashi and Rabbi Menaḥem ben Solomon Meiri (1249–1316, Provence). Rashi bases the principle of "the one who comes forth to kill you, kill him first" in Exodus 22:1, explicitly connecting the two principles, "one who comes forth to kill you, kill him first" and "the one who breaks in through a tunnel." He reasons that the burglar's intentions may be assumed to be homicidal, and therefore the burglar may be killed.

However, Rabbi Halevi argues that the Meiri's interpretation is more cogent. Meiri separates the two principles. He holds that the basis for the principle "the one who comes forth to kill you, kill him first" is based on the divine command to attack the Midianites in Numbers 25:16–18; that God was certain of the Midianites' intention to destroy the Israelites when issuing this command, according to *Midrash Tanḥuma*; and therefore a preemptive strike grounded in the "one who comes forth to kill you, kill him first" principle may be undertaken only when there is absolute certainty that an entire hostile group seeks one's destruction—far different from the assumptions made when a burglar breaks into one's house:

> At the beginning of your letter, you include the principle of "one who comes forth to kill you, kill him first" in the law of "the one who breaks in through a tunnel" because that is the way you found the words ordered in the Babylonian Talmud *Sanhedrin*

72a. However, in truth, they are two independent halakhic concepts. This is the language of the Talmud:

> Rava says: What is the reason for this rule addressing the burglar who breaks into a house through a tunnel? There is a presumption that a person does not restrain himself when faced with losing his money, and therefore this burglar must have thought: If I go in and the owner sees me, he will rise against me and not allow me to steal from him, and if he rises against me, I will kill him. And the Torah stated [the principle]: If someone comes forth to kill you, kill him first.

Rashi explains:

> Why does the Torah say that in regard to the burglar tunnelling, there is no bloodguilt? That is to say, he is like someone who has no blood or soul and it is permitted to kill him: His meaning is clear: this is only a burglar and therefore why is there permission to kill him? There is a presumption that a person does not restrain himself: [is it the case that] when one sees another taking [his possessions], he is quiet? Therefore the burglar knows that the owner of the home will attempt to save his money, and so that burglar thinks that if the owner of the home rises up against him, he will kill him. And the Torah states there is no bloodguilt, and it teaches that "the one who comes forth to kill you, kill him first."

From Rashi's explanation, it seems at first glance that the Torah has taught this since that is expressed clearly in the words "And the Torah states there is no bloodguilt, and it teaches that 'the one who comes forth to kill you, kill him first.'" However, the contextual meaning of the talmudic passage is different, for if the Talmud had intended [linking the two principles], it should have said, "The Torah says, 'The one who comes forth to kill you so on and so forth,'" then the explanation that the Torah said, "There is no bloodguilt" in order to teach this principle. However the language of "And the Torah states ..." makes it clear that this was said in another place.

> The Meiri wrote about this *sugya*, and this is what he said: And the Torah teaches that "the one who comes forth to kill you, kill him first," where is this stated? This was explained in *Midrash Tanḥuma* (Pinḥas section 3) about "Attack the Midianites because they attacked you" (Num. 25:16).
>
> Now, the source for the principle of "the one who comes forth to kill you, kill him first" is the divine command to attack the Midianites and strike them down. Divine knowledge can be completely certain that they are hostile to you. Therefore, when a nation senses with certainty [like the divine command about the Midianites] that its enemies are scheming against it, it can initiate a preventive strike, as follows from the principle of "the one who comes forth to kill you, kill him first." This is also the law for an individual who senses with certainty that his enemy is plotting to strike him mortally or cause him a mortal blow, it is permitted to kill him first. . . .
>
> This is the meaning of the principle "the one who comes forth to kill you, kill him first." He is killed because of his intention, and this is the reason for the permission to kill the burglar who breaks into a house through a tunnel, even though surely he comes only to steal, not to kill . . . , just as we will explain [next].

SECTION C: KILLING THE BURGLAR WHO BREAKS IN THROUGH A TUNNEL

Rabbi Halevi explains that the principle of killing "one who breaks in through a tunnel" is optional, not obligatory. A preemptive strike is only mandated in instances of certain imminent homicidal attack, but it is not completely clear whether the burglar intends to kill:

Killing the burglar who breaks in through a tunnel is optional, not required, just as Rashi, whose words we have cited, said, "It is permitted to kill him." Maimonides wrote in Hilkhot Geneivah [Laws of Theft] 9:7:

> [As for] the burglar who breaks in through a tunnel, there is no bloodguilt for him, but if the owner of the house or another kills him, they are exempt from punishment. Permission is given to anyone to kill him. In any death in which one has the permission to kill, there is no bloodguilt.

The permission to kill him [the burglar who breaks in through a tunnel] is granted because he [the burglar] himself is ready to kill the owner of the house who he stands up against him, and therefore the burglar is a *rodef* [pursuer]. Even Maimonides compared him to a *rodef* in Hilkhot Geneivah 9:9 [using the words] "like a *rodef* who [pursues] another to kill him" and in Hilkhot Rotze'aḥ [Laws of Murderers] 1:6:

> [In regard to] a *rodef* [who is] after another person to kill him, even if the *rodef* is a minor, all Israel is commanded to save the pursued from the *rodef* even at the cost of the life of the *rodef*. It is [also] a negative commandment in that it is forbidden to have mercy upon the pursuer.

If so, why is not required to kill the one who breaks in through a tunnel but only optional? It appears that there is a distinction between [the two cases]. The intention of one who pursues after another to kill him is clear—through his deeds, [one can see] that he has come to kill. Therefore, it is a requirement and a mitzvah to save the life of the pursued by [taking] the life of the *rodef*.

However, this is not the case with the one who breaks in through a tunnel, for it is a presumption that a person will not hesitate to save his money. Because of this presumption, it is reasonable to think that the burglar is also ready to kill, even though it is not totally clear that he is a *rodef*. That is why Maimonides wrote that he is *like a rodef*, not a *rodef*. That is why there is permission to kill him but not a requirement.

SECTION D: THE LAW FOR A HOSTILE POPULATION

Rabbi Halevi insists the suggestion that the principle of "the one who comes forth to kill you, kill him first" cannot be applied as justification to kill any Arab when there is no good reason to assume that the person intends, and has the ability, to carry out a homicidal attack. While he concedes that it is reasonable to assume that the Arab public is generally hostile to the Israeli Jewish population, he argues that only Israel's governmental leadership has the right to declare war on the basis of this principle—and, moreover, only if the leadership is certain a preemptive strike is necessary to defend Israel against an imminent attack:

> Now how can one think that it is required to kill any Arab, or even an option to kill him, because of the principle of "the one who breaks in through a tunnel." The law of a pursuer certainly does not apply to him. Just any Arab [minding his own business] is not a pursuer at that moment. Even an Arab subject to the law of "the one who breaks in through a tunnel," it is not a mitzvah to kill him but only a permitted act. Just any Arab [minding his own business] is not subject to the law of "the one who breaks in through a tunnel," since he is not doing anything that serves as evidence for an intent to kill. How would one think that there is permission [to kill the Arab]?
>
> Perhaps the many that you referred to think that because of the general hostility of the Arab public toward us, the law of "attack the Midianites and strike them down for they attacked you" applies. This is a very serious error: this does not make it permissible to kill an individual. . . . Only in the case of defense of

the nation is it permissible to declare war with a hostile nation, like Midian. If the leadership of the nation ever decides a nation is preparing to launch a war against Israel, then it is permissible to strike first in a war of deterrence. However, it is not permissible to kill individuals from that nation, just as it says it was not permissible to kill individual Midianites except during war.

PESAK DIN

Rabbi Halevi states categorically:

> The principle of "the one who comes forth to kill you, kill him first" is dependent on circumstances that clearly prove that he comes with deadly intent, as in the war with Midian.... Therefore, if it is not apparent from a person's deeds that he endangers the life of another, one cannot kill him.
>
> It is not permitted to kill an individual, even if he belongs to a public that is hostile, even extremely hostile, as long as the hostility is not expressed in action; because individuals from among them who commit homicidal assaults on us are difficult to identify, [one might think that it is permitted, but it is not]. However just as it is permissible to launch a preventive attack against an enemy who is planning to attack ... it is permissible to use defensive means in order to identify those terrorists or to prevent them from attacking. The authorities may undertake appropriate actions, such as imposing a lockdown and the like, in the measure necessary to prevent those individuals from harming us, and these actions are permissible because of the support that they receive from a hostile public....
>
> May we be blessed with complete redemption soon! May Jacob reside in quiet and tranquility, and none shall make him afraid.[10]

Text 9.3. Friedman, "A Responsum on the Issue of 'the Greater Land of Israel' and Halakhah"

TESHUVOT VA'AD HA-HALAKHAH, 2

Born in the United States, Rabbi Theodore Friedman (1908–92) spent his rabbinic career in the United States and Israel. He received his undergraduate degree at the City College of New York, was ordained by the Jewish Theological Seminary, and earned a PhD from Columbia University.

Rabbi Friedman was a man ahead of his times. In 1963 he called for all members of the Rabbinical Assembly to advocate on behalf of Soviet Jewry. That same year, under his leadership as president of the International Rabbinical Assembly, a delegation of Conservative rabbis traveled to Birmingham, Alabama, to protest police brutality. He additionally urged his fellow rabbis not to forget to focus on their personal spiritual lives amid the demands of their communal work.

He served as a visiting professor at the Jewish Theological Seminary of America and the Schechter Institute of Jewish Studies. He was also deeply involved with the rabbinical students of the Seminario Rabinico Latinoamerica. He published six books and authored over two hundred articles, most popular and some scholarly.

He also served as chair of the Rabbinical Assembly's Committee on Jewish Law and Standards and, when he subsequently retired to Israel, as chair of the Va'ad Halakhah, the Rabbinical Assembly's responsa committee addressing questions specific to Israel. Here he examines a question addressed to the Va'ad Halakhah concerning the public declaration by the (Orthodox) Chief Rabbinate of Israel that the boundaries of the Land of Israel must be defined as the widest extent found in Jewish textual sources and that none of "the Greater Land of Israel" can be relinquished for the sake of a peace treaty.

QUESTION

Rabbi Friedman is asked:

> The Chief Rabbinate has published an article and an ad in the press stating that according to halakhah it is forbidden to cede even an inch of any part of the Greater Land of Israel. What is the position of the Va'ad Halakhah of the Conservative/Masorti movement on this?

SECTION A: "THE GREATER LAND OF ISRAEL" IS NEVER MENTIONED[11]

Rabbi Friedman states categorically that the sources will demonstrate that contrary to what the (Orthodox) Chief Rabbinate has declared, the borders of the Land of Israel were flexible and that no such concept as "the Greater Land of Israel" exists in the Bible or in the Mishnah, the Talmud, or the books of midrash. Characteristic of a Conservative/Masorti rabbi, he highlights historical development:

> Our sources, whether in the Bible and in classical Rabbinic sources, and in the *rishonim* and *aḥaronim*, do not mention the concept of "the Greater Land of Israel" or even a concept similar to it. The reason for this is very clear. Anyone who takes even a modest survey of the issue of the borders of the Land of Israel will conclude that in the biblical period and the Rabbinic period the borders of the land expanded or contracted for political reasons. In the period of the Rabbis, one cannot speak of stable borders at all, but about places that were mentioned as part of the Land of Israel and cities and towns that were mentioned as outside the Land of Israel.

SECTION B: WHERE IS THE BORDER?

Rabbi Friedman demonstrates the ambiguity of the borders stated in the divine promise to Abraham in Genesis 15:18:

Let us open with the divine promise to our father Abraham . . . [in] (Gen. 15:18), "To your seed, I have given this land from the Egyptian river to the great river Euphrates." In identifying "the Egyptian river," there is a disagreement among the classic biblical commentators. According to the *Targum [Pseudo-Jonathan]*, Rashi, and Radak [1160?–1235?, Provence], this refers to the Nile River, and this is the contextual interpretation accepted by modern commentators. However, Saadiah Gaon, Ibn Ezra [1089–1164, Spain, Italy, England], Baḥya ibn Pakuda [second half of eleventh century], and Abarbanel [1437–1508, Portugal, Venice] interpret it . . . as Wadi el-Arish. Between Wadi el-Arish and the Nile River is a distance of nearly a hundred kilometers.

SECTION C: BIBLICAL BORDERS

Rabbi Friedman points out that elsewhere in the Bible, only one border was fixed—the Mediterranean Sea—but it was unclear which parts of the Mediterranean seashore belonged to the Land of Israel:

> As for the changes in borders in light of geopolitical reality, we will start with the one that occurred thanks to the conquests of King David. David's conquests . . . invested the Judahite-Israelite state with Ammon, Moab, and Edom east of the Jordan, and the Aramaean lands in southern Syria, primarily the kingdom of Aram Tzova. In the heyday of the reign of David and Solomon, the kingdom of Israel stretched from the borders of the kingdoms of Tyre and Hamath to the north and from the Euphrates River in the north to Eilat in the southeast to the kingdom of Egypt in the southwest (1 Kings 5:1, 2:26). The term "the Land of Israel" took on a much broader meaning at that time than in the previous period.
>
> However, this geographical spread did not last long. . . . Far-reaching changes took place as early as the end of the reign of King Solomon and definitely after the division of the

monarchy ... when it is narrated (1 Kings 9:11–13) that Solomon ceded "twenty cities in the land of the Galilee" to Hiram of Tyre, probably in exchange for the materials of the Temple and palace that Hiram supplied. From then on, this area remained in the Upper Galilee within the territory of the kingdom of Tyre.

The rule of the kingdom of Israel on the eastern side of the Jordan also decreased. Until the death of King Ahab, the kingdom of Moab was included in the border of the kingdom of Israel, and when it threw off the rule of the kingdom of Israel, it became independent and a rival of Israel. The changes that took place in the borders of Israel since the division of the kingdom until the end of the Second Temple period are an overly complicated affair. . . . .

One clear lesson emerges from this—that it is impossible to install boundary markers and declare that here the border of the Land of Israel begins and here it ends. Only one boundary remained fixed without any change—the Mediterranean Sea as the western border. But among the classical Rabbis, a dispute emerged as to which part of the Mediterranean Sea is to be considered as the Land of Israel and which as outside the Land of Israel (Babylonian Talmud *Gittin* 8a).

SECTION D: THE BORDERS ACCORDING TO THE RABBIS

Rabbi Friedman observes that when the Rabbis discuss the borders of the Land of Israel, they are interested not in political boundaries but in determining which areas were and were not subject to ritual laws tied to the Land. Furthermore, identifying and locating the places mentioned in Rabbinic literature may be a riddle that cannot be solved:

> The interest of the classical Rabbis in the question of the borders of the Land of Israel did not flow from it being a political question. As early as the first half of the first century BCE,

when Pompey, the Roman army minister, intervened in the war between the Hasmonean brothers Hyrcanus and Aristobulus, Jewish political sovereignty disappeared. The Rabbis' interest in and determination of the boundaries of the Land stemmed from the question of which areas, cities, and villages were subject to the laws of the mitzvot that depended on the Land, such as *terumot* [offerings], *ma'asrot* [tithes], and *bikkurim* [first fruits], and which areas were considered free and exempt from these mitzvot.

The meaning of this latter determination is that a Jew who goes outside the Land of Israel automatically becomes ritually impure. This was quite a blow to the priests because it would prevent them from serving in the Temple while it was in existence and also prevented them from eating *terumah* even after the destruction of the Temple. Therefore, the Rabbis employed the language of permission [*heiter*] and prohibition [*issur*] regarding certain cities and areas. When they spoke about a certain place, like Caesarea (Tosefta *Oholot* 18:16), as permitted, the meaning was that it is considered part of the Land of Israel and priests were allowed to live there, its inhabitants were required to give *terumot*, *ma'asrot*, and the like. On the other hand, when they spoke about a certain place as forbidden, meaning that it was outside the Land of Israel, the priest who entered it became unclean and that place was exempt from *terumot* and *ma'asrot*.

This issue, the determination of the boundaries of the Land according to the Rabbis, is one of the most serious. The main difficulty stems from identifying and locating the places mentioned in the sources.... Places appearing in one list are absent in other lists. In different manuscripts of the same existing source, there are spelling differences. Sometimes the differences are substantial. Differences in spelling may cause different identification of the same place. For example, the Palestinian Talmud mentions a place called SKL. In an inscription from Beit

Shean, the same place is mentioned by SGL. These places are far apart. What is the correct terminology? There are differences of opinion among the researchers. Moreover, the booklet includes two maps, one of the Land of Israel and one of the Galilee.... One line marks the boundary according to the [academic] researcher S. Klein... and the other indicates the borders according to the [academic] research of Yeshayahu Peres.... Between these two lines is considerable difference. What has been said above comes to teach us how little agreement there is about the boundaries of the Land of Israel in the talmudic period.... This issue continues to vex contemporary scholars.

SECTION E: THE RABBIS' CRITERION FOR DETERMINING ISRAEL'S BORDERS

Rabbi Friedman argues that the Rabbis' sole criterion to determine whether a place was to be deemed part of the Land of Israel was its percentage of Jewish versus non-Jewish inhabitants. As a consequence, as the Jewish population of a given city in the Land of Israel waxed and waned, the Rabbis' determination as to whether that city was part of the Land of Israel often changed as well. Furthermore, he points out that there are instances where a city was determined to be part of the Land of Israel according to one benchmark but not according to another:

> We will try to prove that in their considerations the Rabbis were very pragmatic and were not guided by historical factors or abstract ideology. Their sole consideration was the number of Jewish inhabitants of a place: if the percentage of the Jewish population of a place was considerable in contrast to the non-Jewish population, they determined that the place was part of the Land of Israel, and if not, not. The Rabbis also disagreed on whether one place or another was part of the Land or Israel.

Moreover, the Jewish population in several places was unstable. Over time it could grow or shrink. So we find several cases where one city begins was considered outside the Land of Israel, but when its Jewish population grew, the Rabbis determined that the city was considered part of the Land of Israel. That is to say, from one halakhic point of view the place was considered part of the Land of Israel, and in another respect it is considered outside the Land....

Let us consider one example. As is well-known, the city of Caesarea was rebuilt by Herod in 10 BCE. The city was a typical Roman city in all its polytheistic customs, and the Rabbis did not delay in declaring it outside the Land of Israel. One may speculate that its polytheistic culture dissuaded Jews from settling in it (Tosefta *Oholot* 18:13). However, later, especially after the destruction of the Temple and the Bar Kokhba revolt, most of the Jewish population was in the Galilee and nearby places. The number of Jewish residents in Caesarea increased, and the city soon became a Torah center. Therefore, in light of the reality, the sages have repeatedly stated that Caesarea is included within the boundaries of the Land of Israel (Tosefta *Oholot* 18:16)....

Sometimes the Rabbis made a compromise regarding a specific place, in that from one perspective it was considered part of the Land of Israel and from another, not. As an example, we will take the city of Ashkelon and its suburbs. Initially, the Rabbis determined that the city of Ashkelon was outside the Land of Israel (Palestinian Talmud, *Shevi'it*, 6, 5, 35c). However, from another source (Tosefta *Oholot* 18:15) we learn that the Rabbis determined it to be pure and part of the Land of Israel. This source was based on a count made in the days of Rabbi Judah the Patriarch. Despite this, the city of Ashkelon was considered in several respects outside the Land, and the rules of *terumot* and *ma'asrot* did not apply nor the rule of *shevi'it* (Tosefta *Oholot* 18:4).

PESAK DIN

Rabbi Friedman concludes:

> From this brief survey, it is clear that, in determining which places were part of the Land of Israel and which places were outside the Land, the Rabbis were guided by pragmatic considerations. The consideration of the boundaries was never fixed and rigid, but the opposite: flexible in accordance with the pragmatic reality of the time. To claim that the concept "the Greater Land of Israel" forbids us from conceding any part of the geographic land that happens to be under Jewish sovereignty has no support in the halakhah. The disagreement relative to "the Greater Land of Israel" concept is strictly a political dispute with no halakhic relevance whatever.[12]

Text 9.4. Yosef, "Ceding Territory from the Land of Israel When There Is *Pikku'aḥ Nefesh*"

TEḤUMIN 10 (1989): 34–47

Since the 1970s, when a peace treaty was negotiated with Egypt, rabbinic decisors have debated whether halakhah prohibits or mandates ceding of territory in a peace treaty with the Palestinians. Rabbi Ovadiah Yosef (see chapter 3) published two versions of his responsum on ceding territory for peace: an early version in 1980 and a more extensive version in 1989.

At the time of his writing, the Israeli government was refusing to negotiate with the Palestinian Liberation Organization, generally recognized as representing the Palestinians, but as a result of the 1979 Egypt-Israel peace treaty, much debate was ensuing over whether the Israeli government's stance should change. Meanwhile, there was no Arab partner except for Egypt with whom to make peace, and the various military and political experts Rabbi Yosef confers with advance cogent argument both for and against ceding territory.

While at the beginning of his *teshuvah* Rabbi Yosef states that he is not issuing a ruling, at the end he reaches a conclusion that territory may be ceded for the sake of peace (under certain conditions).

SECTION A: AT THIS POINT THE QUESTION IS MOOT/IMPRACTICAL

Rabbi Yosef lays out the purpose of his *teshuvah*: to examine the opinion that the mitzvah of settling the Land of Israel is greater than that of the mitzvah of *pikku'aḥ nefesh* (mortal danger to human life), and hence a Jew is obligated to risk one's life to settle the Land. Thus the question becomes: does the principle of *pikku'aḥ nefesh* suspend the mitzvah of settling the Land of Israel?

> At the beginning, I would like to make clear that I am not issuing a halakhic ruling whether the government of Israel should return territories of the Land of Israel or not, and this for two reasons. First, the question is merely theoretical today. There is, at present, no negotiating partner, since the Arabs are demanding the return of the entire Land of Israel, including Jerusalem, to which all the military commanders and politicians are opposed. This situation is embodied in the verse "I am for peace; but when I speak, they are for war" (Ps. 120:7).
>
> Second, I have conferred with four experts concerning the military and political aspects of the question, and they completely disagreed, each offering persuasive arguments. One side argues that, in light of modern weapon systems, such as long-range missiles, chemical warfare, and ... missile-bearing airplanes, there is no significance to the location of the border or whether we return parts of the Land of Israel. The more important issue is the stationing of the miliary and the demilitarization of evacuated areas. The peace accords with Egypt show that Egypt is fulfilling the accords and has diverted most of its budget from military procurement to economic development. Therefore we may assume

that an agreement with the inhabitants of Judea and Samaria will reduce the chances of war with our neighboring countries....

The opposing side argues that Judea and Samaria are vital, since they provide strategic depth. It is too great a risk to cede these territories, even in return for peace, since the danger of terrorism remains even in peacetime. Furthermore, even if we sign a peace accord with some Arabs, this will not restrain the more extreme terrorist organizations, who will continue to fight. They argue that the defense of Tel Aviv and Jerusalem is dependent on retaining Shechem [Nablus] and Hebron. Finally, they argue that the true aim of the Arabs is to seize all the Land of Israel....

Given this situation ... I support the prime minister, the deputy prime minister, and all the other ministers in their endeavors and completely endorse their recent actions, whose purpose is to ensure security and peace for all the inhabitants of the Land of Israel....

My goal here is to analyze the position advocated recently that the importance of the mitzvah of settling the Land of Israel is greater than that of the mitzvah of preserving life and that one is obligated to risk one's life for the settlement of the Land.... [The question is] whether the principle of *pikku'aḥ nefesh* [mortal danger] suspends the mitzvah of settling the Land of Israel ... or whether, to the contrary, political stalemate will lead to a situation in which *pikku'aḥ nefesh* must be invoked?

SECTION B: THE MITZVAH OF SETTLING
THE LAND OF ISRAEL

Rabbi Yosef highlights that the classical Rabbis emphasized the importance of the mitzvah of settling the Land of Israel:

> The basis for our discussion is ... the statements of our Rabbis concerning the importance of the mitzvah of settling the Land of Israel, its sanctity, and the obligation to live in the Land of Israel.

Sifrei comments on the verse, "You shall dispossess them and dwell in their land" (Deut. 12:29):

> It happened that Rabbi Judah ben Beteira, Rabbi Matia ben Ḥeresh, Rabbi Ḥanina the nephew of Rabbi Joshua, and Rabbi Joḥanan were leaving the Land of Israel. They arrived in Paltum and remembered the Land of Israel.
>
> They raised their eyes in tears, tore their clothes, and recited the following verse: "You shall dispossess them and dwell in their land." They returned to their homes. They said: Dwelling in the Land of Israel is equivalent to all the mitzvot of the Torah.
>
> It happened that Rabbi Eleazar ben Shamu'a and Rabbi Joḥanan the sandal-maker were going to Netzivin to study Torah with Rabbi Judah ben Beteira. When they came to Sidon, they remembered the Land of Israel. They raised their eyes in tears, they tore their clothes, and recited the following verse: "You shall dispossess them and dwell in their land." They returned to their homes. They said: Dwelling in the Land of Israel is equivalent to all the mitzvot of the Torah.

SECTION C: *PIKKU'AḤ NEFESH*

Investigating the scope of *pikku'aḥ nefesh*, Rabbi Yosef demonstrates that this major halakhic principle mandates the waiving of other mitzvot (with certain exceptions) if there is immediate danger to human life. This sets the stage for his argument later in his responsum that *pikku'aḥ nefesh* may require the ceding of territory:

> It is a major halakhic principle that *pikku'aḥ nefesh* suspends all the mitzvot, except for the prohibitions of *avodah zarah*, *arayot* [forbidden sexual relations], and murder. The Babylonian Talmud *Sanhedrin* 74a interprets the verse "You shall observe My statutes and judgments, which a human being shall do to live

by them" (Lev. 18:5) to mean "to live by them and not die by them." ...

The Palestinian Talmud *Yoma* 8.5 states: "One who asks a rabbi [whether to desecrate Shabbat or Yom Kippur in order to save a life] is shedding blood [since the person is liable to die while he goes out to ask]; [the rabbi] who is asked is worthy of censure [because he should have publicized this law]; and he who is prompt [to act and desecrate Shabbat or Yom Kippur] is to be commended."

Rabbi Yosef is saying, first, that settling the Land of Israel is not listed as one of the three mitzvot that one should die for and, second, that hesitating to act when human life is in danger is itself a sin. He needs to investigate the scope of the principle of *pikku'aḥ nefesh* in order to demonstrate that it would apply even to the important mitzvah of settling the Land of Israel.

SECTION D: DOES THE PROHIBITION OF *LO TEḤONEIM* APPLY TO CEDING TERRITORIES TO ARABS?

Rabbi Yosef decides to address another issue, the prohibition of *lo teḥoneim* (they shall not dwell), before delving into the implications of *pikku'aḥ nefesh*, because if this prohibition supersedes *pikku'aḥ nefesh*, then territory in the Land of Israel could never be ceded to non-Jews.

He then examines whether the biblical verse "Do not grant them encampment" (Deut. 7:2), understood as preventing idol worshipers from living in the Land of Israel, does or does not apply to Muslims living in Israel today:

Is there a prohibition to cede territory of the Land of Israel when there is no *pikku'aḥ nefesh*? Maimonides (Hilkhot Avodah Zarah [Laws of Idolatry] 10:6) writes:

> If the Jews have dominion over the nations, we are forbidden to leave a non-Jew among us [in the Land of Israel]. Even if his residence is temporary or if he is passing through on business, he may not pass through our land before accepting the seven Noahide commandments, as it is written: "Do not grant them encampment" [*lo teḥoneim*; Deut. 7:2] even temporarily.
>
> It appears from Maimonides that this law applies to Moslems even though they are not idolaters. The Ra'avad [Rabbi Abraham ben David, c. 1125–98, Provence] disagrees: "We have never heard of such [an interpretation]. The verse he quotes refers to the seven nations...."
>
> The great scholar of Jerusalem the Rishon Lezion Rabbi Meyuhas Bekhor Shmuel (*Mizbaḥ adamah*, Salonica 5537 [1877], 12b) testifies that he knew of several great rabbis who sold their houses or courtyards to Moslems, and maintained that the prohibition applies only to idolaters, but not to Moslems.

In other words, it is acceptable for Muslims to live in the Land of Israel. By this determination, Rabbi Yosef refutes the argument that no territory can be ceded because then non-Jews would be living there.

SECTION E: *PIKKU'AḤ NEFESH* SUSPENDS *LO TEḤONEIM* AND ITS APPLICABILITY IS DETERMINED BY EXPERTS

Rabbi Yosef argues that we must rule leniently when there is immediate danger to life. If military commanders and political experts believe that ceding territory lessens danger to life, then parts of the Land of Israel should be relinquished:

> If our military commanders and political experts decide that if we do not cede sections of the Land of Israel, danger to life exists, that there is a danger of imminent war with the neighboring

Arab countries... while on the contrary, ceding land will reduce the danger of war, with a chance for a lasting and genuine peace, it would definitely be permitted to return the territories for this purpose, as *pikku'aḥ nefesh* suspends all prohibitions.

Just as in the case of a sick person on Yom Kippur, the decision [that the patient must eat] will be made by a physician, even a non-Jewish one. If [the physician] decides that fasting is dangerous, or even if it will worsen [the patient's] condition, which in turn might lead to danger, the patient is required to eat (see Shulḥan Arukh *Oraḥ Ḥayyim* 618:1). The patient is not allowed to be more strict and fast; on the contrary, he would be considered responsible for the loss of life were he to do so....

The same principle applies in our case.... The Shulḥan Arukh (*Oraḥ Ḥayyim* 618:4) rules that if physicians disagree, with some requiring that the patient eat and some believing that this is not necessary, we give [the patient] food, as a doubt in questions of *pikku'aḥ nefesh* is resolved leniently.... The same, therefore, applies to our case. If the experts disagree, with some of them stating that there is no *pikku'aḥ nefesh* in our situation, while others declare there is a danger of immediate war and *pikku'aḥ nefesh* and that without ceding territory, doubt should be resolved leniently, the territories must be ceded in order to prevent loss of life.

SECTION F: TRUSTING IN GOD

Rabbi Yosef argues that we should not rely on miracles and think that God will save us in war. To protect ourselves, we must continue to abide by the principle that saving life overrides ceding territory:

> Given our spiritual state today, it would appear that it is prohibited for us to rely on a miracle and risk a war with our neighboring Arab countries, for perhaps [our sins will be the

cause] that God will not perform a miracle.... Hence, we return to the principle that *pikku'aḥ nefesh* suspends the prohibition of ceding territories—indeed, all Israeli governments refrained from annexing the territories in order to allow for the possibility of negotiations based on ceding territories for peace.

SECTION G: PREVENTING IMMINENT DANGER TO AVOID POSSIBLE FUTURE DANGER

Rabbi Yosef argues that halakhically the danger of life lost in an imminent war would call for Israel to relinquish territory proactively:

> It is always more important to prevent an imminent danger of war than to be concerned about the possibility of a future one. This is comparable to the statement of Rabbi Ezekiel Landau on *Yoreh De'ah* 2:210 that *pikku'aḥ nefesh* does not suspend a prohibition unless the danger is before us. The possibility of future danger is not considered *pikku'aḥ nefesh*; otherwise, all Shabbat prohibitions would always be suspended on the possibility that it might help some critically ill person.... In our case, there is a present danger before us, since if we do not return the territories, it may lead to immediate war. On the other hand, the danger that a war will result in the future if we allow the border to come closer to our settlements is not a present danger....
>
> In our case... if the military commanders and political experts conclude that there is no danger in returning territories, there will be no reason to refrain from returning territories in order to avoid the danger of an imminent war.

Thus Rabbi Yosef adds the proviso that military and political experts must weigh in on whether or not ceding territory will present a danger.

PESAK DIN

Rabbi Yosef rules:

> If it can be determined without any doubt that a genuine peace between us and our Arab neighbors will result from ceding territory, whereas not ceding the territories will increase the danger of immediate war, then the territories should be returned, as nothing stands in the way of *pikku'aḥ nefesh*. The matter must be analyzed carefully after consultations with military commanders and political leaders who are expert in these matters.
>
> May God inspire the government ministers and advisors to do everything for the good of the community in the Land of Israel, and grant them wisdom.... "Nation shall not bear sword against nation, nor shall they study warfare" [Mic. 4:3]. "Jacob shall return and be calm, and none shall make him afraid" [Jer. 46:27].[13]

Inasmuch as Rabbi Yosef concludes that territory may be ceded, he puts strict limits on whether it can be put into practice, aware that his ruling is very controversial. Indeed it was, prompting another leading rabbinic decisor, Rabbi Shaul Yisraeli, to respond.

Text 9.5. Yisraeli, "Ceding Territory because of *Pikku'aḥ Nefesh*"
TEḤUMIN 10 (1989): 48–61

Born in Belarus, then part of the Russian Empire, Rabbi Shaul Yisraeli (1909–1985) studied in secret yeshivot in the Soviet Union. After the Communist government denied him an exit visa, he tried to flee the country but was caught. Only through the direct intervention of Ashkenazic chief rabbi Avraham Isaac Kook was he released and allowed to immigrate to Mandatory Palestine. He served as the *rosh yeshiva* of Yeshivat Merkaz Harav and became one of the most influential rabbis in the Religious Zionist community.

In 1989 Rabbi Yisraeli responded to Rabbi Yosef's opinion on whether territory may be ceded for the sake of peace. He disagrees sharply with most of Rabbi Yosef's analysis of halakhah and politics. While Rabbi Yisraeli does not believe that the State of Israel should start a war to gain Transjordan, the rest of the Land of Israel in his opinion, he does maintain that it must hold land gained in a defensive action, such as the Six-Day War.

SECTION A: THE VALIDITY OF THE CONQUEST OF THE LAND ACCORDING TO NAHMANIDES IN OUR TIME[14]

Rabbi Yisraeli employs Nahmanides's conviction that the mitzvah to conquer the Land of Israel is operative at all times to argue that once the modern State of Israel has conquered territory that is part of the Land of Israel, that territory must not be relinquished. He then introduces the concept of the three oaths. Rabbinic tradition holds that (1) God made Jews swear not to rebel against their non-Jewish sovereigns and (2) not to seek to conquer the Land of Israel by force, and (3) God made non-Jews swear to not oppress Jews.[15] He cites the United Nations vote for an independent Jewish state, the establishment of the State of Israel, and the opening of the new state's borders to all Jews as proof that those oaths are no longer in force. All the more so, he contends, Israel's establishment "reinstitutes the original national obligation of conquest [of the Land of Israel]":

> Nahmanides (addenda to *Sefer ha-mitzvot* 4) writes:
>
>> We may not leave the land in the hands [of the seven Canaanite nations] or of any other nations at any time throughout the ages.... So [we see that] the mitzvah of conquest applies in all times.... This is a mitzvah required of every individual in all times, including the time of exile....

> Naḥmanides explicitly states that the mitzvah to conquer [the Land of Israel] applies in every generation, even during the exile....

The vote of the United Nations for an independent Jewish state, followed by the establishment of the State of Israel on 5 Iyar 5708, together with the unrestricted opening of the new state's borders to all Jews, constitutes the revocation of the oath "to not ascend the wall" by force [that is, to not go forth in military action to reconquer the Land of Israel].... Accordingly, the whole of the Jewish people is again obligated to come to the Land of Israel and fulfill the mitzvah of conquest wherever possible.... The establishment of the State of Israel reinstitutes the original national obligation of conquest.... Since the Land of Israel was a mandate of the United Nations, where decisions are formulated by majority vote of the members, the opposition of the minority [of nations who voted against] is irrelevant and immaterial.

SECTION B: THE OBLIGATION TO THANK GOD FOR THE OPPORTUNITY TO COME TO ISRAEL

Rabbi Yisraeli expresses astonishment that observant Jews are still living outside the Land of Israel. Now that the three oaths are revoked, Jews should recognize God's providence by returning to Israel:

> I cannot refrain at this point from once again expressing my amazement that a significant number of Torah-true Jews, who affirm faithfully that God's providence is the cause of everything that happens to humanity, especially everything that has befallen the Jewish people, ignore the enormity of the miracle that took place when the State of Israel was established, when we were liberated from the oaths that hung over us throughout the exile without our being able to escape.... One might

argue that we have not yet achieved full redemption.... Why should we be ungrateful for the kindness God has bestowed upon us? Only through gratitude to the one who granted us all these blessings will we merit a continuation of God's mercy, blessing, and sustenance. In my opinion, this negative attitude is the result of a sinful tendency to disparage God's gifts and to absolve ourselves with lame excuses.

SECTION C: WHY DOES RABBI YOSEF NOT DISCUSS THE THREE OATHS?

Rabbi Yisraeli sharply critiques how Rabbi Yosef analyzes the situation. If the question of ceding territory is solely viewed through the lens of *pikku'aḥ nefesh*, and if there is a definitive world consensus for Israel to cede territory, then Israel will have to relinquish essential land, including parts of Jerusalem:

> Why then does he treat the entire subject [only in relation to the principle of *pikku'aḥ nefesh*]?...
>
> If the opposition of the nations is determinative, this will apply to parts of Jerusalem as well [including] the Old City, the Western Wall, and all of East Jerusalem. We should be obligated to return them even before negotiations start. Furthermore, the inclusion of the new city of Jerusalem in the borders of Israel and its status as the capital is in opposition to the nations of the world, including our erstwhile friend, the United States, which continue to maintain that it should be an internationalized city.

SECTION D: THE AGREEMENT OF THE NATIONS CANNOT BE REVOKED

Rabbi Yisraeli argues that ever since the oath not to seek to conquer the Land of Israel by force has been revoked, it cannot be renewed. Once the Balfour Declaration recognized the rights of the Jewish people over the entire Land of Israel, such an international declaration cannot be undone:

> [Rabbi Simḥah Hacohen of Dvinsk] stated shortly after the first international declaration endorsing the return of the Jews to their country:
>
>> Through divine providence, the conference of the civilized nations in San Remo has issued an edict that the Land of Israel should belong to the people of Israel. Since the terror of the oaths is eliminated, and the mitzvah of settling the Land of Israel, which is the equivalent of all the mitzvot, is reestablished by the permission of the kings ... one can perhaps apply to this situation the verse "How long will you avoid [Me]?" (Jer. 31:22).
>
> The Balfour Declaration recognized the rights of the Jewish people over the entire Land of Israel.[16] The *aliyah* that followed the declaration serves as an act of acquisition for all that was then included in the borders of Palestine, according to the halakhic rule "If he sold ten fields in ten areas—once he takes possession of one of them, he acquires them all" (Babylonian Talmud *Bava Kamma* 12a). The nations do not have the power to retract. Hence, the removal of Transjordan from the Land of Israel by the mandatory powers was illegal. It is even more obvious that the partition resolution, which divided the West Bank of the Jordan River [from the rest of the Land of Israel] and created the present-day distinction between the two sides of the "green line," was outright robbery. Robbery, even when committed by governmental powers, has no validity.

SECTION E: CONQUEST DOES NOT MEAN DOMINATION

Rabbi Yisraeli then argues that the commandment to uproot idolatry does not apply to Christians or Muslims, and therefore they are permitted to reside in the Land of Israel:

> According to the conclusion of [Rabbi Moses Isserles, *Oraḥ Ḥayyim* 156] that non-Jews are not enjoined from associating another being with God [*shittuf*], Christians do not violate the prohibition of idolatry, as they worship the Creator of the world.... Since, according to [Rabbi Isserles], Christians are not idolaters, it is not necessary to do away with their churches....
>
> As far as Muslims are concerned, Rabbi Yosef cites several rabbinic decisors who hold that they are not included in the prohibition *lo teḥoneim*. Accordingly, it is permitted to sell them land in Israel.

SECTION F: THE LAWS OF CONQUEST APPLY TO TERRITORY ALREADY CONQUERED AND POSSESSED

Rabbi Yisraeli holds that Jews have every right to reside in territory they conquered during a defensive war, even at the risk of losing life. Furthermore, Rabbi Yosef's claim to the contrary, ceding territory is more likely to result in loss of life than retaining it:

> Based on the preceding arguments, we may conclude that the occupation of territory by the Israeli military during the Six-Day War, a war forced upon us even though we made strenuous efforts to avoid it, together with the subsequent act of acquisition through possession of the land accomplished by government-aided settlements founded during the ensuing years [after it became clear that the Arabs still hoped to drive us into the sea], constitutes a fulfillment of the mitzvah of conquest regarding those territories.

This applies even if we agree, as I do, that we are not obligated today to go to war, with the attending possibility of loss of life, in order to conquer new territory within the Land of Israel [such as Transjordan]. However, those territories that were liberated through the grace of God in a defensive war and were subsequently settled, showing our intention to possess them, have the status of conquered territories, and even according to the axioms of Rabbi Yosef's article, we are obligated to go to war in order to defend them, ignoring the principle of *pikku'aḥ nefesh*. . . .

Rabbi Yosef has been somewhat inaccurate in quoting the claims of our adversaries. Even the most moderate of our antagonists demands not the return of territories, but of "the territories" as a condition for signing a peace treaty with us. The definite article is of major significance here. They explicitly declare that they will not settle for less than seeing their flag waving over the holy city of Jerusalem. Why should we delude ourselves with slogans about "peace, peace—and there is no peace" (Jer. 6:14)?

By the use of their formulation of "returning territories" that we have allegedly stolen from them, we are ourselves giving partial credence to the claim that the problem is one of "return," that is, that we have taken their land, whereas the sole basis of our link to this land is that "the Land of Israel is an inheritance to us from our forefathers," and they are living on foreign soil. The halakhah does not recognize the possibility of the alienation of land from its proper owner, even if he has despaired [*yei'ush*] of its return. We, in any event, never gave up hope, and the connection of the Jewish people to this land was never forgotten (Babylonian Talmud *Sukkah* 30; Tosafot ad loc.). Our claim is rooted in our steadfast assertion of the justice of our cause, based on God's promise to the Jewish people, and the undeniable historical fact that Jewish culture flourished in this land until we were forcibly exiled. The books of the prophets and the extensive literature of the Talmud [and other literature of that age] are witnesses that this land is ours for all time. . . .

Rabbi Yosef raises another distinction . . . [when he writes,] "It is always more important to prevent an imminent danger of war than to be concerned about the possibility of a future one." . . . Therefore, Rabbi Yosef concludes, "In our case, there is a present danger before us since if we do not return the territories, it may lead to immediate war. On the other hand, the danger that a war will result in the future if we allow the border to come closer to our settlements is not a present danger." . . . Furthermore, Rabbi Yosef's whole argument is based on the judgment that the danger of immediate war with our neighbors is a more prevalent one than that posed by ceding territory. This appears to be pure guesswork. If we are really concerned about the chance of war, we should consider the northern front, where the danger is not reduced at all by returning Judea, Samaria, and Gaza but is in fact increased. Therefore, it is clear, on the basis of the ruling in the Shulḥan Arukh, that ceding any territory whatsoever is prohibited. It does not eliminate danger—rather, it increases it.

PESAK DIN

Rabbi Yisraeli rules:

> It is completely prohibited to cede the territories that we liberated by the grace of God in a defensive war. This does not diminish the danger of loss of life—it increases it.
>
> Let us strengthen ourselves by faith in God, the guardian of Israel, who will guide and keep us safe in difficult times, grant us deliverance and redemption, and bless us speedily with the ingathering of the exiles of Israel.[17]

Life in the United States   10

Jews had been living in North America since their arrival in the Dutch colony of New Amsterdam in 1654, but it wasn't until the late nineteenth century that their numbers in the United States started to increased dramatically. By the early twentieth century, the largest population of Jews outside of Europe was to be found in North America, and today the country with the largest Jewish population outside of the State of Israel is the United States.

The responsa in this chapter demonstrate how American rabbis have sought to navigate between halakhic principles and the reality of American life. The Committee on Responsa of the Committee on Army and Navy Religious Activities (Reform, Conservative, and Orthodox) answers questions arising during military service, from reciting *Kaddish* without a minyan to wearing a cross in emergency situations. Rabbi Moses Feinstein argues against observing the quintessential American holiday of Thanksgiving. Rabbi Jeremy Kalmanofsky addresses one of the most controversial issues in American civic life—the death penalty—considering what roles Jews may play in capital cases.

Text 10.1. Committee on Responsa of the Committee on Army and Navy Religious Activities, "Responsa in War Time"

American Jews have served in the United States military since the Revolutionary War. In 1917, at the onset of direct U.S. involvement in World War I, Congress passed a bill authorizing additional chaplain positions for the duration of the war, and rabbis were given the opportunity to become military chaplains. A number of Jewish organizations serving Jewish military personnel joined together to create the Jewish Welfare Board, which had the authority to recommend rabbis as military chaplains.[1] Rabbi Elkan Voorsanger, a Reform rabbi already in Europe serving as a private in the American Expeditionary Force, became the first official Jewish chaplain in the American military. His presence and exploits on the front line earned him the sobriquet of "the fighting rabbi," a Purple Heart, a French Croix de Guerre, and eventually the rank of captain.[2]

The beginning of World War II saw the establishment of the Committee on Responsa of the Committee on Army and Navy Religious Activities, a rabbinic committee uniquely composed of Reform (Rabbi Solomon B. Freehof), Conservative (Rabbi Milton Steinberg), and Orthodox (Rabbi Leo Jung) rabbis formed to answer halakhic questions pertaining to military service. As Committee on Responsa chairman Rabbi Solomon Freehof explains in *Responsa in War Time*, a collected volume of responsa published after the war (in 1947):

> A coastguardsman asked how could he say Kaddish on his yahrzeit when he was on lonely patrol service for a week with only one other comrade, a Gentile. Could Kaddish be recited without a quorum of ten worshippers, a minyan? Another soldier asked whether he could have a pidyon haben in absentia. He was in service in Colorado and his wife had given birth to their firstborn son in Brooklyn.[3]

In principle, Rabbi Freehof comments, it would seem difficult for the Committee on Responsa to find common ground in its responses, given that each of its three rabbinic representatives (Reform, Conservative, and Orthodox) had a different attitude to Jewish law, but that turned out not to be the case:

In practice almost no difficulty at all was ever experienced in arriving at a decision. The decision was based upon classic Jewish law. Because of the exigencies of wartime, the more lenient authorities were generally chosen, and when even the liberal decision would be contrary to the practice of Reform Jews, their exceptional point of view on the matter was specifically provided for.

Sometimes, too, the Orthodox member of the Committee would record his disagreement. On this basis it was possible to come to a decision on virtually every question which confronted us with almost no disagreement either among the members of the Committee or from the complete Committee of the CANRA [Committee on Army and Navy Religious Activities], when these reports were presented to it. . . .

We limited ourselves very early as to the type of questions with which we would deal. At first we discussed a number of questions with regard to marriage and divorce, but we very soon decided to stop dealing with such matters. The basis of our decision was that we were concerned primarily with such questions as were involved essentially in a man's or woman's service in the armed forces. While the soldier was profoundly interested in having the status of his marriage or divorce settled, it was clear that this status dealt with his whole life which is overwhelmingly civilian. Even in matters such as kosher and trefah food which were vital to many a soldier's welfare, we confined our decision only to the part of the question which dealt primarily with life in the armed forces, and we avoided general decisions that might be applied to civilian life. Thus we restricted ourselves to matters that dealt with the war emergency. In this way not only was the subject matter limited, but it was also understood that even on these matters our decisions applied only to the period of emergency. Even in army matters they applied only to wartime and thus were *horaath shaah* [leniency that addresses a single extraordinary circumstance and does not create a precedent for use in general].[4]

Rabbi Freehof elucidates the committee's thinking about publication of their wartime responsa in this light:

> It is for this reason that CANRA decided to limit the publication of these responsa so as not to create the impression that a new series of religious standards has been set up for Jewry in general.
>
> It may perhaps be that some of our decisions, even though they were meant as "guidance for the hour," may prove to be of assistance in case, heaven forbid, war comes again. At all events, they will be of interest to chaplains and workers in the war effort, and perhaps to many of the soldiers and sailors. It is chiefly as a memento of wartime that these are now published. The very existence of these responsa is an evidence of the eagerness of our government to be scrupulously careful of the religious rights of its citizens. It is also an evidence of how widespread was the desire not only on the part of the chaplains but of the soldiers themselves to maintain the observances of their faith under the strain and danger of a world war.[5]

Five wartime responsa from the Committee on Responsa follow. Most are printed here in full. All are brief, citing a minimum of sources. Each exchange appears in its own section.

SECTION A: QUESTION AND ANSWER ON A *KOHEN* CLAIMING CONSCIENTIOUS OBJECTION

A questioner asks about the status of a *Kohen* (or *Cohen*) serving in the military:

> May a man who is a kohen claim conscientious objection to war because he is not permitted to come into contact with dead bodies?

In other words, can a person who according to family tradition is descended from priests (officiants in the Jerusalem Temple then required to follow rules of ritual purity) refuse to fight in a war because of this descendant's familial status?

The Committee on Responsa clarifies what remains to be determined:

> The old priestly laws that a priest avoid defilement by contact with the dead are still observed. The question is to what extent this customary observance of the law of uncleanliness with regard to the dead is sufficient ground for claiming conscientious objection to war.

The committee rules that it is not sufficient:

> A soldier may not necessarily come in contact with the dead at all. He is drafted and therefore must be considered [forced into a forbidden action], and he certainly cannot refuse to serve upon this basis.[6]

SECTION B: QUESTION AND ANSWER ON WEARING A CROSS

A Jewish nurse questions if she is permitted to wear a cross in a war zone in case she is marooned:

> A question was brought to us through a chaplain with regard to the inquiry of a Jewish nurse as to her wearing a cross with her "dog-tag." The chaplain stated that the question was raised with reference to the possibility of becoming stranded somewhere in the South Pacific area where in many instances the natives had come to recognize the cross as the only sure symbol of friendship.

The Committee on Responsa weighs issues of concealment:

In the discussion in Yore Deah 178:1, where the question is raised about Jews wearing the garments of non-Jews as to when that is prohibited and when permitted, the commentor Siftei Cohen [Rabbi Shabbetai ben Meir Hakohen, 1621–62, Lithuania, Poland, Germany] says that in times of persecution it is certainly permitted for a Jew to disguise himself by wearing non-Jewish clothes. Thus, if, for example, the question were whether Jewish soldiers fighting on the European continent might not be permitted to conceal their Jewish identity by wearing "dog-tags" without the letter "H" so that, if captured by the Nazis, they would not be mistreated, the answer would be that this is certainly permitted.

However, such concealing of Jewish identity cannot be permitted in the South Seas where there is no question of persecution of Jews. The question specifically, however, is not one of concealing Jewish identity, but of wearing the cross in order to win the friendship of natives in the South Seas who are accustomed to consider the cross as a symbol of friendship.

The committee rules:

The law on this matter is quite clear.

Shulchan Aruch, Yore Deah, 141:1, Joseph Karo, discussing which statues are to be considered idols and which are not, says that the statues in villages are to be considered idols since they are meant to be bowed down to. Those in great cities are not to be considered idols since they are merely for decoration. To this Moses Isserles comments as follows: "A cross which is meant to be bowed down to is forbidden, but one that is worn around the neck is merely a memento and is not forbidden." Thus, the law is clear: To use a cross as the nurse intended to is not forbidden by law, but since it is clearly against general Jewish sentiment, the Committee refrains from advising her on this matter. She herself must judge how grave the danger is and how much help the symbol would give her.[7]

SECTION C: QUESTION AND ANSWER ON FRIDAY EVENING SERVICE IN ARCTIC REGIONS

One of many questions about Shabbat concerns the timing of its observance in unusual situations:

> When should Sabbath services be held by troops of Jewish faith in the northern latitudes—Iceland, etc.?

The Committee on Responsa explains what is being asked:

> The problem involves the extent of the period of twilight.
> Twilight in rabbinic law marks the end of the day and the beginning of night. Hence, the beginning of the sabbath depends upon the extent of twilight in the various latitudes. However, in the far northern latitudes the normal twilight is extended in the summer months by what is known as the astronomical twilight, which often lasts all night; hence, there is continuous twilight or half-twilight for months in succession. Therefore, it is impossible to know when the sabbath should begin or end.

The committee references multiple sources on similar situations:

> This problem is referred to by Chaim Mordecai Margolis [d. 1818, Poland], Shaarey Teshuva, to Shulchan Aruch Orach Chayyim, no. 344. The Shulchan Aruch there discusses the question of the man who is travelling in the desert and finds he has lost count of the days. Rabbi Joseph Caro, basing his opinion on the Talmud, says that he must begin counting days from the time that he became aware of his forgetfulness and must celebrate the

seventh day as [the] Sabbath and mark it with kiddush [prayer marking the Sabbath] and havdalah [prayer marking the end of the Sabbath]. This traveller, not knowing the exact day of the Sabbath, selects a day and observes it as the Sabbath.

Shaarey Teshuva (ad loc.) applies the same principle of the selection of a time for the sabbath to those who live in the northern latitudes and do not know the day and the hour of sabbath, just as the man in the desert does not know the day of the sabbath. The statement of Margolis is as follows: "Those who journey near the North or South Pole, where the day lengthens into a month or two months and sometimes even six months, should count six days of twenty-four hours." In other words, the Jew in the Arctic latitudes selects a time and an hour-length equivalent to those in the lower latitudes. This is the best that he can do.

Rabbi Dr. Pool reports that such is actually the practice among communities of northern Norway and Sweden. They follow the hours for the Sabbath independently of their sunset and follow that of Hamburg.

The committee rules:

> Jewish soldiers in the northern latitudes should pick the hours of the Sabbath as observed in New York or Seattle and fix their Sabbath service accordingly, regardless of whether twilight (in summer) or darkness (in winter) has yet come.[8]

SECTION D: PERFORMANCE OF MARRIAGE OF PROTESTANT GIRL TO JEWISH LIEUTENANT; CONVERSION

A question arises as to whether a Jewish chaplain can officiate at a marriage of a Jewish soldier and a non-Jewish woman who also wishes to convert to Judaism:

A lieutenant returnee from the Aleutians intends to marry a Protestant girl in the next month or so. The girl is very anxious to accept the Jewish faith, a desire which has not been influenced by the wishes of the lieutenant. The lieutenant wants the chaplain to perform the marriage ceremony and would like to know whether he will convert her. There is no civilian rabbi within a radius of 250 miles. As the chaplain sized up the situation it is a question of keeping a Jew in the fold (he has a Reform background) by converting the woman whom he definitely will marry, or have a Justice of the Peace marry them and losing both.

The Committee on Responsa answers:

The general practice recommended by CANRA with regard to the conversion of proselytes is that the chaplain refrain from such conversion, referring all such cases to a nearby civilian rabbi. The reasons for our decision are, first, the general disinclination of Judaism to encourage proselytism, especially cases connected with marriage, and, second, the fact that the military conditions where the chaplain is often in charge of men of different faiths (Catholic, Protestant or Jewish) lead us to the wish to discourage any kind of proselytism which might involve the conversion of soldiers. However, it is clear that there are certain special cases under which the chaplain must make his own decision guiding himself by his own conscience and by the specific religious background of the families involved. In the case mentioned by the chaplain there is no civilian rabbi within 250 miles. Secondly, the young lady is sincerely desirous of accepting Judaism, and according to principle of Rav [Palestinian Talmud *Kiddushin* 65b] such proselytes must be received in friendliness, for we may assume that they are converting out of sincere motives. Thirdly, the young man is of Reform Jewish background and according to the Reform Jewish practice such proselytes are accepted after instruction without ritual requirements. In these circumstances, the chaplain may use his own initiative and judgment as to the conversion.[9]

SECTION E: QUESTION AND ANSWER ON RECITING *KADDISH* WITHOUT A MINYAN

A questioner asks:

> May a soldier or sailor who is on lonely outpost duty for a considerable period of time (as for example, men on coast guard duty) in the event of yahrzeit say kaddish alone, since he cannot possibly assemble a minyan?

The Committee on Responsa responds:

> Just as in the case of the [*Amidah*] it is preferable to say it with the congregation and yet it is permitted to be said silently alone, so the kaddish which is primarily part of the congregational response may also be recited silently alone.
>
> Furthermore, the CANRA will arrange for kaddish to be recited in a congregation in honor of the departed relative of any soldier or sailor who writes in to CANRA or makes such arrangement with the chaplain. The soldier or sailor should report the date of the yahrzeit and the name of the relative.[10]

Text 10.2. Feinstein, "American Thanksgiving"

IGGEROT MOSHE, 4, *YOREH DE'AH*, NO. 12

Born in Belorussia, Rabbi Moses Feinstein (1895–1986) studied with his father, a rabbi, as well as in yeshivot in Belorussia and served as a rabbi there until he immigrated to the United States in 1937.[11] He built Metivta Tiferet Jerusalem in Manhattan into a leading

Ultraorthodox yeshiva, and after World War II he became a leading, if not the leading, rabbinic decisor in Orthodox and Ultraorthodox circles in the United States, publishing a voluminous number of responsa, especially in medical ethics. Notably, his responsa are often brief, about one to four pages. One reason there are so many responsa is that he includes every letter he wrote on a Jewish matter in his responsa.

Rabbi Feinstein served as chairman of Mo'etzet Gedolei Hatorah of Agudat Israel of America, an Ultraorthodox communal group, and, from 1966 until 1976, as president of the Union of Orthodox Rabbis in America and Canada. He also wrote novellae on the Babylonian Talmud.

It has been said that the number one thing that any American Orthodox rabbi needed to know in order to be ordained was Rabbi Feinstein's telephone number. He sought to distance Orthodox Jews from Conservative and Reform Jews and from general American culture: he disallowed secular studies to the extent allowed by government regulations, was antagonistic to coed classes, and was adamant that the height of a *meḥitzah* (divider in an Orthodox synagogue between men and women) be higher than what was the norm when he wrote. He also appeared to view the American political system less as representing citizens with equal rights and more akin to medieval Europe under the direct protection of a monarch, as one of his responsa intimates:

> Regarding the mercy that our government, the United States of America, that with great mercies for the remnant of the Jewish refugees from all the countries of Europe and the remnant of the great Torah scholars and their students, God, may He be blessed, has brought us here where venerable Torah institutions of Europe as well as new ones have been established, and through the grace of the government whose entire purpose is to do good for all the residents of the land created a number

of programs to help students in all the schools in the land to study and advance in their studies, including Torah institutions, which have benefited greatly from aid to their students, certainly all *rashei yeshiva* [the highest level of teacher and leader at a yeshiva], administrators, and students recognize all the boons from the government and utter blessings for the welfare of the state and all those who govern it.[12]

In the following responsum, Rabbi Feinstein considers whether American Jews are permitted to celebrate Thanksgiving.

SECTION A: REASONS FOR NOT
CELEBRATING THANKSGIVING[13]
Rabbi Feinstein summarizes his previous writings about why celebrating Thanksgiving yearly is forbidden:

> To my dear grandson, beloved to me very much, Rabbi Mordecai Tendler, peace and blessing forever.... Regarding the day of Thanksgiving of the United States, I have already written about it this year that to make a party and festive meal in honor of the day of Thanksgiving is forbidden according to religious law, not because of the prohibition of "their festive day," since it is not one of their festive days that their priests invented but because there is a prohibition from "you shall not walk in their ways" (Lev. 18:13). And recently in another responsum to another rabbi, I wrote that there is no prohibition in making a party with a meal nor in eating turkey, but it is certainly forbidden to make this obligatory and a mitzvah but [only] a voluntary party one time and extemporaneously that could also be done in another year. I determined that in any case it is forbidden in my opinion to establish a particular day of the year to have this festival: even in the case of King Yannai who made a party and festive meal when he conquered Kohalit in the desert, as

in Babylonian Talmud *Kiddushin* 66a, this was his conquest and not [celebrated] in later years. I have also written that this is because of "do not add [observances]" according to Naḥmanides on Deuteronomy 4:2.

SECTION B: THANKSGIVING IS UNIMPORTANT

Rabbi Feinstein argues that what happened to the colonists was not of sufficient importance to warrant a permanent national celebration. He does not present the history of Thanksgiving and the reasons why George Washington, Abraham Lincoln, and Franklin Delano Roosevelt set aside a day for public thanksgiving, repentance, and devotion to God,[14] but instead presents an unsubstantiated claim: there was plenty of food, and it just happened by chance that a certain group of colonists, unsuccessful in hunting large wild animals, did not have any.

In this light he introduces Rabbi Moses Isserles's ruling that Jews should not follow the styles of other nations unless it is for a good, necessary reason:

> What Rabbi Isserles meant is that establishing a practice for an unimportant matter, that in itself is the way of the Amorites [and is forbidden]. And this is [what happened] in establishing a day for a party for this matter—that those people ate when they came to this country because it happened that one time they did not have anything to eat and so they ate turkey—this is not a major issue in the settlement of America. For at that time in America there was much to eat, many kinds of fruit, other kinds of found, domesticated animals and wild animals, and fish in the seas and rivers. But it just happened to certain people that they happened to be in a place where there were no fruit, it was hard for them to obtain domesticated animals and big wild animals, and they ate turkey [a small wild animal]. Even if these people do not have anything to eat, since America was already

known in the world, other people would come in ships with all types of foods and seeds... and America would have been settled even without this. Hence, [the event commemorated by Thanksgiving] is really nothing.... It's really unnecessary to celebrate centuries later an event that happened to [a few] people. This is to be considered like an Amorite practice... and therefore the prohibition of "do not walk in their ways" applies.[15]

Text 10.3. Kalmanofsky, "Participating in the American Death Penalty"

COMMITTEE ON JEWISH LAW AND STANDARDS OF THE RABBINICAL ASSEMBLY, ḤOSHEN MISHPAT 2:1.2013

Rabbi Jeremy Kalmanofsky has served as rabbi at Ansche Chesed in Manhattan since 2001. Ordained at the Jewish Theological Seminary of America, he served fourteen years on the Rabbinical Assembly's Committee on Jewish Law and Standards (CJLS). He tries to approach halakhah less as a set of rules demanding conformity as its own end, but rather as shared norms that make Judaism virtuous, reverent, and spiritual.

In addressing the following question on whether Jews may serve as witnesses, prosecutors, judges, and prison personnel in a capital case, Rabbi Kalmanofsky seeks to steer between halakhah and the reality of American life.[16]

QUESTION

In 2013, as the death penalty continued to be the subject of fierce debate in the United States, Rabbi Kalmanofsky addresses:

> May a Jew participate in capital criminal cases in the American legal system?

SECTION A: INTRODUCTION

Rabbi Kalmanofsky stresses that there are divergent opinions in halakhah regarding the death penalty. The Conservative/Masorti movement's Committee on Jewish Law and Standards ruled against its use in the United States in 1960. Given this reality, what are Jewish citizens to do when called to play roles in capital cases?

> Jewish tradition is ambivalent regarding the death penalty. On one hand, Torah is replete with capital punishments.... On the other hand, rabbinic tradition is generally averse to capital punishment.... There is yet a third side to the argument.... The [Babylonian Talmud *Sanhedrin* 46a] recognized that desperate times can call for desperate measures....
>
> The classic Mishnah (Makkot 1:10) on capital punishment captures this ambivalence:
>
>> A Sanhedrin that executes once in seven years is called bloodthirsty. Rabbi Elazar ben Azariah said: even once in 70 years. Rabbi Akiba and Rabbi Tarfon said: had we been in the Sanhedrin, none would ever have been put to death. Rabban Shimon ben Gamaliel said: then these sages would have created more murderers in Israel.
>
> In good rabbinic fashion, this [disagreement] remains unresolved. It seems that each side has a point...
>
> More than 50 years ago, the CJLS affirmed its opposition to the death penalty, in this 1960 statement by Rabbi Ben Zion Bokser [1907–84, United States]:
>
>> Only God has the right to take life. When the state allows itself to take life, it sets an example which the criminal distorts to his own ends. It proves to him that man may take into his own hands the disposition of another man's life. The elimination of capital punishment would help to establish

a climate in which life will be held sacred. The sense of the sanctity of life needs to be bolstered in our time, and it will be perhaps the greatest contribution toward deterring crime and violence....

The abolition of capital punishment will be an important step forward in the direction of a more humane justice. It will free America from a black spot of barbarism which still disfigures the good name of our country.

We reaffirm that position today.... We believe that in virtually all cases, even the worst murderers should be imprisoned rather than executed....

However, we are asked not only about an ideal penal system, but about the one we actually have in the United States (the only country with significant Jewish population that applies capital punishment today). Given that the death penalty exists at the federal level and in 32 states, what should Jewish citizens do when called to play roles in capital cases? Should Jewish judges and prosecutors refuse to play their parts in what Justice Harry Blackmun called "the machinery of death"? Should Jewish citizens refuse to serve on juries that might send a person to execution? Should witnesses withhold testimony that might help send someone to death row? Or, alternatively, does halakhah consider it within a government's legitimate authority to execute criminals, though based on values we would argue that they should elect not to exercise that power? If this is the case, then Jewish citizens could take part in capital cases, albeit reluctantly or under protest. Certainly Jews are generally bound to obey the laws of the land, even those laws they oppose. Yet some laws may be so incompatible with our norms that Jews should refuse to follow them, by civil disobedience or conscientious objection. In which category does capital punishment belong? Is it beyond the bounds of what Judaism can tolerate? Or might it be bad policy, but not *prima facie* illegitimate?

SECTION B: ABOLITION IN THEORY

Rabbi Kalmanofsky stresses that halakhah institutes stringent rules to forestall the death penalty. Halakhic courts very rarely imposed it:

> Perhaps the most famous teaching in all rabbinic literature (Mishnah Sanhedrin 4:5) is that each human life is as valuable as the entire world, so killing a person is tantamount to destroying the world. That homily is presented as what judges should say to impress a healthy fear of heaven upon witnesses in capital cases, in which some human beings decide whether others will live or die....
>
> This expresses the sages' well-attested tendency to view capital punishment with suspicion, as in the aforementioned Mishnah Makkot 1:10. Halakhic criminal procedure and rules of evidence are "rigged extravagantly to bring about the acquittal of the accused."... A particularly interesting feature of these procedures is the ban on accepting circumstantial evidence against a defendant. Even if one witnessed an armed man chase another into an enclosed space, then later saw him, bloody sword in hand, standing above the corpse of the other man, dead of stab wounds, this would constitute inadmissible conjecture, not hard enough evidence for conviction (Babylonian Talmud Sanhedrin 37b)....
>
> While not overturning its many death penalties, [the Rabbis] construed criminal procedure so narrowly that they rendered biblical capital punishment all but theoretical. The sages reported further that the Sanhedrin, by relocating, renounced its power to impose the death penalty in the early first century (Mishneh Torah Sanhedrin 13.11). And so it has remained these two millennia.
>
> Formal renunciation is only half the story, however. As elaborated pragmatically through history, halakhah is more complicated. All societies must restrain and punish evil doers,

as the Torah states nine times (Deut. 13:6, for example): "And you shall uproot the evil from among you." A society that fails to punish criminals, even in the name of the humanity of its own rules, effectively encourages crime. . . .

Relevant for our inquiry . . . are emergency powers granted to rabbinic courts to impose penalties not warranted by standard procedures. The Babylonian Talmud (Sanhedrin 46a) authorizes religious courts to flog and to execute malfeasors—"not to violate the Torah, but to make a fence around the Torah"—if they deemed the situation exigent enough; that is "if the hour demands it." Indeed, Jewish courts throughout history cited this passage in asserting their own power to issue sometimes violent punishments. . . . History attests that this power was not merely theoretical; in rare cases, Jewish courts actually imposed the death penalty.

SECTION C: NOAHIDE AUTHORITY

Rabbi Kalmanofsky then moves to analyze how halakhah understands the authority of non-Jewish governmental courts:

> We must [also] consider the *halakhic* status of non-Jewish governments and their powers to inflict violence as a means of preserving social order. . . . Halakhah not only *permits*, it *requires* non-Jewish authorities to create legal systems that maintain social order and restrain crime. The Babylonian Talmud (Sanhedrin 56a) considers the creation of *dinim*, a fair legal system, as one of the Noahide laws, applicable to all human societies. . . .
>
> It is the role of sovereign government to punish criminals like robbers, thieves and murderers, and its laws in such matters are law.

SECTION D: WHAT IS CAPITAL PUNISHMENT SUPPOSED TO ACCOMPLISH?

Rabbi Kalmanofsky seeks to identify the philosophical basis of punishment in halakhah:

> There are two main arguments for capital punishment....
>
> There is, first, a *deontological* or duty-based explanation for executing the most terrible criminals.... Some crimes are so awful that a moral society must respond with the most severe condemnation possible: that the perpetrator had forfeited the right to live.... Post-biblical Jewish tradition has generally not built law upon the deontological argument, however. Set aside the virtually *sui generis* case of Adolf Eichmann—to this day, the only person executed after a civilian trial in Israel, under a 1950 law specifically written for WWII-era murderers....
>
> Why, then, would certain crimes entail death? When the Torah imposes capital punishment, it often (nine times, all in Deuteronomy) explains the penalty by saying "you shall root out the evil from your midst." On seven of those nine cases, *Sifrei* repeatedly comments "so that you root out evil *doers* from Israel." This amounts to a *consequentialist* or outcomes-based argument for the death penalty. Under this approach, capital punishment is warranted because it helps do what all moral societies must: control crime, imposing the most severe punishments on the worst offenders, and deterring further crime by other potential criminals....
>
> The Judaic legitimacy of capital punishment depends precisely on the claims of deterrence and crime control. If in fact the American death penalty effectively helps control, punish and deter crime, then the consequentialist argument for the death penalty finds relatively easy justification in the Jewish legal tradition. On the other hand, if the death penalty produces no practical positive consequence for society, it really is pointless

bloodshed that Jews should resist by conscientious objection to participation in capital trials.

SECTION E: DOES THE AMERICAN DEATH PENALTY DETER?

Addressing whether the death penalty serves as a deterrent, Rabbi Kalmanofsky observes that the first two chief rabbis of Israel argued against its use by the Israeli court system:

> A *halakhic* analysis of the American death penalty calls for more than *halakhic* judgment. Jewish law ... should consult expert data so that its decisions meaningfully hook on to the world. ... And it must be said that capital punishment is a more complicated question than it might seem at first glance. ...
>
> Measuring deterrence is a most complicated matter. The question is not whether fear of capital punishment would deter crime; it is whether fear of death is a substantially greater deterrent than the threat of life in prison. ... In fact, a number of leading scholars have concluded that empirical data on executions and deterrence is just too small and varies too widely year-to-year and by locale, and is responsive to too many other extrinsic factors to establish either the existence or absence of a deterrent effect. For instance, opponents like to note that death penalty states may have higher homicide rates than non-death penalty states. But too many other factors influence those results. ... Among the member states of the OECD [Organization for Economic Cooperation and Development], only America and Japan practice capital punishment. ...
>
> Most modern Jewish religious leaders have favored abolition. In Israel, when the young state convicted its first murderer, the two chief rabbis, Rabbi Isaac Herzog and Rabbi Ben Zion Meir Hai Ouziel, urged the justice minister to nullify the death penalty, left over from the British Mandate. ...

The most obvious argument for abolition emerging from Jewish sources is that capital punishment all too hastily risks the irreversible horror of executing an innocent person. Killing even a criminal destroys a whole world. Imagine the worlds that would have been destroyed if 142 [and more since Rabbi Kalmanofsky wrote] American death row prisoners had not been released since 1973 after their convictions were reversed. . . .

American death penalty policy deserves our condemnation in numerous other ways. We note the persistent patterns of racial discrimination, consistently poor defense counsel, and inconsistent approaches to appeal across jurisdictions in capital cases. . . . Moreover, the death penalty is tremendously expensive. . . . Couldn't that money have been better spent elsewhere on fighting crime? . . .

SECTION F: SHOULD JEWS REFUSE TO PARTICIPATE?

Rabbi Kalmanofsky weighs whether Jewish citizens in the United States should refrain from participating in capital trials:

The American death penalty is in decline.

Given this advancing trend, it might be argued, the best course for a Jewish citizen is to refuse to participate in capital trials as judge, prosecutor or juror. . . . Such conscientious objection might seem at first glance to reflect a good moral intuition, and might seem appealing as a gesture of protest against a repugnant policy. But before coming to that conclusion, a few points bear consideration.

First, although we believe religious Jews should oppose the death penalty on moral and pragmatic grounds, at [the] same time not everything moral by definition imposes a *halakhic* imperative or a prohibition. Based on all the foregoing . . . we do not find a *halakhic* prohibition on participating or a *halakhic* imperative to refuse to participate in capital cases as witnesses, jurors, prosecutors or judges.

Second, Jewish citizens of the United States are duty-bound to support the state's fundamentally necessary efforts to restrain criminals and control crime. That duty does not lapse because we object to capital punishment. Do Jewish norms really demand that [Jews living in states with active capital penalties] cede that civic obligation to their gentile neighbors whenever a murder is committed?

SECTION G: HOW SHOULD JEWS PARTICIPATE IN CAPITAL CASES?

Rabbi Kalmanofsky delineates which roles Jews may serve in the legal process:

> Witnesses: This is the least morally freighted of the roles. A witness neither convicts nor acquits and assigns no penalty. A witness merely conveys to the court the information, for judges and jurors to evaluate. Even if that testimony proves decisive, it is not the witness who decided....
>
> Jurors: ... Since, by any honest report, halakhah recognizes that the death penalty is warranted in extreme cases, there is no halakhic reason why jurors should assert absolutely that they could never impose capital punishment. Observant Jewish jurors could promise to keep an open mind and vote for the death penalty if prosecutors could convince them execution was "the morally appropriate punishment," even if that applied only to a tiny class of cases....
>
> Judges and Prosecutors: The foregoing applies equally and more strongly to prosecutors and judges. Their work helps keep society safe, and so, in its way, is holy work. Prosecutors have virtually unfettered discretion over when to seek the death penalty or long-term imprisonment. In many jurisdictions, judges are

bound to follow juries' sentencing determinations; in others, judges have discretion to modify those determinations.... Even in cases where American law dictates a capital punishment, Jewish prosecutors and judges can fulfill their professional duties without transgressing the Torah and the decrees of our sages.

Prison Guards and Medical Technicians: ... [There is] the possibility that a Jewish guard may have to strap a prisoner to a gurney, or a Jewish medical aide may be called upon to administer a lethal injection.... There is no escaping the conclusion that when these employees of the state ... carry out their duties, they are not murderers, but duly authorized public servants.

The judges, prosecutors, jurors, and witnesses who play their roles in reaching and executing a capital sentence would not be halakhically guilty of causing an unjust homicide.

PESAK DIN

Rabbi Kalmanofsky rules:

> We urge the American federal and state governments to renounce capital punishment except in the rarest cases. Religious Jews should advocate for that position as the superior moral stance and best public policy. But given the weight of precedent, it would be false to assert that Jewish law forbids capital punishment. Halakhah confers on secular governments the legitimate power to punish criminals to protect the innocent, including the right to impose death, when needed, God forbid. Objection to the death penalty is not halakhic grounds to refuse to participate as judge, prosecutor, juror, police or witness in capital trials.[17]

SOURCE ACKNOWLEDGMENTS

1.1. Rabbi Nina Beth Cardin and Rabbi Avram Reisner, "*Ma'asei Yadai L'hitpa-er*: On the Mitzvah of Sustainability." Committee on Jewish Law and Standards of the Conservative Movement, Ḥoshen Mishpaṭ 175:26, https://www.rabbinicalassembly.org/sites/default/files/2023-02/cjls-sustainability-teshuvah-final-updated-feb-2023.pdf. With permission of the Rabbinical Assembly.

1.2. Rabbi Barry Leff, "Whistleblowing: The Requirement to Report Employer Wrongdoing." Committee on Jewish Law and Standards of the Conservative Movement, Ḥoshen Mishpaṭ 410:8.2007, https://www.rabbinicalassembly.org/sites/default/files/public/halakhah/teshuvot/20052010/leff_whistleblowing.pdf. With permission of the Rabbinical Assembly.

1.3. Rabbi Isaac Jacob Weiss, "About Commercial Encroachment." In *Minḥat Yitzhak*, vol. 2, no. 90, corrected edition (Jerusalem: Minḥat Yitzhak Publishing House, 1993), 194–96. Translated by Pamela Barmash.

1.4. Rabbi Abdallah Somekh and Rabbi Joseph Ḥayyim Al-Hakam, "On Commerce in the Markets of Malabar." In *Zivḥei tzedek* (Baghdad: privately printed, 1899), Ḥoshen Mishpaṭ, no. 2. Translated by Pamela Barmash.

1.5. Rabbi Pamela Barmash, "Veal Calves." Committee on Jewish Law and Standards of the Conservative Movement, Even ha-Ezer 5:14, https://www.rabbinicalassembly.org/sites/default/files/teshuvot/1703225420_108.pdf?id=49666%20. Courtesy of the Rabbinical Assembly.

2.1. Rabbi Moses Sofer, "On Using the Vernacular in Prayer." In *Ḥatam sofer* (Bratislava: privately printed, 1912), vol. 6, *Likutim*, 218–20, no. 84, and 221–25, no. 86. Translated by Pamela Barmash.

2.2. Rabbi Ḥayyim David Halevi, "What Are the Chances That Our Prayers Are Answered by God?" In *Aseh lekha rav* (Tel Aviv: Committee to Publish the Works of Rabbi Ḥ. D. Halevi, 1975), vol. 2, no. 22. Translated by Pamela Barmash.

2.3. CCAR Responsum: "A Sex Offender in the Synagogue," 5765.4, https://www.ccarnet.org/ccar-responsa/nyp-no-5765-4/. Copyright © 2004 by Central Conference of American Rabbis. Used by permission of the CCAR. All rights reserved.

3.1. Ephraim Oshry, "The Case of a *Mamzer* Rabbi." In *Mima'amakim* (New York: privately published, 1968), vol. 3, no. 98, 73–80. Translated by Pamela Barmash.

3.2. Rabbi Elie Spitz, "*Mamzerut*." Committee on Jewish Law and Standards of the Conservative Movement, Even ha-Ezer 4.2000a, https://www.rabbinicalassembly.org/sites/default/files/2022-09/spitz_mamzerut.pdf. With permission of the Rabbinical Assembly.

3.3. Rabbi Shalom Mesas, "A *Pesak Din* in a Matter of *Mamzerut*." *Shemesh u-magen* (Jerusalem: privately printed, 2000), vol. 3, no. 12, 227–29. Translated by Pamela Barmash.

3.4. CCAR Responsum: "Patrilineal and Matrilineal Descent." In *Contemporary American Reform Responsa*, ed. Walter Jacob © 1987 Hebrew Union College Press; Central Conference of American Rabbis. Used by permission of the CCAR. All rights reserved.

3.5. Rabbi Ovadiah Yosef, "On the Status of Ethiopian Jews." In *Yabi'a omer*, vol. 8, *Even ha-Ezer* (Jerusalem: privately printed, 1995), no. 11. Translated by Pamela Barmash.

3.6. Rabbi Pamela Barmash, "The Status of the Ḥeresh [Deaf Mute] and of Sign Language." Committee on Jewish Law and Standards of the Conservative Movement, Ḥoshen Mishpaṭ 35:11, https://www.rabbinicalassembly.org/sites/default/files/public/halakhah/teshuvot/2011-2020/Status%20of%20the%20Heresh6.2011.pdf. Courtesy of the Rabbinical Assembly.

4.1. Rabbi Jacob Lauterbach, "Shall Women Be Ordained Rabbis?" In *Yearbook of the Central Conference of American Rabbis* (New York: Central Conference of American Rabbis, 1922), 32:156–77.

4.2. Rabbi Isaac Herzog, "*Takkanot* on Marriage and *Yibbum*." In *Teḥukah le-Yisrael al pi ha-Torah* (Jerusalem: Mossad Harav Kook, 1989), 3:168–69. Translated by Pamela Barmash.

4.3. Yo'ezet halakhah Michal Roness, "When Staining Renders a Woman Niddah." In *Nishmat Ha-Bayit: Contemporary Questions on Women's Reproductive Health Addressed by Yoatzot Halacha*, ed. Yehuda-Herzl Henkin and Chana Henkin (New Milford CT and Jerusalem: Maggid Press, 2021), no. 42.

4.4. Rabbi Joel E. Rembaum, "Regarding the Inclusion of the Names of the Matriarchs in the First Blessing of the *Amidah*." Committee on Jewish Law and Standards, Oraḥ Ḥayyim 112.1990. In *Proceedings of the Committee on Jewish Law and Standards of the Conservative Movement, 1991-2000* (New York: Rabbinical Assembly, 2001), 485–90. https://www.rabbinicalassembly.org/sites/default/files/assets/public/halakhah/teshuvot/19861990/rembaum_matriarchs.pdf. With permission of the Rabbinical Assembly.

4.5. Rabbi Pamela Barmash, "Women and Mitzvot." Committee on Jewish Law and Standards of the Conservative Movement, Yoreh De'ah 246:6.2014a, https://www.rabbinicalassembly.org/sites/default/files/public/halakhah/teshuvot/2011-2020/womenandhiyyuvfinal.pdf. Courtesy of the Rabbinical Assembly.

5.1. Rabbi Joel Roth, "Homosexuality," Even ha-Ezer 24.1992b. In *Responsa: The Committee on Jewish Law and Standards of the Conservative Movement, 1991-2000*, ed. Kassel Abelson and David J. Fine (New York: Rabbinical Assembly, 2002), 613–75. https://www.rabbinicalassembly.org/sites/default/files/assets/public/halakhah/teshuvot/19912000/roth_homosexual.pdf. With permission of the Rabbinical Assembly.

5.2. Rabbi Elliot Dorff, Rabbi Daniel Nevins, and Rabbi Avram Reisner, "Homosexuality, Human Dignity and Halakhah." Committee on Jewish Law and Standards of the Conservative Movement,

Even ha-Ezer 24.2006b, https://www.rabbinicalassembly.org/sites/default/files/public/halakhah/teshuvot/20052010/dorff_nevins_reisner_dignity.pdf. With permission of the Rabbinical Assembly.

5.3. CCAR Responsum: "Same-Sex Marriage as *Kiddushin*," 5774.4, https://www.ccarnet.org/ccar-responsa/same-sex-marriage-kiddushin/. Copyright © 2014 by Central Conference of American Rabbis. Used by permission of the CCAR. All rights reserved.

5.4. Rabbi Leonard A. Sharzer, "Transgender Jews and Halakhah." Committee on Jewish Law and Standards of the Conservative Movement, Even ha-Ezer 5:11.2017b, https://www.rabbinicalassembly.org/sites/default/files/public/halakhah/teshuvot/2011-2020/transgender-halakhah.pdf. With permission of the Rabbinical Assembly.

6.1. Rabbi Moses Sternbuch, "A Woman Suffering from Alzheimer's Disease Whose Husband Wishes to Divorce Her." In *Teshuvot ve-hanhagot*, vol. 5 (Jerusalem: privately published, 2007), no. 316. Translated by Pamela Barmash.

6.2. Rabbi Tomer Mevorakh, "Eating on Yom Kippur When a Person Is Suffering from an Eating Disorder (Anorexia)." *Teḥumin* 38 (2018): 75–84. By permission of the Zomet Institute. Translated by Pamela Barmash.

6.3. Rabbi Eliezer Waldenberg, "On Abortion in General." In *Tzitz Eliezer* (Jerusalem: privately printed, 1967), vol. 9, no. 51.3. Translated by Pamela Barmash.

6.4. Rabbi Eliezer Waldenberg, "On the Abortion of a Fetus with Tay-Sachs Disease." In *Tzitz Eliezer* (Jerusalem: privately printed, 1978), vol. 13, no. 102. Translated by Pamela Barmash.

6.5. Rabbi Susan Grossman, "'Partial Birth Abortion' and the Question of When Human Life Begins." Committee on Jewish Law and Standards of the Conservative Movement, Ḥoshen Mishpaṭ 425:2.2003, https://www.rabbinicalassembly.org/sites/default/files/public/halakhah/teshuvot/20052010/grossman_partial_birth.pdf. With permission of the Rabbinical Assembly.

7.1. Co-chairs, Committee on Jewish Law and Standards, "Halakhic Guidance from CJLS about Coronavirus," https://www.rabbinical assembly.org/story/halakhic-guidance-cjls-about-coronavirus. With permission of the Rabbinical Assembly.

7.2. CCAR Responsum: "Virtual Minyan in Time of COVID-19 Emergency," 5780.2, https://www.ccarnet.org/ccar-responsa/5780-2/. Copyright © 2020 by Central Conference of American Rabbis. Used by permission of the CCAR. All rights reserved.

7.3. Iggud Ḥakhmei ha-Ma'arav be-Eretz Yisrael, "On a Seder via Zoom," https://www.ynet.co.il/articles/0,7340,l-5701269,00.html #autoplay, https://pic-upload.ynet.co.il/yahadut/01.pdf, https://www.makorrishon.co.il/judaism/214971/. Translated by Pamela Barmash.

7.4. Rabbi Herschel (Tzvi) Schachter, "Washing on Tisha b'Av" and "Regarding the Rule of 'God Protects the Simple,'" https://www.torahweb.org/torah/docs/rsch/RavSchachter-Corona-43-July-21-2020.pdf, https://www.torahweb.org/torah/docs/rsch/RavSchachter-Corona-45-July-29-2020.pdf. Translated by Pamela Barmash.

7.5. Rabbi Pamela Barmash, "Ethics of Gathering When Not All of Us May Attend in Person." Committee on Jewish Law and Standards of the Conservative Movement, https://www.rabbinicalassembly.org/story/ethics-gathering-when-not-all-us-may-attend-person. Courtesy of the Rabbinical Assembly.

8.1. Rabbi Hayyim Eleazar Shapira, "Engaging in a Public Fast in Sympathy with German Jews." In *Minḥat Eleazar*, Likutim (reprinted, Jerusalem: Hotza'at Emet, Or Torah Muncasz, 1996), Oraḥ Ḥayyim, no. 36. Translated by Pamela Barmash.

8.2. Rabbi Jehiel Jacob Weinberg, "On the Burial of a Person Converted by Liberal Rabbis." In *Seridei esh* (Jerusalem: privately printed, 1961–69), vol. 3, no. 100. Translated by Pamela Barmash.

8.3. Rabbi Ḥayyim David Halevi, "Transcendental Meditation." In *Aseh lekha rav* (Tel Aviv: Committee to Publish the Works of Rabbi Ḥ. D. Halevi, 1975), vol. 2, no. 47. Translated by Pamela Barmash.

8.4. Liz P. G. Hirsch and Yael Rapport, "Yoga as a Jewish Worship Practice: *Chukat Hagoyim* or Spiritual Innovation?" CCAR *Journal: The Reform Jewish Quarterly*, Spring 2020. Copyright © 2020 by Central Conference of American Rabbis. Used by permission of the CCAR. All rights reserved.

8.5. Rabbi Reuven Hammer, "The Status of Non-Jews in Jewish Law and Lore Today." Committee on Jewish Law and Standards of the Conservative Movement, Ḥoshen Mishpaṭ 359:1.2016, https://www.rabbinicalassembly.org/sites/default/files/public/halakhah/teshuvot/2011-2020/hammer-non-jews-law-lore.pdf. With permission of the Rabbinical Assembly.

9.1. Rabbi Shlomo Goren, "The Siege on Beirut in Light of Halakhah." In *Torat ha-medinah* (Jerusalem: Ha-idna Rabbah, 1996), 402–23. Translated by Pamela Barmash.

9.2. Rabbi Ḥayyim David Halevi, "The Law of 'the One Who Comes Forth to Kill You, Kill Him First' in Our State Affairs." In *Aseh lekha rav* (Tel Aviv: Committee to Publish the Works of Rabbi Ḥ. D. Halevi, n.d.), vol. 4, no. 2. Translated by Pamela Barmash.

9.3. Rabbi Theodore Friedman, "A Responsum on the Issue of 'the Greater Land of Israel' and Halakhah." In *Teshuvot Va'ad ha-Halakhah shel Kenesset ha-Rabbanim be-Yisrael*, vol. 2 (Jerusalem: Kenesset ha-Rabbanim be-Yisrael, 1987), 72–77. With permission of Kenesset ha-Rabbanim be-Yisrael. Translated by Pamela Barmash.

9.4. Rabbi Ovadiah Yosef, "Ceding Territory from the Land of Israel When There Is *Pikku'aḥ Nefesh*." *Teḥumin* 10 (1989): 34–47. By permission of the Zomet Institute. Translated by Pamela Barmash.

9.5. Rabbi Shaul Yisraeli, "Ceding Territory because of *Pikku'aḥ Nefesh*." *Teḥumin* 10 (1989): 48–61. By permission of the Zomet Institute. Translated by Pamela Barmash.

10.1. Committee on Responsa (later, Commission on Jewish Chaplaincy), *Responsa in War Time* (New York: Jewish Welfare Board, 1947), 1, 4–5, 14, 24, 51.

10.2. Rabbi Moses Feinstein, "American Thanksgiving." In *Iggerot Moshe*, vol. 4, *Yoreh De'ah* (New York: n.p., 1996), no. 12. Translated by Pamela Barmash.

10.3. Rabbi Jeremy Kalmanofsky, "Participating in the American Death Penalty." Committee on Jewish Law and Standards of the Conservative Movement, Ḥoshen Mishpaṭ 2:1.2013, https://www.rabbinicalassembly.org/sites/default/files/public/halakhah/teshuvot/2011-2020/cjls-onesh-mavet.pdf. With permission of the Rabbinical Assembly.

GLOSSARY

The definitions that follow are specific to how the rabbinic decisors use them in this volume.

aḥaronim: Rabbinic authorities of recent centuries.
akhzariyyut: Prohibition against human beings behaving in a cruel way.
Amalek, pl. **Amalekites**: Enemy of the Israelites during the Wilderness period of the Exodus who in tradition become the implacable enemy of the Jewish people.
Amidah: Central Jewish prayer also known as the *Shemoneh Esreh*.
arayot: Forbidden intercourse.
Arba'ah Ṭurim: Code of Jewish law written by Rabbi Jacob ben Asher, 1270?–1340. Its division into four parts (*Even ha-Ezer, Ḥoshen Mishpaṭ, Oraḥ Ḥayyim,* and *Yoreh De'ah*) becomes standard for halakhic codes.
avodah zarah: Worship of polytheistic deities, considered idolatry and contrary to Judaism's monotheistic worship of God.
Avot: First blessing of the *Amidah*.

Babylonian Talmud: Compendium of Rabbinic learning from the third to eighth centuries, structured on the Mishnah, compiled in Babylonia. It becomes the more authoritative version of the Talmud; when "the Talmud" is mentioned, it always means the Babylonian Talmud.
bal tashḥiṭ: A halakhic rule derived from Deuteronomy 20:19 that forbids the destruction of fruit trees when besieging a city during war. In the Middle Ages and early Modern period, *bal tashḥiṭ* was

broadened to prohibit gratuitous destruction of natural and manufactured objects in general while permitting the use of resources for the benefit of human beings in the short term.

baraita: A halakhic opinion or tradition from the period of the Mishnah (the first two centuries CE) that was recorded in the Babylonian Talmud or Palestinian Talmud but not in the Mishnah.

beit din, pl. *batei din*: Court of Jewish law.

beit midrash, pl. *batei midrash*: Academy of rabbinic learning.

Birkat ha-Shaḥar: Initial section of morning prayers.

brit milah: Ritual circumcision.

brit kodesh: Ritual naming of a daughter. Sometimes also refers to *brit milah*.

Caro, Rabbi Joseph: 1488–1575, Turkey, Israel. Author of the Shulḥan Arukh, the code of Jewish law that became authoritative starting in the early modern period, and of the *Beit Yosef*, a commentary on the *Arba'ah Ṭurim*.

Codes: Systematic collection of halakhic rules and principles, such as Maimonides' *Mishneh Torah*, Rabbi Jacob ben Asher's *Arba'ah Ṭurim*, and Rabbi Joseph Caro's Shulḥan Arukh.

darkhei shalom: Peaceful relations within, and between, communities.

de-oraita: Law ascribed to the Torah by the Rabbis.

de-rabbanan: Law promulgated by the Rabbis, in distinction to *de-oraita* law, law ascribed by the Rabbis to the Torah.

erusin: The betrothal ceremony, which consists of two parts: (1) the recitation of *Birkat Erusin*, the blessing of betrothal, over wine; and (2) the legal action of *kiddushin*. *Kiddushin* is a main act of creating a marriage because once it occurs, the personal status of the couple has changed. The couple is considered basically married even if *nisuin*, "nuptials," are still required for the couple to be fully married. Not to be confused with *shiddukhin*, "engagement."

Even ha-Ezer: One of the four sections of the *Arba'ah Ṭurim* and the Shulḥan Arukh. Treats marriage and divorce.

gaon, pl. **geonim**: Rabbinic authorities of the seventh to tenth centuries. Also used as an honorific for later rabbis, especially those of higher-level knowledge and authority.

get, pl. *gittin*: Document of Jewish divorce.

gezerah, pl. *gezerot*: Rabbinic interdiction.

gezerah shavah: Hermeneutic method that derives similar laws from similar words.

giyyur leḥumrah: Conversion to allay doubts about Jewish status.

halakhah: Hebrew "path (of Jewish life); Jewish law broadly defined." The term may also refer to a particular rule or legal institution.

ḥalitzah: Ceremony of rejection of a *yibbum*.

haredi: Ultraorthodox non-Hasidic.

hargashah: Physical sensation accompanying the onset of uterine bleeding that has halakhic significance.

hatafat dam brit: Ritual in place of *brit milah* in which a drop of blood is drawn for someone who has already been circumcised.

heiter: Rabbinic permission.

ḥevra kadisha: Religious association preparing body for burial.

ḥillul ha-Shem: Desecration of God's name caused by inappropriate behavior by Jews.

hora'at sha'ah: Leniency that addresses a single extraordinary circumstance and does not create a precedent for general use.

Ḥoshen Mishpaṭ: One of the four sections of the *Arba'ah Ṭurim* and the Shulḥan Arukh. Treats jurisprudence, economic issues, and personal safety.

ḥuppah: Wedding canopy; also used to refer to a Jewish wedding ceremony.

Isserles, Rabbi Moses: 1525 or 1530–1572, Poland. Talmudist and legal scholar who added glosses about Ashkenazic practice to the Shulḥan Arukh.

issur veheiter: Rules prohibiting and permitting, usually referring to kashrut, but occasionally applied to a wider range of issues.

Kabbalah: Esoteric Jewish mysticism.

Karaites: A group starting in the early Middle Ages that rejected rabbinic interpretation and authority.

kashrut: Kosher food regulations.

kavvanah: Spiritual engagement in prayer.

kehillah: Jewish community.

ketubbah: Document or contract of Jewish marriage.

kevod beriyyot: Human dignity.

kevod ha-met: Respectful behavior toward a deceased's body.

kibbud av va-em: Halakhic principle of respect toward parents.

Kiddush: Prayer marking the Sabbath and festivals.

kiddushin: Betrothal; the legal act of creating a Jewish marriage. Once *kiddushin* is performed, the couple is considered married even if *nisuin*, "nuptials," are still required. If the couple wishes to sever their relationship, a *get* must be issued.

ma'arufya: A Jew serving as the exclusive supplier or financial agent of a non-Jew whose prerogative to do was protected by the Jewish community.

Maimonides: 1135–1204, Spain, Egypt. Outstanding Jewish personality of the Middle Ages, a physician who authored a commentary on the Mishnah in Arabic, a book of Jewish philosophy (*Guide for the Perplexed*), and a code of Jewish law (*Mishneh Torah*), one of the most cited works in responsa.

mamzer, pl. *mamzerim*: Jew with problematic family lineage, not to be confused with the status of bastard.

mara de-atra: Rabbinic decisor for a local community.

matbe'a: Fixed wording of the liturgy.

Messianic Age: Future age when it is said a descendant of King David will once again reign and peace and justice will prevail over all human beings and nations.

midrash: Books of rabbinic interpretation that seek to extract more content from biblical texts.

mikveh: Ritual bath.

minhag: (1) Custom. (2) Set of ritual practices.

minyan: Quorum of ten adult Jews required for public prayer.

Mi Sheberakh: Prayer on behalf of the ill.

Mishnah: Collection of Rabbinic traditions edited by Rabbi Judah Hanasi in the second century CE.

Mishneh Torah: Authoritative code of Jewish law written by Maimonides.

mitzvah: Commandment.

mohel: Ritual circumciser.

Naḥmanides: 1194–1270, Spain. Leading rabbi and kabbalist who wrote biblical commentary, responsa, philosophy, and poetry.

niddah: (1) Halakhic status of a woman who experiences uterine bleeding not due to trauma. (2) Mishnah tractate.

Nine Days: Period leading up to Tisha B'Av in which various mourning practices are observed.

nisuin: Final ritual of a Jewish wedding.

Oraḥ Ḥayyim: One of the four sections of the *Arba'ah Ṭurim* and the Shulḥan Arukh. Treats prayer and liturgy, the synagogue, Shabbat, and holy days.

Palestinian Talmud: Compendium of Rabbinic learning from the third to fifth centuries, structured on the Mishnah, compiled in the Land of Israel. Sometimes termed the "Jerusalem Talmud" or the "Talmud of the Land of Israel."

pesak din: Ruling of a rabbinic decisor (*posek*) or a court of Jewish law (*beit din*).

pikku'aḥ nefesh: Halakhic principle that permits the violation of other laws in order to save a person in mortal danger.

posek, pl. ***posekim***: Rabbinic decisor of Jewish law.

Rashi (Rabbi Solomon ben Isaac): 1040–1104, northern France. Author of commentaries on the Bible and the Babylonian Talmud.

responsum (pl. **responsa**): Answer to a halakhic question by a rabbinic decisor (*posek*). The Hebrew term is *teshuvah*, pl. *teshuvot*.

rodef: Pursuer who seeks to kill someone.

Rosh (Rabbi Asher ben Jehiel): c. 1250–1327, France, Germany, Spain. Leading *posek* of his time. His son's work, *Arba'ah Ṭurim*, incorporated his rulings.

rosh yeshiva, pl. *rashei yeshiva*: The highest level of teacher and leader at a yeshiva.

Saadiah Gaon: 882–942, Egypt, Babylonia. Wrote a translation of the Bible into Arabic, monographs on halakhic topics, and the first Hebrew dictionary, among other works.

Sefardic/Mizraḥi: Jews whose background originates in Islamic lands.

sefirah: *Sefirat ha-Omer* (counting of the Omer [sheaves of barley]) from the second day of Passover until Shavuot.

sha'at hadeḥak: Leniency relying on less commonly accepted precedents in pressing but not unprecedented circumstances.

Shabbat: The Sabbath.

shaliaḥ tzibbur: Person leading public prayer.

sheḥiṭah: Kosher slaughter of animals.

Shema: Central piece of Jewish liturgy consisting of the recitation of three paragraphs from the Torah.

shev ve'al ta'aseh: Halakhic principle of not taking action in certain situations.

shevut deshevut: A restriction that is two steps removed from the *deoraita* prohibition of performing work on Shabbat.

Shulḥan Arukh: Authoritative code of halakhah authored by Rabbi Joseph Caro, with glosses by Rabbi Moses Isserles.

shoḥeṭ, pl. *shoḥeṭim*: One who performs kosher slaughter of animals.

shomer Shabbat: Sabbath observer.

siddur, pl. *siddurim*: Prayer book.

sifrei Torah: Torah scrolls.

State Rabbinate: Official rabbinic organization of the modern State of Israel.

Supreme Religious Court of Appeals: Highest level court (*beit din*) of the official State Rabbinate of Israel.

tahara: (1) Preparation for burial involving washing the body. (2) A woman's ritual purity from not being in *niddah*.

takkanah, pl. ***takkanot***: Formal enactment by an especially authoritative rabbi or rabbinic council.

Talmud: Learning. The term "the Talmud" refers to the Babylonian Talmud. See also Palestinian Talmud.

tanna, adjective **tannaitic**: Rabbi of the period of the Mishnah (the first two centuries CE).

Targum: Translation of Bible into Aramaic.

terumah, pl. ***terumot***: (1) Required offering. (2) Mishnah tractate.

teshuvah, pl. ***teshuvot***: (1) Responsum. (2) Repentance.

tohorat ha-mishpaḥah: Observance of *niddah* regulations.

Tosafot: Novellae on the Babylonian Talmud written in the twelfth to fourteenth centuries.

Ṭur: See *Arba'ah Ṭurim*.

tza'ar ba'alei ḥayyim: The prohibition against causing animals pain and suffering.

yibbum: Marriage of the widow of a man without children to his brother.

Yoreh De'ah: One of the four sections of the *Arba'ah Ṭurim* and the Shulḥan Arukh. Treats kashrut (kosher food), conversion, Torah scroll and mezuzah, charity (*tzedakah*) and some economic issues, visiting the ill, and mourning.

NOTES

INTRODUCTION

1. At the same time that responsa are issued, codes of Jewish law, seemingly the polar opposite of responsa, are also published. Codes represent halakhah in a static compendium, a formal presentation of the law presumably as it is. Versions meant for laypeople seldom acknowledge chronological change and differences within a community or between Ashkenazic and Sefardic/Mizraḥi communities, and other divergences. Versions meant for experts generally attempt to resolve differences between rabbinic authorities.
2. Benjamin Brown, "Teshuvot bazak: Likrat rilism hilkhati" [Instant responsa: Toward halakhic realism], *Diné Yisrael* 35–36 (2012): 111–48. While the term "Ultraorthodox" is contested (and sometimes rejected as having negative connotations), it remains one of the most common words used for a major Jewish stream that contains two major divisions within it: *haredi* (derived from *haredim*, meaning those who tremble before God) and Hasidic. For the sake of intelligibility and accessibility, Ultraorthodox as used in this volume is meant as a neutral designation for this form of Orthodoxy.
3. See Avinoam Rosenak, "Styles of Halakhic Ruling: A Mapping in Light of Joseph Schwab's Philosophy of Education," *Journal of Jewish Education* 73 (2007): 81–106; Mark Washofsky, "Responsa and Rhetoric: On Law, Literature, and the Rabbinic Decision," in *Pursuing the Text: Studies in Honor of Ben Zion Wacholder on the Occasion of His Seventieth Birthday*, ed. John C. Reeves and John Kampen (Sheffield: Sheffield Academic Press, 1994), 360–409.

4. Although Ultraorthodoxy arose originally in Europe, Sefardic/Mizraḥi Ultraorthodoxy developed in the Land of Israel primarily through contact with Askenazic Ultraorthodoxy. See Benjamin Brown, "Keshet ha-teguvot ha-Ortodoksiyyot: Ashkenazim ve-Sefaradim" [The continuum of Orthodox responses, Ashkenazic and Sefardic], in *Shas: Hebetim tarbutiyyim ve-ra'ayoniyyim* (Tel Aviv: Am Oved, 2006), 41–122; and Zvi Zohar, "On European Jewish Orthodoxy, Sephardic Tradition, and the Shas Movement," in *Jewry between Tradition and Secularism: Europe and Israel Compared*, vol. 5, ed. Eliezer Ben-Rafael, Thomas Gergely, and Yosef Gorny (Leiden and Boston: Brill, 2006), 133–50.

5. See the classic essay of Jacob Katz, "Orthodoxy in Historical Perspective," in *Studies in Contemporary Jewry*, vol. 2 (Bloomington: Indiana University Press, 1986), 3–17.

6. While it might seem surprising that the first responsa committee was established by Reform rabbis, innovation as a defining characteristic of Reform Judaism meant that new organizational structures to address contemporary concerns were more likely to be conceived by Reform Jews rather than those seeking to preserve assumed traditional patterns. The precursors to the halakhah committees of the twentieth century are the rabbinic conferences of the nineteenth century. Even if many were only abortive attempts that disbanded quickly or were not followed by successive meetings, they prepared the groundwork for the successful responsa committees of a later century. See Menachem Keren-Kratz, "Jewish Orthodoxy's First Rabbinical Conference," *Modern Judaism* 41 (2021): 273–93. An ad hoc responsa committee formed in Berlin in 1896 as the health of the leading rabbinic authority in German Modern Orthodoxy, Rabbi Azriel Hildesheimer, deteriorated, but each member of the committee issued responsa on his own authority, and the committee disbanded.

7. However, the responsa of certain prominent authorities are not yet available online as of the writing of this volume. For example, the responsa of Rabbi Shlomo Goren, the first chief rabbi of the Israel Defense Forces and a chief rabbi of the State of Israel, are not posted on the Bar Ilan Responsa Project or anywhere else online.

8. The Reconstructionist movement does not produce responsa but does issue statements termed "Guidelines." According to the Reconstructionist Rabbinical Association, their Guidelines, "significant statements of beliefs about, and guidance for, rabbinic Jewish practice and behavior, . . . are the product of considerable study, discussion and deliberation by the entirety of the membership. While not understood as binding *halacha* (Jewish law), they may be understood as *responsa*" (Reconstructionist Rabbinical Association, "A Word about Resolutions," https://therra.org/resolutions-statements-guidelines.php). However, these Guidelines do not cite or analyze the complex and deeply layered textual heritage of Jewish literary tradition and, therefore, are far afield from the genre of responsa.
9. Reorganization of the original responsa content appears in 5.1., Roth, "Homosexuality"; 6.3., Waldenberg, "Abortion in General"; and 9.1., Goren, "The Siege on Beirut in Light of Halakhah."
10. Amy Horowitz, *Mediterranean Israeli Music and the Politics of the Aesthetic* (Detroit: Wayne State University Press, 2010), 10–11. Note that Sefardic/Mizraḥi *posekim* differ in their ideas about their Sefardic heritage; see Joseph Ringel, "The Construction and De-construction of the Ashkenazi vs. Sephardic/Mizrahi Dichotomy in Israeli Culture: Rabbi Eliyahou Zini vs. Rabbi Ovadia Yosef," *Israel Studies* 21 (2016): 182–205.

1. PERSONAL AND BUSINESS ETHICS

1. The original responsum contains a number of section divisions and headers; the present author has added to section A the header from a later section to facilitate reading.
2. This edited responsum does not contain all of the decisor's arguments. For the full text of the original English responsum, approved on December 19, 2019, see Rabbi Nina Beth Cardin and Rabbi Avram Israel Reisner, "*Ma'asei Yadai L'hitpa-er*: On the Mitzvah of Sustainability," https://www.rabbinicalassembly.org/sites/default/files/2023-02/cjls-sustainability-teshuvah-final-updated-feb-2023.pdf.
3. The original responsum contains a number of section divisions and headers; the present author has added section header A to facilitate reading.

4. This edited responsum does not contain all of the decisor's arguments. For the full text of this original English responsum, approved on December 12, 2007, see Rabbi Dr. Barry Leff, "Whistleblowing: The Requirement to Report Employer Wrongdoing," https://www.rabbinicalassembly.org/sites/default/files/public/halakhah/teshuvot/20052010/leff_whistleblowing.pdf.
5. Alexander Carlebach, "Isaac Jacob Weiss," in *Encyclopaedia Judaica*, 2nd ed., 20.734.
6. The original responsum does not contain section divisions or headers; the present author has added them to facilitate reading.
7. The original Hebrew responsum is published in Isaac Jacob Weiss, *Minḥat Yitzhak*, corrected ed., vol. 2 (Jerusalem: privately printed [Minḥat Yitzhak Publishing House], 1993), no. 90, 194–96, and online at the Bar Ilan Responsa Project.
8. Rabbi Somekh called this responsa 90. The present author devised the title "On Commerce in the Markets of Malabar" for purposes of consistency in this responsa anthology.
9. See Abraham Ben-Yaacoub, "Abdallah Somekh," in *Encyclopaedia Judaica*, 2nd ed., 19.6–7; Zvi Zohar, "Abdallah Somekh," in *Encyclopedia of Jews in the Islamic World*, online edition.
10. See Zvi Zohar, "Yosef Hayyim," in *Encyclopedia of Jews in the Islamic World*, online edition.
11. See Zvi Zohar and Nathan Katz, "The Ethics of the Pepper Marts of Malabar in the Mid-19th Century: A Sephardic View," *Journal of Indo-Judaic Studies* 11 (2010): 122–44. The authors include a translation of the question and a summary and analysis of the responsum.
12. The original responsum does not contain section divisions or headers; the present author has added them to facilitate the reader's review.
13. This edited responsum does not contain all of the decisor's arguments. For the full text of the original Hebrew responsum, see Abdallah Somekh, *Zivḥei tzedek* (Baghdad: privately printed, 1899), Ḥoshen Mishpaṭ, no. 2, or the online Bar Ilan Responsa Project.
14. This edited responsum does not contain all of the decisor's arguments. For the full text of this original English responsum, approved

on December 12, 2007, see Rabbi Pamela Barmash, "Veal Calves," https://www.rabbinicalassembly.org/sites/default/files/teshuvot/1703225420_108.pdf?id=49666%20.

2. RITUAL

1. These responsa are called numbers 84 and 86 in the published volumes of Rabbi Moses Sofer. This author revised the title "On Using the Vernacular in Prayer" for purposes of consistency in the responsa anthology.
2. Moshe Samet, "Moses Sofer," in *Encyclopaedia Judaica*, 2nd ed., 18.742–43; Moshe Samet, *He-hadash asur min ha-Torah: Perakim be-toldot ha-Ortodoksyah* [Anything new is forbidden according to the Torah: Chapters in Orthodox history] (Jerusalem: Merkaz Dinur le-heker toldot Yisrael, 2005), 306–19.
3. *Mishnah Sotah* 7:1.
4. *Shulḥan Arukh* Oraḥ Ḥayyim 62:2.
5. *Shulḥan Arukh* Oraḥ Ḥayyim 101:4.
6. Mark Washofsky, "*Halakhah* in Translation: The Chatam Sofer on Prayer on the Vernacular," CCAR *Journal* 51 (2004): 142–63.
7. The original two letters questioning prayer in the vernacular are not available; hence this discussion begins with the responsa author's "Opening Remarks" instead.
8. The original responsum does not contain section divisions or headers; the present author has added them to facilitate reading.
9. *Responsa Ḥatam Sofer*, 6.86.
10. This edited responsum does not contain all of the decisor's arguments. For the full text of the original Hebrew responsa, see Moses Sofer, *Ḥatam sofer* (Bratislava: privately printed, 1912), vol. 6, *Likutim*, 218–20, no. 84, and 221–25, no. 86, or the online Bar Ilan Responsa Project.
11. David Derovan, "Ḥayyim David Halevi," in *Encyclopaedia Judaica*, 2nd ed., 8.267–68.
12. The original responsum does not contain section divisions or headers; the present author has added them to facilitate reading.

13. The original Hebrew responsum is published in Ḥayyim David Halevi, *Aseh lekha rav* 2, no. 22 (Tel Aviv: Committee to Publish the Works of Rabbi Ḥayyim David Halevi, 1975), and online at the Bar Ilan Responsa Project.
14. Joan S. Friedman, "The CCAR Responsa Committee: A History," *CCAR Journal* (Spring 2020): 40–53.
15. This meaning of the Hebrew word *teshuvah*, "repentance," is to be distinguished from another meaning, "responsum."
16. For the full text of this original English responsum see CCAR Responsa, 5765.4, "A Sex Offender in the Synagogue," https://www.ccarnet.org/ccar-responsa/nyp-no-5765-4/.

3. PERSONAL STATUS

1. Anonymous, "Ephraim Oshry," in *Encyclopaedia Judaica*, 2nd ed., 15.503.
2. A translation of this responsum that differs somewhat from the one created by this author here may be found in Rabbi Ephraim Oshry, *Responsa from the Holocaust*, trans. Y. Leiman (New York: Judaica Press, 1983), 190–92.
3. *Mishnah Yevamot* 4:13.
4. Shulḥan Arukh *Even ha-Ezer* 4:13–30.
5. *Mishnah Kiddushin* 4:1.
6. During the period when slavery was operating, a *mamzer* could marry an emancipated slave, and a male *mamzer* could marry an enslaved Canaanite woman. On the latter, see Babylonian Talmud *Kiddushin* 69a.
7. Shulḥan Arukh *Ḥoshen Mishpaṭ* 276:6.
8. Maimonides, *Mishneh Torah* Hilkhot Mamerim (Laws of Rebels) 6:11.
9. Shulḥan Arukh *Ḥoshen Mishpaṭ* 7:2.
10. See Tosafot to Babylonian Talmud *Yevamot* 45b.
11. The original responsum does not contain section divisions or headers; the present author has added them to facilitate reading.
12. Rabbi Oshry alludes to Micah 7:18–20, the textual source for the ceremony of *Tashlikh*, a penitential ritual usually performed on Rosh Hashanah.

13. The original Hebrew responsum is published in Ephraim Oshry, *Mima'amakim* (New York: privately published, 1968), vol. 3, no. 98, 73–80, and online at the Bar Ilan Responsa Project.
14. This edited responsum does not contain all of the decisor's arguments. For the full text of this English responsum, approved on March 8, 2000, see Kassel Abelson and David J. Fine, eds., *Responsa: The Committee on Jewish Law and Standards of the Conservative Movement, 1991–2000* (New York: Rabbinical Assembly, 2002), 558–86; or Rabbi Elie Kaplan Spitz, "*Mamzerut*," https://www.rabbinicalassembly.org/sites/default/files/2022-09/spitz_mamzerut.pdf.
15. Only if a party to a divorce case specifically binds financial matters to the case will it be included, and the *batei din* of the official State Rabbinate must follow civil law on property as decreed by the (non-halakhic) Israel Supreme Court in the 1994 Bavli case, even if it contradicts halakhah. See Avishalom Westreich, "Accommodating Religious Law with a Civil Legal System: Lessons from the Jewish Law Experience in Financial Family Matters," *Journal of Law and Religion* 33 (2018): 481–503. Interestingly, private *batei din* have developed in Israel as a way of resolving disputes outside the official legal system.
16. Amihai Radzyner, "'Ad sheqim'at lo nimtza mamzer meiha-Torah raq keshehayu aviv ve-imo ḥavushim be-veit ha-asurim'—Al pitronot ḥadshaniyyim le-hatarat miqrei mamzerut be-vatei din be-Yisrael" ["No *mamzer* according to the Torah unless his father and mother were imprisoned in a jail"—On innovative solutions to discharge possible cases of *mamzer* status in religious courts in Israel], *Jewish Studies: An Internet Journal* 20 (2021): 1–59.
17. The opinions of the *batei din* of the State Rabbinate are published on a regular basis in the journal *Ha-din veha-dayan*, available at https://rackmancenter.com/din-dayan/ in a number of printed volumes, and through other electronic media, all in Hebrew. The names of parties in cases are kept confidential; only the judges and lawyers are identified.

18. Yohanan Elul, *Orah shel Yerushalayim* (Jerusalem: Yefeh Nof, 2005). This hagiographical biography repeatedly mentions that Rabbi Mesas is to be considered an innovative rabbi.
19. Rabbi Mesas's initials are the same as the word *shemesh*, "sun," and the titles of his books are puns on his initials.
20. Although Rabbi Mesas includes the complete names of the parties involved in the dispute, unusual for a responsum, this author is providing only the first letter of their given names to protect their privacy.
21. A close relative, such as an uncle, may not serve as a witness to *kiddushin*, and if an uncle does serve as a witness, the *kiddushin* is invalid.
22. A witness must be an observer of the mitzvot in order to be a valid witness.
23. The original responsum does not contain section divisions or headers; the present author has added them to facilitate reading.
24. The abbreviation S-Ṭ is often misconstrued as "a pure Sefardi." However, Rabbi Mesas explains it as the Aramaic phrase *sefeih ṭav*, meaning "may his end be good" in *Shemesh u-magen* 4, no. 193 (Jerusalem: privately printed, 2007).
25. This edited responsum does not contain all of the decisor's arguments. For the full text of the original Hebrew responsum see Shalom Mesas, *Shemesh u-magen* 3, no. 12 (Jerusalem: privately printed, 2000), 227–29.
26. The original responsum does not contain section divisions or headers; the present author has added them to facilitate reading.
27. Brother Daniel did eventually obtain Israeli citizenship through naturalization, not the Law of Return.
28. This English responsum is published in Walter Jacob, ed., *Contemporary American Reform Responsa* (New York: Hebrew Union College Press, 1987), 61–68, and online at CCAR Responsa, "Contemporary American Reform Responsa, 38: Patrilineal and Matrilineal Descent," https://www.ccarnet.org/ccar-responsa/carr-61-68/.
29. Rabbi Ovadiah Yosef originally titled this responsum, "On the Immigrants from Ethiopia." The present author has taken the liberty of changing the title to "On the Status of Ethiopian Jews" to clarify that

Rabbi Yosef did not stipulate that his ruling is limited to Ethiopian Jews who make *aliyah*.

30. The title "Rishon Lezion," based on Isaiah 41:17, was first applied to a seventeenth-century chief rabbi in Jerusalem who, along with his colleagues, believed that he should have a modest title. See Anonymous, "Rishon Lezion," in *Encyclopaedia Judaica*, 2nd ed., 17.344.

31. Many of his supporters felt that the law limiting a chief rabbi to two terms should be modified to allow Rabbi Yosef to serve longer due to his preeminent status as the leading scholar of Sefardic/Mizraḥi Jews in Israel, but the politically powerful son of the previous Rishon Lezion Sefardic chief rabbi prevented it. See Zvi Zohar, "On European Jewish Orthodoxy, Sephardic Tradition, and the Shas Movement," in *Jewry between Tradition and Secularism: Europe and Israel Compared*, vol. 5, ed. Eliezer Ben-Rafael, Thomas Gergely, and Yosef Gorny (Leiden and Boston: Brill, 2006), 146.

32. Ariel Picard, "Ovadia Yosef," in *Encyclopedia of Jews in the Islamic World*, online edition.

33. The original responsum does not contain section divisions or headers; the present author has added them to facilitate reading.

34. See, for example, Steven Kaplan, *The Beta Israel (Falasha) in Ethiopia: From Earliest Times to the Twentieth Century* (New York: New York University Press, 1992).

35. H. J. Zimmels, "David ben Solomon ibn Abi Zimra," in *Encyclopaedia Judaica*, 2nd ed., 5.470–72.

36. This edited responsum does not contain all of the decisor's arguments. For the full text of the original Hebrew responsum, see Ovadiah Yosef, *Yabi'a omer*, vol. 8, Even ha-Ezer (Jerusalem: privately printed, 1995), no. 11, or the online Bar Ilan Responsa Project.

37. Sometimes the term *ḥeresh* seems to also refer to the deaf who do speak.

38. This edited responsum does not contain all of the decisor's arguments. For the full text of the original English responsum, approved on May 24, 2011, see Rabbi Pamela Barmash, "The Status of the Ḥeresh [Deaf Mute] and of Sign Language," https://www.rabbinicalassembly.org

/sites/default/files/public/halakhah/teshuvot/2011-2020/Status%20of%20the%20Heresh6.2011.pdf.

4. WOMEN

1. Bernard M. Bamberger, "Jacob Zallel Lauterbach," in *Encyclopaedia Juaica*, 2nd ed., 12.529.
2. Jacob Z. Lauterbach, *Mekilta de-Rabbi Ishmael* (Philadelphia: Jewish Publication Society of America, 1933).
3. Among Jewish women in Cincinnati affiliated with Reform Judaism as well as the male Hebrew Union College faculty, there were active supporters of women's suffrage. See Katherine T. Durack, "Mrs. Molony's Parties: Suffragists Rally from Defeat and Enjoy a Good Laugh," *American Jewish Archives Journal* 73 (2021): 60–65.
4. The original responsum does not contain section divisions or headers; the present author has added them to facilitate reading.
5. Strikingly, Rabbi Lauterbach omits discussion, for example, of women serving as *shoḥeṭim* (slaughterers of animals for kosher consumption), a profession practiced by Jewish women in the Ashkenazic community until the Middle Ages. Since Rabbi Lauterbach surely knew this reality, it may be surmised that either he did not wish to complicate his discussion or felt it was not germane, since most Reform rabbis were not observing kashrut. See Babylonian Talmud Ḥullin 2a; Tosafot on Ḥullin 2a, s.v. *hakol*; Shulḥan Arukh *Yoreh De'ah* 1.1; Rabbi Moses Isserles on *Yoreh De'ah* 1.1.
6. The responsum and the CCAR statement, both written in English, are published in *Yearbook of the Central Conference of American Rabbis* (New York: Central Conference of American Rabbis, 1922), 32:156–77, and online at CCAR Responsa, "American Reform Responsa, 8: Ordination of Women," https://www.ccarnet.org/responsa-topics/as-rabbis-ordination-of/.
7. Helen Levinthal finally received her belated ordination in 1988. See Pamela S. Nadell, *Women Who Would Be Rabbis* (Boston: Beacon Press, 1998), 110–12.
8. Rabbi Isaac Herzog called this responsum "*Takkanot* from the Year 5710 (1950), the Chief Rabbinate of Israel, Jerusalem." This author

devised the title "*Takkanot* on Marriage and *Yibbum*" for purposes of consistency in this responsa anthology. This responsum is published in *Teḥukah le-Yisrael al pi ha-Torah* (Jerusalem: Mossad Harav Kook, 1989), 3:168–69.

9. Jacob Goldman and David Derovan, "Isaac Herzog," in *Encyclopaedia Judaica*, 2nd ed., 9.68–70.
10. His son, Chaim Herzog, would make the same public gesture as the Israeli ambassador to the United Nations in response to the "Zionism is racism" resolution.
11. The original responsum does not contain section divisions or headers; the present author has added them to facilitate reading.
12. Yehuda-Herzl Henkin and Chana Henkin, eds., *Nishmat Ha-Bayit: Contemporary Questions on Women's Reproductive Health Addressed by Yoatzot Halacha* (New Milford CT and Jerusalem: Maggid Press, 2021), xxviii.
13. The original responsum does not contain section headings; the present author has added them to facilitate reading.
14. The original Hebrew responsum, translated into English, is published in Yehuda-Herzl Henkin and Chana Henkin, eds., *Nishmat Ha-Bayit: Contemporary Questions on Women's Reproductive Health Addressed by Yoatzot Halacha* (New Milford CT and Jerusalem: Maggid Press, 2021), no. 42.
15. The traditional text reads, "Grant peace, bounty and blessing … to us and to all Israel [the Jewish people]." The Conservative/Masorti text reads, "Grant peace to the world, bounty and blessing … to us and to all Israel [the Jewish people]."
16. The traditional siddur includes the blessing for men, thanking God "who has not made me a woman," and for women, thanking God "who has made me according to his will." Rabbi Silverman's siddur includes the blessing "who has made me in his image" for both men and women, an echo of Genesis 1:27.
17. The traditional siddur reads, "May it be your will, Adonai … to lead us in joy to our land … where we will prepare the daily and special sacrifices." *Siddur Sim Shalom* includes these additions and modifications: "May it be your will, Adonai … who restores his children

to their land, to lead us in joy to our land. . . . There our ancestors prepared the daily and special sacrifices."

18. In the trio of blessings about not being a woman, slave, or gentile, the traditional siddur includes the wording "you have not made me a male slave" without indicating what a woman should say for this blessing. *Siddur Sim Shalom* voices this trio in the affirmative, thanking God for making one in God's image, a free man or woman, and a Jew.

19. This edited responsum does not contain all of the decisor's arguments. For the full text of this original English responsum, approved on March 3, 1990, see *Proceedings of the Committee on Jewish Law and Standards of the Conservative Movement, 1991–2000* (New York: Rabbinical Assembly, 2001), 485–90; or Rabbi Joel E. Rembaum, "Regarding the Inclusion of the Names of the Matriarchs in the First Blessing of the *Amidah*," https://www.rabbinicalassembly.org/sites/default/files/public/halakhah/teshuvot/19861990/rembaum_matriarchs.pdf.

20. Babylonian Talmud *Kiddushin* 33b–34a.
21. Tosefta *Megillah* 3:21.
22. *Sifrei Devarim*, 'Ekev, 46.
23. This edited responsum does not contain all of the decisor's arguments. For the full text of the original English responsum, approved on April 29, 2014, see Rabbi Pamela Barmash, "Women and Mitzvot," https://www.rabbinicalassembly.org/sites/default/files/public/halakhah/teshuvot/2011-2020/womenandhiyyuvfinal.pdf.

5. LGBTQIA+

1. This edited responsum does not contain all of the decisor's arguments and has been reorganized to clarity the arguments. To read the original, full English responsum, approved on March 25, 1992, see Kassel Abelson and David J. Fine, eds., *Responsa: The Committee on Jewish Law and Standards of the Conservative Movement, 1991–2000* (New York: The Rabbinical Assembly, 2002), 613–75; or Rabbi Joel Roth,

"Homosexuality," https://www.rabbinicalassembly.org/sites/default/files/public/halakhah/teshuvot/19912000/roth_homosexual.pdf.
2. Elliot Dorff, *For the Love of God and People: A Philosophy of Jewish Law* (Philadelphia: The Jewish Publication Society, 2007).
3. Roth responds to the three rabbis' criticism in "Homosexuality Revisited," https://www.rabbinicalassembly.org/sites/default/files/public/halakhah/teshuvot/20052010/roth_revisited.pdf.
4. This edited responsum does not contain all of the decisor's arguments. For the full text of the original English responsum, approved on December 6, 2007, see Rabbis Elliot N. Dorff, Daniel S. Nevins, and Avram I. Reisner, "Homosexuality, Human Dignity and Halakhah," https://www.rabbinicalassembly.org/sites/default/files/public/halakhah/teshuvot/20052010/dorff_nevins_reisner_dignity.pdf.
5. For the full text of this English responsum, see CCAR Responsa Committee, "Same-Sex Marriage as *Kiddushin*," 2014, https://www.ccarnet.org/ccar-responsa/same-sex-marriage-kiddushin/.
6. Rabbi Moses Isserles, *Darkhei Moshe*, Yoreh De'ah 335.
7. This edited responsum does not contain all of the decisor's arguments. For the full text of this original English responsum, approved on June 7, 2017, see Rabbi Leonard A. Sharzer, MD, "Transgender Jews and Halakhah," https://www.rabbinicalassembly.org/sites/default/files/public/halakhah/teshuvot/2011-2020/transgender-halakhah.pdf.

6. MEDICAL ETHICS

1. The original responsum does not contain section divisions or headers; the present author has added them to facilitate reading.
2. This edited responsa does not contain all of the decisor's arguments. For the full text of the original Hebrew responsum, see Moses Sternbuch, *Teshuvot ve-hanhagot*, vol. 5, no. 316 (Jerusalem: privately published, 2007), or the online Bar-Ilan Responsa Project.
3. The quantity of an olive is considered the minimum quantity of food that counts as eating.
4. This edited responsa does not contain all of the decisor's arguments. For the full text of the original Hebrew responsum see Rabbi Tomer

Mevorakh, "Akhilah be-Yom ha-Kippurim lesovelet meihafra'at akhilah (anorekhsiyah)" Eating on Yom Kippur when a person is suffering from an eating disorder (Anorexia), *Teḥumin* 38 (2018): 75–84.

5. See Pamela Barmash, *Homicide in the Biblical World* (Cambridge: Cambridge University Press, 2005), 158–59; and Pamela Barmash, *The Laws of Hammurabi: At the Confluence of Royal and Scribal Tradition* (New York: Oxford University Press, 2020), 256–60.

6. The original responsum does not contain section headers; the present author has added them to facilitate reading.

7. The other Noahide laws require setting up a legal system to establish justice and prohibit stealing, sexual immorality, idol worship, blasphemy, and tearing a limb from a living animal (a practice associated with the mystery religion of Bacchus in the Roman period).

8. Rabbi Waldenberg also analyzes the opinion of Rabbi Jacob ben Tzvi Emden (1697–1776, Germany, known by his acronym Ya'avetz), but since Rabbi Emden's opinion is generally not accepted by rabbinic decisors, it is not included here. Rabbi Emden rules that since a pregnant married woman who committed adultery is subject to the death penalty, her fetus would also die, and therefore it is permitted to abort her fetus. An astounded Rabbi Waldenberg argues against the ruling: while this punishment does appear in the Torah, it is not implemented.

9. This edited responsum does not contain all of the decisor's arguments and has been reorganized to clarify the arguments. For the full text of the original Hebrew responsum, see Rabbi Eliezer Waldenberg, *Tzitz Eliezer*, vol. 9, no. 51.3 (Jerusalem: privately printed, 1967), or the online Bar Ilan Responsa Project.

10. The original responsum does not contain section divisions or headers; the present author has added them to facilitate reading.

11. The original Hebrew *teshuvah* is published in Rabbi Eliezer Waldenberg, *Tzitz Eliezer*, vol. 13, no. 102 (Jerusalem: privately printed, 1978), and online at the Bar Ilan Responsa Project,

12. The original Hebrew *teshuvah* is published in Rabbi Eliezer Waldenberg, *Tzitz Eliezer*, vol. 20, no. 2 (Jerusalem: privately printed, 1984), and online at the Bar Ilan Responsa Project,

13. This edited responsa does not contain all of the decisor's arguments. For the full text of the original English responsum, approved on September 17, 2003, see Rabbi Susan Grossman, "'Partial Birth Abortion' and the Question of When Human Life Begins," https://www.rabbinicalassembly.org/sites/default/files/public/halakhah/teshuvot/20052010/grossman_partial_birth.pdf.

7. THE COVID-19 PANDEMIC

1. For earlier responses to pandemic, see Moshe Dovid Chechik and Tamara Morsel-Eisenberg, "Plague, Practice, and Prescriptive Text: Jewish Traditions on Fleeing Afflicted Cities in Early Modern Ashkenaz," *Journal of Law, Religion and State* 8 (2020): 152–78.
2. For the full text of this original English responsum, posted on March 4, 2020, see the Rabbinical Assembly, "Halakhic Guidance from CJLS about Coronavirus," https://www.rabbinicalassembly.org/story/halakhic-guidance-cjls-about-coronavirus.
3. An omitted section of this responsum addresses the question of whether Reform congregations should strive, although not require, ten for a minyan. The CCAR Responsa Committee had ruled in 1936 that six or seven was sufficient, basing itself on an opinion from an extracanonical (less authoritative) tractate of the Babylonian Talmud.
4. For example, Maimonides urges people to pray as part of communal prayer by contending that God pays special heed to communal prayer. *Mishneh Torah* Hilkhot Tefillah (Laws of Prayer) 8:1.
5. For the full text of this original English responsum, posted in 2012, see CCAR Responsa Committee, "A Minyan Via the Internet?," https://www.ccarnet.org/ccar-responsa/minyan-via-internet/.
6. Shulḥan Arukh *Oraḥ Ḥayyim* 55:14.
7. This edited responsa does not contain all of the decisor's arguments. For the full text of the original English responsum, posted on March 18, 2020, see CCAR Responsa Committee, "Virtual Minyan in Time of COVID-19 Emergency," 5780.2, https://www.ccarnet.org/ccar-responsa/5780-2/.
8. Iggud Ḥakhmei ha-Ma'arav be-Eretz Yisrael (the Association of North African Rabbis in the Land of Israel) did not title their responsum.

The title "On a Seder via Zoom" was devised by this author for purposes of consistency in this responsa anthology.

9. The original responsum does not contain section divisions or headers; the present author has added them to facilitate the reader's review.
10. See Noam Sasi, "Hadlakat ḥashmal be-yom tov le-or mishnatam shel rabbanei ha-Sefaradim" [Turning on electricity on a festival according to the views of Sefardic/Mizraḥi rabbis], *Maḥanekha* 3 (2008): 261–72.
11. This letter was publicized widely in the news media, including in the newspaper *Makor Rishon* on March 25, 2020, https://www.makorrishon.co.il/judaism/214971/ [Hebrew].
12. The original responsum does not contain section divisions or headers; the present author has added the latter to facilitate the reader's review.
13. For the full text of the original responsum, posted on July 21, 2020, see Hershel Schachter, "Washing on Tisha b'Av," https://www.torahweb.org/torah/docs/rsch/RavSchachter-Corona-43-July-21-2020.pdf.
14. For the full text of the original responsum, posted on July 29, 2020, see Hershel Schachter, "Regarding the Rule of 'God Protects the Simple'," https://www.torahweb.org/torah/docs/rsch/RavSchachter-Corona-45-July-29-2020.pdf.
15. *Iggeret Rabbi Akiva Eiger* (Petah Tikvah: privately printed, 1968), 71.
16. *Pesakim ve-takkanot Rabbi Akiva Eiger*, ed. Natan Gestetner (Jerusalem: privately printed, 1971), Hanhagot ve-takkanot, no. 2.
17. Because the intent was to present principles that inquiring rabbis and others could apply during the High Holy Days, Rabbi Barmash did not call this concluding section a *pesak din*.
18. This edited responsa does not contain all of the decisor's arguments. For the full text of the original English responsum, posted on July 22, 2020, see Rabbi Pamela Barmash, "Ethics of Gathering When Not All of Us May Attend in Person," https://www.rabbinicalassembly.org/story/ethics-gathering-when-not-all-us-may-attend-person.

8. RELATIONSHIPS WITH THE OTHER

1. See Efraim Gottlieb, "Shapira," in *Encyclopaedia Judaica*, 2nd ed., 398–99; Allan Nadler, "The War on Modernity of R. Hayyim Elazar Shapira

of Munkacz," *Modern Judaism* 14 (1994): 233–64. Munkacz is now part of Ukraine.
2. The original responsum does not contain section divisions or headers; the present author has added them to facilitate the reader's review.
3. For a study of Orthodox rabbis' changing attitudes toward non-Orthodox Jews in the nineteenth to early twentieth centuries, see David Ellenson, "The Orthodox Rabbinate and Apostasy in Nineteenth Century Germany and Hungary," in *Jewish Apostasy in the Modern World*, ed. Todd M. Endelman (New York: Holmes & Meier, 1987), 165–88.
4. This phrase "the finger of God" alludes to the passage in Exod. 8:15 where Pharaoh's advisors warn him that God unleashed the plagues suffered by Egypt.
5. A pro-Zionist Orthodox political party.
6. An anti-Zionist Ultraorthodox organization founded in Kattowitz, German Empire (now Katowice, Poland), in 1912. Even though both the members of Agudat Yisrael and Rabbi Shapira were anti-Zionist and Ultraorthodox, he opposed them because they supported non-Zionist agricultural efforts in the Land of Israel, established a new fund to support those efforts, and founded a rabbinical seminary in Warsaw that he found objectionable.
7. The original Hebrew responsum is published in Hayyim Eleazar Shapira, *Minḥat Eleazar*, Likutim (Jerusalem: Hotza'at Emet, Or Torah Muncasz, 1996), Oraḥ Ḥayyim, no. 36, and online at the Bar Ilan Responsa Project. An English translation different from this author's can be found in Robert Kirschner, *Rabbinic Responsa of the Holocaust Era* (New York: Schocken, 1985), 21–30.
8. Rabbi Jehiel Jacob Weinberg gave this responsa only a number. This author devised the title "On the Burial of a Person Converted by Liberal Rabbis" for purposes of consistency in the responsa anthology.
9. Mordechai Hacohen, "Jehiel Jacob Weinberg," in *Encyclopaedia Judaica*, 2nd ed., 20.717; Marc B. Shapiro, *Between the Yeshiva World and Modern Orthodoxy: The Life and Works of Rabbi Jehiel Jacob Weinberg* (Portland OR: Littman Library, 1999).
10. The original responsum does not contain section divisions or headers; the present author has added them to facilitate the reader's review.

11. Rabbi Weinberg alludes to the phrase in Ezek. 22:30, where God is portrayed as searching for a leader to reprimand the people for their misdeeds and save them from disaster.
12. The original Hebrew responsum is published in Jehiel Jacob Weinberg, *Seridei esh*, vol. 3, no. 100 (Jerusalem: privately printed, 1961–69), and online at the Bar Ilan Responsa Project. See also the new edition, Jehiel Jacob Weinberg, *Seridei esh* (Jerusalem: Mossad Harav Kook, 2003), vol. 2, no. 99, in which the responsa are numbered differently.
13. The name of the radio show quotes a famous passage from *Mishnah Avot* 1:6, "Select for yourself a rabbi, and acquire for yourself a friend (for studying together), and evaluate people favorably."
14. Phrases built on the motif of a cistern that does or does not leak frequently appear in rabbinic literature. See for example *Mishnah Avot* 2:8, where a rabbi who remembers Torah is praised as a cistern that does not leak.
15. This edited responsum does not contain all of the decisor's arguments. For the full text of the original Hebrew responsum, see Ḥayyim David Halevi, *Aseh lekha rav*, vol. 2, no. 47 (Tel Aviv: Committee to Publish the Works of Rabbi Ḥ. D. Halevi, 1975,) and the online Bar Ilan Responsa Project.
16. This edited responsum does not contain all of the decisor's arguments. For the full text of the original English responsum see Liz P.G. Hirsch and Yael Rooks Rapport, "Yoga as a Jewish Worship Practice: *Chukat Hagoyim* or Spiritual Innovation?," CCAR *Journal: A Reform Jewish Quarterly* (Spring 2020): 200–207.
17. This edited responsum does not contain all of the decisor's arguments. For the full text of the original English responsum, approved on April 21, 2016, see Rabbi Reuven Hammer, "The Status of Non-Jews in Jewish Law and Lore Today," https://www.rabbinicalassembly.org/sites/default/files/public/halakhah/teshuvot/2011-2020/hammer-non-jews-law-lore.pdf.

9. THE MODERN STATE OF ISRAEL

1. Although Rabbi Goren felt he had produced a unified siddur, it contained little in the way of Sefardic/Mizraḥi versions of the liturgy.

2. For an analysis of the impact of the opposition on Rabbi Goren from this decision, see Aviad Yehiel Hollander, "The Relationship between Halakhic Decisors and Their Peers as a Determining Factor in the Acceptance of Their Decisions: A Step in Understanding Interpeer Effects in Halakhic Discourse," *Jewish Law Association Studies* 20 (2010): 96–108.
3. Rabbi Ovadiah Yosef's decision to run for the office of chief rabbi against the incumbent Rabbi Yitzhak Nissim also aroused the ire of Rabbi Nissim's politically powerful son, Moshe Nissim, who fought against removing term limits. See Zvi Zohar, "On European Jewish Orthodoxy, Sephardic Tradition, and the Shas Movement," in *Jewry between Tradition and Secularism: Europe and Israel Compared*, vol. 5, ed. Eliezer Ben-Rafael, Thomas Gergely, and Yosef Gorny (Leiden and Boston: Brill, 2006), 146.
4. Shlomo Goren, *Meshiv milḥamah*, 2nd ed. (Jerusalem: Ha-idna Rabbah, 1984), 1.*10–12. The pagination in this book starts a second time.
5. Yaron Silberstein, *Bein adam limdinato: Medinat Yisrael be-mishnato ha-hilkhatit shel ha-Rav Shelomo Goren* [The State of Israel and its institutions in the halakhic thought of Rabbi Shlomo Goren] (Jerusalem: Magnes Press, 2021), 298–304.
6. The present author has selected new section headings to facilitate reading.
7. Rabbi Simḥah Hacohen's more famous book is *Or same'aḥ* [Joyful light], a commentary on Maimonides's *Mishneh Torah*, and Rabbi Hacohen is often known as the Or Same'aḥ.
8. Rabbi Shlomo Goren added this clarification in the later publication of his *teshuvah*. See *Torat ha-medinah*, 406 (the earlier version) versus 408 (the later addition).
9. This edited responsum does not contain all of the decisor's arguments. The original Hebrew *teshuvah* appears in Shlomo Goren, *Torat ha-medinah* (Jerusalem: Ha-idna Rabbah, 1996), 402–23. Another, not entirely identical version is published in Shlomo Goren, *Meshiv milḥamah*, vol. 3 (Jerusalem: Ha-idna Rabbah, 1986), 239–65.
10. This edited responsum does not contain all of the decisor's arguments. For the full text of the original Hebrew responsum, see Ḥayyim David

Halevi, *Aseh lekha rav*, vol. 4, no. 2 (Tel Aviv: Committee to Publish the Works of Rabbi Ḥ. D. Halevi, n.d.). Volume 1 of *Aseh lekha rav* was published in 1975.

11. The original responsum does not contain section divisions or headers; the present author has added them to facilitate reading.

12. This edited responsum does not contain all of the decisor's arguments. For the full text of the original Hebrew responsum, see Theodore Friedman, *Teshuvot Va'ad ha-Halakhah shel Kenesset ha-Rabbanim be-Yisrael*, vol. 2 (Jerusalem: Kenesset ha-Rabbanim be-Yisrael, 1987), 72–77, or Responsa for Today, "All Volumes," https://responsafortoday.com/en/vaad-halakhah/all-volumes/.

13. This edited responsum does not contain all of the decisor's arguments. To read Rabbi Ovadiah Yosef's complete Hebrew responsum, see *Teḥumin* 10 (1989): 34–47. An English translation differing from this one was published in *Crossroads: Halacha in the Modern World*, vol. 3 (Alon Shvut: Zomet Institute, 1990): 11–28.

14. The section headings shown here reflect the published work in *Teḥumin* 10 (1989): 48–61, and not the version of the essay in *Ḥavvat Binyamin* (Jerusalem: Eretz Hemdah Institute, 1992), 1.69–78.

15. The Rabbis invented this concept to explain why the Jews did not seek to reconquer the Land of Israel after the destruction of Jerusalem but remained living in exile.

16. Rabbi Yisraeli ignores the sections of the Balfour Declaration and the San Remo Resolution that aver that the rights of the Arab population in Palestine must be respected and are not abrogated.

17. This edited responsum does not contain all of the decisor's arguments. For the full text of the original Hebrew responsum, see *Teḥumin* 10 (1989): 48–61. An English translation somewhat differing from this one is found in *Crossroads: Halacha and the Modern World*, vol. 3 (Alon Shvut: Zomet Institute, 1990), 29–46.

10. LIFE IN THE UNITED STATES

1. Albert Isaac Slomovitz, *The Fighting Rabbis: Jewish Military Chaplains and American History* (New York: New York University Press, 1999), 52–53.

2. "Rabbi Elkan Voorsanger Dead, Noted Chaplain in World War I," *New York Times*, May 6, 1963.
3. Commission on Jewish Chaplaincy, *Responsa in War Time* (New York: Jewish Welfare Board, 1947), ii. The name CANRA was changed to Commission on Jewish Chaplaincy after the war.
4. Commission on Jewish Chaplaincy, *Responsa in War Time* (New York: Jewish Welfare Board, 1947), iii–iv.
5. Commission on Jewish Chaplaincy, *Responsa in War Time* (New York: Jewish Welfare Board, 1947), iv–v.
6. Commission on Jewish Chaplaincy, *Responsa in War Time* (New York: Jewish Welfare Board, 1947), 1. All of these responsa were written in English.
7. Commission on Jewish Chaplaincy, *Responsa in War Time* (New York: Jewish Welfare Board, 1947), 4–5.
8. Commission on Jewish Chaplaincy, *Responsa in War Time* (New York: Jewish Welfare Board, 1947), 14.
9. Commission on Jewish Chaplaincy, *Responsa in War Time* (New York: Jewish Welfare Board, 1947), 24.
10. Commission on Jewish Chaplaincy, *Responsa in War Time* (New York: Jewish Welfare Board, 1947), 51.
11. David Derovan, "Moses Feinstein," in *Encyclopaedia Judaica*, 2nd ed., 6.741–42; Joseph Berger, "Thousands Mourn Talmudic Scholar," *New York Times*, March 25, 1986.
12. Moshe Feinstein, *Iggerot Moshe* (New York: n.p., 1985), Ḥoshen Mishpaṭ, 2.29.
13. The original responsum does not contain section divisions or headers; the present author has added them to facilitate the reader's review.
14. Godfrey Hodgson, *A Great and Godly Adventure; The Pilgrims and the Myth of the First Thanksgiving* (New York: Public Affairs, 2006); Abraham Lincoln, "Proclamation 118—Thanksgiving Day, 1864," October 20, 1864, https://www.presidency.ucsb.edu/documents/proclamation-118-thanksgiving-day-1864#:~:text=Now%2c%20therefore%2c%20i%2c%20abraham,Creator%20and%20ruler%20of%20the.
15. The original Hebrew responsum is published in Moses Feinstein, *Iggerot Moshe*, Yoreh De'ah, vol. 4 (New York: n.p., 1996), no. 12, and

online on the Bar Ilan Responsa Project. Rabbi Feinstein also discusses Thanksgiving in other responsa: *Iggerot Moshe*, Even ha-Ezer 2:13; Oraḥ Ḥayyim 5:20:6; Yoreh De'ah 4:11:4.

16. Rabbi Kalmanofsky does not address whether or not a Jew may serve as a defense attorney. To speculate: on the one hand, a defense attorney seeks to prevent a client from receiving the death penalty, surely in accord with Rabbi Kalmanofsky's reading of halakhah, yet on the other, if the death penalty is justified, might that militate against a Jewish defense attorney advocating on a client's behalf?

17. This edited responsum does not contain all of the decisor's arguments. For the full text of the original English responsum, approved on October 15, 2013, see Jeremy Kalmanofsky, "Participating in the American Death Penalty," https://www.rabbinicalassembly.org/sites/default/files/public/halakhah/teshuvot/2011-2020/cjls-onesh-mavet.pdf.

INDEX

Abarbanel, Isaac, 285
Abergil, Elijah, 213
abortion, xxiii, 175, 186–203
Abudraham, David, 136
Agudat Yisrael, xx, 232, 317, 363
aḥaronim, 220, 235, 237, 284, 339
akhzariyyut, 30, 33–34, 339
Al-Ḥakam, Joseph Ḥayyim, xxiv, 2, 22, 29
Alzheimer's disease, 176–79
American Jewish University, 9, 120, 148, 157
Amidah, 39, 42–44, 45, 120–28, 132, 135, 316, 339
androginus, 165–66
anorexia, 175, 179–86
"Anything new is forbidden," 38
Arba'ah Ṭurim. *See* Jacob ben Asher
Ashkenazi, Elḥanan, 119
Ashkenazic chief rabbi of Israel, 68, 88, 90, 96, 101, 111, 234, 264, 266, 298
avodah zarah, 230, 238–41, 244–45, 246–49, 293, 339

Bacharach, Jair, 192–93
Balfour Declaration, 230, 301–2, 366
bal tashḥit, 7–8, 339–40
Bar Ilan Responsa Project, xxi
Bar Kochba, 265
Barmash, Pamela, 2, 29–36, 58, 93–100, 102, 128–38, 206, 221–28, 360, 362
Bellugi Ursula, 97
Benhamu, Shlomo, 213
Berger, Joseph, 367n11
Blackmun, Harry, 322
Bokser, Ben Zion, 321–22
Bouskila, Daniel, 213
Brother Daniel case, 84, 354
Brown, Benjamin, 347n2, 348n4
business ethics, 1–36

Cairo Genizah, 122
capital punishment, 71, 307, 320–29
Cardin, Nina Beth, 1–9
Caro, Joseph, 39, 50, 70, 79, 87, 92, 119, 124, 125, 153–54, 169–70,

369

Caro, Joseph (*cont.*)
177, 182, 183, 184–85, 217, 240, 243, 250, 265, 296, 305, 312, 313–14, 340, 343, 344, 345, 351, 352, 352, 352, 356, 361
CCAR Responsa Committee, xx, 37, 51–56, 58, 81–87, 102, 139, 157–62, 205, 209–12, 247, 348
Chabad, 258, 261
Chechik, Moshe Dovid, 361
Chelouche, David, 215
Cohen, Henry, 109–10
Committee on Jewish Law and Standards: history of, xx, 129; responsa of, 2, 9, 29, 65, 93, 120, 128, 140, 148, 162, 198, 206, 221, 252, 320
Committee on Responsa of the Committee on Army and Navy Religious Activities, xx, 307–16
Conservative/Masorti Judaism, xv, xix, xxvi, 70, 102, 121–31, 128–31 156, 200, 205, 210, 230, 283–84, 307–8, 317, 321, 357. *See also* Committee on Jewish Law and Standards
COVID-19 pandemic, xxiii, 205–28
Creation stories in the Torah, 3–5

darkhei shalom, 274, 340
deaf, 93–100
death penalty, 310–29
Declaration of the Establishment of the State of Israel, 274

"Do not curse the deaf" (Lev. 19:14), 99
"Do not put a stumbling-block before the blind" (Lev. 9:14), 24–28
"Do not stand idly by the blood of your neighbor" (Lev. 19:16), 11, 14
Dorff, Elliot, 139, 148–57, 359
Durack, Katherine T., 356

Egypt-Israel peace treaty, 290, 291–92
Eiger, Akiva, 178, 225–26, 362
Ellenson, David, 363
Elul, Yohanan, 354
Emden, Jacob ben Tzvi (Ya'avetz), 360
Ethiopian Jews, 58, 87–93, 355

Feinstein, Moses, 236, 307, 316–20, 367n12, 368n15
Felder, Gedaliah, 236
Freehof, Solomon, 51, 308–10
Friedman, Joan, 352
Friedman, Theodore, 263, 283–90

Gallaudet University, 97
gender dysphoria, 163, 167–68, 173
Ginzburg, Yitzhak, 261–62
Goren, Shlomo, 68, 73, 263, 264–73, 274, 348, 349, 364, 365
"Greater Land of Israel," 283–90
Grodzinski, Ḥayyim Ozer, 219–20

Grossman, Susan, 175, 198–203

Haganah, 264
Halberstam, Yekutiel Yehudah, 119
Halevi, Ḥayyim David, xxi, xxiv, xxv, 37, 46–50, 230, 237–45, 263, 264–82
ḥalitzah, 113–15, 341
Hamburg Temple controversy, 40
Hammer, Reuven, xxv, 230, 252–62
Haredi Beit Din of Jerusalem, 18, 176
Harlap, Jacob, 111
Haskalah, 234
Hassan II of Morocco, 74
Hebrew, liturgy in, 38–40, 43–45
Hebrew Union College, 102–3, 110, 245, 356
Hebron Yeshiva, 264
Henkin, Chana, 115
Henkin, Yehuda, 115
ḥeresh, 93–100, 355
Herzog, Chaim, 111, 357
Herzog, Isaac (1888–1959), 88, 90–91, 96, 101, 110–15, 326
Herzog, Isaac (b. 1960), 111
ḥevra kadisha, 169–70, 173
Hildesheimer, Azriel, 89, 348
ḥillul ha-Shem, 62, 64–65, 178–79, 341
Hirsch, Liz P.G., xxiv, 230
Hirsch, Samson Raphael, 136, 260
Hodgson, Godfrey, 367
Hollander, Yehiel, 365

Horowitz, Amy, 349
Humane Farm Animal Care, 35–36

ibn Ezra, Abraham, 285
ibn Pakuda, Bahya, 285
Iggud Ḥakhmei ha-Ma'arav be'Eretz Yisrael, 206, 212–16
Isserles, Moses, 70, 79, 80, 218, 249–50, 251, 259–60, 303, 312, 319, 341, 344, 356, 359

Jacob ben Asher, 92, 169–70, 339
Jewish Theological Seminary of America, 2, 30, 65, 120, 128, 140, 148, 149, 156, 163, 198, 252, 283, 320
Judah Halevi, 257–58
Judah Heḥasid, 33
Jung, Leo, 308

Kagen, Israel Meir Hakohen, 12
Kalmanofsky, Jeremy, 307, 320–29, 368
Kanievsky, Ḥayyim, xviii
Kaplan, Steven, 355
Katz, Jacob, 348
Katz, Nathan, 350
kavvanah, 45, 50, 342
Keren-Kratz, Menachem, 348
Kirschner, Robert, 363
Klein, S., 288
Klima, Edward S., 97
Kohen (caste), 64, 82, 83, 91, 92, 98, 128, 145, 310

INDEX 371

Kook, Abraham Isaac, 110–11, 234, 298

Landau, Ezekiel, 185, 297
land for peace, 290–305
Langer brother and sister, 68–69, 264
lashon hara, 12–13
Lauterbach, Jacob, 101, 102–9, 356
Law of Return, 58, 84–85, 90
Leff, Barry, 1, 9–18
Levinthal, Helen, 110, 356
LGBTQIA+, 139–73
Lincoln, Abraham, 319, 367
liturgy, modifications in, 40–42, 45–46, 121–28

ma'arufya, 20–22, 342
Madar, Hayyim, 75
Maharil, Jacob ben Moses Levi Moellin, 218
Mahariqas, Jacob Castro, 89
Maharsha, Samuel Eidels, 233
Maimonides, 16, 33–34, 42, 43, 60, 74, 79, 92, 123–25, 188–89, 190, 192, 259, 265, 266, 267–68, 269–71, 272–73, 280–81, 294–95, 323, 340, 342, 343, 352, 361, 365
Malka, Moshe, 215
mamzer, xxiii–xxxiv, 57–81, 192–93, 195, 264, 342
Margolis, Hayyim Mordechai, 313, 314
matrilineal descent, 58, 82–83

Meiri, Menahem ben Solomon, 259, 277–79
Mesas, David, 74
Mesas, Joseph, 215
Mesas, Shalom, xxiv, 57, 73–81, 215, 354
Mevorakh, Tomer, 175, 179–86
Meyuhas Bekhor Shmuel, Rishon Lezion, 295
milḥemet *mitzvah*, 268–73
milḥemet *reshut*, 268–73
Mir Yeshivah, 234
Mishneh Torah. *See* Maimonides
Mizrahi (political party), 46
Mo'etzet Gedolei Hatorah (international), xx
Mo'etzet Gedolei Hatorah (United States), 317
Mo'etzet Ḥakhmei Hatorah, xx
Mohammed VI of Morocco, 74
Morsel-Eisenberg, Tamara, 361
Munkácz, 18, 230

Nadell, Pamela S., 356
Nadler, Allan, 362
Nahmanides, 44, 182–83, 271–73, 299–300, 319, 343
Nevins, Daniel, 139, 149–57
niddah, 117–20, 170–71, 177
Nissim, Yitzhak, 365
Noahide, 24–25, 189–91, 295, 324, 360
non-Jews, 252–62. *See also* Noahide

"one who breaks in through a tunnel," 274–82
Operation Peace for Galilee, 265, 269–70, 271
Orthodox Judaism, xv, xix, xx, xxvi, 38, 102, 115–17, 205, 213, 216, 229–30, 233, 234, 235, 236, 283, 284, 307, 308, 309, 317, 363
Oshry, Ephraim, xxiv, 57–65, 352
Ouziel, Ben-Zion Meir Ḥai, 46, 69, 101, 111, 215, 326

Palestinian Liberation Organization, 290
Panigel, Rafael Meir, 89
Parashat Zakhor, 209
Passover, xxi, 22, 132, 205, 212–16, 264, 344
"partial birth abortion," xxxiii, 198–203
patrilineality, 82–87
Peres, Yeshayahu, 288
pikku'aḥ nefesh, 10, 14–15, 17, 180, 184, 193, 194, 198, 205, 207, 210, 290–98, 301, 304, 343
Po'alei Agudat Yisrael, xx
prayers answered by God, 47–50
Priesand, Sally, 110
Purim, 208–9

Ra'avad, Abraham ben David, 295
Rabbiner-Seminar (Berlin), 102, 234
Rabbinical Council of America, xx
Radak, 285

Radbaz, 88–89
Radzyner, Amihai, 353
Raphael Aharon ben Shimon, 215
Rapport, Yael Rooks, xxiv, 230, 245–51
Rashi, 20, 27, 50, 119, 188, 189, 190, 192, 219, 275–76, 277–79, 285, 343; script, 217
rebuke, mitzvah to, 13–14
Reconstructionist Judaism, xv, 349
Reform Judaism, xv, xxvi, 38, 67, 101, 230, 245, 247, 307, 308, 309, 315–16, 348, 356, 361; relationship to halakhah, xv; relationship of Orthodoxy and Ultraorthodoxy to, 40–41, 20–33, 234–37, 317; style of responsa, xix. *See also* CCAR Responsa Committee
Reisner, Avram Israel, 1–9, 139, 149–57
Rembaum, Joel, 102, 120–28
responsa committees, establishment of, xix–xx, 51
Revivo, Nissim, 75
Ringel, Joseph, 349
rishonim, 98, 235–36, 284
Rishon Lezion Sefardic chief rabbi, 46, 69, 74, 81, 87, 89, 90, 101, 111, 215, 265, 295, 355, 365; meaning of title, 355
rodef, 187–90, 261–62, 280–81, 344
Roness, Yo'ezet Michal, 115–20

Roosevelt, Franklin Delano, 319
Rosenak, Avinoam, 347
Rosh, Asher ben Jehiel, 182–83
Rosh Hashanah, 221–28, 230, 238
Roth, Joel, 139, 140–48, 152–53, 349

Saadiah (Sa'adia) Gaon, 122–23, 285, 344
Sabbath, 21, 31–32, 40–41, 75, 126, 132, 206–8, 209, 214, 215, 216, 223, 232, 233, 242, 244, 264, 294, 297, 313–14, 342, 343, 344
same-sex relations, 140–48, 148–62
Samet, Moshe, 351
Sanhedrin, 41, 71, 270, 321, 323
San Remo conference, 302
Sasi, Noam, 362
Schachter, Herschel (Tzvi), 205–6, 216–21
Schechter Institute of Jewish Studies, 252, 283
Sefardic/Mizraḥi, xxvi
Seminario Rabinico Latinoamericano, 283
sex offender, 51–56
Shabbat. *See* Sabbath
Shabbetai ben Meir Hakohen, 312
Shapira, Hayyim Eleazar, 229, 230–33, 363
Shapiro, Marc B., 363
Sharzer, Leonard, 139, 162–73
Shas political party, xx, 46
Shema, 8, 39, 98–99, 105, 132, 344
shev ve'al ta'aseh, 194, 344

Shneur Zalman of Lyady, 258
shoṭeh, 94–95, 180, 185
Shulḥan Arukh. *See* Caro, Joseph
siege warfare, 265–73
Silberstein, Yaron, 365
Silverman, Morris, 126, 357
Simḥah Hacohen of Dvinsk, 271–72, 302, 365
Slobodka Yeshiva, 234
Slomovitz, Albert Isaac, 366n1
Sofer, Abraham Samuel Benjamin, 96
Sofer, Moses, xxv, 37, 38–46, 219, 220, 221
Sofer, Simḥah Bunim, 96
Soloveitchik, Joseph B., 216
Somekh, Abdalla, xxiv, 2, 21–29
Spitz, Elie, xxiv, 57, 65–72
State Rabbinate of Israel, 57, 68–69, 73, 87–88, 114, 179, 283–84, 344, 353. *See also* Ashkenazic chief rabbi; Rishon Lezion Sefardic chief rabbi
Steinberg, Milton, 308
Sternbuch, Moses, 175, 176–79
Stokoe, William C., 97
sustainability, xxiii, 2–9

ṭaharat ha-mishpaḥah 115–20
takkanah, 42, 101, 111–15, 344; of Rabbenu Gershom, 177–78, 179
Tanya, 262
Tay-Sachs disease, 196–97
teshuvah (responsum), xv, 343, 352; format of, xvii; influence

of technology on dissemination, of xx–xxi
teshuvah (repentance), 52–53, 55–56
Thanksgiving, American, 318–20
three oaths, 299–305, 366
time-bound positive mitzvot, 131–39
Tisha B'Av, 206, 216–21
Torat Hamelekh, 261–62
Tosafot, 25, 28, 119, 217, 304, 345, 352, 356
Trani, Joseph, 191–92
Transcendental Meditation, 237–45
transgender Jews, xxiii, 162–73
tza'ar ba'alei ḥayyim, 30, 32–34

Ultraorthodox Judaism, xviii, xix, xx, xxvi, 18, 38, 68, 73, 87–88, 176, 177, 230, 317, 341, 347, 348, 363
United Nations, 299

Va'ad Halakhah (Conservative/Masorti Judaism in Israel), xx, 252, 283
Valera, Eamon de, 110
veal, 2, 29–37
video conferencing, 207–9, 210–12, 213–16
Voorsanger, Elkan, 308

Waldenberg, Eliezer, 119, 175, 186–98, 349, 360
Warhaftig, Yaakov, 115
Warschawski, Max, 235
Washofsky, Mark, 347, 351
Washington, George, 319
Weinberg, Jehiel Jacob, 229, 234–37, 364
Weiss, Isaac Jacob, xxv, 1, 18–21
Westreich, Avishalom, 353
whistleblowers, 9–19
White Paper, 111
Willig, Mordechai, I, 119
women, 101–38
women as posekot, xxiv, 101–2, 115–16

Yeshivah Mercaz Harav, 198
Yeshivat Gush Etzion, 179
Yeshivat Porat Yosef, 46, 87
Yeshiva University, 163, 216, 252
yibbum, 110 113–15, 341, 345
Yisraeli, Shaul, 263, 298–305, 366
Yoga, 245–51
Yom Kippur, 132, 175, 177, 179–86, 220–28, 294, 296
Yosef, Ovadiah, xxi, 46, 58, 73–74, 81, 87–93, 214, 263, 265, 290–98, 299, 303–5, 365

Zohar, 257, 262
Zohar, Zvi, 348, 350, 355, 365

IN THE JPS ANTHOLOGIES OF JEWISH THOUGHT SERIES

Exile and the Jews: Literature, History, and Identity
Edited by Nancy E. Berg
and Marc Saperstein

Modern Responsa: An Anthology of Jewish Ethical and Ritual Decisions
Pamela Barmash

Contemporary Humanistic Judaism: Beliefs, Values, Practices
Edited by Adam Chalom
and Jodi Kornfeld

Modern Musar: Contested Virtues in Jewish Thought
Geoffrey D. Claussen

Modern Conservative Judaism: Thought and Practice
Elliot N. Dorff
Foreword by Julie Schonfeld

Modern Orthodox Judaism: A Documentary History
Zev Eleff
Foreword by Jacob J. Schacter

A Kabbalah and Jewish Mysticism Reader
Daniel M. Horwitz

Modern Jewish Theology: The First One Hundred Years, 1835–1935
Edited by Samuel J. Kessler
and George Y. Kohler

The Growth of Reform Judaism: American and European Sources
W. Gunther Plaut
Foreword by Jacob K. Shankman
New introduction by
Howard A. Berman
New epilogue by David Ellenson
With select documents, 1975–2008

The Rise of Reform Judaism: A Sourcebook of Its European Origins
W. Gunther Plaut
Foreword by Solomon B. Freehof
New introduction by
Howard A. Berman

The Zionist Ideas: Visions for the Jewish Homeland—Then, Now, Tomorrow
Gil Troy

To order or obtain more information on these or other Jewish Publication Society titles, visit jps.org.

OTHER WORKS BY PAMELA BARMASH

In the Shadow of Empire:
Ancient Israel in the Long Sixth
Century BCE, edited with
Mark W. Hamilton (2021)

The Laws of Hammurabi: At
the Confluence of Royal and
Legal Traditions (2020)

The Oxford Handbook of
Biblical Law (2019)

Exodus in the Jewish Experience:
Echoes and Reverberations, edited
with W. David Nelson (2015)

Homicide in the Biblical World (2005)